QUEEN BEES
& WANNABES

QUEEN BEES & WANNABES

Helping your daughter survive cliques, gossip,
boyfriends and the new realities of Girl World

ROSALIND WISEMAN

piatkus

PIATKUS

First published in the US in 2002 by Three Rivers Press, an imprint of the
Crown Publishing Group, a division of Random House, Inc. New York
This revised and updated edition published in 2009
First published in Great Britain in 2002 by Piatkus Books Ltd
This revised and updated edition published in 2010 by Piatkus

17 19 20 18

A CIP catalogue record for this book
is available from the British Library.

ISBN 978-0-7499-2437-9

Designed by Debbie Glasserman

Printed and bound by CPI Group (UK) Ltd, Croydon, CR0 4YY

Papers used by Piatkus are from well-managed forests
and other responsible sources.

MIX
Paper from
responsible sources
FSC® C104740

Piatkus
An Imprint of
Little, Brown Book Group
Carmelite House
50 Victoria Embankment
London EC4Y 0DZ

An Hachette UK Company
www.hachette.co.uk

www.littlebrown.co.uk

*To my students and all the young people
who have contacted me over the years.
You inspire me to do my best work.*

Contents

QUEEN BEES & WANNABES

Introduction

I just overheard my 8-year-old daughter's friend tell her that she'll only hang out with my daughter at our house because everyone else in the class thinks she's weird. And my daughter agreed! I'm having a very hard time not hating this girl and everyone else in the class. Meanwhile, what is wrong with my daughter that she's OK with this? I didn't raise her to be a doormat. —Patty

My 12-year-old daughter has a great relationship with my brother, and she just told him that she had two boys in the house when we weren't there. Of course he told me but now I don't know what to do. It's totally against our rules but if I punish her she'll know her uncle told me and she'll stop talking to him. If I don't do anything, she'll do it again! What do I do? —Leah

What do you do when your daughter is the Queen Bee? My daughter talks so badly about other people that she's starting to lose all her friends. I'm having a hard time liking her myself. —Marianne

I just went through my 14-year-old daughter's text messages and want to throw up. I couldn't believe the language she was using about herself and other kids in her class. —Todd

Eight years ago I sat down to write a guide for parents about their daughters' friendships. Well, I don't know about you, but my life certainly hasn't been the same since. People talk about *Queen Bees* at work, on television, and in their preschool playgroups. You can buy *Queen Bee* T-shirts, backpacks, and pencil cases—as if being one is something your daughter should aspire to. Every day people ask me questions or share their experiences about Girl World and Queen Bees. For better and for worse, our awareness of Queen Bees and Mean Girls is now commonplace.

Meanwhile, girls are still in the thick of Girl World—where people won't tell you why they're mad at you, friends tease you and then dismiss your feelings with "Just kidding!," and everyone texts and instant messages every rumor and embarrassing photograph about you. So the first time your daughter tells you that all her friends have stopped talking to her and she has no idea why, you want to know what to say and what to do—beyond wanting to yell at all those horrible children you now hate. But then things get more complicated when you pick her up the next day at school and there she is arm in arm with one of those Mean Girls like nothing ever happened. You stare at your daughter as she opens the door and begs you to let this kid come over, refusing to acknowledge that she has been co-opted by the Mean Girl World and ignoring your "Are you kidding me?" expression.

Welcome to the wonderful world of your daughter's adolescence. Ten seconds ago she was a sweet, confident little girl. Now you can't breathe in her direction without getting that really annoying eye roll, followed by the equally irritating sigh. Or maybe, one day she's insecure and wants to sit on your lap, but the next day she's threatening to run away and you're ready to pack her bag. She's facing the toughest pressures of adolescent life—test-driving her new body (while you're giving her a big sweatshirt to cover up that figure she seemed to have developed overnight), navigating changing friendships, surviving crushes, trying to keep up with school—and intuitively you know even though she's sometimes totally obnoxious, she needs you more than ever. Yet it's the very time when she's pulling away from you.

Why do girls so often reject their parents and turn to their friends instead, even when those friends often treat them so cruelly? One day your daughter comes to school and her friends suddenly decide they hate her. Or she's teased relentlessly for wearing the wrong clothes or having the wrong friend. Maybe she's branded with a reputation she can't shake. Or trapped, feeling she has to conform to what her friends expect from her so she won't be kicked out of the group. But no matter what they do to her, she still feels that her friends know her best and genuinely want what is best for her. Or worse, she knows they aren't good for her, but she would rather put up with being treated like dirt than be alone. In comparison, she believes that you, previously a reliable source of information, don't have a clue. For parents, being rejected by your daughter is an excruciating experience. But it can really make you mad and doubt your child's sanity when you're replaced by a group of girls with all the tact, sense of fairness, and social graces of a pack of hyenas.

Most people believe a girl's task is to get through it, grow up, and put those experiences behind her. But your daughter's relationships with other girls have deep and far-reaching implications beyond her teen years. Your daughter's friendships with other girls are a double-edged sword. First, let's talk about the positives. These friendships can be the key to surviving adolescence. Many girls will make it through their teen years precisely because they have the support and care of a few good friends. These are the friendships in which a girl truly feels unconditionally accepted, understood, and sometimes even challenged when she's doing something that's not good for her—like dating a guy who doesn't treat her with respect.

But I wouldn't be writing this book and you wouldn't be reading it if that's all there was to girls' friendships. Girls' friendships are often intense, confusing, frustrating, and humiliating; the joy and security of "best friendships" can be shattered by devastating breakups and betrayals. And beyond the pain in the moment, girls can develop patterns of behavior and expectations for future relationships that stop them from becoming competent, authentic people who are capable of having healthy relationships with others as adults.

But your daughter is too close to it all to realize the good and bad influence of her friends. She needs guidance from you despite the fact that she's pulling away. My job is to give you my best suggestions for what kind of guidance to give her and how that information should be presented so she listens and your relationship with her is strengthened through the process.

As this is the updated version of *Queen Bees*, there's no way I could write it without addressing two things: (1) how technology and the media influence your daughter's social life for better and worse; and (2) how these issues are impacting younger girls and what you can do about it.

I can't emphasize enough the effect that constant connectivity to the Internet, e-mail, cell phones, and texting has on your child's landscape—not to mention online social networking like MySpace, Webkinz, Club Penguin, Stardoll, Facebook, Twitter, or the ten other new websites the girls will be regularly using by the time this book is published. These things are in your daughter's life—even if you don't let her have a cell phone or you don't think she has an e-mail account.

Before you assume I think all of those things are bad, let me assure you I don't. What I think is that most parents haven't realized that as soon as their child interacts with technology in any way, they have to explicitly tie her use of this incredibly powerful tool to their values. If parents don't, they have missed the most important opportunity to teach her how to be a decent, ethical person.

The worst thing you can do is be in denial. About a year ago I realized that teens weren't watching music videos that often. I knew this because I often show music videos of popular songs in my classes where it was common for my students to see them for the first time—even if the same song was one of their ring tones. But in researching for this book, I figured out who *is* watching them—fourth, fifth, and sixth graders. How are they doing this when you'd never let them watch MTV? On YouTube (or Vimeo, Hulu, or Yahoo Video)—where they can see all of those videos in their entirety for free. But it's not just the music videos. Any social networking site can be used to bring people of like interests together. These sites can build a sense of community in a positive way. But they can also do the opposite.

If you don't believe all of this, listen to these fifth graders:

> Last year, a girl I used to be friends with got mad at me and went into my Webkinz account and destroyed everything. She did it because she knew my password. Everything, everything I had was gone. —Kara, 11

> My friend loves Stardoll.com and her grandmother gave her these star dollars so she can buy all the best things. My parents don't have the money to buy me things like that and she makes me feel bad because then she looks at the things I do [on the site] and tells me how ugly it is and how the girl doesn't have any money. It's like she's telling me I'm ugly and poor. —Natalie, 10

Fast-forward three years later to an instant message between two eighth graders:

> Everyone knows what you did . . . your life is now over
> What are you talking about!!!!
> I'm not going to say . . .
> Seriously, you have to tell me
> No, I don't, but you'll find out soon

I will give you all the strategies I use to stop that kind of exchange from occurring again—and you won't have to become a technology expert. Technology is instantly and continuously transforming our world, and we have got to teach our children how to use it and and still keep their dignity and sense of human decency intact.

What girls fight about with technology is what this book has always been about. So, of course, we'll still examine cliques, "frenemies," reputations, gossiping, rebellion, bullying, crushes, and boyfriends. I'll show you how your daughter is conditioned to remain silent when intimidated by more powerful girls—and the lessons she learns from these experiences. I'll teach you how to recognize which friends will support her and which could lead her into situations that threaten her emotional health and even her physical safety. I'll show you how your daughter's place in her social pecking order can affect how she will or won't participate in humiliating others, staying silent, or being the Target. Finally, I'll make a connection between what your daughter learns in her early life and how those lessons impact her future.

I will do this by walking you through key rites of passage your daughter is likely to experience: the first time people get mad at her and won't tell her why; her first breakup with a friend; the first time she gets into a fight with you because she wants to go to school or a party in the latest style that you think is totally inappropriate; the first time you realize she's no longer talking to you about her problems; the first or seventy-fifth time she receives a nasty text message. Just as these moments can be excruciating for her, they can be equally challenging for you. I'm not talking only in terms of the extent to which they make you angry or try your patience; mishandling them can prevent you from getting her the help she needs and weaken your relationship with her. I'll help you navigate them together.

Understanding your daughter's friendships and social life can be grueling and frustrating. Parents often tell me they feel totally shut out of this part of their daughter's life, incapable of exerting any influence. This book will let you in. It'll show how to help your daughter deal with the nasty things girls do to one another, minimize the negative effects of what's often an invisible war behind girls' friendships, and recognize the truly strong relationships she may already have.

Before I go any further, let me reassure you that I can help you even if you often feel helpless or at war with your daughter.

It's perfectly natural at this stage that she:

- Stops looking to you for answers.
- Doesn't respect your opinion as much as she did before.
- Believes that there's no possible way that you could understand what she's going through.

- Is absolutely certain that telling you her problems will only make her life worse.
- Lies and sneaks around behind your back.
- Denies she lied and snuck behind your back—even in the face of undeniable evidence.

On the other hand, it's natural that you:

- Feel rejected and angry when she rolls her eyes at everything you say.
- Have moments when you really don't like her.
- Wonder whose child this is anyway, as this person in front of you can't possibly be your sweet, wonderful daughter.
- Feel confused when conversations end in fights.
- Feel misunderstood when she feels you're intruding and prying when you ask what's going on in her life.
- Are really worried about the influence of her friends and feel powerless and angry to stop her hanging out with them. (Because, of course, she'll keep the friends you don't like if you expressly forbid her from seeing them.)
- Feel sad because you don't know how to deal with problems she won't even discuss with you.

THE MOTHER/DAUGHTER MAELSTROM

Moms and daughters seem to have the hardest time with each other. Your daughter craves privacy, and your very presence feels like an intrusion. You feel you have so much to offer her. After all, you've been through the changes she's experiencing, and you think your advice will help. Although this privacy war is natural, it creates a big problem. Girls are often so focused on resisting the influence of their parents that they rarely see when their peers are influencing them in the wrong way. Girls often see things in very concrete, either/or ways. You, as the parent, are intrusive and prying, which equals bad; her peers are involved and understanding, which equals good.

But there's another issue that complicates everything, especially for moms. In the words of one mom who wrote me:

When I was a senior in high school, my best friend since third grade dumped me and had our entire clique turn their back on me. I was devastated. I found more friends, but the experience left me very insecure in my relationships—something that haunts me to this day (I'm 36). The anger and betrayal I felt at the time has never fully left me, despite my fervent desire to leave it behind. In short, she is the person that I would run out of the grocery store to avoid. The most difficult aspect of all this is that I am trying very hard to "check" this baggage as I witness MY daughter's blossoming best friendship . . . and my deeply wired desire to protect her.   *—Ellen*

So if you're a mom reading this, it's important to remember that your experiences as a girl are both your greatest gift and liability as your daughter navigates her own friendships. They're a gift because they enable you to empathize. They're a liability if your past makes you so anxious or reactionary that you can't separate your experiences from hers.

Don't Dismiss the Dads

This book isn't only for mothers. I know, I know, most fathers would rather do anything else than read any kind of parenting book. Believe me, I've talked to and laughed with plenty of dads at my presentations who have been dragged there by their wives. But whether you're this kind of dad, or the one who e-mails me knowing all the seventh-grade girl drama in your daughter's class, almost all dads want to be emotionally engaged with their children and struggle coming to terms with the young woman who just moments ago was "Daddy's little girl."

So if you only read one paragraph in this book, make it this: Never forget or dismiss that your perspective can help your daughter. Just because you were never a girl, don't know what a menstrual cramp feels like, and have never liked talking for hours about other people's lives doesn't mean you're clueless or useless. I know lots of dads feel rejected and pushed aside when their little girl suddenly dismisses them with "You just wouldn't understand." But in reality, this is an opportunity for you to become a genuinely cool dad. I don't mean you let her get away with stuff, side with her against her mom, or drive her wherever she wants. I'm talking about the dad who patiently waits around until she wants to talk, then listens without being judgmental, isn't afraid to look foolish or show his emotions, shares the "boy perspective," holds her accountable when necessary, and is able to communicate his concerns without coming across as controlling and dogmatic.

You're probably dying to warn your daughter off of every hormone-crazed boy who walks through your door because you may remember what you or guys you knew were like. But if you launch in with "what boys really want" and come across as the crazy-control-freak-doesn't-have-a-clue father, you've lost a golden opportunity. Your job is to present your wisdom in a credible manner so she won't blow you off. Through your relationship with her, you can teach her that she has the right to expect that relationships with men must be mutually respectful and caring. This book will help you.

BELIEVE IT OR NOT, YOUR DAUGHTER STILL WANTS YOU IN HER LIFE

When I ask girls privately what they need most from their parents, they tell me they want their parents to be proud of them. You may look at her in the middle of an argument when she's screaming that she hates you and think there's no way you can get through to her, but you can and will if you learn to see the world through her eyes.

Parents don't realize that their children look up to them. When I know that deep in my mother and father's heart they really don't agree with what I'm doing, that really hurts. —Eve, 12

I know I should listen to my parents, even if they're wrong. —Abby, 16

DEVELOPING YOUR GIRL BRAIN

One of the hardest truths for parents is that as their daughter gets older they have less control over which people she hangs out with. It's terribly stressful knowing that they can't always be there when their daughter faces the difficult decisions that could impact her health and safety. When your daughter was little and got hurt, she'd run to you and you'd kiss the pain away. Now you're lucky if you have a clue what the problem is. Worse, if you sweep in to save the day instead of teaching your daughter how to handle it, she'll either be angry with you for intruding or she won't learn to take care of herself. How can you help her? Start by thinking the way she does.

The key to maintaining your relationship with your daughter is understanding how and why she's turning away from you and toward her friends, and being there for her anyway. In this book I will teach you to develop or restart your girl brain. It's like looking at the world through a new pair of glasses. And even though she may be acting as if you aren't an important influence in her life, you are—she just may not want to admit it because either it feels like she's becoming too mature to need your help or afraid of what you'll take away from her if she tells you what's really going on. If you can learn how to be her safe harbor when she's in the midst of Girl World conflicts, your voice will be in her head along with your values and ethics.

The first step is to understand what your daughter's world, Girl World, looks like. You need to know who intimidates her, where she feels safe, and where she doesn't. If she has a problem, does she think going to an adult will make the problem better or worse? Who does she go to for advice? What kind of music does she listen to and why? Why did she choose the ring tones on her cell phone and what does that say about her? What common things can ruin her day or make her feel on top of the world?

An even harder task is taking a closer look at her social interactions. What is she being teased about? Why are other children mean to her? Or the worst to ask yourself, why would she be cruel to others? What would make her lie or sneak behind your back? Get inside her head, and you'll understand where she's coming from.

REMEMBERING THE LUNCH TRAY MOMENTS

It helps to remember what it was like to be your daughter's age. Think back to your experiences, the role models (both good and bad), and the lessons learned from your family, your school, and your community. Suspend the worry, the common sense, and the wisdom you have accumulated over the last years. Think back to what you were like and what was important to you back then. Now if you're really struggling to remember, like seventh grade is just a black hole in your mind, you may have to do some reconnaissance. That's right, you know what I'm talking about. It's time to take out the yearbooks and read what people wrote you— or even scarier, open up those diaries and start reading and remembering.

Parents, teachers, and other adults are telling you what to do— and especially what you can't do. You have a close group of friends, but for some reason one of your best friends comes up to you between classes and tells you that one of your other friends is spreading rumors about you. Your face feels hot; you can feel everyone looking at you. Thoughts race through your head. What did you do? Why is she mad at you? Are your friends going to back you or side with her? What can you do to fix the problem? All of a sudden, a question drives an icy stake of fear through your heart as you stand there clutching your orange plastic lunch tray in the cafeteria line: Where are you going to sit at lunch?

Can you remember what it was like? Not too pleasant. As adults, we can laugh at how immense and insurmountable problems like those "lunch tray moments" can feel when you're young. But in Girl World they're vital issues, and to dismiss them as trivial is to disrespect your daughter's reality. And within those moments are ethical choices and complex dynamics that are just as challenging as negotiating a peace treaty. Who says anything when someone is being excluded and treated cruelly? Who believes that seeking revenge or teaching someone "her place" justifies humiliating someone? What issues are more important than that? If you want your daughter to be a morally courageous person, it starts in these moments. And frankly, although the core issues remain the same, it's probably harder for her than it was for you at her age. Did you have to deal with telling someone a secret and then having them forward it to everyone in the school? Did anyone ever set up a webpage dedicated to destroying you and making you feel that everyone hates you? You didn't. I didn't. But your daughter does.

THE GIRL WORLD POLICE

Girls (like all of us) absorb the cultural messages of what a girl should wear and own, and how she should conduct herself, and then they take that information and develop strict social hierarchies based on it. At no time in your daughter's life will it probably feel more important to her to fit these elusive girl standards than during adolescence. But it's also confusing because girls don't know what these rules are because they're invisible. You only really learn them when you break them or you see someone else break them and live with the fallout. And who is the prime enforcer of these rules? The movies? The magazines? This is definitely where it starts, but what is often overlooked is that it is the girls themselves who are usually the enforcers. They police one another, conducting surveillance on who's breaking the laws of appearance and clothing, boys, and personality—all of which have a profound influence on the women they become. Your daughter gets daily lessons about what's "in" from her friends—and who has the "right" to wear those things. She isn't watching television, movies, or websites by herself. She processes this information with and through her friends.

I'm not saying "the media" isn't responsible for putting powerful images in our daughters' heads, but it isn't unfairly demonizing or blaming girls to ask them to admit that they play a part in their own degradation. Instead, it's being honest about the complexity of this problem so that we can create effective solutions. We also have to point to ourselves (i.e., adults) for not challenging a culture that so often adamantly portrays girls and women as hypersexual, unintelligent, and materialistic. For example, musical groups go on morning talk shows in lingerie and talk with straight faces about how they're good role models for girls—and the producers of those shows, who are often parents, let it slide. Many journalists are parents too, yet often they don't ask substantive questions when interviewing people who create girl-degrading content or play those roles. And we all buy magazines that are obsessed with being mean. Who's fat this week? Whose boyfriend dumped her for that younger blond actress? Who got pregnant and ruined her career? Who has the most or worst plastic surgery? Lots of mothers rationalize reading these magazines as a guilty pleasure. But, honestly, when you do this, you're not being the strong woman your daughter needs you to be. Never mind the fact that it's impossible to read one of those things and not suck in your stomach and think about those ten pounds you need to lose.

Last, we often don't want to admit how little supervision we really exert over what our children are watching. To be fair, it's really hard to do. You can pick out appropriate TV shows, but then the ads during the commercial breaks are horrible. You can get on a plane, let your child listen to the audio channel, and not know that the song they're listening to is one on the radio station you have forbidden. We need to sit down with our daughters (and of course our sons as well) and walk them through how to think about the relentless messages they're getting—we also have to educate ourselves without being afraid to be labeled as the uptight parent. We must, as must our daughters. Girls will only reach their full potential if they're taught to be the agents of their own social change. As we guide girls through adolescence, we have to acknowledge it, name it, and empower our girls so they can go into that store with the Queen Bee backpacks, and tell the manager to take them off the shelf.

SO WHY LISTEN TO ME?

During a recent fifth-grade assembly, a student asked me, "Are you wise at what you do?" I said, "It's really up to you to decide if I am. Listen to what I say and then tell me." I'd say the same thing to you. Although I'm a mom now myself and have worked with tens of thousands of children and teens over many years, I don't know your individual child. I'm going to give you my best analysis and suggestions for what's going on in the lives of most girls. And I'm going to ask you to engage with me, your daughter, and the important girls in your life in the process. The only thing I know for certain is that each person's dignity is not negotiable. Everyone is worthy. Everyone has the right to have her voice heard.

I'm frequently asked how I got into this line of work. Or said another way, "Were you a victim of a Queen Bee?" or, as kids love to ask me, "Were you popular?" Well, here's the short version of why I do this work.

Until fifth grade I'd grown up in a close community in Washington, D.C., and attended a small, public elementary school. I had many friends of different races, nationalities, and economic backgrounds. I was part of a clique, but I was friends with lots of students. The summer after I completed fifth grade, my family moved to Pittsburgh, Pennsylvania, and I attended a well-respected, private all-girls school. That's where I had my first really miserable lunch tray moment when girls wouldn't let me sit at their tables. But there were also girls who saw that happening to me and invited me to sit with them instead (thank you, Madeline McGrady and Melissa McSwiggen).

I returned to Washington the next year and enrolled in another private but coed school where I ran into more Mean Girls—but this time they became my friends and they were incredibly charismatic and fun. Looking back, I see that one of them in particular was any parent's nightmare. She was stunningly beautiful, brazen, funny, and had a house with MIA parents, a fabulously exciting older sister, and a cute older brother who was always bringing his even cuter friends over. Honestly, from my eighth-grade perspective, there was nothing better than going over to her house and just waiting to see what exciting and dangerous thing would happen after school. And her family presented well, meaning my parents didn't have a clue about what I was seeing and experiencing in that house and I certainly wasn't going to tell them.

That's when it got confusing. Think of it this way: when girls are mean to you all the time, it's easy to hate them back and/or pretend they don't exist; but it's a world of difference when the Mean Girls can also be really nice and exciting. In the scheme of things, it seemed like a good trade-off. So what if they would turn on me at any second or make fun of me for the things I was the most self-conscious about? I was willing to pay the price, because speaking my mind meant losing the friendships and all the exciting things that went with it.

Then the first day of ninth grade arrived, and I fell in love—hard. Unbelievable to me at the time, the boy liked me back. And just like that, my friends stopped teasing and humiliating me. It was like I had an insurance policy against how badly my friends could treat me. Why? Because he had the boyfriend "trifecta." He was cute, charming, and wealthy. I had proven myself to my friends.

Unfortunately, my relationship with him became incredibly serious and then incredibly abusive. How did I, someone with no violence in my family and parents who loved each other, get into an abusive relationship at such a young age and stay in that relationship for five years? On paper, I was no one's idea of a likely target for abuse. I would have known exactly what to say on any self-esteem test. I was a competitive athlete. I had a supportive and loving family. I didn't abuse alcohol or drugs. So what was going on?

Like so many girls, I was amazingly good at fooling myself. I'd convinced myself that I was in a mature relationship and I was in control of the situation. But more important, my boyfriend made me feel like I was the only one who understood him. I was the special one. It was like having the BFF I'd always wanted with all the other benefits that go with having a boyfriend. I was in complete denial that I could get into situations that were over my head, even when I had clear evidence to the contrary.

But looking back, I realized I already knew how to be in an abusive relationship by the time I met him—thanks to my friends. I believed I didn't have the right to complain when people who were supposed to care about me treated me badly. I had already learned it was more important to have the relationship than how I was treated within it. And last, when the relationship was at its worst and even I had to admit things were bad, I felt horribly ashamed and powerless to change my situation and that I couldn't go back to my friends for help.

I stayed with him until I graduated from high school. When I was in college, I started studying karate and it gave me a new sense of purpose and personal strength. After my college graduation, I moved back to Washington, D.C., and began teaching self-defense to high school girls. That's where I started hearing stories remarkably similar to my own. I began to wonder: Where did these girls learn to be silent? Where did they learn to deny the danger staring them in the face? Why didn't girls trust other girls? Why were they so willing to throw away friendships if a better offer came along? And the most complicated question of all that's confused women forever: How in the world is a girl supposed to be sexy enough that she gets boys' attention but not so sexy that other girls turn against her?

Clearly, girls are safer and happier when they look out for one another. But, paradoxically, during their period of greatest vulnerability, girls' competition with and judgment of each other weakens their friendships and effectively isolates all of them. Honestly, I hate that. After all these years doing this work, I still get really worked up about it. And this is what the power of the clique is all about, and why it matters so much to your daughter's safety and self-esteem.

As I taught self-defense, schools asked me to develop other classes that would teach girls self-esteem, confidence, and social competence. And that is exactly what I do today—in addition to working with boys, educators, and parents around the world. And although some things have changed since *Queen Bees* was first published, many challenges are still as true today as they were then. Parents often feel overwhelmed by the challenges of parenting a teen, whether they're trying to deal with a cruel message left on their daughter's voice mail, helping her survive the morning bus ride safely, or rescuing a daughter in an abusive relationship. And whether I'm teaching in the most exclusive private school or the largest public school, the girls all bring similar concerns and fears. No matter their income, religion, or ethnicity, they're struggling with the same issues about the pleasures and perils of friendships and how they act as a portal to the larger world.

I love what I do. There's nothing like the adrenaline rush of trying to engage my students. But as I talk with girls and boys in school hallways and cafeterias, and as I teach in their schools, athletic teams, and church groups, something is clear. Adults are struggling. Many of us feel overwhelmed by this new relentless culture. Some of us still dismiss girls' experiences as teen drama; others overreact and get overinvolved so that the girls don't learn how to handle these situations for themselves or stop going to any adults for help.

On the other side, some adults won't get involved at all because they think the "girls should learn to work it out themselves," providing no guidance or ethical standards about how the girls might do that. Some of us also feel helpless or are stuck in the same patterns as the girls themselves. And of course, parents often see their daughters' behaviors as a reflection of the success or failure of their parenting, so it's just that much harder to see their daughters for who they really are.

How the Book Works

Many parents have told me that one of the things they appreciated the most about the first version of *Queen Bees* is that they could read it in small bites—like when they're stuck in traffic or car pool line. I took that to heart, so I didn't mess with how the book is organized. Most chapters will begin with a thorough analysis and description of a specific aspect of Girl World. In the "Checking Your Baggage" section, I'll challenge you to answer a few questions about your experiences when you were your daughter's age, because understanding your own biases and preconceptions can show you how they've affected your behavior toward your daughter. Then I'll give you specific, step-by-step strategies to help her and you.

Just like the first time I wrote this book, I've reached out to girls, boys, parents, and educators to take an active role in its development. I've shown multiple drafts of every chapter to girls of different ages, races, cultures, communities, and socioeconomic levels. They've helped me fill in missing perspectives, pushed me to delve more deeply into certain issues, and offered their "political commentary," which you'll find throughout the book. They've anonymously shared personal stories, feelings, and opinions—all to help you know how to reach out to your daughter in the best possible way. And last, I have added specific questions from girls and their parents with my solutions.

The girls have also taught me about the "land mines" you'll find throughout the book: things parents do and say that are guaranteed eye rollers and shut the door to effective communication. They usually seem insignificant (e.g., you can't roll *your* eyes when your daughter says something that irritates you), but they can make the difference between your daughter listening to you or tuning out completely. As you read this, you may be thinking that pointing out land mines is a lost cause, since *anything* you do, including breathing or looking in her direction, makes her roll *her* eyes, but I promise that there are ways you can decrease the number of embarrassing things you do. (For some reason, the way dads sneeze and moms laugh are also land mines, but you can't change everything about yourself!)

The one thing you aren't allowed to do while you read this book is beat yourself up for being a bad parent. Parenting is really difficult, and the reward is way down the road when she emerges as a cool adult. Allow me to quote my own mother, who said, "When my children were teens, if I liked them for five minutes a day, that was a good day." And now I can say with absolute authority that if I have gotten through a week without screaming at one of my own children, this is a very good and very rare week.

So let's be honest. You don't have to like your daughter all the time. One father I know refers to his increasingly distant daughter as "the exchange student." You're allowed to wonder why you had kids in the first place. Once you acknowledge these rotten—and believe me, universal—feelings, their power over you tends to decrease and you don't feel so guilty.

BEFORE YOU GET INTO THE HEART OF THE BOOK

Your task is difficult. Instilling values, respecting your daughter's growing individuality, influencing her to make good decisions, and protecting her while giving her the freedom to make mistakes is hard, hard work. A lot of the time you'll feel as if you're banging your head against a wall.

This book will give you strategies to make your daughter's adolescence bearable for both of you. It will teach you to talk to your daughter in a way that doesn't make her groan when you speak. She may even walk away from your conversation admitting to herself (but not to you, never to you) that you know what you're talking about.

You can help your daughter develop a strong sense of self. You can teach her personal responsibility, confidence in her abilities, and empathy toward others. You want her to be an authentic person able to realize her full individual potential while being connected to her loved ones and community. You can build a strong, healthy relationship with your daughter as long as you take a long-term view, focus on the overall goal, and challenge yourself to be as honest as you can. I also promise to answer the biggest questions of all: Should I read her e-mail/Facebook/MySpace/text messages/diary? When do I know she's lying to me?

JUST BETWEEN YOU AND ME

This book may be painful to read. If you decide you hate me, have no idea what I'm talking about, or I hit a nerve, I have only one request. Take a moment to reflect. Ask yourself why what you read bothered you so much. Did it call up memories of your own experience as a victim, bystander, or perpetrator? Did it give you a sinking feeling that your daughter is a target or evildoer? Is it hard to face the fact that your daughter is thinking and acting in ways you aren't happy about? Acknowledge the pain you feel, but don't let it stop you from learning all you can about your daughter's world. Everything in this book comes from what people have told me over the years, from my teaching experiences, and from girls' comments as they have read drafts of this book. I'm not accusing girls of being bad people, judging parents as incapable, or predicting which daughters will be failures as adults. I'm reaching out to you, as parents, educators, and role models, to show you what I think girls are up against as they struggle to become healthy young women who will make our communities better. Now, let's start by looking at one of the main reasons I had to rewrite *Queen Bees* in the first place: how technology impacts girls' social lives.

Technology, the Media, and Girl World

My child got 3,000 texts last month. What in the world do I do about that? I've already given her a cell phone and all her friends have one. It feels like I can't go backwards. —Mark

It really does feel like I am the only one who isn't letting my sixth grader have a cell phone. Aren't there any other parents like me out there who think that giving all this technology to kids is getting completely out of hand? —Diana

If you don't text, you don't exist. —Hallie, 13

Every time I get off IM I'm confused and upset. —Tina, 14

Being online is like being drunk. Instead of liquid courage, it's virtual courage. —Emily, 18

When should I start talking to you about the impact of technology on your daughter's world? After a lot of debate (i.e., should it be in the gossip section, the talking-behind-your-back section, the flirting section?), I finally realized that the best place to put it is right here, at the beginning. Because to truly understand a girl growing up in today's world, you have to have a basic comprehension of the technology she uses to connect and live in it. After this 101 course, you'll have the keys to unlock the confusing electronic and digital issues that crop up throughout the rest of this book and in your daughter's everyday life.

It amazes me how much technology has changed my work since I first wrote *Queen Bees*. Google, Facebook, YouTube, and ten-year-olds with cell phones didn't exist. The only things my students used to communicate with each other were e-mails. Now e-mail is the most antiquated form of virtual communication they use. Every day children and teens contact me through various social networking sites. It is part of every presentation I do in almost every class. It enables me to reach children and help them in a way that was impossible a decade ago. But no matter what your age, it can also be used as a weapon of mass destruction.

Your daughter lives in two worlds simultaneously—the real world and the virtual world. In her mind, they are interconnected. What happens in one impacts the other, and vice versa. Unfortunately, where adults have struggled is realizing and then knowing how to give our children moral guideposts in the virtual world just as they do in the real world. This book will give you a lot of information on both because one of the most important things I'd like you to take away is seeing your daughter's use of technology as a way to teach her your family values. You have to embrace it as a critical opportunity to show what you stand for.

First, we have to understand why parents give their children access to technology so easily.

1. The tools of technology became cheaper and more readily available.
2. *"I just feel better knowing my child has a cell phone."* Parents believe that if their child has a cell phone, they can reach him or her at any time and they will know where their children are at all times.
3. Having cell phones, iPods, and Game Boys has become so normal that we don't question whether and when our children should have them.

4. Parents worry that if children don't have these tools, they will be at a disadvantage compared with their peers and suffer academically.

What parents don't realize are the other consequences, including the following:

1. They are status symbols among kids and a prime place for children to become mindless, relentless consumers (think about how many times your child has begged you for the latest technology).
2. Cell phones make it more difficult to know where children are because they can lie and say they are exactly where they are supposed to be. Technology makes it much easier to sneak behind parents' backs and have increased freedom of movement.
3. Technology increases the spread and intensity of gossip, humiliation, and drama.
4. We, the adults, can get so hooked on it ourselves that we role-model horrible behavior.

My Truths About How People of All Ages Interact Online

1. They do things online they wouldn't do in real life.
2. People fight over technology in ways they never would face-to-face because they can say their version of events without getting immediate feedback that might challenge it. It allows people to throw more intense self-righteous temper tantrums.
3. It's quicker and easier to disseminate information, which then becomes harder to get rid of—there is no digital janitor to paint over our Facebook walls.
4. People give personal information online, knowing that their privacy can very easily be violated. This fact, however, does little to stop them from posting that personal information or being surprised when that information becomes public.
5. Technology fans the flames of paranoia. Almost everyone has

had the experience in middle school or high school when they've done something really embarrassing and then walked down the school hallway thinking, "Everyone is looking at me. Everyone knows what I did or what happened." Well, yesterday's teen paranoia is your daughter's reality—everybody really *does* know.

6. They are addicted to being connected. Having been raised in a connective culture, many children feel like there is no way the information stream would stop, or that it should. Even if your child disconnects, she understandably believes that she "can't ever stop the chatter." All these people in her school and community now feel like they're in your house and in her room. Technology provides a constantly updated picture of everyone's life.

The limit of how mean and vicious a girl can be is beginning to disappear. If girls are pretty certain that other girls won't be confrontational face-to-face, they have the freedom to be super nasty and never have to own up to it.   —Lily, 18

How do they hide what they're doing from you?

I type an IM and then I quickly minimize it. Then I pull up a game really fast.

I put the IM down under the screen so no one can see.

I have four different e-mail accounts. My parents think the only one I have is the one I got in fourth grade.

I text while they are talking to me. It looks like I'm paying attention and I sort of am, but I'm always doing my own personal business too.

I have a more than one Facebook account.

I have more than one MySpace account.

My parents don't let me on the computer unless they're around, so I go down to the basement because there's a computer down there I can use.

I wait until my parents are asleep.

CELL PHONES

I'm not going to tell you to take away your daughter's cell phone because, even if I did, I'm pretty sure you're not going to. I can, however, give you my best suggestions for tying your daughter's ethical development with her use of one.

When Does She Need a Cell Phone?

If you have a child between the ages of five and twelve walking around with a cell phone and it has any other capabilities beyond calling you, their grandparents, or 911, you have lost your mind. Beyond that, the following are my absolute standards for when a child needs access to a cell phone—which doesn't mean she needs one for her exclusive use. Again, please notice that, based on my criteria, no one in elementary school should have a cell phone.

Why your daughter needs a cell phone
1. She's going to a concert or any event where there will be a lot of people and it'll be easy to get lost.
2. She's going to a party where she may have to leave because she's uncomfortable.
3. She is going to more activities after school, so she needs to be able to call you or vice versa if anyone has a change of plans.
4. She drives a car.
5. She starts doing most things without parental supervision.

Tips to Keep Your Kids Safe While Using Technology
1. Under no circumstances should your child share a password with their friends or people they are dating—not even when someone is harmlessly sitting at the computer with your daughter right next to her and they say "Hey, what's your password, I can't get access to . . ." Instead, your daughter should put it in herself and then change it when they leave.
2. Do your best to know your child's password. This is easier said than done because your child could always change it

later. If you really feel that she should give you her password, you can always do random checks by going up to her when she's at the computer and force her to log in. The problem, however, is that this strategy can become a power struggle between you and will convince her that she's justified to up the ante (i.e., do whatever is necessary to stop you from seeing her information).

3. Look at your phone or cable bill. You need to track when your child is texting. If she is texting at 2:00 A.M., that is a problem, starting with the resultant lack of sleep.

4. The same goes for her Facebook and MySpace wall. If you are in their network, you don't have to read the content of their messages to be able to see the time and date stamps of their communication. If you really want to see what's going on, go to sleep, but set your alarm for about an hour after your bedtime. Wake up and go to her room or downstairs and see if she's on the computer. It's the same concept as when you called your boyfriend or girlfriend once your parents were asleep when you were younger.

5. Understand that online games are what chat rooms were five years ago. When your child meets people online and plays games, they develop relationships with them. Those people become known to them (i.e., trusted). Not all these people are scary and horrible, but some are.

6. The majority of girls who meet people in real life whom they initially met online do so willingly. Most girls know it is beyond stupid to meet someone in real life whom you only know online. But if the girl is socially isolated, doesn't have other good adult relationships in her life, and wants to be special in someone's eyes, her desperation might make someone she meets online become much more enticing and believable.

7. Have a designated adult be the only one in your house allowed to clear the browser cache of what websites have been visited, and keep a log of the last time it was done. Kids are often smart enough to figure this out, so establish and maintain a rule for them not to clean the history.

8. Take advantage of all usage controls your cell phone plan

and/or Internet provider offers. Most allow you to see ingoing and outgoing information, including texts and pictures. Some allow you to control the times your child's cell phone works—which means you can stop them from sending or receiving information in the evening when they should be hanging out with family, doing homework, or sleeping.

LAYING DOWN THE LAW

This is what you say in preparation for giving your daughter or allowing her to use any kind of technology (cell phones, social networking sites, online games, etc.):

> Technology can be really fun to use and it gives us incredible access to the world. But it is a privilege, not a right. And because it is a privilege, you have a responsibility to use it ethically. What using technology ethically looks like to me is that you never use it to humiliate, embarrass, send personal information, misrepresent yourself or someone else, use passwords without the person's permission, share embarrassing information or pictures of other people, put someone down (elementary school), or compromise yourself by sending pictures of you naked, half naked, in your bra (junior high/high school). Remember that it is so easy for things to get out of control. You know it. I know it. So I reserve the right to check your online life, from texting to your Facebook page. If I see that you are violating the terms of our agreement, I will take all of your technology away until you can earn my trust back. This is my unbreakable, unshakable law.

THE DEFINITION OF PRIVACY HAS CHANGED

Your definition of privacy is probably very different from your daughter's. Although it would never occur to you to put your personal thoughts and experiences online, your daughter may think there's nothing wrong with that. But let me ask you a question: Have you ever put pictures of yourself and your family on your Facebook page or Flickr? Do you forward personal pictures to friends and family on any kind of social networking site? Although it may be to a lesser degree, it's the same thing as what your daughter does when she puts up pictures of the party she went to last weekend. The only difference is that most girls' lives are way more dramatic than your last trip to see your parents, and girls may not have the ability to decide what's appropriate. Either way, many of us are putting personal information online for the whole world to see, and we can't just blame it on our kids. Recently, someone who blogs for my website was notified that a "guest" was looking at pictures he had recently posted, including ones of his six-year-old daughter playing at a pool. He went to the guest's account and found hundreds of pictures of girls in similar situations. As a collection, the pictures were incredibly disturbing. He had the person blocked.

How Do We Teach Kids to Have Personal Boundaries Without Scaring Them to Death?

As a general rule, I think we approach these issues with the same philosophy we use to teach our children about people in the real world. You say:

As much as I wish this weren't true, there are some people in the world who want to hurt kids. This doesn't mean everyone is like that, but some people are, and you need to be smart about whom you communicate with, trust, and give personal information. You're a smart kid, but no matter how smart you are, it can be incredibly easy to give away personal information without even realizing you're doing it. For example, if you record something in your room or house and post it on YouTube, do you say something or have things in the background that give away your personal information? If you're playing online games and they say they go to a school nearby and are in a certain grade, how do you know what they're saying is true and do you respond by giving them your information?

Why Is There a Disconnect in Kids' Minds Between Public Versus Private?

Many adults are baffled by young people's enthusiasm for putting pictures of themselves and very personal information all over social networking sites, but those same kids think it's an invasion of privacy when it comes to parents or teachers viewing the same information. Take a step back and realize that, from your daughter's perspective, you aren't supposed to see it. That information is up there for her world to see it. You're supposed to be on another planet.

What is very confusing and painful to see is kids who are really surprised when their personal information is used against them. I see this as a version of invincibility and an example of the mentality that "it won't happen to me" that many of us have. I know it's hard to believe when we see kids shocked that their privacy has been violated, but as far as I can tell, their reaction is genuine. They don't seem to get it until it happens to them.

ONE-TO-ONE LAPTOP SCHOOLS

Parents and schools alike have associated giving kids laptops with educational opportunities, but it creates as many problems as it solves. The thinking behind it, which I'll grant makes sense, is this: if you want to prepare students for the future, you have to introduce them to technology as early and often as possible. But one-to-one laptop programs aren't that simple, because students distract themselves by sitting at their desks writing instant messages, watching videos, or checking their Facebook page (I know there are schools who block Facebook and YouTube, but most students know how to get around that using proxy sites) while they're in school. How do I know this? Because I e-mail with students all the time, and it usually takes them about five minutes to get back to me—during the school day. So you have to have structured, sophisticated, responsive guidelines to enable these programs to actually achieve the stated goal—to make students better able to work, not sitting in class writing mean messages to each other about the teacher or other kids in the class.*

Constant Connectivity Weighs on Kids

You can never escape your social network. The easiest way I can explain this is that the majority of students I see sleep with their cell phones by their beds. Some kids even sleep with their phone on their chest.

This is a serious problem.

Ironically, many parents closely monitor what movies and television shows their children watch, put all sorts of filtering devices on the computers, and harshly judge those parents who don't. To their minds, their home is a protected bubble. But as soon as you let your daughter take her cell phone to bed at night there is no safety zone except the one that exists in your mind. Why? Because it's 2:00 A.M. and your daughter just got a text message about how everyone in the school hates her, or she was just sent pornography because someone in her class thought it would be funny.

The last time I wrote this book, just seven years ago, unless your daughter was physically sneaking out or someone was physically sneaking in, once your daughter was in her room at night, you could sleep peacefully knowing that she was safe and no one could do anything to hurt her. Now, if she has a cell phone or any kind of device that gives her Internet access, at some point she's going to bed at 4:00 A.M., exhausted and anxious. Three hours later, you walk by her room and get annoyed because she was supposed to be up a half an hour ago. At 7:30, she comes downstairs, barely eats breakfast, and is in a foul mood that you attribute to being a moody, lazy teenager. In frustration, you say, "How do you plan to do well in school if you aren't taking it seriously? Life doesn't wait for late people." She just looks at you like you're crazy and blows you off, making you even more irritated.

And, even if she's not getting hateful text messages, the fact that

---

*If you would like more information or examples of these guidelines, I have them in my curriculum, *Owning Up*, under the "Social Justice Guidelines" section.

she's spending precious sleeping hours chattering away with her friends, unable to pull herself away from the constant conversation, infringes on her ability to do well in school. We need to help kids set boundaries with technology—not only to keep them safe, but also to let them know it's OK to be disconnected, even in a culture that tells us that that's not an option.

Now, if and when you disconnect your daughter in any way, you are going to get serious pushback. She's going to be mad, resentful, and indignant. If it helps at all, girls get mad at me, too, and I want to share with you a recent experience.

In the beginning of this school year, I met with a group of parents at a wonderful Catholic all-girls school in the Midwest. During the presentation, I challenged them to take their daughters' cell phones away when they returned home that night. The problem was that the next day, I had a presentation with their daughters. As I watched the girls file into the auditorium, I couldn't help but notice the death stares I was getting. So I went over to a group of girls to ask what was going on.

The girls did hate me. Or better said, they resented me. Why? Because to my surprise, their parents had actually listened to me and gone home and taken their daughters' cell phones away. Trying not to laugh, I asked the girls if they would hold off hating me until I had an opportunity to explain myself—then they could hate me as much as they wanted. My only request was that if I said anything that made sense to them, even if they didn't like it, they had to tell me. These are two of the responses I got after the assembly.

> *My mom took my phone out of my room at night. I thought it wouldn't help, but I actually slept better. I don't know how to tell her I think she was right. We have been getting into a lot of fights recently and I don't want to give in to her.*

> *My mom came home from the presentation and told me my cell phone was no longer allowed in my room . . . and I still liked you!*

The lesson of this story is critical. Parents today seem to be afraid to lay down rules because they don't want their child being angry at them. Your daughter is your child. If she's not mad at you when you enforce rules, there is something wrong.

THE BLACKBERRY DOESN'T FALL FAR FROM THE TREE

Let's be honest, teens aren't the only ones addicted to being connected. I cannot tell you how many times I've heard middle and high schoolers complain about their parents' constant texting. Here are a few examples:

> *It's 11 in the morning. I've only been up since 7:30. I've literally received fifteen messages from my mother since that time—the most important of which informed me that she was "driving through Richmond" with my "sisters sleeping in the back of the car" and that "Gma's flight is delayed, but not really that much." Really, Mom? Was it that crucial I know my sisters' nap schedule? Shouldn't you be paying attention to the road?* —Katelyn, 18

> *I can't move without my mom texting me at school. Like, "How's your day? Is everyone being nice to you?" She never stops, and don't even get me started on how often she e-mails my teachers.* —Bella, 11

So if you're wondering how your daughter gets into the thousands with her message count each month, remember that you might be playing a large part in her accumulation of texts. If you set the example that she constantly needs to be in communication with you, you will absolutely normalize her need to always be a text away from talking to a friend. You've given her the OK to hit that three-thousand-message mark with your example. More dangerously, she might simply start ignoring your messages. Not a good thing when you have an emergency on hand and she ignores the constant buzzing of her phone as your usual addiction to text messaging.

> *My mother has a serious problem with her BlackBerry—she whips it out at red lights, or sets the car on cruise control and asks me to watch the wheel while she responds to an*

e-mail. We took it away from her for a day, and she went through withdrawal—your BlackBerry is our Facebook. —Mia, 18

My mom texts me ALL THE TIME. Maybe 1% of the time it's important, but it's so annoying that I ignore those ones too. My personal favorite? "Ewwww . . . im sooo grossed out . . . this guy at the gas station who is missing half his teeth was coming on to me. . . . ICK!" —Alex, 18

Do You Have the Right to Check Your Daughter's Text Messages/Facebook Page/Etc.?

Yes, you do. That said, don't do it every night because your daughter does deserve some privacy. There are only a few specific times I think you should preemptively check: (1) when you have made plans to be out of town and she isn't coming with you. You need to do this because cell phones and Facebook are the de facto ways teens get the word out about parties. If you are unclear about what I am referring to, please skip to Chapter 11, "Sex, Drugs, Alcohol, and Partying in Girl World." (2) When her behavior is really frightening you/causing concern and she won't tell you what's going on.

When Should I Let My Child Get a Facebook Page, Cell Phone, Etc.?

A counselor I work with advises parents that letting a seventh grader have a Facebook page is like giving a sixteen-year-old a Ferrari—it's simply too much power in the hands of someone too impulsive and inexperienced. Of course, you don't have a lot of control over whether your child gets one or not, because all she needs to do to get a Facebook page is say, "Yes, I am fourteen." As powerless as that makes you, take hope: guess who *is* effective in getting younger teens off Facebook? Their older brothers and sisters.

My older brother won't let me use Facebook. He told me I was too young and he wouldn't even friend me. He said that I should do it when I'm older. —Arval, 12

Never underestimate older siblings' ability and desire to protect their younger siblings, even if those older children act badly themselves. Also, recognize that they know better than you do what's going on online.

TECHNOLOGY MANNERS

There's never an excuse for bad manners. I don't care if you're a moody teenager or an adult who's had a bad day. When you are with other human beings, you need to show interest in their presence and be polite. This is not only the right thing to do, but also a demonstration of basic social ability and competence. So, parents, if you want your child to be socially inept, by all means allow them to play handheld video games at dinner. Take them to social gatherings and let them sit in the corner, completely oblivious to those around them. Watch as people try to engage them and receive only a grunt in response. This is not only rude, but will also result in other people's not getting to know your child and your child's not getting to know them.

For the record, I completely understand wanting to conduct a conversation without interruptions from whining children. I myself am not above putting my children in front of a movie while I have dinner in the next room with friends. That doesn't mean we should let our children off the hook for participating in social functions. Few things annoy me more than watching a kid sit completely unaware of her surroundings because her parents are letting her talk on the phone, text, or play games. Games are a distraction, meant for mundane things like waiting in line at the post office. Playing games is not a substitute for daily human interaction.

It is also rude to talk on a cell phone at the dinner table, which means you can't do it either. And having a family dinner where everyone is answering their phone and texting doesn't count as quality family time. There needs to be a family rule that, when people walk into your house, their cell phones go in a basket in the hallway or the kitchen. You get a pass if you are a doctor or therapist and you're on call—but only when you're on call. This also should go for any other child who is over at your house.

USING TECHNOLOGY FOR RECONNAISSANCE

If you want to know if your child is going where she says she's going, have her take a picture of her location and e-mail it to you. If you have a *very* sneaky kid, make her take a picture that includes something to indicate the date and time—that way, she can't use a picture from another time and trick you. Some parents make kids take a picture of the scoreboard if they say they're going to a game. Other parents make their children hand over their cell phone to the adult wherever they are to verify the plans and get that person's cell number.

Technology can be your friend if you use it to strengthen your communication with other parents. If you have their cell numbers or have friended them on Facebook, it will be a lot harder for girls to exploit information vacuums between parents because there won't be any. This weapon, however, must be used strategically. You want your daughter slightly paranoid that you have the capacity to get in touch with other parents, but you don't want her so freaked out that she countersneaks or doesn't tell you her problems because she's so worried you're going to immediately sit down and fire off a nasty e-mail to some other person.

When you have a teenager, your goal is to keep one step ahead of them. This has been and always will be the goal. Likewise, teens will always be looking for the next way to get one over on you. Don't take it personally. And remember, a small degree of fear and paranoia can literally save your child's life.

IF YOU DECIDE TO LET YOUR CHILD HAVE A FACEBOOK PAGE

Say your child has been begging for a Facebook page and you decide to let them. This is what you should say:

> If I give you permission to have a Facebook page, number one, I want you to know that I want to be there when you determine what e-mail address it's connected to. We are going to walk through all the privacy settings and together decide what the boundaries will be. You will authentically represent your age

and not give information about where you live. If you would be embarrassed if I found out anything you put up, that should be your cue that what you've put up isn't appropriate.

At the time of this writing, Facebook has over 200 million users. Even if you have no desire to be on it yourself, chances are good that someone you know and trust *does* have a Facebook page. They should friend your child so that they can check information when and if needed.

Signs That the Social Networking Page You Set Up Is Not the One Your Child Is Actually Using

A child who is using a different site may have any sort of message on the wall that says, "Hey, do you ever use this anymore? Where have you been?" If the messages are dated from two weeks ago, she's set up another account. Ten minutes equals a day. If she has been begging you to allow her to get an account, it's not like she is not going to be online.

Want to Know If She's a Decent Person?

If you want to check if your daughter's a decent human being and following your rules, go look at her text messages of the last two weeks. It might also be helpful for her to be self-reflective: ask her to go through them and think about what she's been communicating as well.

What If Your Daughter Makes a Mistake and Sends Information About Herself?

If she reveals personal information, she has to do everything she can to immediately pull that information down. Be careful to not make her feel stupid about it in that process though—avoid saying things like, "How could you have not realized that our address was written right behind your head when you posted that thing on YouTube?" Honestly, it's really easy to make these kinds of mistakes. Your daughter knows by now that it wasn't an intelligent thing to do. The first time it happens, I'd say:

> Look, we made an agreement about how you could upload things onto the Internet. I know it was a mistake, but I need you to take responsibility for your actions. You are going to pull it down wherever you posted it. You are also going to ask your friends if anyone forwarded it to any other social networking site and you're going to do whatever you can to pull that down as well. You will lose your computer privileges for one week. I really do get that this was a mistake and you didn't intend to do it, but you also have to understand that if it happens again, I will be forced to take away more computer privileges because you're showing me you aren't ready to use it safely.

If She's Part of the Problem

Make no mistake, forwarding is not being an innocent bystander. She has made a choice to make the problem bigger. If she participated in the creation of negative information or forwarding of that information about someone else, she has to apologize to that person in person (see p. 227 for apologies), and she has to send an e-mail to all the people she knows it went to acknowledging what she did. It would look something like this:

> To everyone in the ninth grade,
> Last week, I wrote stuff on my Facebook wall about Allison that wasn't true. I shouldn't have done it. I have apologized to Allison in person, but I also needed to write to you so you would know it wasn't true.

You will be standing over her and watching her press "send" while she does this. And yes, she will hate you for making her do it. Too bad. Someone has to take a stand about this stuff, and that someone is you.

What If She Embarrasses Herself?

There is nothing you're going to say that she hasn't already thought herself—avoid anything along the lines of "How could you have been so stupid?" She's going to feel humiliated, dumb, possibly defensive (like, "that never would have happened if . . ."), hurt, and paranoid that everyone she's ever had contact with knows about what she did. So don't say, "Everyone will forget about it tomorrow. Don't let it bother you." Because you are asking for the impossible. Just hold her and tell her how sorry you are. No matter what she did or how embarrassed you are by it (and under no circumstances should you say you're embarrassed), this is the time to tell her you will get through this as a family. Everyone makes mistakes. It's how you conduct yourself after messing up that shows what kind of person you are. Work on figuring out how she is going to walk down the hallway the next day.

After comforting her a bit, have her give you her phone for the next seventy-two hours. She may balk at this suggestion because she may be trying to convince herself that there's something she can do or say that will fix it. Let her know that the way she's going to fix it is by holding her head high in real life. To have any chance of that, she has to disconnect from what people are saying to her or each other about what she did. It'll just make her feel worse.

Second, she has to acknowledge what she did and why. If she sent a picture of herself to a boy because she wanted him to like her, she's not the first person who has done something they regretted to get someone to like them; however, she does need to acknowledge why it was so important to her to get this boy to pay attention to her that she was willing to make that choice. This may be too excruciating of a conversation for her to have with you, so I would strongly recommend asking if she'd rather speak to her ally (see information on allies in Chapter 2). You would then make sure that the goal with the ally is to come up with a strategy where she can ask for help if she's feeling desperately embarrassed or can't face going to school. Regardless, I'd give her a day to lick her wounds, go for a hike, window-shop, or just spend some time with her. While you're out, prepare her for going to school.

What Happens If Someone Teases Her About It?

Tell her to take a deep breath. Then she can say, "I made a big mistake, which I'm really trying to deal with. Your bringing it up is making me feel worse. I'm not sure if that's your point, but I promise you that I would never make you feel bad if you were in my situation, so I'm leaving now."

SEXTING: GIRLS BETRAYING THEMSELVES

Your family is hanging out in the living room on a normal Monday evening. Your son, age ten, is doing his homework on his laptop on the couch while your fourteen-year-old daughter lies in her favorite chair, texting away with her friends, half paying attention to the TV. The Cowboys are playing the Redskins, and your spouse is reading. You look up for a minute and think to yourself, "How awesome that my family can hang out like this. The kids are getting older, but we still spend time together, and everyone's not hiding in their corners of the house." At halftime, you and your daughter banter back and forth about that insane pass Jason Campbell just threw, and she goes to the bathroom before the game comes back on. Little do you know that while she's in there, she flips open her phone, pulls up her shirt, and takes a picture of her boobs. You don't know it, but during the game she's been texting with a guy in the grade above her whom she has a crush on. Their flirtatious texts have escalated and as she hits "send" on the explicit shot captioned "u like?" she feels a little adrenaline rush and hopes that he'll ask her to homecoming. She was worried he'd think she was a prude because she's a freshman, but she's pretty convinced he'll think differently now. She deletes the photo from her phone's memory card, runs the water in the sink for a second, then comes back out and flops down in her chair. She's been gone all of two minutes.

It may seem odd to you that we have a common reality in which girls are voluntarily sending seminude or nude pictures of themselves. You may reasonably ask yourself, "What is wrong with kids today to make them think this is a sane thing to do?" It's a perfectly good question, and it's one that girls need to ask themselves. A reasonable fifteen-year-old girl in real life would never stand in front of a guy she liked, take off all her clothes, and ask, "Now do you like me?" Nor would she think it was acceptable for that boy to bring all his friends over to weigh in on the decision—yet a lot of girls send naked pictures of themselves to boys they're trying to impress. Note that those pictures are usually a follow-up to unbelievably graphic text messages going back and forth between those two kids, who really don't see what they're doing as a problem because it wasn't really graphic since no pictures were involved.

Sometimes as the principal, I have to read the printouts from these conversations and it is so embarrassing. My last one, I had thirty pages brought to me but honestly I didn't need to read beyond the first couple.   —Robert

Sometimes boys will find their friends' stash of naked girl pictures and forward them to themselves or their other friends.
                                                            —Dylan, 18

Land Mine!

Don't say, "I'm never going to hear anything about you doing this sexting stuff, am I?" with your eyebrows raised, shoulders hunched, and lips pursed. If you're too uncomfortable to ask these questions and have a discussion in a real way, even if what you're saying is valid, it automatically gets annoying and she will absolutely blow you off.

WHAT SHOULD SCHOOLS DO TO TEACH RESPONSIBLE TECHNOLOGY USE?

At my school, there have been girls who get into fights and use each other's passwords to forward e-mails that gossip about people to those people. Or other girls make fake AIM [AOL In-

stant Messenger] accounts and show them to everybody at
school the next day.   *—Carolyn, 16*

*This year I had a girl save an old e-mail from a girl when they got
into a fight. Then, they got into another fight, and the first girl
copied and pasted the original e-mail to a new one so it looked
like it had just been sent. Somehow, our IT person figured it out,
but if you had told me when I first got into education that I would
be dealing with this, I wouldn't have believed you.*

                                                —Brian, Principal

Unless you work in schools on a day-to-day basis, there really is
no way to fully appreciate how technology has impacted the
school environment. It is not unusual for school administrators to
spend hours with their technical/computer support people trying
to figure out which students started the latest bullying smear campaign against someone else in the school. And this is absolutely
certain—teens will never stop coming up with new and creative
ways to use technology to go after each other and the adults in the
community.

Schools, and by default school administrators and educators,
are on the front lines of the battle to teach young people how to
use technology ethically. To say the least, this is an incredibly difficult task, one that no one in education today got their professional
degree in. I know I didn't. But I, just like many people in education, have had to become an expert. We all want to be proactive,
and many people are—to the best of their ability—but the nature
of the beast means we will always have to be on the lookout for
"next iteration of." How has it changed schools? Here are some
examples:

- Students can cheat and plagiarize more easily (yes, there are
  programs teachers use to deter and control plagiarism, but it's
  still easier).
- Students are better able to hide drugs and other contraband.
  In schools where police and school resource officers conduct

random drug checks, as soon as the first students know about it they text their friends. Within minutes everyone knows a search is under way and can take the necessary precautions to avoid being caught.
- Students can bully and harass each other more intensely, more ruthlessly, in any and all forms.

In response, almost all schools have tried to block inappropriate material from getting through their computer systems with firewalls and filters. This doesn't work anymore because most students have cell phones with Internet service. Ironically, it's come to the point where a student who wants to research sexual harassment can't, because the filtering devices on the schools' computers restrict access to the information; but it wouldn't stop a kid from sexually harassing another student from his phone as he walks down the hall.

As my area of expertise is bullying, I'm going to focus on that aspect of technology in schools. The harassment you grew up with is most likely completely tame compared with what the average high school person experiences on a daily basis. Again, you didn't have cell phones with Internet access so there was no possibility anyone could download pornography and show it to you as walked down the hallway. There was no way you'd be sitting in math class and an instant message pops up from the girl sitting in the front row about what an ugly fat cow you are. There was no way you were going to get a text from the guy sitting behind you about how hot you are. There was no way you'd be sitting at home doing your homework while receiving repeated voice mails from three boys in your class about all the graphic sexual things they want to do to you, and then have the school administration say the next day that they can't do anything to the boys because they did it at home and the technology they used wasn't the school's.

Clearly, not all school administrators are incompetent, but some are, and the consequences are much larger than what happens with the individual case. The unfortunate reality is if these situations aren't handled well, the abusive kids are in control of the school.

First let me show you how school administrators handle it badly and then I'll show you how it's handled well.

Sorry, our hands are tied. It didn't happen on school property and they didn't use their school e-mail, so we can't do anything.

I get so angry when I hear school professionals say that, and to put it right out there, this response is the most naive, irresponsible answer we could ever give our children. It doesn't matter if it's abusive voice mails, kids posting videos on YouTube trashing someone, sending humiliating pictures, or any other of the countless ways kids are destroying each other, some parents and school administrators believe the school has no power or authority to discipline the offenders.

Technology obliterates the boundary between home and school. If this is our response, here's what happens. The target has to go to school knowing that no adult will protect them there, and they therefore feel anxious, depressed, and isolated. The perpetrators know that they are in control of the school environment because they know what they do outside of school will have a profound impact inside the school, yet the school will do nothing to stop them.

The terrible consequences of ignoring these situations are teens and children who hate going to school and believe the educators who are supposed to keep them safe are incompetent at best and that there is no point in standing up to bullying and harassment because it is so prevalent. The adults don't get it, so why in the world would children take the chance to fight this battle when the grown-ups won't? In their minds, all the adults do is have assemblies or put a kindness banner at the entrance of the school.

At the end of the day, no one has any stake in each other (and why would they?) in a world where adults give them no reason ever to take actual interest in the well-being of their colleagues. Why would we?
                                                              —Max, 21

But not all school administrators are like this. There are a lot who are doing their absolute best. In my experience, those people understand the following:

- They realize that what happens in the school affects what happens outside the school and vice versa. This is what many of the schools I work with include in their technology contract: *Bullying often occurs outside of the school's physical grounds yet these actions impact the safety of our students as though they have occurred on school grounds. Any bullying behavior demonstrated at school or outside of school that affects our school community will be addressed by the school.*
- They believe discipline means to teach. They understand that there are various levels of culpability, and it takes time to figure out who has done what and to what extent. Doing that, however, takes a great deal of skill and finesse because while you are uncovering the facts, you're dealing with angry parents and defensive, embarrassed kids who are often trying to hide what they've done.
- They understand the relationship between transparency and confidentiality. The people in a position of leadership in a school need to share enough information with their community so that people feel informed about how issues of bullying in any form will be handled, but be clear that in specific cases, the people involved and any disciplinary actions against them will be confidential to respect their privacy.

In my experience, there are waves of how these things go. The first wave is gathering the data and interviewing the people involved. The second wave is giving out the disciplinary action—that is based on an understanding of the various levels of individual responsibility and accountability. The third wave is the reaction of the parents in the larger community. Sometimes it's a ripple and sometimes it's a huge wave.

—Stewart, Head of School

Land Mine!

When you're sitting on the bleachers at your child's athletic event or waiting in car pool and another parent tells you a horrible story about bullying in the school and describes the counselor as incompetent or says the head of the school "did nothing," there is a chance they are accurate. But there is a larger chance that the parent has no idea what he or she is talking about. This is not to take away from any child's bad experience with an uncaring or ineffective school person, but in my experience parents who know nothing about the actual events spread gossip around the school while these school personnel are working their hardest to figure out what happened and what the best response should be. The problem is no principal, teacher, coach, or counselor can divulge to the community at large the exact circumstances that would explain their decision making without compromising their integrity and breaching confidentiality.

Schools can't be safe places of learning without your help. If you have a bad principal, who won't take the leadership role necessary, go to that person with a plan of action created by different stakeholders in your community (including the students) so she is compelled to make the necessary changes.

Support school administrators and educators when they take a stand—especially when your child has been identified as part of the problem. Back them up when parents start the rumor mill. And if you think the school personnel are part of the problem, at least demand that people demonstrate civil thoughtful disagreement.

Be very, very nice to your school's computer specialist. He, along with the custodians, is often the most underappreciated person in the building.

So You Hate Their Music (or Think You Should)

"Has anyone had the experience of an adult telling you they hate your music? That it sends the wrong message? That it's too violent? Hypersexual? That it's disrespectful to women?"

Of course, when I ask teens these questions, all hands go up. Just as their parents' hands would have if I had asked them when they were teens.

Music is and always has been powerful, and never more so than during the teenage years. Think about the music that brings back your strongest memories—isn't it from when you were young? When I was a teen, I loved Depeche Mode (in fact I still do). One of my favorite albums was *Violator*. If you don't know every word of every song like I do, take my word for it that the whole thing is about a guy having hypnotic control over a girl. It was pretty much as if Edward Cullen in *Twilight* joined a rock group and sang to me. And for those of you who love the classics, your music isn't off the hook either. Do you love Robert Plant when he sings, "Squeeze my lemon 'til the juice runs down my leg"? Bon Jovi's "Slippery When Wet"? Or Jimi Hendrix when you're rocking out to "Crosstown Traffic" as he sings, "Tire tracks all across your back / I can see you had your fun"?

Music means something to us because it touches the most profound aspects of our lives. Love, lust, jealousy, alienation, confusion, anger, loneliness, insecurity: it's all there. And, more often than not, the times we feel these emotions the most strongly occur when we're teens.

What's different about music today is how it comes into our lives. It has interlinked with all the other forms of technology to combine into one relentless stream. And, more than any other time in human history, music is about selling things to the listener. Mainstream music is a constant advertisement for the "Act Like a Woman" box. (Information on the Act Like a Woman box is presented in Chapter 3, and see information in Chapter 8 about the Act Like a Man box.)

That's why it's absolutely critical to engage in the music your daughter is listening to in just the way I'm suggesting you engage in all the other forms of technology she uses. This can be really hard for some adults. Why? I think it's for three main reasons: (1) you feel overwhelmed by the crassness of the message; (2) the images and sounds put you into sensory overload; or (3) you kind of like the music too.

To be a competent thinker in today's society, your daughter

must consider critically the messages she's receiving through music and examine how those messages relate to the culture of Girl World and Boy World.

You can find almost all the music your daughter is listening to in two ways. One: type the name of the song followed by the word "lyrics" in your favorite search engine. Two: type the name of the song followed by "official video" into YouTube to view the music video for free.

Also, you don't have to limit yourself to music, because that is by no means the only form of media that can be analyzed. Your daughter also needs to become an informed observer of television shows, movies, video games, websites devoted to TV shows, blogs, gossip/teen magazines, and advertisements. In other words, her brain should always be on.

"I Just Like the Beat"

Of course she does. So do I. Let me give you an example. Personally, I can't stand Justin Timberlake. To say it another way, the man has serious issues with women. As far as I can tell, he has never done a song or music video with a woman where she's wearing even half the clothes he is. If you're a woman and you're going to do a duet with him, you have to literally climb all over him while he assures you that "you're the one" (countless songs) who "might get the keys to the castle" ("What Goes Around . . . Comes Around") with good behavior. If you're *really* good, he may even "give you [his] ring" ("My Love"). But, if you misbehave, then you deserve to die in a car explosion ("What Goes Around . . . Comes Around").

However, when I am in my car and his music comes on, do I start singing the words and dancing in my seat? Yes, I do. Why? Because the music is good—that is, it's catchy. It's really easy to not pay attention to the messages in the songs, so you can listen to it. You can even dance along, but you have to know what it's telling you so you can withstand its influence.

Most Artists Aren't All Bad or All Good

Every once in a while, the adult media labels an artist or a type of music a really bad influence for the nation's youth. Don't buy into that. Things are never that simple, and if you believe it and try to talk to your daughter with that standpoint, she'll dismiss you for your unfounded judgments and assumptions. It is common for an artist to create an amazingly poignant song about racism, child abuse, or domestic violence and then to turn around and perform a song that has women shaking their butts in his face while they throw money at the camera. It's common for women artists to talk about how they are into female empowerment and positive self-esteem for girls, and then sing about how all they want is for people to envy them and they'll take away another girl's boyfriend because they're hotter. For example, one of my favorite artists, Ciara, a couple of years ago did an amazing music video with a female video producer that challenged gender stereotypes. This year, she teamed up again with the same producer and made a video where she is imitating a stripper with a dog collar around her neck and Justin Timberlake is pulling on it. Now, you don't have to keep up with each and every artist and what he or she is doing. You just have to keep this in mind when you are talking to your daughter so she takes you seriously.

Do I Overanalyze Things Too Much?

High school and college students love to ask me this question, and I understand where it comes from. If you do what I'm asking you to do, it seems like you'll never be able to watch or listen to anything mindlessly again. I get that. And I also admit that I do have a tendency to analyze things—a lot. But do you know who does it more than me? The artists who sell the music. My one brain is nothing compared to the army of marketing people working with the artist to sell the listener everything, from the artist's image to cell phones, laptops, places in a music video, brands of alcohol, and the clothes the artist sings about. This is about who has control over your daughter's brain—is it your daughter, or other people whose single purpose is to make her a relentless thoughtless consumer?

Talking to Her About Her Music

All of what I just wrote doesn't take away from the fact that music can be deeply personal and powerful for young people. Music can be positively transformative. Asking teens to share their music and other preferred forms of media with you can be like asking them to share their diary.

Before you can have any chance of a successful dialogue with your daughter, it is critical that you process and manage your own emotional reactions to the media. I don't care if it's music or a video game. You can't sit across the table from her with a look of disgust on your face and hope to have a successful conversation. Try this instead:

> I know I've been complaining about the music you've been listening to, but I've decided that I really need to learn about it and why you like it. After that, I'd like to talk about it. Just like you, I have media coming at me all day, and I want us both to be more aware of what messages are coming at us. I want us to be informed, so I'd really like for you to show me what you like and tell me why. Then I want to ask you a couple of questions so I can understand it better.

You can point out that, according to a report by the Federal Trade Commission, teenagers (ages twelve to seventeen) see an average of thirty-one thousand ads per year on television alone. That doesn't include product placements, web ads, text message marketing, billboards, magazines, catalogs, games, or other forms of media.*

How I Break It Down

As a way of understanding how media work, you can separate what you see and hear into three distinct categories of expression: aspirational, relational, and oppositional.

*Holt, D. J., Ippolito, P. M., Desrochers, D. M., & Kelley, C. R. (June 1, 2007). Children's exposure to TV advertising in 1977 and 2004 (Federal Trade Commission Bureau of Economics Staff Report). www.ftc.gov/os/2007/06/cabecolor.pdf

Aspirational music and media shows a desire or ambition to achieve something through material success and being better than other people. Aspirational music and music videos are ones that reinforce the Girl World and Boy World boxes; most pop music fits into this category.

Relational music and media involves expressing a relationship with the viewer or listener. The artist is saying that he or she understands and identifies with what the listener is going through.

Oppositional music and media shows an actively hostile attitude toward something or a resistance stance against something in the culture. The artist is opposing the Girl World and Boy World box.

If your daughter is willing, watch the videos together and ask her the following questions:

> What were your initial feelings while watching the video? What was your gut reaction?
> What do the people who created this video want you to think?
> What do the people who created this video want you to feel?
> What do the people who created this video want you to buy?
> Did you see any product placements?
> Going back to your initial reaction, do you think the video works?
> Did you see the Act Like a Woman and Act Like a Man boxes being reinforced? Where and how?

You Want a Critical Thinker

Everything I'm writing about in this chapter comes down to this: technology and how it is used in the media is constantly changing our world. It either empowers your daughter to be more engaged, curious, and thoughtful about her world or it turns her into a thoughtless consumer of ideas and products. Don't waste this opportunity to teach your daughter to be a critical thinker—it's the only way she'll grow up to be a competent person capable of reaching her full potential.

SAMPLE TECHNOLOGY CONTRACT

A tangible way to instill your family values in your daughter is to create a family technology contract. Start by sitting around the kitchen table and asking her what your values are and how they would look when using technology. Here's a sample one to get you started.

We, the Edwards family, believe our family values include integrity and compassion. Every member of the family understands that our use of technology must reflect our values. Therefore, we recognize that the following are in direct contradiction to our values:

- Using someone's password and identity without his/her consent
- Spreading gossip
- Making or forwarding sexually suggestive photographs
- Sending viruses
- Participating in Internet polling
- Creating or participating in insulting websites and blogs
- Using Facebook, MySpace, Xanga, LiveJournal, YouTube, or any other website with the purpose of creating, viewing, or participating in the humiliation of others

If any family member is found acting in violation of this contract, the following will occur:

- First violation: Computer or cell phone privileges ended for ____ amount of time.
- Second violation: Computer and cell phone privileges ended for ____ amount of time.
- Third violation: One of the person's most valued privileges is taken away. (Remember, an iPod is a privilege and so is participating in team sports—no matter how good your child is.)

While we understand that any of us can make a mistake, we believe that living according to these values is critically important.

Signed on this day _____ of this year _____

Child _____ Parent(s) _____

If you're a religious family, make this an opportunity to show the relationship between family and religious values, and sign it in front of your religious leader. If you aren't religious, consider signing it in front of a notary. Either way, you want your children to understand that your family stands for treating people with dignity and that your word is your bond. Last, frame the contract and put it near the family computer as a visible reminder.

As you'll see, this chapter is written to provide a framework for how technology impacts your daughter's life. In the following chapters, you'll see it interwoven into every aspect of girls' lives.

We're now going to look at the social conflicts of younger girls, like the parents who recently told me that their five-year-old came home in tears because the Queen Bee told her, "Princesses don't wear pants, so you can't play with us!" So if you've ever been shocked at the manipulative behavior of the other eight-year-olds in your child's class or just want to know how the seeds of your daughter's social dynamics are planted in her younger years, the next chapter is for you.

Is It Really Happening
So Much Younger?

Second grade is when everything exploded.   —Ana, 9

My sister is 9, and in third grade, and already there are signs of cliquey mean behavior from some of her classmates. Glad you're stressing that it's not just middle schoolers—it IS starting earlier.
           —Lucy, 14

Several years ago a small package arrived in my mail that immediately caught my eye. It was expertly wrapped in a brown paper bag. An Oklahoma return address was written on the top left-hand corner. Wondering how people wrap things so perfectly, I opened it and was surprised to see a copy of *Queen Bees & Wannabes* along with a note in beautiful looping handwriting that immediately reminded me of Mrs. Clarke, my fifth-grade teacher at John Eaton Elementary School.

Dear Rosalind,
I bought this book because my ten-year-old granddaughter is having problems with her friends. But when I read it I was very upset with you to see the bad words in it. I can't in good conscience give this to my granddaughter because I do not want to introduce her to this world. Couldn't you talk to girls about these

things without using all those bad words? In the meantime, I am
respectfully sending you the book back because I have no further
need of it.
   Sincerely,
   Margaret Garrison

Well, Margaret, you're right. I did need to write something for younger girls because they are experiencing Queen Bees, cliques, and social cruelty. So this chapter is for you and all the other grandparents, parents, aunts, and teachers who have asked me to write something specifically for younger girls in a way that you could read together.

Adults are often so surprised that younger girls can be so mean. Maybe it's because they look cute (i.e., harmless), and they still give us hugs and listen to our advice. Maybe it's because we assume kids can only be so mean without using "bad words" to humiliate someone. Unfortunately, there's no age minimum for cruelty.

Here are some questions I have received from seven- to eleven-year-old girls:

Why do you think people are so exclusive to people they don't get
   to know?
If you were from another country and kids were making fun of
   you, what would you do?
How do I deal with someone who won't let me be friends with
   someone else?
If someone was mean to you earlier in the year and you see them
   getting made fun of now, what should you do?
If I was a bystander and the bully told me not to tell or else I
   would get beat up, what should I do?
What if your best friend is the bully and she doesn't know it?
What do you do when your clique doesn't accept you for who you
   are but for what you have?
How do you feel about racism and how do you stop it?
Will I always be a reject loser?

And my personal favorite:

How many bad influences are there in the United States?

These questions reflect the hardest issues a person will ever face. Why do people discriminate against others? How do I stand up against injustice? How do I get help for myself when I am being disrespected or humiliated? How do I help someone I care about when he or she is hurting? When you look at your daughter, remember that even at her age, she's already dealing with profound and complicated problems.

Things to Keep in Mind with Younger Girls

- Although it's true that she's telling you things that are going on in her life, don't assume she's telling you everything.
- Girls aren't only being mean to each other. They can be just as cruel to boys—just like some boys can be mean to them.
- Even if your daughter's only interaction with technology is Club Penguin and Webkinz, she can still use those things to be mean to someone or vice versa.
- By the time girls are in fourth and fifth grades, most of them cite YouTube as the website they go to most often. While on YouTube they can and do watch any music videos they want. Most parents I work with refuse to admit this.
- By fourth grade there will be girls in your daughter's class (or your daughter) who are going through puberty.
- Around the same time, there will also be girls who are incredibly boy crazy.
- Not withstanding the very serious questions written above, girls can get into very intense conflicts about things like, "she knows purple is my color." Use whatever issue is bothering them to teach them about ethics and friendships.
- Inside jokes, secret languages, and clubs are normal at this age, but they quickly become hurtful effective

weapons precisely because they can be excused as harmless games.

IS IT STARTING EARLIER?

I have been asked this question countless times by people who have already made up their mind about the answer. It's as if parents think there's something in the water that's making girls nastier. You may not like my answer. It's not in the water, it's in the mirror. Parents are buying into a culture that believes it's "cute" to buy trendy, sexy clothes or funny that an eight-year-old can lip-sync the latest Britney Spears or Katy Perry song. So funny that the adults then put it on YouTube for everyone to see. It has become a custom for moms and their prepubescent daughters to get manicures and pedicures. When I was growing up, I went to the salon with my mom and it was a bonding experience — as I watched her get her hair done. But having a good time with her didn't depend on getting to do the same things she did.

So it's not that girls are being pushed to be meaner. It's that they are being pushed to be older (as opposed to more mature, which would lend itself to increased sense of responsibility, etc.). Being mean is just a by-product. Adults are the ones who create and give young girls access to content that assumes they are already teens, or want to be. Cartoons are based on reality shows that depict girls as superficial and catty; toys and websites teach them to be famous and "celebrities" with all the accompanying clothes, jewelry, clothes, and entitled spoiled attitudes.

So why do parents buy into pushing their daughters to be older? Honestly, a lot of parents simply don't realize what they're doing because they're sucked into the sophisticated marketing just like their daughters. Marketing campaigns aimed at girls and their parents present a false image of girls' empowerment that girls with high self-esteem and confidence act like miniadults with the latest styles and narcissistic attitude. So we buy the messages without really looking at the content underneath.

Likewise, girls at younger ages are being pushed to present themselves in increasingly sexual ways—and there hasn't been an effective parenting response to address the problem. Girls at dance class recitals are wearing costumes women wear in music videos. Parents are often so happy to see their daughter reading a book instead of watching TV or texting that they don't read the books themselves and see what cultural values those books are imparting. And even if you are aware, many parents don't want to complain because they don't want to come across as the over-bearing uptight helicopter parent. These dynamics combine to encourage mean, materialistic, more typically adolescent behavior in younger girls.

And of course, sometimes you might just be so beyond exhausted that you just don't have the energy to fight one more battle. I really get that. But this is the battle we have to fight.

You can counteract this problem and give your daughter and other girls in your life the knowledge and strategies to navigate her way through this process as soon as possible. Let's start with an exercise you can do with your daughter. Sarah Silverstone and Adele Paynter are two teachers at the Sheridan school in Washington, D.C., who came up with this exercise for their students. I liked it so much I wanted to share it with you.

Circle the words that best describe you right now.

Bossy
Outgoing
Go with the flow
Quiet
Shy
Leader
Follower
Helpful
Anxious
Moody
Pushy
Sarcastic

Remember, you can always reinvent yourself. You are in charge of who you become. So looking back at the words above, answer these three questions:

What words would you like to do more of?
What words would you like to minimize?
What words would you like to become?

What's the Difference Between Good Teasing and Mean Teasing?

One of the most confusing aspects of bullying is that it is so easily dismissed as harmless teasing. Here's how you tell the difference.

Good Teasing
You feel liked by the teaser.
You don't feel the teaser's motivation is to put you down.
If you decide you don't like it, you can say something and it will stop.

Unintentional Bad Teasing
You don't like it.
The teaser either doesn't know how you feel or dismisses your feelings because he or she doesn't understand how strongly you feel.
If you tell them to stop, they won't tease you more.

Mean Teasing
Teasing is done to make you feel bad, insecure, or embarrassed.
You're teased about something that other people know you feel insecure about.
If you defend yourself, you're made fun of or blown off because "you're too sensitive" or you can't take a joke.
The teasing never stops.

Why "Just Joking" Is Never Funny

When someone says something mean and then follows it up with "Just kidding!" what they're really doing is hurting you and then denying your right to be upset about it. This is a supermanipulative thing to do because it gets them off the hook for taking responsibility for their actions. Even more annoying, it allows the person to dismiss and ridicule you if you complain.

> I hate when my friends say "just joking" to me. They pick on me and pick on me and I try to hold it in and then sometimes I just can't anymore. Then I explode and they say, "Fine, if you're so sensitive then we don't have to be friends!" But I want to be friends, so I end up begging to get back with them. I hate it.
> —Samantha, 10

Samantha is completely right. It's bad enough that your friend is making fun of you and refusing to admit it. Worse, your friends can threaten to break up with you. So then it can feel like you have to make the following choice: either I put up with the ridicule or I lose the friend. What lots of people do (no matter what their age) is bury their anger and frustration at having someone close to them be mean and then not admit it. But this is the kind of burying that isn't good because the requirement for being accepted is the right for the person to treat you badly. You never want these kinds of relationships.

What's the Difference Between Tattling and Telling?

Tattling means all you want is for the person to get in trouble.
Telling means that you believe there is a problem you can't solve by yourself so you need to tell a trusted adult.
Telling means your goal is to right a wrong.
A person reports a problem because they want the problem resolved.
A person tattles because they want the problem to get bigger or more public so everyone knows.

The really tricky thing, however, is that sometimes it can be confusing to tell the difference between the two, because when you report something you're bringing attention to it. It's like the problem was in a dark cave and you're going in there with a big flashlight and shining a light on it. So, if you report something and people get mad at you, the most important thing to remember is that the people who are now in trouble are not in trouble because you reported them. They're in trouble because they acted in ways that were against the rules. If you want to say something about it, here's a suggestion: "They didn't get in trouble because I told the teacher (parent, coach, etc). They got in trouble because they did (say specifically what they did)."

What Should You Say When Your Child Tells You Someone Is Being Mean to Them?

First let's put out there some common and understandable responses parents say that *don't* help:

> *They're just jealous.*
> *They're just insecure.*
> *You're better off without them.*
> *Just show them what a good friend is.*
> *Just be nice.*
> *Just be strong.*
> *Just don't let it bother you.*
> *Just ignore it.*

Just to be really clear here: the reason "Just be nice" and "show them what a good friend looks like" don't work is because when and if your daughter says this to kids who are mean to her, it doesn't look like she's being nice in their eyes. In their eyes, she looks weak and easily manipulated.

What you *do* say:

> *I'm so sorry.*
> *Thank you for telling me.*

I'm going to help you think this through so you feel better about how it's being handled.

But what if your child says, "Mom, I'm going to tell you but you have to promise not to do anything."

I really understand any parent wanting to make this promise. It makes common sense. You want your daughter to continue talking to you so if you don't make this promise, you have an understandable fear that she'll stop. So in the moment, it makes sense to make that promise. *Not so fast.* Instead, this is what I want you to say, "I would love to make that promise, but I can't. The reason I can't is because you may tell me something that's too big for us to handle alone. But this is what I can promise. If I think we need to get another person's opinion, you will know about it and you can help me pick the best person to go to."

Please notice that I didn't say that the child gets ultimate decision-making power here. You are the adult, that's your responsibility. But kids can tolerate your decisions, even if they really disagree, if you include them as part of the process. When they stop talking to you is when they get blindsided and don't feel respected.

THE SEAL STRATEGY

Throughout this book, you'll see I use a strategy, which you can teach your daughter, for thinking through a situation when I'm angry or upset about something. I call it SEAL and it stands for these four things:

Stop and Strategize: Breathe, listen, and think when and where, now or later?

Explain: What happened that you don't like and what do you want?

Affirm: Admit (recognize) anything you did that contributed to the conflict but affirm your right to be treated with dignity by the other person and vice versa.

Lock: Lock in the friendship, take a vacation, or lock the friendship out.

It's totally understandable if you read this and think, "There's no way my daughter is going to do this. It's not going to work." This is probably because girls, like most of us, usually define success in a confrontation by either being best friends afterwards or destroying the other person. You're asking your daughter to redefine what it means to be in a confrontation with someone. SEAL helps whenever you're in a situation where you're really angry at someone and you think about the perfect thing to say but then when you get around the person you're mad at, you lose your words. SEAL helps get you clear about what you think, so you can be clear about what to say to the person and how to say it. So any part of it that you do is a success. If you get mad at someone and you do the "S" for stop and that's it, that's great. Next week, you can try to do the "E."

So here's a common situation between two girls where you could use SEAL. This one involves a girl bystanding, seeing something another girl is doing and not liking it but not knowing what to say.

KATIE: Did you see Sara trying to guess what we were talking about? She's so stupid, she totally copies everything I do!

AMANDA: I know. She's so annoying!

KATIE: During recess, let's just pretend she doesn't exist. Like she's invisible.

AMANDA: I guess . . .

KATIE: I mean what else are we supposed to do? It's like she thinks she can be with us all the time, and when we don't let her, she's so mean about it!

The thing about being a Bystander is that often it's really hard to know what to do exactly at the moment it's happening. But that doesn't mean Bystanders can't go back later and say something.

Stop and Strategize: Amanda puts her bad feelings to words and chooses the time to talk to Katie.

Explain: *I don't want to do the secret language now or pretend Sara is invisible. It looks like a game but it's not.*
Affirm: *You don't have to be friends with Sara, but we can't be mean to her. Pretending she's invisible is mean.*
Lock: *This was really hard but you're my friend and I wanted to tell you.*

We will examine this further in Chapter 6, Mean Girls, but take note that when girls use the word *annoying*, they need to tell you exactly what they feel, because it can mean the girl stood up to the other girls.

Likewise, when girls use the word *mean* to describe a girl's behavior, they can really be describing the girl expressing anger. It is very important for girls' emotional health to realize expressing anger is not necessarily mean.

Now we'll look at several common experiences younger girls and parents have and use SEAL in some of them to see how to walk through them.

Sleepovers

First of all, sleepovers are a horrible idea. It's true. Admit it. The girls eat terrible food, stay up way too late, which means you do too, and someone usually ends up crying, furious, or telling you that she has to go home because she doesn't "feel well," which is girl code for "the other girls are being really mean to me."

So we need to have some commonsense rules about sleepovers.

1. Ideally only one girl sleeps over.
2. Bedtimes—while not as early as school nights—are reasonably sane, midnight at the latest.

3. Which movies they see and computer and cell phone use are strictly monitored and/or limited.

Why?

1. If you have more than one girl over, you're just paving the way for girl drama. From who sleeps next to whom, to inside jokes that someone doesn't know — it's a mess.
2. If the parents are going to let the children go to bed at 2:00 A.M. so that you pick up a horrible nasty cranky brat masquerading as your child, I think you should turn around and let your daughter stay at their house the next day too.
3. Sleepovers have always been drama central. But when you add instant messaging, social networking sites, and cell phones into the mix, the drama goes from containable to combustible. One of the most common is when one girl holds her cell phone or sits in front of a computer keyboard while the other girls feed her what to say. In this manner, a text, voice mail, or instant message that starts out with "Heyyyyy whats up?" can transform into an all-out gossip war.

So if your daughter is invited to someone's house, give the parents a call before taking your daughter there and have the following conversation.

YOU: Hi, Alan, thanks so much for inviting Sydney to sleep over tomorrow night. She's really excited about it. I just wanted to check in with you about some things.

ALAN: Sure, of course!

YOU: Sydney usually goes to bed around 9 or 9:30. I know they'll probably go to bed later than that but if she could get to sleep by 10:30 that would be great. Also, can you tell me what you let the kids watch on cable or do on the computer? I know a lot of the kids in the class want to watch X (the latest movie all the kids want to see and the parents are arguing about whether to let their kids do it) but we think it's too mature/scary/violent/sexual for her.

ALAN: Sure, but don't we want the kids to have fun too?

YOU: Of course. If you watch out for those things I'd really appreciate it.

On the other side, if you're inviting a girl to come over to your house, call the parents and check in with them so you're all on the same page.

Technology and Sleepovers

Before so many fifth graders had cell phones, if a girl wanted to go home she would have to call from a landline in your house. You would know what was going on and you wouldn't be surprised when an upset parent knocked on your door because their daughter called them from the bathroom crying. Now chances are that you'll be blindsided. Or there's always the possibility you won't know until a few days later when you find out there's been a flurry of e-mails between parents in your community about how horrible the girls were at your house.

To guard yourself against this, make it absolutely clear to your daughter what the technology use rules are during a sleepover—which should be exactly the same rules as every other night in your house. Just know as tempting as it is to abuse those rules when she's by herself, the temptation is much worse during a sleepover.

Whispering

Your daughter walks down the hallway and two girls start whispering as soon as she passes them. Does she say something to the girls? I think if it happens once, let it pass, because she may be making an incorrect assumption. But if it happens more than once, then she needs to address it, using SEAL as a way to prepare what she wants to say. Remember, put no pressure on her to do

SEAL in real life while she does her preparation. Ask her what it feels like when she sees the girls in the hallway. Have her put it into words for herself. The thing you need to get across to her is that while she can't control whether the girls will stop whispering, she can control what she does. Using SEAL, she can do the following:

Stop and Strategize: She decides she's going to say something to them the next time it happens.

Explain: *Three times today you've been whispering when I walk by. I can't stop you from doing it and I guess your point is to make me feel bad.*

Affirm: *I have the right to walk down the hall without people making me feel bad by whispering whenever I'm around. If there's something you need to tell me, then you need to tell me to my face.*

Lock: *If you want to tell me, that'd be great. I'll be around all day.*

Then she should walk away so she's not waiting around for the girls to slam her. Now remember that when you SEAL something, chances are high that the bullies are going to respond by denying it and then getting mad at your daughter because she's being "mean" to them or saying something obnoxious, like "what-

If your daughter has been bullied and you are going to have a meeting with a teacher or a school administrator about it, before you go, sit down with your daughter the night before and have her tell you what the kids have said and done to her. As much as she can, she should tell you exactly the words the bullies said. While she speaks you should write it down. Then, when you get to the meeting, she should try her best to say what she told you the night before. But she needs you as a backup because sometimes it's too hard to say what happened or the bad words that were said. That's why kids sometimes say, "I don't re-member" when people ask them what happened.

ever" or roll their eyes, or laugh. If they do this, it doesn't mean you or SEAL has failed. Think about it this way; you're taking away power from the bullies and they feel like they have to get a little back. Denying it or making fun of what you say is the easiest way to do it. But in the long term, you are showing that you can hold your own.

Your Daughter's Friend Is Treating Her Hot and Cold

It is 4:30 P.M. and I have just dropped off a girl who came to play with my daughter for the first time. This is the conversation I overheard while reading in the living room and they were doing art in the dining room.

PLAYDATE: The reason I didn't want the teacher to tell anybody I was going to play at your house is because my other friends might dump me. I can't be your friend, but I can still have playdates with you.

MY DAUGHTER: Just don't tell your friends and they won't be mad at you.

PLAYDATE: They won't be mad, they will make fun of me.

DAUGHTER: Why will they make fun of you?

PLAYDATE: Because they think you are weird. Another classmate told me she felt sorry for me for having a playdate with you.

This woman's daughter shouldn't turn herself inside out trying to be nice to this girl. It will only come across as trying too hard and chasing her. At best, the old friend will treat her well when they are one-on-one, but she'll turn her back on her when she's around her new friends.

This is how she'd SEAL it:

Stop and Strategize: How does she feel about what the girl said? Where does she think is the best place to talk to her?

Explain: *When you were over at my house, you told me that peo-*
  ple are making fun of you for being friends with me. I want to
  hang out with you, but I don't want to worry about when you
  will be my friend and when you won't.
Affirm: *I want a friend who treats me nicely no matter who's*
  around.
Lock: *I would really like to keep being friends.*

If the girl agrees and then goes back to treating your daughter
hot and cold, then I would ask your daughter to consider the "take
a vacation" or "lock out" option.

What if the girl says, "It's not my fault. You always want to hang
out so I never feel like I can see my other friends"?

As much as this may hurt your daughter's feelings, she needs to
respect what the other girl is saying. So if the other girl says that
she wants to play with someone else at a certain time, then your
daughter needs to respect her friend's boundaries. Instead, take
the long view; that this is an opportunity to help your daughter
build social skills. As the parent, don't focus on how mean the
other child is or how weak your daughter is for accepting her
second-rate status.

Car Pool

I remember this one girl in fifth grade and no one would sit next
to her. She'd go into her shell and sit in the back looking out the
window.   —Cherise, 14

For field trips in third grade, my school basically let the kids or-
ganize the car pools because we didn't have buses. So the par-
ents would sign up to drive and then we'd tell our parents who
we wanted to take.   —Sara, 13

I always thought it was funny that there were parents who
wouldn't let their kids go to McDonald's on the way back from
games, but then there were the parents who would let us and
they wouldn't tell the other parents.   —Molly, 14

I get a lot of questions from parents about car pools. And truth be told, I personally didn't have a lot of experience with them because I grew up in a city. But I did have one, and the memories of the annoying boys I was surrounded by and the mom who never smiled are vivid.

Kids tell me that there are two basic car pool conflicts. The first is when someone in the car pool is really mad at someone else in the car pool. As the driver, you would notice that no one is talking. At best there is a decided chill in the air. The other is when someone in the car pool has been assessed as a social liability by the other kids. In this case, as the driver, you would notice that all the kids are talking but that kid—unless that child has social skills deficits and she would try to interact but be ignored.

What do you do if the kids are in a fight? You would use SEAL to frame your strategy.

> Stop and Strategize: Identify which situation you have and which children have social power (this is usually the ones who are most verbal/persuasive) and what children if any push your buttons. Remind yourself to do your absolute best to perceive your child in their role in the group first rather than your daughter.
>
> Explain: *Girls, for the last few days I've noticed that you aren't talking to each other* (or whatever is going on is that you're seeing). *Do you want to talk about it and see if we can resolve it or should we just keep pretending that everything's fine?*

> GIRL ONE: I don't know what you're talking about.
> GIRL TWO: Whatever (rolling her eyes).

> Affirm: *You don't have to be friends with each other, but we do have to ride in the car pool together, so I expect at the least that you treat each other civilly. For example, that means to me no snide comments about anyone else.*

I asked two students to draw a map with basic car pool social dynamics to get us started.

"THE MINIVAN"
An Analysis of Car Pool Dynamics

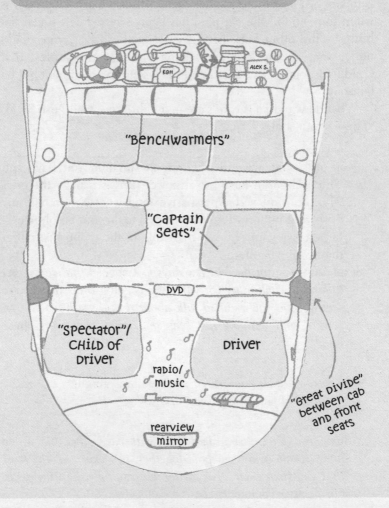

"BENCHWARMERS"

"Captain Seats"

DVD

"Spectator"/ Child of Driver

Driver

radio/ music

"Great Divide" between cab and front seats

rearview mirror

THE BENCHWARMERS

- *Physically the worst seats, which means the kids who are the youngest or least socially powerful will sit there because they are the hardest seat to get to and have loud "batman" windows, you can't control heat, and you have very little legroom.*
- *Everyone else in the car pool has their back to them.*
- *One positive is if three people are close friends, they might capitalize on the isolation of these seats and exclude everyone else from their conversation or do things without the parent seeing (i.e., show inappropriate pictures, share embarrassing text messages, write mean notes back and forth). Note: This might also take place if the captains turn their backs.*

THE CAPTAINS

- *Location, location, location! The best seats in the car: the most space, you don't have to share, closest to DVD player, control back temperature.*
- *Conversation is easy; can turn around and lean forward or backward to talk to whomever you want.*
- *Easy to do things the parent can't see.*
- *Last in the car and first to get out.*

SHOTGUN/CHILD OF DRIVER

- *Isolated from rest of friends; has to talk to parent.*
- *Conflicted because they have to be on their best behavior in front of their parent but their friends do not in the back.*
- *Stuck helping Mom or Dad with directions.*
- *Has to take orders from the back (i.e., changing the radio, raising the volume).*
- *Can't see DVD player (if applicable).*

THE DRIVER/PARENT

- *Must focus on the road, even though they are talking on their cell phone or trying to figure out directions: generally not paying any attention to the backseat.*
- *Can't hear the conversation due to the blaring music.*
- *Can't see all the way to the back because of the Captain seats and the DVD player.*

Lock: *I know I can't make you all get along but I hope you do because* (say something positive about each girl). *Thanks for hearing me out.*

What if you have the situation in which everyone is ignoring a child? This is what I'd say to all of them (minus of course the child you are talking about):

Stop and Strategize: Where you can get all the other kids together.

Explain: *I've noticed that most of the time everybody is ignoring Constance.* (Wait for denials to end.) *I'm not saying you have to be friends with her, but I am asking that you include her in your conversations as best you can. How can we do that?*

Affirm: *Everyone can have moments or be in situations where you don't feel comfortable. And I think it's important to do your best to reach out to people.*

Lock: *Thanks for hearing me out.*

I'm suggesting you do this not because I think all the kids will change their behavior. What you are doing by speaking out is showing the kids you aren't clueless and that you are an adult who demands civil behavior.

When Do You Start Teaching Her About How to Use Technology?

Anne, Grace, and Jenny are students in my third-grade class. Last weekend, Anne and Grace used Jenny's password to access her Webkinz account and destroy all of her hard work. Anne did this because Jenny had built up a land of clothing, accessories, and rooms in bubble-gum pink . . . and Anne felt SHE owned that color. Jenny went to her account to find her world obliterated.

—John

Last year, a hacker got into my Webkinz account and stole all my rare things. I went into my house and all my things were gone. I was outraged. —Emma, 11

It was easier when we were younger, like when we were in first grade, because we didn't have screen names and cell phones. —Claire, 10

Last year I got a text message that said, "You're so ugly you should go back to another country. I hate you." —Marisol, 10

As soon as your child starts using technology, you have to teach her how to use it ethically. This means that if your six-year-old is on Club Penguin, it's time to sit her down and talk about how you expect her to conduct herself and her Penguin Avatars.

When Your Daughter Is the Really Mean Girl

Two girls in my fifth-grade class just paid a boy $5 in our grade to go ask another girl to go out with him and then break up with her the next day. The girl isn't very attractive and doesn't get the social dynamics swirling around her at all. She never saw it coming. She thought he was serious. —Ana

When the teacher who was working with me told me that story my heart broke for the girl. Why was it so important that those girls would go out of their way to humiliate another girl in their class—one who's already struggling socially? This is one of those times as a parent or someone who works with girls that you need to remember two things: (1) we are on a long road to making decent human beings; and (2) we have to take ownership of our children's behavior when it's messy and embarrassing, not just when our kids make us look good.

So if your daughter is one of the Mean Girls, here's how SEAL could help you talk to her. Now, it is a little different because you're also using SEAL to role-model what you want and as a way to hold her accountable for her actions. To make it more realistic, I have also included common girl responses when confronted in situations like these.

> Stop and Strategize: As soon as you hear this, go somewhere quiet and breathe. Remember, your child is not the worst child in the world and you aren't the worst parent. She has made a big mistake, and it's up to you to make this an opportunity for her to see your values in action. Do not think about how much more or less guilty the boy or your daughter's friend is. Your daughter was involved— that's all you need to know. Now think, where can you talk to her where you have the best chance of her listening to you? If at all possible, both parents are there but no one else.

YOU (Explain): It has come to my attention that you paid a boy five dollars to ask a girl to go out with him and then dump her. Is that accurate?

YOUR DAUGHTER: OMG, it wasn't like that at all! We were just joking around with Will. How was I supposed to know he was actually going to do it?

YOU: Did you give him money or not?

YOUR DAUGHTER: No! McKenna did. It's not my fault!

YOU: I need you to answer this question with a yes or no. When Will asked Kara to be his girlfriend, were you completely surprised, like it was the first time you ever heard of the possibility of him doing this?

YOUR DAUGHTER: What? I don't know. If you say it like that, fine, no. I wasn't COMPLETELY surprised.

YOU: OK, now that we have that clear, here's the deal. You will sit and write a letter of apology to Kara. While you are doing that I'm calling Kara's parents and asking if we can come over so you can apologize to her in person, in front of her parents. After I do that, I'm calling McKenna's parents and telling them what you are doing to take responsibility for your actions. After you are done with the letter and if Kara's parents agree to allow you into their house, we will immediately go over there so you can apologize. If you apologize with a fake or mean tone in your voice or the content of your words comes across as giving a fake apology, then I will apologize on your behalf. And since you did it at school, you are also going to apologize to your teacher and principal for going against the school's rules of treating people with dignity.

YOUR DAUGHTER: There is no way you can make me do those things!

YOU: Why don't you want to do it? Is it embarrassing?

YOUR DAUGHTER: What do you think?

YOU (Affirm): I'm not saying you have to be friends with Kara but you are never allowed to do something to deliberately make her feel miserable. I hope you'll remember that the next time you're tempted to do something so mean to someone. And if you do something like this again, you will force me to increase the consequences to you. I love you with all my heart, but this is something I have to take a stand on.

YOUR DAUGHTER: Do you have any idea how much I hate you?

YOU (Lock): I have a pretty good idea, but I'm willing to accept that. But for what it's worth, if you do take responsibility for what you did, that will mean a great deal to me. So can I make you a cup of tea while you write your letter?

There's a lot more material that is relevant to younger girls in the other chapters (like the apologies section in Chapter 6), but I hope this gives those of you with younger girls a good foundation to help them as they bump into their first experiences with Queen Bees and Mean Girls. In the meantime, the following pages I wrote specifically for girls.

JUST FOR GIRLS

Who and When Do You Tell?

Sometimes it's easy to tell when someone is being mean to you. Usually that's when someone physically hurts you or threatens your safety. But people can be mean in other ways, like when they make fun of you, ignore you, or get other people to gang up on you. So if that happens to you, when should you tell an adult?

You may be worried that if you tell, the situation will get worse. The bully may have even told you that as a way to keep you quiet. So let's break it down. If you don't tell, do you think the person will stop being mean to you or hurting you? In my experience, bullies don't stop because you cooperate. They know that they have power over you. And there's no way adults can help if they don't know the problem. That said, you have to be smart about whom you tell because some adults are better than other adults at knowing how to handle problems.

Finding an Ally

Sometimes girls have feelings or experiences that they don't want to tell their mom or dad. If you're having that feeling, that is completely normal. The problem is that sometimes it's really helpful and important to tell an adult what's going on. So I'm going to give you an assignment to find an ally. An ally is someone you can rely on to talk about what's going on in your life, who's really smart and thinks clearly (meaning they don't freak out). To find an ally, I want you to sit down at a table with an adult in your family. Each of you should have a piece of paper and something to write with. I want you to think of all the adults you are close to in your family, at school, or in your neighborhood and come up with a list of people you think are cool and smart enough that you would want to talk to them about important things going on in your life. While you do that, I want the person sitting across from you to write down their list of adults you know that they trust to give you good advice. When you're finished, compare your lists. Ideally there would be someone who is on both of your lists, and that's the person you would ask to be your ally—someone whom you can talk to on a regular basis for big and little stuff, who can help you think through maybe difficult problems. And the agreement is that these conversations between you are private unless your physical safety or mental health is in danger.

Cliques and Popularity

Hi, I'm Lauren and I'm a 13-year-old girl in seventh grade. I read your book Queen Bees & Wannabes *and I must admit most everything was true. I mapped out my clique (popular). I found out that I am the Banker/Floater. Even though I feel as though the girls and boys I hang out with are my friends, my self-esteem is lower when I'm with them. And within the clique is an even more exclusive girls' clique which I am very proud to be a member of. That's where I want to belong. BUT, I'm part of EVERY clique. My best friend is in a less popular clique that I am also friends with. Those are the people I feel most comfortable around. They understand I'm part of another clique but they choose to tell me every little piece of gossip they know, which I tell to everyone in my other clique. But anyway after reading* Queen Bees & Wannabes *I learned which clique I wanna stay with and that being the Banker isn't a good thing. Because I don't like my friends living in fear of me. So thanks.*   Truly Yours, Lauren*

Are you horrified at Lauren's unapologetic social climbing and manipulation? Mystified at her simultaneous self-awareness and off-center moral compass? Or are you counting your blessings that you aren't in seventh grade anymore or, better yet, wondering why these seventh-grade personalities persist with the adults you know in your neighborhoods and workplaces?

Welcome to my world. If you want to understand girls, you have to start by examining how and what your daughter understands about the nature and dynamics of friendship, cliques, and popularity. Why? Because on a daily basis, she learns what kind of girl she is "required" to be in order to be accepted by a group or the consequence of standing her ground. And for better or worse, what she learns will profoundly influence her—from her appearance and academic and extracurricular interests to her core values and ability to hold her own against intimidating people and situations.

This chapter will help you analyze and understand the nature of cliques so you can better understand what your daughter is going through, identify her position in the clique, help her develop healthy boundaries with friends, and if necessary, take responsibility for cruel behavior. The common definition of a clique is an exclusive group of girls who are close friends, but I see it a little differently. I see them as a platoon of soldiers who have banded together to survive adolescence. There's a chain of command, and they operate as one to the outside world, even if there may be dissatisfaction within the ranks. Group cohesion is based on unquestioned loyalty to the leaders and an "us-versus-the-world" mentality.

> *Some members may not even like other members within cliques. There are those you hang out with just because certain people seem to come in a set, like markers, but then there are those you actually trust and respect.*   —Amelia, 15

Cliques reinforce your daughter's bonds with her friends. They can also break apart or weaken the bond between a daughter and her parents. This is painful for you, but it also can be dangerous for your daughter, because the clique teaches her to turn to and exclusively depend on the members of her clique when she's in trouble, instead of asking for help from you or another adult. But the worst thing some girls learn from cliques is that it's more important to *maintain* a relationship at all costs instead of realizing that how they are treated *within* that relationship should be the basis for whether or not they stay in it.

> *It's also true that girls learn it's more [about] high-status relationships instead of pursuing and/or keeping healthy positive friendships.*   —Amelia, 15

Many parents believe that there's one particular time in a girl's life that you can predict when cliques will be the worst. Unfortunately, it doesn't work like that. You can't watch your daughter's eighth-grade graduation and breathe a sigh of relief that all the girl drama is now over. In my teaching, I've seen shocking examples of cliques even in kindergarten. So, more important than trying to figure out a precise time when these issues will start and stop is to always keep in mind that children and teens often operate in groups, and this can produce intense power struggles.

There are times when you can reliably predict when these dynamics intensify. For example, when your daughter is new to a school, when her grade is receiving a large number of new students, or when she's in the youngest grade of a school are all times the problems increase, because the social hierarchy is challenged and people want to know how any changes to that hierarchy will shake out.

Before I go any further, I want to make clear that I don't think there's anything wrong per se with cliques or groups. Girls tend to have a group of girlfriends with whom they feel close, and often these friendships are great. They can be themselves, share secrets, hang out, and act silly, and have confidence that they will be supported no matter what. Having said that, the way girls group together can sow the seeds for cruel competition for popularity and social status.

Why is that? Because girls, like all of us, are vulnerable to being controlled by the power of the group. Equally common is conflict or power struggles between individuals within the group. This is why what I speak and write about isn't simply addressing the issue of girls being nice or friends with one another. I don't care if girls are nice. What I'm talking about is how we maintain our ethics and moral compass when we are in a group. I don't care if you're in third grade, sixth grade, the principal of a school, or the president of a country. How does the group respond when an individual within it believes the group is acting unethically? What will the price of speaking out be? What will the price of silence be? Will the person be seen as disloyal and kicked out? I believe it is through understanding your relationship to the group and your right to speak out within it that girls develop their ethics and moral courage, ability to think critically, and belief that their actions can affect change. Here's an excellent example of a girl who understands the process.

I went to a public school until fourth grade and I was very sure of who I was. When the girls weren't allowed by the boys to play soccer at recess I, quite literally, petitioned for change. Eventually the boys let us play just to shut me up. I started at this school in fifth grade and didn't fit in. I had plenty of "lunch tray moments" until it was discovered midyear that I could sing, something that I guess is an attractive trait in a friend. Same old story, I ended up compromising who I was, working my way up the social ladder, tailoring personalities trying to find one that fit. I'd toss off new friends for newer friends until I reached the heights of Middle School Hierarchy. I wasn't that confident fourth grader or that awkward fifth grader; I was way worse, I was nothing. I was anything my friends wanted me to be and because of that, I was nothing without their guidance. I was called weird by my friends for my infatuation with musical theater, pressured to give up extracurriculars, told I was only liked because I was pretty, mocked for being feminist and anti-drinking. I lost myself; I was the sidekick of the same girl who had made me miserable in grade school. She made me miserable in middle school too, but this time I victimized myself. End of eighth grade I ran against her for class president—that was my idea of taking a stand. The cattiness was ridiculous. I refused to succumb, not so much because I was above it, mostly because I knew that acting like the bigger person could buy votes. It's terrible and I don't want you to think I'm heartless, I hate who I was. I won the election but realized it wasn't worth the fight. I quit. I quit drama and popularity and competition. I've been clean for two years now.

—Allison, 16

POPULARITY

For some girls, popularity is magical. Popularity conveys an unmatched sense of power. Some girls think that if they can achieve it, all their problems will disappear. Some become obsessed and measure the popularity barometer daily, then issue constant weather reports. Others dismiss it, thinking the whole thing is ridiculous. Some are angry and deny they care, although they often actually do. Some feel so out of it they give up.

Imagine you're invisible, and walk with me into a classroom (feel free to imagine any grade from third grade up) where I'm going to discuss cliques and popularity. This is what you'll see: thirty girls grouped together in clumps of usually four or five. They're sitting on chairs, or on each other's laps, doing each other's hair, texting, reading, or sitting by themselves. Some are even studying. I start the class by asking the girls to close their eyes and answer by a show of hands how many of them have had a friend gossip about them, talk behind their back, force them to stop being friends with someone, or be exclusive. All hands immediately shoot up. I ask the girls to keep their hands up and open their eyes. They laugh. Then I have them close their eyes again and ask them to answer by a show of hands how many of them have gossiped, backstabbed, or been exclusive about a friend. Much more slowly, some bending from the elbow instead of extending their hand, all the hands go up. I tell them to keep their hands up and open their eyes. They look around. They laugh again, but nervously.

After five minutes or so, almost without exception, the following occurs: a girl, usually generically pretty and surrounded by four or five girls, will raise her hand defiantly and say, "Ms. Wiseman, maybe this happens at other schools you work at, but at this school we don't have exclusive cliques like that. It's not like we're all best friends, but we all have our groups and people are fine with it. People just can't be best friends with everyone." As she's speaking, there are many expressions of disbelief and eye rolling from the other girls in the room, making it difficult for me not to laugh out loud. But no one speaks up to challenge her declaration. Almost always, three things will be true about this girl: first, she'll always be one of the meanest, most exclusive girls in the room; second, she honestly believes what she's saying; and third, her parents will be in total denial about how mean she is and completely back her up. It's enough to make your head spin. So how do we get the girls to tell the truth? There's only one way: anonymity.

I tell the girls to take out a piece of paper, sit wherever they want around the room except next to their friends, and anonymously tell me if the girl who spoke is correct. As you watch them find a place to write, the power of the social hierarchy is clear. The girls can't wait to write, but most want to hide as they scribble away. Especially if the girls are younger, they sit in closets, under their desks, under the teacher's desk, and even in lockers (if they're small enough).

When they're done, they get to fold the paper in any way they want—and how they do it also tells me a lot about what they think. Some girls condense the paper into a small ball or the smallest square. Others hand me the paper unfolded and defiantly tell me they don't care who knows what they wrote. I put all the answers in a box and take it with me to the front of the room.

Everyone sits in a circle and the air is tense with expectation. Before I begin, I remind the girls to "own up" to their own behavior and not focus on figuring out who wrote what. I tell them to stare at the ground so they can resist trying to telepathically communicate who they think wrote what. I read aloud most of the responses (girls can write "for your eyes only" if they don't want their answer to be read out loud).

Not surprisingly, the girl who initially raised her hand and declared that there are no cliques holds the minority opinion. Here are the responses from a typical sixth-grade class.

From the bottom of the social totem pole:

I'm uncool. Let's face it. There are many cliques among the "cool."   *—Emily, 11*

In this grade there are cliques and I hate it. Popular people put other people down all the time. I know I'm part of a clique, but my clique was formed of the girls that were excluded and shunned. We like each other for who we are, and not by our hair, looks, clothes, or popularity. These girls are my real friends.   *—Michelle, 12*

From the middle:

I guess, for want of a friend, girls are willing to hurt anyone and don't care what stands in their way.   *—Kiana, 12*

There are cliques and even exclusive clubs. There are about three or four cliques and some are nice. The rest are exclusive and mean. Sometimes I feel like I have to conform and be boy crazy.   *—Kim, 12*

And from the top:

There are cliques in this class and everybody is popular in their own group. The cliques are intertwined. I think the popular people are really nice. There is gossip but no backstabbing.   *—Paige, 13*

I think there are cliques, but we aren't mean to each other mostly. But there are occasional breakouts of trouble.   *—Carrie, 12*

Can you picture what Carrie means by "occasional breakouts of trouble"? This is a classic popular girl understatement, which usually consists of one girl completely humiliating another. Why were the girls so reluctant to admit the gossiping and exclusivity out loud? What was silencing the girls from telling the truth? The power of cliques silences them, because those in positions of power are often blind to their behavior or justify it so they won't have to take responsibility for their actions. Those not in positions of power fear the consequences of speaking out in public. When girls do talk about it, they only talk with their friends and in private places like school bathrooms, their bedrooms, or by text, phone, or e-mail. So, most of the time, the girls who aren't afraid to speak out in public are those who are so out of the social pecking order that they have nothing to lose by saying what they really think.

Popular girls, like any other group of privileged people, often don't recognize their privilege because they are blind to it. It's all they know, and they haven't had to go through the experience of understanding what it feels like to be on the outside. They know little to nothing about people outside of their group and are reluctant to admit what they do to put other girls down. In contrast, the girls on the outside usually know a lot about what's going on with the popular girls. But what's critically important about this exercise is that it enables the adult to teach a fundamental value: each person's truth is of equal value. No one gets to speak for anyone else or dismiss an opinion just because it's not shared by the people who have the most power. Once the silence is broken, the truth comes out. Girls want to talk about what's really going on between them. They just have to be in an environment where they can speak their truth. And in the age of texting, e-mail, MySpace, and so on, it's essential to create a space where they can express these truths both by themselves and within a group. The classroom can be a great place for this.

Land Mine!

Some girls can't stand the word *clique* and will be immediately defensive if you use this word to describe their group of friends. They assume you're accusing them of being exclusive. If you want to ask a girl about her group of friends, just say the word *group* and she'll be less reactive.

Good Popularity Versus Mean Popularity

I'm not saying it's inherently bad to be popular, but girls have had to help me realize that I sometimes make it sound as if it is. When I first started teaching, an adorable sixth-grade girl in pigtails politely raised her hand and asked me, "Ms. Wiseman, why do you think all popular people are bad?" She totally caught me off guard and enlightened me. Of course she was right—there are popular girls whom people really like. From then on I defined "the popular girls" in two ways: the good kind is a girl who is genuinely liked. The mean kind is when other girls are grateful if she's nice to them and terrified when she's angry.

My students usually want to talk about good popularity for about thirty seconds. They are much more interested in knowing why the definition of good popularity doesn't usually describe the popular girls they know. Very quickly, the questions start to fly: Why are popular girls so mean? Why is everyone so afraid of them? No one likes the most popular girl, so why does she have the most friends? They're describing the bad kind of popularity. In the girls' words:

> "She's the meanest to everyone."
> "She has all the power and she'll crush you."
> "She'll influence you to be her friend, and then backstab you, ruining your life."

Who personifies mean popularity? I bet you have a picture in your mind right now.

THE QUEEN BEE AND HER COURT

We need to give girls credit for the sophistication of their social structures. Our best politicians and diplomats can't match a girl who understands the social intrigue and political landscape that lead to power. Cliques are sophisticated, complex, and multilayered, and every girl has a role within them. However, positions in cliques aren't static. A girl can lose her position to another girl, and she can move up and down the social totem pole. The reality is that few girls are stuck in one role, and they can often have moments of being something else. Here are the different roles that your daughter and her friends might play:

Queen Bee
Sidekick
Banker
Messenger
Pleaser/Wannabe
Torn Bystander
Target
Champion

A Queen Bee can have a Champion moment. A Champion can get into such a tough situation that she becomes a Torn Bystander. Also, your daughter doesn't have to be in the "popular" group to have these roles within her group of friends, but it is true that the higher up the social pecking order, the more rigid the group's rules tend to become.

Because girls' social hierarchies are complicated and overwhelming in their detail, I'm going to take you through a general breakdown of the different positions in the clique. However, when you talk to your daughter about cliques, encourage her to come up with her own names and create roles she thinks I've missed. If you can answer yes to the majority of items for each role, you've identified your daughter.

The Queen Bee

Think of a combination of the Queen of Hearts in Alice in Wonderland and Barbie. She's the Queen Bee, the epitome of teen girl perfection. Through a combination of charisma, force, money, looks, will, and social intelligence, this girl reigns supreme over the other girls and weakens their friendships with others, thereby strengthening her own power and influence. Never underestimate her power over other girls (and boys as well). She can and will silence her peers with a look and then turn around and be incredibly nice. But the bottom line is you're on her side or else—you are with her or against her.

She will do anything to have control. She will humiliate you in front of your whole grade, just if you are getting a little attention from boys, even if the boys are just your friends. —Kelly, 14

Your Daughter Is a Queen Bee If . . .

- Her friends do what she wants to do.
- She isn't intimidated by other girls in her class.
- She complains about other people copying her, never leaving her alone, or being too sensitive.
- When she's hanging out in a group, she's in the center. When she moves, they follow.
- She can argue anyone down, including friends, peers, teachers, and parents.
- She can make another girl feel "anointed" by declaring her a special friend.
- She's strategically affectionate. For example, she sees two girls in her group, one she's pleased with and one she isn't. When she sees them, she'll throw her arms around one and insist that they sit together and barely say anything to the other.
- She won't (or is very reluctant to) take responsibility when she hurts someone's feelings.
- If she thinks she's been wronged, she feels she has the right to seek revenge and will do so.

She thinks she's better than everyone else. She's in control, intimidating, smart, caring, and has the power to make others feel good or bad. She'll make stuff up about people and everyone will believe her. —Anne, 15

If that sinking feeling in your stomach stems from just realizing your daughter is a Queen Bee, congratulate yourself. Honesty is the first step to parenting successfully. If you are thinking, "How can my daughter already be a Queen Bee at the age of seven?" accept it and realize you are not alone. As I say to Queen Bees all the time, we just need to use your power for good and not evil. As FDR and Spiderman have said, "With great power comes great responsibility."

What Does She Gain by Being a Queen Bee?
She feels power and control over her environment. She's the center of attention, and people pay homage to her.

What Does She Lose by Being a Queen Bee?
Her friendships are defined by power, not mutual support, trust, or care. She can be incredibly cynical about her friendships with both boys and girls. She may easily feel that she can't admit to anyone when she's in over her head because her reputation dictates that she always has everything and everyone in control.

I want to share with you a recent experience I had in a junior high. It resonates with me because it's not often that I come across Queen Bees who admit their fall from power. I'd just finished an assembly with the sixth grade when the counselor asked me if I could talk to a couple of girls. I looked over in the corner to see two beautiful girls with stick-straight brown hair, button-down shirts, plaid skirts, and Ugg boots throwing furtive glances in my direction.

"Hi, girls, what's up?" I said.

Both girls scanned the room anxiously. The smaller one pushed her long bangs out of her face. "OK, we were in this clique with four other girls but they kicked both of us out. They now talk bad about us and have code words for my name. It's really bad . . ." She looked away, obviously trying not to cry. "When I try to talk to any of them, they just walk away and whisper to each other and laugh."

The other girl broke in, "And we've tried to talk to them. But they just throw it back in our face. I know we used to be the Queen Bees, but now I cry every night. And I know the school didn't like us in the group because sometimes I guess we were mean to people. Now . . . I guess I know what it feels like . . . I guess they were never my friends."

For twenty minutes we talked candidly. One admitted that she had "a serious problem wanting to know everyone's business all the time." They knew they abused their power, and their victims weren't sympathetic to their plight. I left them with a plan based on the idea that this could be a life-changing moment for both of them. Could they learn from this and use their dynamic, powerful personalities for good? Would they remember what it felt like to be excluded and betrayed and speak out when it was happening to someone else?

But my other reason for sharing this experience is that a lot of people love to see Queen Bees get brought down. Of course, we need to hold the Queen Bees accountable for wielding their power unethically, but we also need to be there to catch them when they fall. What I want you to take away from this is the understanding that even Queen Bees experience the negative effects of cliques, and you should encourage your daughter to show compassion, even when her instinct is to have the last laugh.

The Sidekick

She's the lieutenant or second in command, the girl who's closest to the Queen Bee and will back her no matter what because her power depends on the confidence she gets from the Queen Bee. Together they appear to other girls as an impenetrable force. They commonly bully and silence other girls to forward their own agenda. The Queen Bee and Sidekick are usually the first to focus on boys and are often attracted to older boys. This is particularly true in seventh and eighth grade (and their behavior is even worse if they're physically mature and going to high school parties, but that's another chapter), but remember, it's happening at younger ages. The difference between the two is that if you separate the Sidekick from the Queen Bee, the Sidekick can alter her behavior for the better, while the Queen Bee would be more likely to find another Sidekick and begin again. On the other hand, sometimes a Sidekick can stage a coup against the Queen Bee and take over her position.

Your Daughter Is a Sidekick If . . .

- She's jealous of someone else being friends with the Queen Bee.
- The Queen Bee is your daughter's authority figure, not you.
- She feels like it's just the two of them and everyone else is a Wannabe (see the Pleaser/Wannabe section).
- You think her best friend pushes her around.

> *She notices everything about the Queen Bee. She will do everything the Queen Bee says and wants to be her. She lies for the Queen Bee, but she isn't as pretty as the Queen Bee.*
>
> *—Madeline, 14*

What Does She Gain by Being a Sidekick?

A Sidekick has power over other girls that she wouldn't have without the Queen Bee. She has a close friend who makes her feel popular and included.

What Does She Lose by Being a Sidekick?

If she's with the Queen Bee too long, she may forget she ever had her own opinion. She doesn't go through the process of thoughtfully deciding what she wants in a friend and how she should act in a friendship.

The Banker

Information about other people is currency in Girl World—whoever has the most information has the most power. I call that girl the "Banker." She creates chaos by banking information about girls in her social sphere and dispensing it at strategic intervals. For instance, if a girl has said something negative about another girl, the Banker will casually mention it to someone in conversation because she knows it's going to cause a conflict and strengthen her status as someone in the know. She can get girls to trust her because when she pumps them for information it doesn't seem like gossip; instead, she does it in an innocent, "I'm-trying-to-be-there-for-you" kind of way.

> *Her power lies in getting girls to confide in her. Once they figure out she can't be trusted, it's too late because she already has information on them, and in order to keep her from revealing things, girls will be nice to her.* —Leigh, 17

The Banker is almost as powerful as the Queen Bee, but it's easy to mistake her for the Messenger, the next in line in the hierarchy. She's usually really cute, quiet, and withdrawn in front of adults. This is the girl who sneaks under adult radar all the time because she seems so harmless.

Your Daughter Is a Banker If . . .
- She is extremely secretive.
- She thinks in complex, strategic ways.
- She seems to be friends with everyone; some girls even treat her like a pet.
- She's rarely the subject of fights.
- She's rarely excluded from the group.

What Does She Gain by Being a Banker?
She gets to create drama. The Banker is very confusing to other girls because she seems harmless yet everyone is afraid of her.

What Does She Lose by Being a Banker?
Once other girls figure out what she's doing, they don't trust her. With her utilitarian mind-set, she can forget to look to other girls as a trusted resource. If girls do organize against her, it can be really hurtful and unsettling because she's never been on that end of it.

> *The girls can't oust the Banker from the clique because she has information on everyone and could make or break reputations based on the information she knows.* —Charlotte, 15

The Messenger

The Messenger also trades personal information and gossip about others; however, she differs from the Banker in that her motivation is to reconcile the parties in conflict. By doing this, she hopes to gain recognition and social power. Parents can easily misread their daughter if she's the Messenger because they see her peace-making efforts as being entirely altruistic.

Your Daughter Is a Messenger If . . .
- She lives for drama, and she's obvious about it.
- She loves to "help" people out when they are in fights, which most parents describe as "just wanting everyone to get along."
- When a conflict arises between girls, it's all she's thinking about.
- She gets an adrenaline rush from being in the middle of a conflict (but it looks to unsuspecting adults as if her only motivation is caring too much, wanting everyone to get along, and trying to make peace).
- She feels better about herself when other girls come to her for help.

What Does She Gain by Being a Messenger?
She feels valued because friendships will be made or broken based on her involvement.

What Does She Lose by Being a Messenger?
Her position is precarious. Others can easily turn on her, especially if she gets information wrong (which she inevitably will because it's too hard to keep all the details right) or others deny what she's claimed. She can be easily used, manipulated, and then discarded when no longer useful.

The Pleaser/Wannabe

This person will do almost anything to be in the group or gain favor from the Queen Bee or the Sidekick. She often observes and imitates their behavior, clothes, and interests but never feels completely in the group—that's why she's always proving her loyalty to the more powerful girls. As a result, she can give up what's important to her and/or what she enjoys. She constantly anticipates what people want from her, but doesn't ask herself what she wants in return.

Your Daughter Is a Pleaser/Wannabe If . . .
- Other girls' opinions and wants are more important than her own.
- Her opinions on dress, style, friends, and "in" celebrities constantly change according to what the Queen Bee does and says.
- She has trouble developing personal boundaries and communicating them to others.
- She can't tell the difference between what she wants and what the group wants.
- She's desperate to have the "right" look (clothes, hair, etc.).
- She'll stop doing things she likes because she fears the clique's disapproval.
- She avoids conflicts. Her common response when asked her opinion is, "Whatever you want, doesn't matter to me."

What Does She Gain by Being a Pleaser/Wannabe?
The Pleaser/Wannabe has the feeling that she belongs.

What Does She Lose by Being a Pleaser/Wannabe?
Frankly, almost all girls and women have moments of being the Pleaser. Here's the deal. Because girls are rewarded for being "nice," pleasing behavior is reinforced because it is socially condoned. Therefore, it's really hard to see when a girl is sacrificing her personal boundaries. As a result, many pleasers have low self-

esteem from sacrificing their needs and judgment. Pleasers often assume that the more they please, the more liked they will be or positively recognized for their actions. But ironically, that's not true. Instead, the more Pleasers accommodate, the worse people treat them.

> She thinks she belongs, but the Queen Bee and the Sidekick are just using her; she'll lose all her friends, then the Queen Bee and her Sidekick will destroy her reputation. Don't be a Pleaser/Wannabe if you can help it.   —Trinity, 16

The Torn Bystander

She doesn't want to go against the more powerful people in the group and usually convinces herself not to challenge them. She wants to help the Target, the next in line, but she is not sure how or thinks it won't make a difference. She may rationalize her own silence or apologize for others' behavior.

Your Daughter Is a Torn Bystander If . . .
- She's always finding herself in situations where she has to choose between friends.
- She tries to accommodate everyone.
- She's not good at saying no to her friends.
- She wants everyone "to get along."
- She can't imagine standing up to anyone she has a conflict with; she goes along to get along.

> She's confused and insecure because her reputation is over if she doesn't stick with the Queen Bee, but she can be really cool when she's alone.   —Anne, 13

What Does She Gain by Being a Torn Bystander?
Her silence buys her acceptance into the group. In high-social-status groups, that also means she has increased access to popularity, high social status herself, and boys.

What Does She Lose by Being a Torn Bystander?

Her fear of the Queen Bee or other girls in power can be so terrifying that she never learns to take a stand. She can't imagine having the personal power to do it. So she's smart enough to know something's wrong but feels incapable to exert any influence over the situation.

The Target

She's the girl who gets set up by the other girls to be humiliated, made fun of, and/or excluded. Targets are assumed to be out of the clique, one of the class "losers." Although this is sometimes true, it's not always the case. Just because a girl is in the clique doesn't mean she can't be targeted by the other members. Often the social hierarchy of the clique is maintained precisely by having someone clearly at the bottom of the group's totem pole. Girls outside the clique tend to become Targets because they're perceived to be trying too hard or because their style of dress, behavior, or personal background is outside the norms acceptable to the clique. Girls inside the clique tend to become Targets if they've challenged someone higher on the social totem pole (i.e., the Queen Bee, Sidekick, or Banker) and need to be put in their place.

Your Daughter Is a Target If . . .

- She feels helpless to stop the girls' behavior.
- She feels she has no allies. No one will back her up.
- She feels isolated.
- She can mask her hurt by rejecting people first, saying she doesn't like anyone.

This role can be harder to figure out than you would think, and your daughter may be too embarrassed to tell you. She might admit she feels excluded, or she might just withdraw from you and "not want to talk about it." That's why I'll discuss how to talk with your daughter in the next chapter.

> *Targets don't want to tell their parents because they don't want their parents to think they're a loser or a nobody.* —Jennifer, 16

What Does She Gain by Being a Target?

This may seem like an odd question, but being a Target can have some hidden benefits. There's nothing like being targeted to teach your daughter about empathy and understanding for people who are bullied and/or discriminated against. Being a Target can also give her objectivity. She can see the costs of fitting in and decide she's better off outside the clique because at least she can be true to herself and/or find good friends who like her for who she is, not for her social standing. Remember the girl who wrote that she was in the loser clique but at least she knew her friends were true friends? A lot of girls don't have that security. But in general, the benefits of having these experiences usually become clear to girls as they get older. In the meantime, being the Target can be excruciating. At the least, it doesn't seem like a very good trade-off for being made fun of now.

What Does She Lose by Being a Target?

She can feel helpless in the face of other girls' cruelty. She feels ashamed of being rejected by the other girls because of who she is. She'll be tempted to change herself in order to fit in. She feels vulnerable and unable to affect the outcome of her situation. She could become so anxious that she can't concentrate on schoolwork.

> *If a girl's stuck in a degrading clique, it's the same as when she's later in a bad relationship. She doesn't expect to be treated any better.* —Ellen, 15

The Champion

> *In every girl there is a Champion who wants to get out.* —Joanna, 17

In the last edition, I called these people the "Floaters" but I don't think that was a clear enough definition—and way too many people insisted to me that their daughter was one. So now, I'm calling this person the "Champion." The main goal of this book is to help your daughter have more Champion moments at every age. These moments are so important in shaping a girl's character, and if encouraged by parents and other adults, these Champion moments will profoundly change not only her life but also the lives of those around her. The Champion is not confined or controlled by the Act Like a Woman box. She can take criticism, doesn't make people choose friends, and doesn't blow off someone for a better offer. She has friends in different groups and doesn't treat people differently when groups are together. She can and will stand up to the Queen Bee in a way that treats them both with dignity.

You can usually spot this girl because she doesn't associate with only one clique. She has friends in different groups but can move freely among them (but remember so did the Banker who wrote to me in the beginning of the chapter). She's more likely to have higher self-esteem because she doesn't base her self-worth on how well she's accepted by one group.

Your Daughter Is a Champion If . . .

- She doesn't want to exclude people; you aren't always having fights with her about spending time with people she considers "losers."
- Her friends are comfortable around her and don't seem intimidated; she's not "winning" all the conversations.
- She's not exclusively tied to one group of friends.
- She can and is willing to bring another person into a group of friends.

What Does She Gain by Being a Champion?

Her peers like her for who she is as a person. She'll be less likely to sacrifice herself to gain and keep social status.

What Does She Lose by Being a Champion?

The only thing bad about being a Champion is when she stands up for someone and, in response, people turn on her. I'll talk about this later in Chapter 7, but suffice it to say, it can be lonely and scary to do the right thing.

. . .

Now, if you just read all those roles and have come to the conclusion that your daughter is the Champion, just take a moment. It isn't that I don't believe you, but I have a lot of experience with parents believing their children are something they're not. We all want to believe the best about the people we love, but sometimes our love blinds us to reality. It should go without saying that just because your daughter isn't a Champion doesn't mean she won't become an amazing young woman or that you haven't done a good job raising her. But, if you insist on seeing her in a way that she isn't, you won't be able to be as good a parent as she needs you to be. Most important to remember is, who among us can be a Champion all the time? Our goal is to have more Champion moments—in all of our lives, not just those of our daughters.

Treacherous Waters

OK, now you know the different roles girls play in cliques. The next questions are: How were these roles created in the first place? Who and what determine these positions and power plays? Why are girls able to get away with treating each other so badly?

Imagine you and your daughter are on a cruise ship. The cruise director's job is to make sure your daughter is reasonably happy and entertained. There are scheduled activities, and if by chance she hurts herself, someone will be there to get her back on her feet. She knows most of the people on the ship and everything is familiar. But all of the sudden, girls start telling each other the ship is stupid and boring and it's time to get off. As you watch helplessly, she leaves behind everything that is safe and secure, gets into a life raft with people who have little in common with her except their age, and drifts away.

Once in the raft she may ask herself how she got there or why she even left in the first place, but when she looks around, she sees that the ship is impossibly far away, the waves are too big, and there are a limited number of supplies; she quickly realizes that her survival depends on bonding with the other girls in that life raft. But your daughter isn't stupid. This realization is quickly followed by another one: she's trapped.

I know this is a dramatic metaphor to demonstrate girls' fear, but it shows how trapped many girls feel, forced to be a certain way in order to be accepted by their peers. They perceive their only choices as being stuck in the life raft or thrown into the water. To girls, the life raft of the clique can truly feel like a matter of life and death.

When I'm teaching girls in a class, I get them to talk about these feelings by giving them the following exercise: I ask them to describe what a girl or woman who has high social status is like. This is a person everyone "knows." If she has an opinion, everyone listens and agrees. What does she look like, and how does she act? Then I ask them to describe what a girl or woman who doesn't have high social status is like. This is someone who is likely to be teased, ridiculed, and/or dismissed. What does she look like, and how does she act?

Next, we put the characteristics of high social status within a box and place the characteristics of low social status outside the box (off the raft), as demonstrated in the following "Act Like a Woman" box.

	Pretty	Right brands	Poor
Tries too hard	Popular	of clothes	Uptight
Gay/ dyke/lez	Thin but right curves	Cell phones, etc.	Wrong style/brands
Inexperienced with guys	Good hair	In control	of clothes
Bad skin	Athletic but not bulky	Smart but not too intense about it	Slut
Fat	Confident	Guys think	Disabilities
Too masculine in appearance	Money	you're hot	Passionate about uncool things

The box shows what girls think they need in order to stay in the life raft and what characteristics will get them thrown out. I visualize most of the girls I teach as squeezing into this raft and hanging on for dear life. They'll tolerate almost anything to stay in—and there's always the threat of being cast out.

Are there some girls who are comfortable swimming in the waters? Are there girls who would rather drown than be in the raft? Sure, and sometimes these girls are stronger because of the struggle. But in many ways, every girl has to deal with the life raft, because her society's social pecking order is based on this metaphor. Even if she doesn't care, her peers do, and they're judging her accordingly. So no matter where your daughter is—sitting securely, teetering on the rails, bobbing in the waters with a life preserver, swimming strongly, treading water, or drowning—it is imperative to understand and accept the reasons why she bonds so tightly with her friends and why the idea of being cast out can be so frightening and paralyzing. Her fear also makes it more difficult to ask for help. From her perspective, that cruise ship is very far away, and you probably couldn't get her back on board even if you tried.

But how do people get thrown out of the life raft? Look at the words outside the box. These are weapons. For example, imagine your daughter is in the popular group. One of the girls in her group teases another girl for being overweight. Your daughter may feel bad, but what would happen if she stood up to the teaser? Any challenge to the powers that be is seen as an act of disloyalty and, in turn, she might be thrown out. Just the threat of being thrown out is powerful enough to silence most girls.

Cliques are self-reinforcing. As soon as you define your role and group, you perceive others as outsiders. It becomes harder to put yourself in their shoes, and therefore it is easier to be cruel to them or watch and do nothing. It doesn't matter if we're talking about social hierarchies, racism, sexism, homophobia, or any "ism"; this is the way people assert their power, which really translates into discrimination and bigotry. You've probably raised your daughter to stand up to and for people. But you're a long way away on the cruise ship, and heeding your advice—and perhaps her conscience—won't put her back on board with you. She's the one who has to stay on the raft with the girls. See why your daughter is so tempted to "do the wrong thing" even when she knows better?

If you want to really understand what your daughter's world looks like, ask her to draw a map of her school that shows who hangs out where. I asked two sixteen-year-old girls to do this exercise, an Indian-American girl from the East Coast and a junior

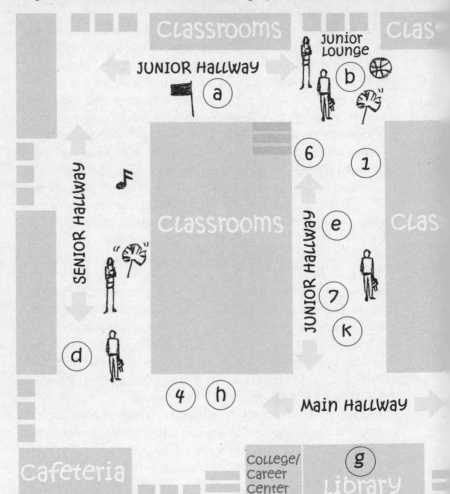

(a) Available for flirting, but there's a few jerks among them... a few dorks too.

(b) Gauntlet #1 - the guys are checking you out, esp. if you're someone that they semi-know.

(c) Oh Lord - Bitches, Incorporated. These are the <u>real</u> drama queens.

(d) Gauntlet #2 - the <u>real</u> test. These are the older guys, the ones everybody wants, the ones that judge your looks right as you walk by instead of waiting till you're pas

(e) Uh oh! physics teacher - didn't turn in my last problem set.

(f) These are the cute little girls who want to be part of the older group - annoying, but cute.

from the Southwest. I flinched when I saw their artwork. Their
worlds are harsh, judgmental places—but they're typical of
what many girls tell me their school experience is like.

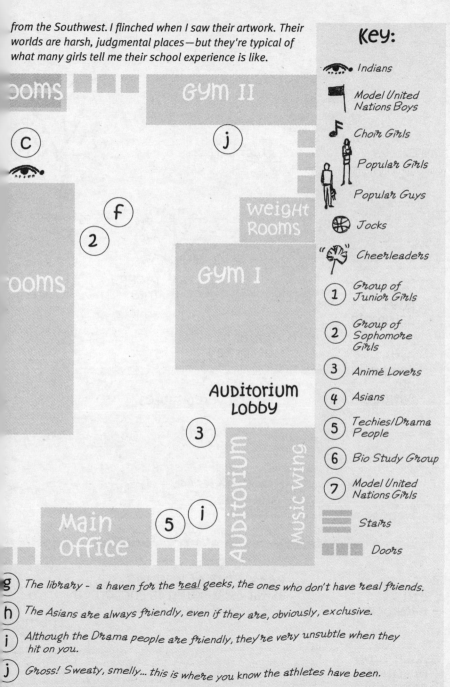

KEY:

- Indians
- Model United Nations Boys
- Choir Girls
- Popular Girls
- Popular Guys
- Jocks
- "Cheerleaders"
- (1) Group of Junior Girls
- (2) Group of Sophomore Girls
- (3) Animé Lovers
- (4) Asians
- (5) Techies/Drama People
- (6) Bio Study Group
- (7) Model United Nations Girls
- Stairs
- Doors

GYM II

c

j

f

2

WEIGHT ROOMS

GYM I

AUDITORIUM LOBBY

3

5   i

AUDITORIUM

MUSIC WING

Main Office

ooms

oms

g) The library - a haven for the <u>real</u> geeks, the ones who don't have real friends.

h) The Asians are always friendly, even if they are, obviously, exclusive.

i) Although the Drama people are friendly, they're very unsubtle when they hit on you.

j) Gross! Sweaty, smelly... this is where you know the athletes have been.

k) <u>So</u> ditzy - but sweet.

TECH ED. BUILDING

Preppies & Skaters

Preppies
(It's shady over here.)

"Sex Tree"

LOCKER BAY
(Mature Freshman & Sophomores)

Juniors mostly   Jocks

People make out over here.

Preppy Tree

BOYS' BATHROOM

GIRLS' SMOKE-OUT BATHROOM

SENIOR LOCKER BAY

Drugs here, too.

COVERED TABLES

Hispanics	Football & "Easy" Girls	Populars	Populars
Arabs	Football & "Easy" Girls	Populars	Populars
Blacks	Wrestlers	Sophomore Girls That Judge	Freshman Girls That Judge

ACADEMIC BUILDING

WORST STRIP OF WALKING AS FAR AS JUDGING IS CONCERNED

GIRLS' BATHROOM

VENDING MACHINES

BOYS' DRUG-DEALING BATHROOM

More Hacky-Sack Kids

OFFICE

ROTC
kids

Asians

GotHics/
Gays/Lesbians Tree

BOYS' GYM

LOCKER BAY
(Freshmen
& Juniors)

Pot Smokers *here*

BENCH

Nerdy Freshmen
(ones who
don't "belong")

AUDITORIUM

Hacky-Sack-Playing Kids

(Built up so
there are stairs)

Fat Girls
& Scrawny Boys

If you go   instead of
walking by the weird kids by
the auditorium, you get
judged and called names.

Unpopular Party Kids & Ecstasy
& Acid Users (mostly juniors)

Cafeteria

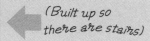

Entering/Exiting - you get
judged and you, naturally,
compare yourself to them.

Popular Girls -
Judgers *Anorexic*

More
Goths

SMOKING
BATHROOMS

Preps

Preppies

B-Ball Boys   B-Ball Juniors

Attitude Girls   Wannabe populars

Immature Boys   Preppy Girl Judges

PAY PHONES

Sex Table   Drug-dealer Table

How School Looks to Your Daughter

Some of us remember middle school and high school only too well. Others might need to jog their memory to recall what the hallways looked like. I asked a few girls to draw maps of their schools. You might ask your daughter to do the same. No matter what the details of her drawing, you'll discover the lay of the land your daughter traverses every day. And, if your daughter is willing to share her map with you, how does it compare with your school experience?

Checking Your Baggage
- Where did you fit in middle school?
- Where did you fit in high school?
- What did you get from being a part of this group?
- Did you ever want to leave the clique but felt like you couldn't?
- Were you ever tormented by someone in a clique?

Her Cliques and You

Accept the following:

You'll often have to rely on second-hand information. You won't be around when she gets into trouble. Your influence is limited to what you can do before and after. The only people guaranteed to be around her when she does get into trouble are her peers. Think of it this way: Where does your daughter hang out with her friends? How often do you hang out in these places? What exactly is she texting or twittering or posting on her favorite social networking site? Teens have access to each other in ways no adult does. This means that she'll have to stand up for herself with your support, but not your physical presence.

You have to get out of denial. Your daughter will make poor choices, behave in cruel and unethical ways, and/or be on the receiving end of both. If you want to raise a girl who survives adolescence (I mean this literally) and develops into a responsible, ethical woman, you have to accept the reality that there will be hurdles along the way and even some seemingly insurmountable mountains to scale.

Remember the life raft. When she's having a problem with friends, when she dreads going to school because she's having a fight with another girl, remember how terrifying it can be to swim in an ocean with predators all around and no rescue in sight.

Talking to Your Daughter About Cliques

It can be really hard to talk to your daughter about her role and experiences in the clique. As a general rule, unless she brings it up, don't begin the conversation by asking about her personal experiences. Instead, start the conversation by asking her opinion. Ask her to read this chapter and tell you what she thinks, or summarize it for her if reading it feels like homework to her. What rings true for her and what doesn't? If she tells you that there's nothing in the chapter that applies to her experience, don't let that be the end of your conversation. Ask her what does. You're looking for a starting place, which you might find by watching a TV show or movie together.

Approach your daughter as an observer of other girls. Then, when she's opened up to you about what she sees, you can ask what she thinks her role is. Most likely she'll start talking about herself as she talks to you about her friends. You can use the definitions I use in this book, but be ready to discard them if she's reactive. Let her define her experience for you. As I said earlier, it's great if she comes up with her own names for roles in the clique. Some good questions to ask are:

- What do people gain and lose from their role?
- Why does she think that person is in that role?
- How does it impact her to watch these things happen with her friends?
- How does she feel when it happens to her?

In the chapters that follow, I'll give you more specific advice on how to help your daughter, depending on the situation and where she stands on the social totem pole. For now, I'll describe your key task as a parent depending on your daughter's general position in the clique: from a powerful position, in the middle, or as the Target.

Position of Power (Queen Bee, Sidekick, Banker)

If she's operating from a power position, it'll be hard for her to admit when she's in the wrong, and she's unlikely to show empathy for other girls. Always emphasize taking responsibility for her actions and not blaming others.

If your daughter is in a position of power, she'll be focused on revenge. If you try to talk to her, she'll either put up fierce resistance or be as smooth as silk. Don't be fooled by the smooth approach. She's only doing that because she's smart enough to know that placating you will get you off her back faster.

Caught in the Middle (Torn Bystander, Pleaser/Wannabe, Messenger)

Don't create a situation in which she feels that she has to choose between you and the person described above because that girl is cooler than you are. Tell her you know she's in a difficult position, but encourage her to take responsibility, because her torn feelings look like two-faced behavior to other girls.

Ask her, "Who's making the decisions in your life?" She doesn't like when you make decisions for her, so she shouldn't like it when the Queen Bee makes decisions for her. But remember, no matter how close you are, you can't provide the social validation she gets from her friends, or convince her that she doesn't need it in the first place. The key to success in this conversation is to make your daughter understand that, by following the clique, she's not in control of what she wants. Don't blame her for not being able to stand up for herself. Give her credit for talking about it openly. Practice with her what she wants to communicate to the more powerful girls.

Target

If you identify your daughter in this role or if she ever has an experience where she's a Target, let her talk about it at her own pace. These situations can be very humiliating, so give her space but make sure she knows you are available to talk to anytime. If she tells you she's a Target, don't freak out and threaten to call the school or other parents unless she asks for your help. If she really doesn't want to talk to you, respect her feelings. In the next chapter, I'll talk more about the importance of finding an ally for your daughter in those cases where she's not comfortable talking to you. In Chapter 6, I'll discuss how to help your daughter stand up to those in power in the clique.

Land Mine!

Don't read this chapter and immediately ask your daughter what clique she's in! While we're on the subject, there are some parents who have asked me whether their child should read this book. First I think you need to read the whole book and decide which parts are appropriate. If you do have her read it, under no circumstances should you say something like, "I think you should read this book because . . ." Instead say, "I just read this book (and this goes for anything you see, read, hear about to do with one's children) and I want to know if you think the writer is realistic, completely wrong, or out of her mind. So will you read it and tell me what you think?" The important thing is that you talk about it and get her opinion.

No Matter What . . .

Whatever position she's in, always affirm your daughter in some way. Tell her that you recognize that these situations are really difficult. Most adults struggle with these same issues. If you think a story about when you were a teenager will be something she can relate to, tell her. But don't tell her what to do. Instead, describe the behavior you respect. Work with her as she comes up with a

plan that describes specifically what she wants to happen differently, and how she can make that happen. (Tell her she can always
blame you if her friends come down on her.) Your daughter will
feel better knowing that you respect the challenges she's up
against and want to help her through them.

Passport to Girl World:
Communication and Reconnaissance

I didn't understand why I was so unhappy in sixth grade. I couldn't have told my parents that girls were being mean to me.
— Erin, 17

If you've done something wrong, you don't want to tell your parents. Because you know you've been mean so it's uncomfortable. So maybe I'll tell my parents the little things I've done.
— Meredith, 13

I last told my parents in second grade about a problem I was having with a friend and then they told all their friends and my family. So then my cousins knew and teased me. So now, I just tell my brother and he just listens.
— Abby, 14

Parents tell me they want a passport that admits them to Girl World and the ability to translate this foreign language and understand the customs they find once they get there. But you don't want to be a casual tourist; you want to really get inside the culture. In this chapter, I give you general strategies to help you communicate more effectively with your daughter and translate what she's saying. (In later chapters I'll show how to apply those strategies more specifically.) I also show you how to get the information you need to tour Girl World without reading your daughter's diary or snooping through her text messages or Facebook page (although you do have the right to do that as a last, last, last resort).

But before I stamp your passport, I'm going give you some general things to keep in mind and then challenge you to evaluate your parenting style and how that impacts your daughter. If you don't have an effective parenting style, you can't be an effective communicator.

Always remember: No parent wakes up in the morning wanting to be an enabling, micromanaging, in denial, or irresponsible parent. And it's easy not to be when the social waters are calm in your child's life. But the minute you find out that she's caught up in a storm of Mean Girls, it gets infinitely harder. So the question is, Why are we so challenged?

Here's my short list:

1. We hate the people who are mean to our kids.
2. We love our children and we don't like thinking badly of people we love.
3. It's embarrassing when our children are mean, rude, or obnoxious because they make us look like bad parents. So rather than just sit and deal with our embarrassment, it's just too tempting to excuse the behavior. From saying she's "overtired" when she's little to saying "She's moody" or "You know, girls are just catty at this age" when she's a teen, we often miss opportunities to see our children's behavior for what it is.

WHAT'S YOUR PARENTING STYLE?

In my work with parents I see a variety of parenting styles and philosophies. Most of them are based on love, but as you probably know, there's a lot of anxiety, fear, and denial out there. Look over the following styles. Yours is probably a combination—I know mine is—but see which ones resonate with you the most. You can also ask your daughter what she thinks.

The Lock-Her-in-a-Closet Parent

This parent believes it's possible to control a daughter's move-ments and choose her friends and boyfriends. This parent also be-lieves that telling her to "just say no" to drugs, alcohol, and sex will work. I can't tell you how many times I've run into these parents only to find out that their daughters are doing all of the preced-ing—they're just really good at hiding it. Even if you could lock your daughter away until she's eighteen, you're only prolonging the inevitable. When she comes out, she'll want to experience things on her own, but without the opportunity to have had any guidance from you. If this is your parenting philosophy, you're teaching your daughter to sneak behind your back and get herself into serious trouble without giving her the skills to get out or the resources to help herself.

The Best-Friend Parent

Best friends? Some of you may laugh at this because you count as a good day one in which you and your daughter are on speaking terms. Most parents today who fit into this category know better than to say, "I'm best friends with my daughter." But how about, "I know my daughter isn't perfect, because no child is, but I'm just really lucky because she tells me everything and we're just really close." Never assume that your daughter isn't doing something solely because you don't approve of it or because you believe she tells you everything. *Just because she talks to you a lot doesn't mean she isn't selective about what she's saying.* In any case, your daugh-ter doesn't want you to be her best friend. She wants you to be her mother or father. Your connection with her is profound and unique.

Sometimes parents really are their daughter's best friend. How-ever, most often this ends abruptly sometime in early adolescence. These parents can feel terribly rejected. A few parents manage to think of their daughter as their best friend through high school, but I've rarely seen this work out well. The daughter feels torn be-tween resenting the overinvolved parents and feeling guilty about rejecting them. Or she's so dependent on the parents that she never learns to form her own independent relationships. In the first case, the daughter is forced to take extreme measures to separate from the parents. In the second case, she never grows up.

The Hip Parent

This parent will do anything to be liked by the daughter and her friends. In elementary and middle school, this is the parent who has inappropriate theme parties or buys things for their daughter and her friends in spite of the other parents' fervent wishes. In high school, this is the parent who buys beer for parties, often justifying this behavior (usually after a party has gotten out of hand and other parents are furious) by believing that if the kids are going to drink, they may as well do it under their own roof. At first glance, it seems like a good point—teens are going to drink, and it is better to have them in a safe place than driving around looking for parties. But by buying the beer, the Hip Parent is condoning the abuse of alcohol and its use as a social crutch.

I've never seen a child who respected the Hip or Best-Friend Parent. Both types are easily manipulated and disrespected by their children, especially in front of others. So while it may feel good in the short term, this method isn't responsible parenting. And forget discipline. Once you go down this road, it's almost impossible to set guidelines and rules that your daughter will take seriously. Your child wants and needs you to be a parent, not a friend with the ID.

The difference between a best-friend parent and a hip parent is that the best-friend parent's goal is to develop a relationship with their child and be close to them. But the hip parent's goal is to be close to the child's friends so they think they're cool. They'll put their own children down in order to be seen as cool by their kid's friends.   *—Katelyn, 18*

The Believer Parent

There's one thing I haven't ever gotten used to: parents believing that their child's perspective is the one and only truth. I get countless e-mails from parents describing something that happened to their child as if they were actually present at the event, like the Believer Parent was actually at lunch, the playground, or the school hallway when the incident occurred. Or the Believer Parent automatically believes their child when they say, "Mr. Edwards is so unfair! He totally yelled at me after he gave us a pop vocab test today! I swear he gave us the words yesterday!" Ask yourself: Have you ever argued with your daughter and you heard in response, "Mom, Dad, you are totally yelling at me!" And your thought to this accusation could be summed up to be something like, "You call this yelling? You haven't even seen yelling yet. In fact, I should be getting an award right now for how calm and mature I am being." There's a chance that something similar could be going on here. In fact, Mr. Edwards gave out the vocab list a week ago and reminded your child of that fact when he handed back the test results. But the Believer Parent never takes that under consideration while furiously typing and then sending an aggressive e-mail to Mr. Edwards or marching over to the school.

Land Mine!

Do not e-mail or call anyone right after your child has told you something that makes you angry! If your child is safe, standing in front of you, then whatever you need to do or say needs to be done when you are relatively calm and sane.

I'm not saying your child's truth isn't valid. It is. But if you don't consider the possibility of other perspectives, three things happen: (1) you won't find out what's really going on; (2) when you find out that there's another side to the story you can get embarrassed because your child has just made you look like a fool; and (3) your embarrassment turns into massive denial and defensiveness and then you think the other person is lying. None of these reactions creates a situation for effective parenting.

The "You Mess with My Kid, You Mess with Me" Parent

Just a little more extreme is the "You Mess with My Kid, You Mess with Me" Parent. Now I know this comes from a really natural place of feeling like a mama or papa bear when someone is hurting your child, but these parents can't pick their child's battles. Everything to do with their child is a battle and they are always ready to wage war. They rush in, without letting their child either advocate for themselves or be held responsible for bad behavior.

The "Let's Let Them Work It Out" Parent

On the face of it, this makes perfect sense. Your daughter needs to learn how to handle difficult social situations like being teased or bullied. But the big problem with this is: (1) these parents rarely have this attitude when their kid's on the receiving end; and (2) they don't get involved at all—which means they provide no moral guidance and structure as their child navigates through complex difficult social dynamics. To this parent, "involvement" means micromanaging a child's life; and they're going to leave that to the helicopter parents they love to make fun of. But what all parents need to realize is that sane involvement means being behind the scenes, asking your child the right questions and knowing enough of the details to hold your child accountable when necessary.

The Pushover Parent

The only girls who don't wish they had this kind of parent are the girls who actually do. Daughters of Pushover Parents are primarily left to make their own mistakes with no guidance and no parental consequences. Teens want rules and boundaries. They may rebel, but deep down they know that rules and boundaries make them feel safe, that there's order to the world, and that someone's look-ing out for them.

There's another kind of Pushover Parent, though he or she may not look like it on the surface. This is the parent who isn't around a lot because of his or her job (long hours or they travel a lot) or a divorce. These parents can be really aggressive to everyone else in the child's life (the other parent, a teacher, a coach) but will do anything to be on the child's side.

> *What's the difference between the two? I would say that the Pushover lets you change the rules whenever you want and the Hip Parent has rules but they are really cool, like "No beer in the bedroom."* —Becca, 16

The Benign Neglect Parent

This parent wants to do the right thing but is simply too exhausted and distracted by work and other obligations to create the struc-tured environment a daughter needs. The biggest problem is in-consistency—the parent initiates rules but then they're forgotten because the parent is distracted or just too tired to enforce disci-pline. When the daughter breaks a rule, she can take advantage of the parent's guilt and insecurity to transition the conversation from the daughter's behavior to the parent's bad parenting.

The No-Excuses Parent

This parent has some wonderful qualities, demanding the best from a child and holding her to a high standard of accountability and personal responsibility. Through their words and deeds, No-Excuses Parents show their daughter that she should always get up no matter how many times she's pushed down. These parents usu-ally raise girls who would make any parent proud: girls who get good grades, are respectful to others, and so on. There's only one problem with this kind of parenting: since the daughter has been taught that she should take care of whatever problem faces her, she can be reluctant to ask for help. If she's in over her head, she can easily feel ashamed that she isn't strong enough to overcome her problems on her own. Shame is a powerful feeling and it can make girls feel so bad that they've let the family down that they internalize their feelings and become self-destructive and/or disconnected from the family.

The Private Parent

This close relative of the No-Excuses Parent believes that family problems should stay within the family. Daughters raised in this style get the message that imperfection, fear, feelings of insecurity, depression, and helplessness may be something other people have but not "us." The Private Parent's daughter can grow up afraid to reach out for help and/or not know how. Although privacy is important (especially to a teen!), anyone can get into situations that are over her head, and her health depends on reaching out.

The No-Privacy Parent

On the other end of the spectrum, and more publicly embarrassing, is the No-Privacy parent. This parent believes that anyone, often unsuspecting strangers or unlucky dinner guests, should be included in family disputes, even if—or especially if—they include the revelation of embarrassing and humiliating information about individual family members. Because teens are often sensitive about sharing any personal information beyond their name, most parents could be innocently accused of this parenting style, but there's a difference between giving factual information and telling your new best friend about the gory details of the last fight you had with your daughter. Girls with this parent will go to great lengths to create privacy—usually by sneaking behind their parents' backs.

The Don't-Ask, Don't-Tell Parent

Through an unspoken agreement, the daughter doesn't tell the parent what's going on and the parent doesn't ask. When parents feel unprepared and/or don't have the support they need, they often feel that ignorance is bliss. This makes for pleasant yet superficial conversations at the dinner table, but in the meantime, the daughter can be foundering.

The Overbearing Parent

This parent's love, anxiety, or fear combine either to overwhelm and incapacitate the daughter or drive her away. She often feels suffocated and fights back by becoming defiant. Everything between the parent and child becomes a battle of wills and control; and in the process, everyone in the family suffers. Spouses feel they have to choose between their children and their partner, ex-spouses feel they have to defend their child, and siblings lay low to avoid the fire. In short, the home becomes the last place any of the children want to be.

The Loving Hard-Ass Parent

Of course, this is my favorite parent. The one I now aspire to be. Parents with this philosophy know there may be things their daughter hides from them, like e-mails, texts, or early and sometimes troubled relationships with boys, but they don't take it as a personal insult or an indication that their relationship with their daughter is weak. When they make mistakes, they own up to their behavior and right the wrong, and they encourage their daughter to do the same. They demonstrate that you can learn from mistakes and be better for it. They love their daughter unconditionally but hold her accountable for decisions and behavior that go against the family's values and ethics. When they're told that their daughter may have done something wrong, they listen and don't blame other people for their daughter's behavior. At the same time, they never make her feel ashamed of who she is. They also realize, especially as their children get older, that they may want to confide in someone else about a problem. This parent realizes that the most important goal is that their daughter has someone reliable and sane to talk to—even if it's not them.

Here are some things Loving Hard-Ass Parents do:

- If their daughter has done something really wrong, they go with their daughter and apologize.
- They don't gossip about children while waiting in car pool lanes and watching athletic events.
- They laugh at their own mistakes and use them to inform better judgements in the future.
- They aren't quick to judge other parents.
- They are not afraid to admit when they feel overwhelmed or unsure about how to handle a difficult situation with their kids.

I hate to say it, but my parents really are pretty cool! And all the other parents I can think of that are cool are really very similar to mine. They're laid-back, but not oblivious or completely separate from my life. They trust me. They genuinely like me and like spending time with me. They know what goes on in my life, but they can take a hint when it's time for them to leave me alone. Of course there are the occasional fights or disagreements, but in the end, I think they only help make our family life stronger.
—Julie, 16

I urge every parent to become a Loving Hard-Ass Parent.

SOMETIMES LOVE ISN'T ENOUGH

As I said in the introduction, the biggest difference in my life between when I first wrote this book and now is that I am the mother of two boys who are six and eight. I'm in the thick of it just like you! I regularly face many of the same problems I discuss in my work. Have I gotten calls from the principal? Yes—and it wasn't about how wonderful my child was in a certain situation. My children have been the bully, the target, and the bystander, and I, like you, have experienced the unbelievable anxiety of not knowing how to help my child through a challenging problem. So let me

assure you that just because I do this stuff for a living, I am not immune to experiencing these problems firsthand. One experience I
went through this year rocked me to my core.

A few weeks into the new school year, my husband and I were
notified that our older child, Elijah, was acting out in school. He
was disrespectful to his teachers, he wasn't participating in class,
and he was physically aggressive with other students. While it was
upsetting to get this news, we had seen similar behavior at home in
the form of tantrums and saying negative things about himself,
like he was a "loser" and he wished he'd "never been born." Up to
that point, we weren't sure how seriously to take his behavior. But
it got worse and worse until the school referred him to see a therapist in the school—someone I had trained, by the way. As I sat in
her office, close to tears, scared to death, I looked up to see all my
books and curricula on her bookshelf. You may think I'd be embarrassed that someone I'd trained would see the problems I was
having within my own family. I had that feeling but it was fleeting,
because at that point, I was so desperate that all I felt was gratitude
that someone I thought was competent could help him.

Four weeks later, after seeing Ms. LaNail Plummer twice a
week, he was doing better with her and at home, but he was still
struggling in the class. Then the Tuesday before Thanksgiving,
Ms. LaNail called me and said Elijah had been beat up at school
by a group of boys and that I needed to take him home. I rushed
over to the school, where she was waiting for me. She gave me a
hug and took me to him where he was waiting in her office. I
wrapped my arms around him, told him I loved him, and took
him home. During the next few days Elijah told us that since the
beginning of the year, a group of boys had been telling him before
lunch and recess that they were going to beat him up. Sometimes
they would. Sometimes they wouldn't. But he didn't tell us because they told him not to.

Of course I felt like I had failed my child. And I, of all people,
hadn't seen the signs? I, who have said two things to countless
teachers over the years: "Kids almost always have a good reason
for what they do. You may think what they're doing is horrible or

annoying, but there's always a reason." And, "You always see the second hit, you rarely see the first." Most teachers first see the retaliation, not the act that initiated the conflict. Yet my frustration and anxiety blinded me to look behind my own child's actions.

The night before he returned to school, we sat down with him and he described to me the details of how the kids had threatened him and physically hurt him. While he spoke I wrote it all down. My husband and I prepared him for the meeting we would have the next day with the principal, Ms. Perez. We asked him to think of questions he wanted to ask her and his teachers. We encouraged him to talk as much as possible, but we assured him that we would both be there as backups.

As soon as the meeting started, Ms. Perez asked Elijah to describe what he'd been going through. He said nothing. She asked again and he said he didn't remember. Then I noticed he was nodding in my direction and lifting his eyebrows, clearly communicating, "Come on, Mom, tell her what I said last night!" I asked him if he wanted me to tell the principal what I had written down the night before. He nodded with relief that I was getting it. As I spoke, his eyes were glued on Ms. Perez. After I was done, Ms. Perez looked him straight in the eye and said, "Elijah, I'm sorry and we're going to do better." I almost lost it. I don't know about you, but the feeling of relief when you witness another adult doing right by your kid can make the hardest among us weep.

From there we created a safety plan for him, and the school supervised recess differently. Slowly but surely Elijah's behavior improved. The negative self-talk and tantrums stopped. The calls home about his disrupting the class ended. And then one day, Elijah and I were in the kitchen and he told me he was worried that he may have a hard time in school the next day. My pulse quickened. "Do you want to talk about it?" I asked. He shook his head and said matter-of-factly, "Mom, you really aren't good at that." I sputtered, "Excuse me?????" He shrugged. "You're not really that good at talking to me about this stuff." I laughed. "You're kidding me with this, right?" He shook his head. I asked, "OK, can you talk to Ms. LaNail about it?" Without a moment's hesitation he replied, "Oh yeah, she's way better than you are."

What did I learn from this experience? That frankly, while no one can take the place of a child's primary caretaker when you need a hug at the end of a horrible day, sometimes our love and anxiety stops us from giving the kind of guidance our children need. Ironically, our love can make us so close we can't see what to do. For as good as I am at my work, in the darkest of those days, I couldn't see how to help him. It is not an exaggeration that Ms. LaNail changed my son's life. She offered him the kind of support and guidance he needed at the time he needed it.

THE APPLE DOESN'T FALL FAR FROM THE TREE

Just as I challenge girls to own up to what they do that contributes to their being their own worst enemies, I'm also challenging you to own up to what you do that contributes to girls' social hierarchies. Leave behind the assumption that Queen Bee girls always have Queen Bees as mothers—"after all, the apple doesn't fall from the tree." Because I don't think that's a helpful way to think about it. First, when we say that, we aren't looking at (i.e., blaming) the dad for nurturing a Queen Bee. Second, we never say the same things about the Pleaser/Wannabe girls or any other position in the group. Third, since almost no one identifies themselves as Queen Bees, if you believe this line of thinking, you'll never be able to see Queen Beeism in your own child. And fourth, I've seen too many variations on the Queen Bee girl/parent dynamic to feel confident telling you I think there is a correlation. And in any case, it really doesn't matter which girl has which parents. Instead, what is much more important to understand is that if you're a parent or someone who is around girls in any capacity, the way you handle yourself is profound.

I am the coleader of a Girl Scout Troop and our girls are Cadettes (seventh and eighth grade), and have been together since Daisys (kindergarten). New girls have come along almost each year, and most have stayed. The newest girl is being ignored and avoided at best and shunned and dumped on by the Queen Bee daughter of the Queen Bee troop leader. I am horrified. I am angry at myself because I did not/cannot do more to help Irene. I am angry at the other adults for being clueless, or unwilling to see. After an overwhelming desire to resign as a tactic to avoid the discomfort and pain . . . I now know that I have to stay and effect change.   *—Mary*

My 8-year-old daughter had just started at a new school when the mother of a Queen Bee approached me. She wanted to invite my daughter to her daughter's birthday party, but she told me to keep it quiet because the two other new girls hadn't been invited. For a moment I was elated that my daughter had made the cut, but then I realized both my daughter and I were being co-opted by the clique. I was so torn. I wanted my daughter to be included, but at what price?   *—Roger*

It's now time to ask yourself some very difficult questions: you're your daughter's role model; are you talking about other people in a way that you're proud of? What is she learning from you? When you run up against a Queen Bee, how do you react? Do you want your daughter acting the same way? Are there girls you want your daughter to be friends with (or not) because of social status? And the biggest question: are you living according to your values—not just when things are easy and you're getting along with people, but when it's hard? When you're so angry that the last thing you want to do is treat someone with dignity? Asking yourself the following questions can help clarify your rights and responsibilities in relation to your daughter.

Your Parental Bill of Rights

- What do you need in your relationship with your daughter? I have the right to get the information I need to keep my daughter safe.
- What are your responsibilities to your daughter? I'm responsible for helping her become an independent adult through being a good role model and holding her accountable for her actions.

- Under what circumstances would you ask someone for help with a problem you're having with your daughter? When I believe it's too uncomfortable for my daughter or the issues she's tackling are making me so crazy and anxious that my input will only make the problem worse.
- Does your daughter know your answers to these questions? I'm not sure, but I should find out.

Your daughter also needs a Bill of Rights with you. Here are some questions she can answer.

Your Daughter's Bill of Rights with You
- What do you need in your relationship with your parent(s)?
- What are your responsibilities to your parent(s)?
- Under what circumstances would you ask someone for help with a problem you are having with your parent(s)?

I want to come to them with problems and get advice and sympathy—not anger or controlling behavior. My responsibility is to keep them informed of where I am, what I'm doing, never lie, uphold their values, and try my best.   —*Tanya, 16*

OPENING UP THE LINES OF COMMUNICATION: TEETH-PULLING 101

I know, I know. You just want to visit Girl World and talk to your daughter about what's going on in her life. Why does she respond by disclosing nothing more than name, rank, and serial number to the evil interrogator? Before you even think of engaging your daughter in an in-depth conversation, know that there are a few certainties that make your task more difficult:

1. If you press her to answer more completely than "fine" and "okay" when you ask her how school is, she'll initially see your interest as an invasion of privacy and a waste of time. This is a common reaction. Don't take it personally.

2. If you tell her you want to "talk" to her, she'll sigh, roll her eyes, or assume you're blaming her for something.

I have some suggestions to get around these common hurdles. First, appreciate that those monosyllables and grunts in response to the daily question of how things are going at school are normal. Asking your daughter a general question like "How was school today?" is too difficult (there was that horrible math test, then Anna and Kenya ignored her at lunch, then the buttons on her shirt popped open in front of the boys . . .). Instead, ask her specific questions. For example, asking "Read anything interesting in English class today?" or "Learn anything relevant in health class today?" gives her more freedom to answer.

When you ask her about her life ("So, what's new?"), she might assume you know something bad or that she's in trouble and immediately go into defensive mode. Once she's defensive, you'll never get anything out of her.

Maybe starting with "You're not in trouble. I just want to know what's up with you" would work better.   —Katherine, 17

As a newly minted Loving Hard-Ass Parent, you certainly don't want every conversation short-circuited, so you need to better communicate with your daughter. Make it a priority. Look for opportunities to bond when you have no other agenda but to check with your daughter just to see that she's okay. Make the most of your time together when you're making dinner, watching TV, driving around on errands. But don't limit yourself to spontaneous opportunities for sporadic conversations. I strongly recommend that you create more focused time just to connect.

At least once a month, take your daughter out to a coffee shop or some other place she likes to go where the two of you can sit down and hang out, away from other siblings and distractions. Take her to school one day and leave early so you can stop for bagels and juice. Avoid going to a place where either one of you may run into someone you know. At any point, but especially in the beginning, refrain from making any comments about what she's wearing, homework she's supposed to be doing, or the room she's supposed to be cleaning. Don't talk about schedules, upcoming events, or things you need to get information about—unless she brings it up. Just as important, watch out for those land mine remarks, like "You should wear your hair pulled back like that more often. You're so pretty when you can see your face."

Get your daughter her favorite drink, and don't make faces when she orders something you think is disgusting or unhealthy. (That's another talk.) Sit down at a table she chooses, get comfortable, and start: "Thanks for getting up early today so we could do this. There's really no pressure to do or say anything. We just don't get a lot of time to talk without a million things going on at the same time so I thought we could spend some time together and you can tell me what you feel comfortable with. So what's up with X?

Don't be afraid of silence. If she just sits there for a while and it looks like that's the way it'll stay, remind her there's no pressure so it's totally acceptable for the two of you to just sit together and read. But just one rule: she can't use technology. No games on her cell phone or texting her friends.

Eventually, you'll get answers from her if you set up a comfortable environment and listen respectfully. Even if she complains later to her friends, believe me, she appreciates your effort. If, however, you've never done something like this before, expect her to say something during this talk that sets your teeth on edge. She's your daughter so she's an expert button pusher. Let's say she reacts to your overture by being obnoxious. Take a deep breath and remember your goal for the conversation: to connect. For example, she might say disdainfully, "Why do you care all of a sudden? Are you feeling guilty because you're never around? Don't think you can be parent for a day and I'll start telling you things . . . because that's not happening." At this moment, you may wonder why you bothered and whose child this is anyway. Instead of shutting down and fighting with her, ask, "Do you really feel that way? Because if

you do, I really need to hear why you think that." Then be prepared to listen.

LISTENING: THE HARD PART

*Sometimes when I tell my parents stories, I specifically don't
want their advice. All I want them to do is listen.   —Keisha, 16*

Truly listening can be incredibly challenging! Without even realizing it, you're asking leading questions and/or coming across as a
scary interrogator bent on fixing the problem. None of these will
work on your daughter. You might as well pay for the coffee and go
home.

*Don't sigh, roll your eyes, or click your teeth. These are all very
annoying when you're talking to your Martian parents!*
—Alexa, 13

So how to best keep these inclinations at bay? First, be honest
with yourself about your agenda and goals. Are you keeping an
open mind and trying to get information from your daughter's perspective, or are you out to confirm your preconceived opinions?
For example, let's suppose you don't like one of her friends and
you want to know more about what your daughter does with this
girl after school.

YOU: So what's up with Emily? You seem to be spending a
    lot of time with her.
DAUGHTER: (Silence for two seconds)
YOU: Are you sure you want to be doing that? I have to tell
    you that I think she's hanging out with the kind of people
    you don't want to be associated with.
DAUGHTER: Mom—don't worry about it. She's fine.
YOU: I'm just worried about you. I'm sure she's a nice person
    but I just wouldn't want you to make a bad decision about
    a friend and end up regretting it.

If you say things like this, let's admit that the goal is not "finding out what's up" with your daughter but instead to communicate your anxiety that Emily isn't a good influence. Now, you may be absolutely right that Emily is a bad influence, but the problem is that this conversation will result in the opposite of your goal. Your daughter will now be less likely to tell you anything about Emily (or anyone else, for that matter) because you weren't trying to connect, but leading the conversation to confirm your own suspicions. Girls see through this easily and will shut down. Anyone would. Let go of your agenda and allow your daughter to take the lead.

> I think one main reason kids don't tell their parents anything when they are fighting with friends is that things so quickly turn around and if my parents don't see every detail of the turn-around, then they have this image of this bad kid that did something so mean to their child. I told my mom about something that happened on my soccer team and now her one image of that person is horrible because she's not actually there. She doesn't see when the girl does nice things. One girl is kind of tagging along evil and there's one girl who is actually legitimately evil. The girl who is tagging along, she's really nice when she's alone. I told my mom this one incident so my mom tells me that they are a bad crowd.
> —Julia, 13

Mark these get-togethers in your calendar; they're unbreakable dates. You want to establish a pattern that says you're there just for her, you don't want to get involved only when there's a problem, and you're capable of having a conversation that doesn't revolve around your role as the enforcer or a logistics coordinator. The younger (starting at a young age is very important now) your daughter is when you start these one-on-one conversations, the more she'll see that you're someone she can turn to when she needs support.

Unfortunately, you can't depend on your daughter coming to you when she's upset. The older she gets, the less she'll want to involve you in her problems (often because she considers you one of the main sources). At twelve, she may come crying to you when a girl has been mean to her, but at fifteen, she'll more likely keep it inside or talk to her friends. Even when she can't bring herself to approach you and say, "I really need to talk to you," she may broadcast signals that she wants your help. Here are some signs to watch for:

- She hangs around where you are but doesn't necessarily say anything.
- She says she doesn't feel well and wants to stay home with you, but there doesn't seem to be anything physically wrong.
- You're about to drive somewhere on an errand and she volunteers to go with you. In the words of Joanna, sixteen, "I like this strategy because she has to focus on driving and can't freak out about what you're saying."
- She asks to watch a show with you.
- She slips a very casual reference to her problem into the conversation.
- She tries to get other people out of the house except you.

If your daughter wants to talk to you but also couches it as "no big deal," don't believe her. If she actually wants to talk to you, she's already telling you that she thinks it's a big deal. Anytime your daughter wants to talk, pay attention. You're ready to talk when she's ready to talk.

In any conversation like this with your daughter, there are two goals. The first is having a productive conversation with her. This means that through the process of your conversation, you want to affirm her and show that you're a good resource and a nonjudgmental listener. The second is helping her develop realistic strategies to confront her problem effectively. You'll never accomplish the second goal without the first. Later in the book I'll walk you through when you need to contact others for additional help (see Resources) but in general, here's what you say when your daughter approaches you with a problem:

1. "I'm so sorry that happened."
2. "Thank you for telling me."

3. "Together we're going to think through a strategy where you feel that you have regained some control in the situation."

Now let's break it down a little more:

- **Affirm your daughter's feelings.** Don't be a Truth Cop, intent on verifying the accuracy of everything she tells you right away. The facts will come out over time, but your daughter's emotional truth is what is important, and you should affirm that. Having said that, don't make this a Hallmark moment where you freak your daughter out by stopping everything you're doing, look her in the eyes, and make this the most intense bonding moment ever. This is why it can be very effective to have these conversations while you are doing something else, like hiking, driving in the car, shopping, or even sitting in front of the TV.
- **Don't use the slang your daughter uses.** There's nothing more ridiculous than an adult who tries to be hip by using teen slang. Slang changes so fast that it's impossible to keep up anyway. Nevertheless, some parents think that if they use it, they'll relate to their daughter better. Not true. It only looks like you're trying too hard—and there's nothing worse to a teen. If she uses a word you don't understand, ask her to explain it to you. She may laugh at how clueless you are, but it demonstrates that you respect and are interested in what she has to say and how she describes her world.
- **Share your own experiences/stories from when you were her age, especially the ones where you made mistakes and learned from them.** As a general rule, it's better to avoid telling stories about your adult experiences because you need to maintain boundaries with her. The purpose of this storytelling is to empathize—"I know what you've been through, because something similar happened to me"—not to preach.
- **Don't just do something, stand there.** In other words, don't try to fix all of her problems. You want to empower her so she develops the skills to think through and get through her

problems. Sometimes your daughter just wants to voice her concerns about something and isn't looking to fix it right away. If she does want to take action, ask her, "What ideas do you have for fixing this?" "Do you want to sound any of them out with me?" Only after you've worked through her ideas might you suggest, "I think I may have some other ideas that could work, too. Do you want to hear them?"

- **Give her ownership of what she does (good and bad) and let her make mistakes.** Even if her solution is completely ridiculous, the fact that it's her idea means that she's working toward independence. Encouraging that is more important than making sure she tries the best (i.e., your) solution.

- **Remember to accept silence.** You are her parent. This means that when you discuss difficult or uncomfortable topics with your daughter, she may not respond right away. Don't think you always need to fill the silence. You can ask her about it after a while by saying, "You just got really quiet when we talked about X; why is that?"

- **Don't make fun of her.** In your daughter's most dramatic moments, you may be tempted to make fun of the situation in an attempt to make her realize this problem isn't the end of the world. This effort will look like you are teasing her. So keep the joking comments to yourself and substitute supportive questions.

What if she says, "Mom, Dad, I'm going to tell you something but you have to promise me you won't do anything!"

OK, this is one of those moments that prove how incredibly confusing parenting is. Common sense would dictate that you want to make that promise because, if you don't, your daughter won't talk to you. And if she won't talk to you, then you can't help her. But what if you make that promise and she tells you something you need to do something about? Like a friend who is hurting herself? Then you are in the situation where you would be forced to break a promise—never a good thing.

Here's the way out. Tell your daughter that while you would love to make that promise, you can't because if she or someone

HOW TO STOP THE EYE ROLLING

If your daughter excels in the art of eye rolling, sighing, or crossing her arms, this may be slightly annoying to you. Here's my suggestion for addressing the problem. At base, your daughter wants something from you—either she wants to do something or she wants you to see her opinion. So this is what you say:

> Charlotte, here's the deal. You want X from me. When you roll your eyes and sigh when I'm speaking, there is no chance you'll get what you want from me because your behavior is so irritating and disrespectful. But if we can have this conversation without eye rolling, there's a chance we can come to some kind of agreement. Eye rolling—you have no chance. No eye rolling—you have a shot. So I am going to leave for five minutes, let you think about it, and then we can continue the conversation.

else is in need of help, you may need to call on a professional or contact a counselor or another parent. But what you *can* promise is that if you do decide you need to bring someone else in, she will always be informed. She'll never be surprised and blindsided. In fact, she can help you decide who would be the best person with whom to talk. In my experience, kids don't stop talking to their parents when their parents make decisions they don't like—as long as they are respected and brought into the process.

After your conversation, or anytime she's feeling bad, affirm her and tell her you love her. Do something for her that will make her feel special and taken care of. Buy her flowers or a scented candle. Let her watch a movie—and don't let anyone else in the family change the channel. If she enjoys them, let her take a bath without her brothers or sisters bothering her.

And please remember you aren't a bad parent if your child goes to someone for help. The following story demonstrates how allies can bring a parent closer to their child. I received an e-mail from a thirteen-year-old girl who needed advice telling her widowed dad that she had gotten her period and needed extra money to buy tampons. She was too embarrassed to tell him, and he couldn't figure out why their conversations were ending up in fights and crying. As part of my advice, I suggested she tell a woman she was close to what the problem was so they could go to a store and get what she needed. The girl took my advice and talked to her older cousin, who immediately took her to the drugstore and bought her a six-month supply of tampons. But the cousin also told her mom (the sister of the dad), and then I got this letter.

> I feel like a bit of a fool that my own kid had to write to a stranger for help. She was the little girl who began her period. I guess I am what you call old-fashioned. I run a construction company full of men. My daughter has really been one of the guys till now. I forgot she has different issues than her brothers. But over the past few months, there have been tears and attitude and eye rolling. I was scared she was trying drugs, but her brothers assure me she is not part of that crowd. Last year she got me a Homer Simpson T-shirt on my birthday and I am afraid this is pretty much the level of sensitivity and intelligence you're dealing with. Thanks for giving her good advice.   —Frank

Your Little Angel Is a Liar and a Sneak

Many teenagers lie. I'm not saying "all," because there are some teens who don't. I, however, was not one of them. When my mother reminisces about my adolescence, it always begins with, "You give birth to this wonderful kid and you can never imagine in your wildest dreams that this person that you love so much would lie to you. And then they do. All the time." I did—I lied to my mother all the time. Even when I didn't need to. I lied about everything: where I was going, who I was going with, why I wanted to go in the first place. I lied when there was no reason to lie. I just didn't want her to know anything about what was going on in my life. Not all girls are as bad as I was, but I've yet to meet a girl who is *always* honest with her parents. Don't take it personally if your daughter lies to you. I know that's hard. I've had students I've been very close with who have lied. It's very hard to take, and it made me incredibly angry. But lying is often about testing boundaries—your own and the authority figures in your life and/or wanting something so badly that you'll do anything to make it happen—including deceiving the people whom you perceive to be standing in the way. I'm not excusing it, but it needs to be seen in context so you can hold your child accountable for the right reason in the right way.

What Makes a Good Liar?

- She bases every lie on a grain of truth. This truthlet can be used later if she's caught, and she'll hang on to it for dear life. This is why a girl can be so self-righteous when she's caught.
- She is a detail queen. When she's trying to hide something from you, she overloads you with so many details that you end the conversation completely confused.
- She approaches you when you're distracted and/or tired.
- She gets friends to back up the story. (You can undermine this strategy by developing close relationships with the parents of your daughter's friends, as I'll describe shortly.)
- She truly believes what she's saying.
- She's angry with you for something else, so she feels justified in lying.

My mom recently got divorced and I was really upset about it. So I thought it was totally okay for me to tell her I was sleeping at my girlfriend's house when I was really at my boyfriend's house.
—Molly, 15

How Can You Tell When She's Lying?

Some parents believe they have the magic power to look their daughter in the eye and the truth will come spilling out. Maybe. If you're really good, your daughter may crumble under the stern, unflinching parental lie detector. But a good liar can pass this test easily. A good liar is cool and collected and continues to hold her ground no matter what

So here's how you figure it out.

- Trust your gut—if it sounds funny, it is.
- When she tells you her plans, stop what you're doing and pay very close attention to what she says she's doing, where, when, and with whom. Write it down and keep a copy of your school directory or other lists handy (see Reconnaissance Strategies section) to double-check parents' numbers.

If your daughter tells you she's going to be at a friend's house, there's a very good chance she is—for about five minutes. Just enough time to go into her friend's house, check out what her friend is wearing, borrow some clothes, grab something to eat, and then they're out the door to their real destination: a party, a boy-friend's house, or some other place you'd rather she not go. Some girls will try to weasel their way out of trouble by telling their parents they're sleeping over at a friend's house. Technically, she isn't lying, because eventually she planned to end up back at the house where she said she'd be. How was she supposed to know the party she went to would be so far away that she got stuck there, and that the party got so out of control that another parent called you at three in the morning?

If you suspect something like this could be afloat, here's what you do. Of course, confirm the sleepover with the friend's parent. But if you forget or tried to and didn't get in touch in time, here are some backup strategies: the easiest, of course, is to drop her off and actually go into the house and talk to the parent. But if you're not dropping her off, when your daughter arrives at the friend's house, she must call you using her cell phone and hand the phone to the other parent, who will confirm what your daughter has said. If you get any evidence that your daughter is lying to you, like you run into another parent at the grocery store who tells you "how surprised she was that you let your daughter go to the concert tonight," you immediately call your daughter and report what has just been said to you. Ask her if any part of what that parent reported is true or any part of what she told you is untrue. If she's steadfast in her denial, remind her that there are consequences for breaking rules but once she lies to you the consequences are going to be way more severe. Ask her again and then tell her that just so everyone's clear, you are on the way to meeting her so she can tell you to your face.

If She Says "You Don't Trust Me!"

You don't, nor should you!   —*Fran, 17*

What's the difference between lying and sneaking? Think of lying as untruthful words and sneaking as untruthful actions.

What Makes a Good Sneak?
- She takes advantage of your exhaustion, distractibility, and denial that she would sneak behind your back in the first place.
- She has strategic backup plans. If the first plan to sneak out of the house doesn't work, she always has an alternative.
- She's patient and intelligent. She can think three steps ahead to get what she wants.

Let's say you've told your daughter that she can't go to a party because she's not old enough. If your daughter easily accepts your decision and it's clearly contrary to what she wants, she could be placating you and planning to sneak behind your back. Don't take it personally. She isn't sneaking against you. She just thinks that what she wants is way more important than anything you have to say.

You know what would be funny? Put a tracking device on your daughter so you could compare where she tells you she's going and where she actually goes.   —*Zoe, 17*

If you don't trust your daughter, admit it. But be very clear about why before you talk to her. If she really can be trusted, but you're having a hard time with her growing independence, you have to own up to that. She has to earn your distrust by her actions, not because of your own baggage or because you think teens are inherently untrustworthy. It's a painful fact of life that your daughter may lie and sneak, but to be a good parent, you're still going to need to know what's going on in her life. You need to lay a pipeline for a reliable flow of information from credible sources. You need reconnaissance strategies.

RECONNAISSANCE STRATEGIES

1. Become friendly with the parents of your daughter's friends. This doesn't mean you have to be BFFs, but you need to know you can go to them when necessary. At the least, get their e-mail addresses and cell numbers. But if you can get together with these parents at all, like having a potluck dinner or meeting for dinner, drinks, or coffee, that would be even better. Knowing that her parents and her friends' parents are meeting on a regular basis may make your daughter slightly paranoid, which is exactly what you want.

2. If your school has a directory, keep a hard copy in a secret place because some girls have been known to hide them so it'll be harder for you to contact other parents or school personnel. For example, label a folder "Taxes 2007" and keep it there. Most public schools don't have these directories, so try to pull together as comprehensive a phone list as possible from the sports team roster, Girl Scout troop list, church group, and so on.

3. Whenever possible, get as complete a list as possible of your daughter's friends' cell phone numbers and keep them in a secret place. Although I went into cell phones in much greater detail in the technology chapter, suffice it to say that if your daughter has a cell phone, you may feel reassured that you can reach her and vice versa when necessary. But cell

phones also make reconnaissance much more difficult. It's common for girls to give their parents their friends' cell numbers and lie about where they're supposed to be. So keep these numbers handy for comparison.

Everyone has a cell phone. It's simple to say you're going to someone's house and then give your parents an alternate number of one of your friend's phones; I've made my friends change their voice mails. I'm brilliant!   —Molly, 16

Oops, I Did It Again: Should You Read Your Daughter's Diary, E-mail, Text, Facebook Page, MySpace, Etc.?

When parents tell me that they "accidentally" found their daughter's diaries when they were cleaning their rooms or just happened to run across their daughter's private e-mail, I just laugh. They sound just like their daughters when they're caught doing something they weren't supposed to do. And just as you don't believe her when she gives you a ridiculously weak excuse, she doesn't believe you either. Believe me, you don't have to read her diary or go through her e-mails to find out what's going on with her. She'll tell you what you need to know if you follow the strategies in this chapter. The only time I can possibly see a reason for reading a diary or an e-mail is if your daughter has totally shut down, you have followed the communication strategies in this book, you're getting nowhere, and you're really worried she's doing something dangerous to her health.

I say things in my diary that I don't mean all the time. It's not like you'll write when you walked the dog, did your homework, and went to bed. You write in your journal when you're very happy, very miserable, or very angry.   —Paloma, 16

The issue of privacy and trust between parent and child is immense. Here's how I suggest you think about it. Your child thinks of her privacy as her most precious treasure. When you violate her privacy, it feels like you are stealing that treasure away. Now, there are times when you have no choice but to violate her privacy (which is almost always when you don't trust what she's saying), but you need to be very thoughtful and considered when you take such a huge step. Because you can't do it that many times without it seriously backfiring on you; that is, she stops trusting you entirely and really starts lying and sneaking behind your back.

The other challenge is that some kids would never consider sneaking and lying in the way I describe. Some kids do it once, feel really bad about it, and never do it again. Some develop a pattern where it's all they do. So here's another conversation you can try:

> *I respect your privacy. But the way you are acting [describe exactly what she's doing] is making me feel I have no choice but to second-guess what you are telling me. I don't want to do this. I don't want to constantly read your text messages, Facebook page, call other parents, etc., but you aren't giving me a lot of options here. So you and I have to figure this out; what do you want to do?*

What to Do If You Catch Your Daughter Lying

The reconnaissance has paid off, and you've caught your daughter lying. The only thing more difficult than talking to your daughter when she's upset is when she's done something wrong. Some girls are amazingly good at dodging and evading. When they're caught and they know they're going to get in trouble, they'll obsess on their evasion tactics. You, too, should be similarly focused, but in a more positive direction.

Here's the trick: information is power. Never let your anger get the best of you, because then you'll be more likely to divulge what you know. Approach your daughter with the strategy that you really want her opinion about what happened and knock down her defenses. By doing this, you demonstrate that you respect her perspective (note that I didn't say agree), but you're also getting as much information as possible without letting on what you know. Any girl worth her weight will know when she's in trouble. The key is to first figure out how much her parents actually know. There may well be things you don't know. Her goal is to keep it that way.

Write down what your daughter is saying as she's saying it. I know this sounds over the top, but you'll notice any contradictions in her story much more quickly. You'll also have a record, so she can't deny you said something you're sure you said or vice versa. Girls take advantage of how tired and distracted parents are, so it may make her nervous and she may lash out and accuse you of not trusting her. If you don't trust her, remember, it's okay to admit it. Or at the least, don't lie and tell her you do when you don't. Just tell her you want to make sure you get her side of the story.

Never Confront Her in Front of Her Friends!

Either wait until later, or ask her to join you in the kitchen. Saving face is very important to your daughter. If you confront her in front of her friends, you'll embarrass her and she'll snap—most likely at you. Think of it this way: she knows you'll always be her parent, so there's more freedom in how she can treat you. That's a downside to being a parent who'll always be there, and your daughter may take your relationship for granted. Her friends are different. She constantly has to prove herself to them. One way she can do this is if she shows how independent she is by talking back to you. You're not giving in to her or letting her get away with something if you wait until she's alone. In fact, waiting is a punishment unto itself. Remember when you got in trouble? Often the worst part was when you knew you were caught and were waiting for the ax to fall.

If you do have good reason not to trust her, tell her why. Describe the specific actions that led to your suspicions, explain how you feel and what you want, and what she can do to gain back your trust. Remember, your daughter may give you incremental information. Give her the space to do it. Whether she's in trouble with you or she's had a bad experience that she wants to share with you, she'll probably parcel out the story in chapters, if not sentences.

Having the Conversation

You found out an hour ago that your daughter has lied to you about where she went last night. She told you she was at a friend's house, but she went out with her friend and some boys. You found out when a mother called you, thinking her daughter was sleeping over at your house. You've taken some time to calm down and plan your strategy.

YOU: I want to talk about what happened last night. Tell me what you think happened.

YOUR DAUGHTER: How should I know? I don't even care, because I'm just going to be punished anyway.

YOU: Well, what do you think I think happened?

YOUR DAUGHTER: You think I lied to you; which I didn't, by the way, because I was supposed to be sleeping over at Maggie's house and I went out instead. But you didn't tell me that I couldn't go out with them and I did sleep over at Maggie's house.

YOU: You did lie to me because you told me information to mislead me about where you would be. Do you agree or not?

YOUR DAUGHTER: I didn't lie!

YOU: You're not answering my question: Did you give me information to mislead me because you didn't want me to know what you were doing?

YOUR DAUGHTER: Whatever [which means in this context, if you say it that way, I guess you're right].

YOU: Well, first I want to know why.

YOUR DAUGHTER: Because you'd get mad and I was obviously right because you're freaking out over nothing.

YOU: I'm freaking out for two reasons. First, you intentionally misled me. Two, by misleading me and Maggie's parents, no adult knew where you were. I know that was the point, but the reality is when you make decisions like that, if you get in a situation you want to get out of, it may get considerably harder if no one knows where you are.

YOUR DAUGHTER: So what's my punishment?

YOU: You lied because you wanted me out of your face. The consequence is that I'm now going to be much more in your face. Your lying forces me to act like a controlling parent and treat you like a child. You can't use the phone and e-mail for two weeks. And you will have to build back the trust you have lost. I'm not sure how long that'll take, but I do know that it'll be a process over time.

If She's Sneaking Out of the House

Don't get bogged down in the details so that you're arguing about whether she sneaked out on Thursday or Friday. The important thing is that if she's sneaking out, you have to address the issues of dishonesty and safety. You could say:

> I know you're sneaking out of the house. I don't want to argue about it, but I want you to know that I know it. I could lock you in the room every night and treat you like a child and a prisoner in your own home, but I don't think that would be an effective way of dealing with this problem, because I'll become the enemy and you'll sneak out whenever you get the chance. I assume you don't want to be treated like a child, yet you're forcing me to treat you like one. If you continue to sneak out then I'll worry about you until I know you're safe, and I won't trust you. Then we have a relationship of mutual distrust and you see the house as a prison. So what do you want to do about this?

If she doesn't back down and have a reasonable conversation with you after you've said this, then take away something concrete or a privilege that you do have control over. Remind her that the reason you are treating her like a child is because her actions leave you no alternative.

What Is the Worst Punishment You Can Give Her?

It's very clear what girls consider the worst punishment. Time and time again, they all say the same thing. The worst punishment is losing your respect and disappointing you and taking away their ability to communicate with their peers. Countless girls have told me a variation on the quotes below:

> *I have deep respect for my dad and I talk to him about it a lot. The worst punishment he could give me is to lose his respect and trust in me.*   —*Jane, 16*

> *I hate when I get into trouble because my mother cuts off my computer and cell phone. I don't know anything that's going on!*   —*Claire, 14*

Anytime you take away your daughter's ability to communicate with her peers, it's a serious punishment. Putting a hold on e-mail and phone and grounding her so she can't go out—all these consequences hurt where it matters most to girls. And no matter what, don't hand down a punishment and then change your mind or don't enforce it—unless you want to lose all credibility as her parent.

Overall, my general strategy when disciplining children (either my own or my students) is to frame my response in this way:

1. Tell them exactly what they did that was a problem.
2. Tell them that those specific actions are against what I believe in (as their mom or a teacher).
3. Tell them specifically what privilege will be taken away and for how long.
4. Give them a "way out"; that is, a way to make amends that will make them and me proud.

What Your Daughters Want You to Know

Frequently girls will ask me to share things with their parents that are a little too difficult to tell their parents themselves. Here are the girls' most common requests to tell you:

I wish my parents . . .

> *Dropped me off and picked me up at places on time. This is a very big deal!*
>
> *Taught me more about my culture.*
>
> *Asked to meet my friends.*
>
> *Let go of stereotypes about other races and religions.*
>
> *Let me have the freedom to make more choices.*
>
> *Stopped worrying about my messy room.*
>
> *Were more patient with me.*
>
> *Paid more attention to their own lives.*
>
> *Understood that I want freedom but we can still be close. I'm my own person. Don't limit my abilities or who I am, let me follow my intuition and be supportive.*
>
> *Knew I really want to make them proud of me.*

And what do they really want me to make sure I tell you about how to communicate with her?

I wish my parents . . .

> *Had more real conversations with me.*
>
> *Told me when they're proud of me.*
>
> *Talked to me more about what I'm passionate about.*
>
> *Understood that when I need to be left alone, my bedroom door is shut. This means I really need to be left alone. Your interference will only make me more irritated.*

My parents need to know . . .

> *That sometimes we just want to vent, but that doesn't mean we want you to interfere.*
>
> *I don't want them to e-mail all the other parents about some problem I am having! It only makes it worse!*

I do want to talk to you but not about everything. If it was my fault or I'm superinvolved, I'll probably wait until after it was resolved to tell you.

Sibling loyalty can be stronger than parental loyalty. I might not tell you something my siblings don't want you to know.

My dad is very sexist with me sometimes. I hate it. For example, my younger brother can talk to girls on the phone without no one bugging or interrupting him to ask who he is talking to. But when I'm on my cell they are constantly telling me to get off the phone and especially when they think I'm talking to a guy.

What works:

- When I have problems I go to my mom usually because she doesn't give me specific ways to deal with it; she says, "I have some suggestions."
- She always listens and pays attention. And she says, "I love you," even if I do something wrong. And she's read a lot of books.
- I feel more comfortable with my dad because with my dad he's not really "let's go tell the teachers," he's more like "let's talk about this or try this to make it better." Often I go to my dad to complain about stuff because he listens. I can tell my dad anything.
- She gives me steps. She says, "If this doesn't work, then try that," and "What do you think will work better?"
- My dad makes me laugh. It makes me relax.
- Taking to my grandfather. I know he's older but he seems to understand what's going on.
- Talking to my babysitter. She doesn't give me advice. She just listens to me and lets me figure it out. Plus, my mom's so involved in the school that I just can't.

What doesn't:

- My mom is so intense that I don't tell her much. If I do, it's when I see someone else do something I don't like. If I know

*I'm involved deeply like it was my fault or I really made a
mistake, then I don't tell because then she'll really be on my
back. So I only tell her things when I know she'd be happy
if I tell her that I've done the right thing.*

- *If I go to my mom, she tells me to stop whining.*
- *When I give my mom a situation, either she gets crazy or she
immediately says we need to talk to your teacher or the
principal about this. I say, "Mom, we don't need to talk to the
principal," or she just says, "Deal with it."*

YOUR DAUGHTER WILL TAKE YOU SERIOUSLY IF . . .

For any of this to work, you must practice what you preach. You
can do nothing worse to undermine your authority than be hypocritical. Your daughter can smell it on you a mile away. Don't lay
down your values, expect her to follow them, and then act differently yourself. If you gossip about other people (especially other
children she knows), don't expect her to do anything different. If
you lie or sneak around, expect her to do the same. If you make a
mistake and don't own up to it, don't expect her to hold herself accountable. If you're defensive and refuse to apologize, she'll be
self-righteous. It doesn't mean you can't make mistakes and admit
that to her (in fact, that in itself can be a great bonding moment
for both of you). Being a credible role model depends on you consistently demonstrating the core values you believe in and want
her to practice.

YOU AREN'T A FAILURE

Many parents I work with tell me they feel like a failure when their
daughter struggles so much and so often. Or they hear me say
something in a presentation that is different from what they've
done. Please let go of all that. The only way you can fail is if you
don't try, you disconnect from her and her world, you don't hold
her accountable for her behavior, or you don't teach her and role
model empathy, thoughtfulness, critical thinking, and the belief

that everyone deserves to be treated with dignity. Be kind to your-self. Parenting is often overwhelming, and very few of us are taught to develop effective coping skills.

It's so hard for us [parents] to be reflective. It's too painful to be aware of our choices—what we've given up and what they've embraced. When I look at my own daughter, I often feel like a failure. I feel responsible and guilty that I can't fix her pain, I can't fix society overnight, and I can't find her the help she needs.

—Kara

There's so much shame when your daughter has problems. Other parents talk about their kids' activities and school. It's so hard to discuss what's going on because I feel different and that every-one else is perfect. Part of me knows better and part of me won-ders . . . —Michaela

I went to a couple of parent meetings and talked about the prob-lems my daughter was having with other girls. All I got was stony silence or people being nice in a patronizing way by expressing sympathy at best, but never suggesting that what I or my daugh-ter are going through has ever happened to them or their daugh-ters. Never did I hear "I know what you mean—this happened to my daughter." So I felt like a freak, and didn't trust what other parents would say about her, so I shut my mouth. —Susan

I went to a parenting class and I was really glad I went. Not just for the strategies I learned but because so many parents were going through the same problems. —Belle

You are not alone. If you reach out, you will find a community of parents that will support you through the hardest moments.

Always Remember

Parenting isn't a popularity contest. You don't need to be your daughter's best friend. You need to be her parent by setting limits and holding her accountable when those limits are broken. Even if she says she hates your interference and accuses you of violating her privacy, rest assured her hatred is temporary and will be replaced with respect as she gets older. If you continue to be a Loving Hard-Ass Parent, no matter how much of a pain in the butt she is now, she'll apologize later, thank you, and raise her own kids well. Now we're ready to go back to Girl World and take a closer look at how girls enforce the rules on a daily basis. It's the way girls get tossed out of the raft—the Beauty Pageant.

The Beauty Pageant: Who Wants to Be Miss Congeniality?

Your thirteen-year-old daughter has just been invited to a party, and she's convinced you she needs new shoes. Your selective memory kicks into gear and you temporarily forget about the last time you attempted a shopping expedition with her. Off to the mall you go. As soon as you walk in, you're bombarded by monitors flashing videos, neon signs proclaiming the brands your daughter covets, and perky store assistants barely older than your daughter offering their assistance. You begin to feel exhausted, defeated, and slightly paranoid that the whole situation is conspiring against you. Which, of course, is true.

Then it happens. She sees the pair that she *must* have. You groan. They look ridiculous, they're too expensive, the heels are too high, and they're too sexy for a girl her age. You hold up a pair you like: "What about these?" Your daughter rolls her eyes, then begs, then barters, "Just let me get these shoes and I promise I'll walk the dog, clean my room, and do the dishes every day for a month!" When you are less than persuaded, she launches into an outright self-righteous tantrum to the strains of "You're so mean!"

You begin to feel the watchful eyes of the other mothers. The saleswoman hovers. You think of all the girls in your daughter's school, so many of whom are wearing the shoes your daughter wants. Your resolve starts to crumble. If all the parents are allowing their daughters to have these shoes, maybe you should get them. They're just shoes, after all, and not having them seems like more trouble than it's worth and look! They're 40 percent off. There are bigger issues to worry about with your daughter . . . and so it goes until you find yourself handing over your credit card.

Okay, on the face of it, this is a ridiculous fight over shoes, but why is this situation so contentious? First, it's hard to see your daughter grow up. Those shoes could symbolize your daughter's developing sexuality and you could understandably (and correctly) think she's growing up too fast. Even if you think of yourself as a fairly relaxed parent, when your daughter wants to be sexy, it can be very unnerving. But those shoes are equally meaningful to her. Why is she acting like it'll be the end of the world if she doesn't get them? Until recently, you may have believed your daughter was a reasonable person. What's motivating her to act like this? What may be hard to remember in situations like this is that those shoes are a lot more than just something she wears on her feet.

Remember, it's *never* just about the shoes.

It's about style, beauty, and image, and how they impact your daughter's relationship with the clique and her social position in her culture. In her mind, those shoes are the key to maintaining or gaining social acceptance or complete social destruction. She could really believe that if she gets them, her life will be better.

Is there anything you can do to help you daughter regain her sanity? Can you stop your daughter from wearing revealing tops, tight pants, or shoes that make her six inches taller? What do you do if she feels ugly, no matter what you say to the contrary? How do race and class impact your daughter's definition of beauty? These are the questions this chapter addresses.

Ironically, when I first started teaching, it was easy to overlook beauty's impact on girls because it's as common and invisible as the air they breathe. Beauty and style are so important to the Girl World that it wouldn't exist without it. When you look at your daughter, you see a beautiful girl. She, however, probably can't look past that too-big nose, her "fat" stomach, or that pimple on her chin. Those issues are a constant source of humiliation. Girls have told me for years that they struggle to survive in a painful world where the value of self-worth is too often tied to an impossible standard of beauty. The following sums up how they see the world.

WHAT YOU SHOULD KNOW

- Issues of beauty for girls start at really young ages, so don't be surprised if your eight-year-old has very definitive opinions about who is beautiful and who isn't.
- Girls are constantly comparing themselves with each other.
- If there's something about their physical appearance that they do like, most girls will never admit it because they're afraid other girls will accuse them of being vain.
- If there's something about their physical appearance they don't like, they're obsessed by it.
- Girls need constant reassurance from each other that they fit in and look good.
- Girls know they're manipulated by the media to hold themselves to an impossible standard of beauty, but that doesn't stop them from holding themselves to it anyway.
- Most girls are obsessed with their looks. If they aren't, they've found another way to express themselves through a talent or skill that builds their self-esteem.
- For most girls, when a girl has a friend who's starving herself, she's often torn between worry and envy.
- The way a girl decides to "mark" herself—from piercing a nose or lip or coloring her hair to the choice between wearing Gap or BCBG—identifies how she sees herself and to what group she belongs. Her markers reveal her relationship to the Act Like a Woman box and her opinions about living as a girl in this culture.

Adolescence is a beauty pageant. Even if your daughter doesn't want to be a contestant, others will look at her as if she is. In Girl World, everyone is automatically entered. How does a girl win? By looking like she is standing right in the middle of the Act Like a

Woman box. However, winning often comes at a high price if it means she has to sacrifice her individual identity, she thinks her inherent self-worth is tied to conforming to the beauty standard, or she becomes a vapid, noncritically thinking person because she has spent her formative years thinking her appearance is the most important thing she should focus on.

If you're raising your daughter to value her inner worth more than her external appearance, you may be appalled to find that your daughter is so heavily judged by her looks or how ruthlessly judgmental she can be. But regardless of your very understandable feelings, you need to acknowledge the power of these issues and that it is almost inevitable that she'll have experiences where she feels like she's competing in this pageant. And like a pageant, there are many individual competitions leading up to the crown.

> *It is impossible to win the contest . . . but I think a lot of girls perceive others to be the winner, but in actuality those girls are just as competitive and unsure of themselves as everyone else.*
> —Isabel, 17

FEMININITY: THE RULES OF THE PAGEANT

Your daughter doesn't need special classes to learn how to be a girl in our culture. From the moment she wakes up until she goes to bed, a girl learns with constant reinforcement how she's supposed to behave. What she wears and how she cuts her hair, says hello, and shakes hands all reflect how our culture has taught her to be a girl.

Trying to get it right can be overwhelming for girls. They're afraid to make mistakes and often aren't even sure what those mistakes are. Frequently they feel as if they not only have to be perfect but achieve that perfection effortlessly. Girls are bombarded with the Victoria's Secret definition of femininity, which means having hips and curves (but only in the right places) and being skinny, hairless, fresh and clean, and smelling good. This kind of femininity appears powerful and simultaneously elusive. The ingredients to win the pageant, however, aren't based on looks alone. It's about coming to terms with how others perceive you as a whole package. Your appearance is merely the wrapping.

Like any present, if you're "wrapped" well, people will think the gift is more valuable.   *—Zoe, 17*

Of course, definitions of femininity have become progressively more complicated and nuanced, and girls and women can be seen as strong, aggressive, and competitive athletes. Still, look at the female athletes who have the most commercial success off the field or court. They all fit right into the Act Like a Woman box as well. Just like these athletes, to get social validation, girls must still be soft, pretty, and nonthreatening. So while it's wonderful that so many parents encourage their daughters to play competitive sports at young ages, we still have a long way to go to free them of such rigid definitions of beauty.

Everyone wants to be in shape to be skinny. Nobody wants to be ripped. You want to be toned but no bulging muscles.
—Corinne, 18

If you want your daughter to grow up to be president (or at the least have people take her seriously), teach her these four seemingly small things:

1. Shake hands by extending her hand confidently, looking the other person in the eye. No dead wrists or hands allowed.
2. Sneeze naturally. She's not a kitten.
3. Do not speak a declarative sentence as if she's asking a question, meaning her voice doesn't rise on the last word she says.
4. If bothered by the presence of an insect or small animal, walk away or calmly remove it with a container or paper towel.

HERE SHE COMES . . . MISS AMERICA

Every school has one. The golden girl who bears aloft the holy grail of beauty. When she's around, boys lose their power of speech. Girls are intimidated or envious of her and think her life is perfect. Some girls constantly try to be her friend. Others talk behind her back, looking for signs of weakness. But listen to what one of these icons has to say:

> *People think being pretty is going to make your life way easier but it's not that simple. My mom puts a lot of pressure on me to always look right. She always tell me it's important to look good and present yourself well but sometimes I think that's what is most important to her. As long as I look good, she's happy. And I'm not happy, I'm pretending—but when I tell people that they don't believe me. They say sarcastic things like, "Yeah, I know it must be really tough to be you." It's like if you're pretty you're not allowed to have any problems.*   —*Gillian, 16*

I'm sure it wouldn't surprise you that this girl typifies the classic definition of beauty: tall, thin, blond, and beautiful. If this girl—the one so many girls want to be like, the one girls envy—can feel unworthy, can you imagine what other girls feel?

Your daughter, like every girl, has moments when she has similar feelings. I often ask girls, "In an average day, how many times do you think about your weight and/or your appearance, and what percentage of those comments are negative versus positive?" they laugh at me for thinking they ever have positive comments. For some, these moments of insecurity are just that, moments when they feel good or bad, secure or insecure. But for far too many others, these moments dictate an entire self-concept of who they are and what they can be.

Girls are also constantly comparing themselves with one another, and rarely do they feel they measure up. I teach countless girls who are beautiful by anyone's standards, yet they're absolutely convinced that their flaws are all anyone sees, because they're either constantly evaluating themselves according to the girls they see in the media or the "perfect" girls around them. So when your daughter tells you how incredibly ugly she is, how fat her thighs are, or how big her nose is, you have to realize that she believes it—no matter what you tell her.

> You may have wondered why your daughter doesn't believe you when you tell her she's beautiful. You're being blown off because you unconditionally love her. That's why she says, "Mom, that's what you have to say; you're my mom." It begs the question that if you were more conditionally loving, your opinion would matter more. This doesn't mean you shouldn't say it, because you should. But it's important to know why it feels like sometimes the things you say don't matter.

It's critical that moms and dads keep telling girls they are perfect and beautiful (instead of some treacherous parents I know who urge their girls to lose weight or get a nose job, etc.), even though it doesn't seem to matter to their daughter. It does. We don't show it. But it matters that you think we are precious and gorgeous and beautiful. —Maggie, 18

I have never met a person who thinks she's pretty. You sit and pick apart every flaw. The combined list of how you don't measure up really adds up. —Joni, 15

THE EVENING GOWN COMPETITION

The pursuit and attainment of the elusive standard of beauty is one of the most critical components of girls' power structure. Girls are keenly aware of these dynamics, and, unfortunately, very few of them feel there's anything they can do to stop them. Ironically, it isn't so much about the individual girl's look that will get her into the clique but her willingness to conform to the group's look that grants acceptance. If your daughter conforms, they'll support her. If she rebels and strays from their norm, she'll be ostracized.

The Queen Bee always asks "What are you wearing?" but not like what are you wearing you look cute but OMG what are YOU wearing? —Gabriel, 11

Both my parents work in the city and we often cannot afford the luxuries my friends can. Of course I would like to fit in so I'm always asking my mom for money so I can buy the right clothes and look like I belong with them. But not wearing anything twice a month [unwritten rule of the popular cliques] is hard when you're given a budget like mine. —Abby, 15

When I was younger I didn't really go after the sexy high shoes as much as the most expensive ones with the designer logos flashing all over them (Kate Spade, Lilly Pulitzer, Abercrombie, etc.). In my opinion, with younger girls especially, it's not just about sex appeal but it's also about getting and showing off the most expensive brands/stuff. —Ana, 20

The Queen Bee doesn't necessarily create the look, but she's a conduit of information on the look from the media to the rest of her clique. The irony of all of this is that Queen Bees are copying too—they're just really good at looking like they're not imitating anyone around them. A Queen Bee strictly adheres to the rules (because she made them up) and quickly corrects those who break them and stray outside the set definition of cool. The fear of censure is so strong that it can largely dictate who gets into the "higher" cliques and encourages all girls to be Wannabes. The result is that the girls in these cliques all start to look the same.

It's not that they're all beautiful, but those girls all look alike. They seem like they're all sisters. They have the same body structure and they're all petite. —Lynn, 16

WHY MARKERS MATTER IN YOUR DAUGHTER'S WORLD

Markers control girls' minds whether we like it or not. —Jade, 17

A marker is the signifier of how your daughter accepts or rejects Girl World, her place in her community's social hierarchy and her group. Her choice of clothes, hairstyle, and overall style are all markers. So are the sports she plays, what clubs she belongs to, how well she does in school, or how much money you have. Markers for a particular clique might be more specific; for example, the soccer team clique (usually the older or more athletically inclined girls plus one or two anointed freshmen) might all wear a particular sports headband in their hair.

Unfortunately, parents often have difficulty seeing their daughter's markers for what they are—a wealth of information about her and the key to knowing how and when to reach out to her. When their daughter suddenly makes different choices about her appearance, parents take it so personally that they literally can't see what's in front of them. Unless she feels that she isn't getting enough attention from you, the way she dresses and does her hair usually has nothing to do with you until you freak out about it and get into a huge fight. Many parents see these displays as a sign of disrespect toward them. They're not. They are expressions of identity. Your children want your affirmation. They want you to be proud of them and the choices they make. They want to be accepted by you for who they are, bad clothes and strange makeup included. If you don't accept her, she'll think you're squashing her, which will make her feel rejected at the precise time in her life when creating and exploring her sense of self through her image is her greatest priority. When you tell her that her tongue piercing is distracting (and you're a little worried about the dental bills), you may believe you're only looking out for her best interests, but she can't hear what you're saying. Instead, she hears that you don't accept who she is or what she stands for. That's why she fights back so hard. She feels as if she's fighting for her soul, that you're denying the person she is. Also be careful: if you freak out, you'll convince her that the only people who unconditionally accept her are her clique.

Land Mine!

Not all piercings are equal! Where and what a girl pierces is a clear indicator of what she thinks about Girl World. For example, piercing her belly button is an "in the box" act, where piercing her lip is an "outside the box" act.

THE SWIMSUIT COMPETITION: WHO GETS BOOBS FIRST

Breasts are one of the most obvious signifiers of femininity, and with the increasing frequency of breast augmentation, their cultural currency has increased significantly. Girls see so many enhanced breasts around them that all look exactly the same, real breasts start to seem abnormal.

But even without so many women having boob jobs, do you remember the girl who developed breasts first in your circle of friends? Most likely, it was a significant moment for everybody. Were you that girl? Remember the taunting from boys and comments from other girls? Like the first daffodil of spring, this girl signals that puberty has officially begun. Many boys are transfixed by the changes her body is going through, and the other girls can be simultaneously anxious, intrigued, and envious. She's a lightning rod for all the other children to bounce their preadolescent anxiety and excitement off of. And, if you're a twelve-year-old girl in full bloom, the chances of your handling this situation well are slim to none.

This dynamic can be even more confusing if and when the girl notices the power of her sexuality. All of a sudden, this girl is getting attention and she gains popularity because she literally embodies the girl ideal. She can be conflicted between wanting and liking the attention and being disturbed by what it means. She likes being objectified because she's getting attention, but is it the kind of attention she wants? Yes and no.

When I was younger, girls were worse than the boys about my boobs getting bigger. I remember in sixth grade I went to a pool party. There was only one other girl who was developing like me. I had been running around—it never occurred to me then to be self-conscious—but she had purposefully stayed in the pool to hide.   —Olivia, 16

I developed over the summer before I began seventh grade. I wore big sweatshirts all year.   —Haley, 15

A boy asked me if I would wear shoes if I didn't have any feet. I said no. Then he asked, so then why do you wear a bra? Boys are so mean.   —Marcy, 16

One of the girls in our class obviously stuffed her shirt with tissue paper and it was coming out during class. The girls destroyed her.   —Evan, 11

In seventh grade, when we knew a girl stuffed her bra, we would sneeze and say to her, "Hey, we need a tissue!" and then everybody would laugh. So bad but so funny.   —Alex, 18

When I was in fifth grade, one girl developed DD breasts. Her breasts were the topic of everyone's conversation. It got her a lot of attention. Maybe it was a front, but she seemed to like it. Girls were so envious. When I had a birthday party, we all made fun of her by putting towels down our shirts and pretending to flirt with invisible boys.   —Simone, 17

Simone's making fun of an early-blooming friend is a somewhat self-deceptive act. In fact, Simone and her friends were emulating her and trying on what it would feel like to have the power and ability to flirt with boys. Now, it is absolutely true that some girls are comfortable being objectified and don't feel subjugated if they are. They have bought into the philosophy that flaunting their sexuality doesn't come at the expense of their personal power but is in fact a *source* of power. A side note for the older girls who really do believe that showing off your body is the way to have power—I think it's a trick. If you flaunt your body to get attention or manipulate men, your power is almost always superficial because the culture (in the form of the people around you) will demand you act accordingly. And that means acting like a five-year-old. Think of the Playboy bunnies who get to live in the Mansion. They're fun, silly, and cute. Nothing about that is authentically powerful.

BODY HAIR

The first time someone teases a girl or a friend about their leg hair, girls realize being hairless is a critical yet invisible Girl World rule. Truly, it is one of the first issues that push little girls into Girl World and the Act Like a Woman box, and it is coming at girls at earlier ages. A generation ago the teasing would start when the girls were between twelve and fourteen. Now it starts around ten or even younger. It also used to be the case that African American and Latina girls who didn't shave were immune from censure—but not anymore. Now for all girls, having body hair is one of the first things our culture tells our daughters is wrong, unacceptable, and shameful about their bodies that they must fix to be valued.

Meanwhile, you have an eleven-year-old girl in your house who is begging to shave. So when are you supposed to let her?

First of all, understand that this is often a rite of passage for both you and her. I know it's tempting to say "No way! Talk to me when you're fourteen!" or hand her a razor and be done with it, but this is truly an important moment. Here's what I'd do. Remember that your primary job is to be kind and nonjudgmental throughout the conversation because she's probably embarrassed. And as you are being kind, ask her the pros and cons of shaving. In my opinion they are: pro—she doesn't get teased; con—she changes herself to please others. If after all that she still wants to, I'd let her—because otherwise she just may be too much of an open target for other kids' cruelty. Even if you disagree with the choice she ultimately makes, your conversation hasn't gone to waste. You've had an open, thoughtful dialogue about an uncomfortable subject—these are the kinds of precedents you need to establish for later talks about other aspects of puberty, dating, and sex.

However, even though I said let her shave, this is not a free pass about all things to do with body hair. Under no circumstances do I think it's appropriate for you to be paying for or allowing her to get Brazilian bikini waxes or anything else like it. It needs to be said that this is just a bad idea all around. If you don't believe me, ask your daughter's doctor the next time you see her. A "Brazilian" is when people get most or all of their pubic hair removed, which buys into the cultural message that the sexiest women are hairless. But the only females who are hairless are prepubescent girls. That's really messed up.

The Competition No One Wins

I have struggled my whole life with my weight. Two years ago I was much heavier and people made fun of me. I would cry every day after school.   —Anne, 15

My parents have always been relentless with my sister about her weight. They say things like, "Do you really need to eat that?" or they tell her they'll give her things if she loses weight. She's 22 now and they still do it. I feel really bad for her but I have no idea how to get her to stop and the weird thing is my parents have no idea that everything they say just makes it worse.   —Mark, 20

I don't have a big butt. People compare me to a white girl. I'm teased a lot for being too skinny. I wanted to hang out with people who would accept me for not being so curvy.   —Aliesha, 17

I go to a boarding school and sometimes I swear it feels like every girl in our dorm has an eating disorder. I really think some of it is because girls aren't taken seriously here and they don't have strong friendships with other girls. We just get so mad and don't know how to express it. But that still doesn't take away from the fact that one of the seniors was teaching three sophomores how to throw up. I hate that girl.   —Katie, 18

For way too many girls, their weight from the earliest of ages is their ultimate measure of worth. But it is also much more. It can represent control—especially when you feel like that's the last thing you actually have. Whether girls worry about being too thin or having curves in "all the right places," it's a given that whatever they weigh is never good enough. And one of the saddest things about girls' friendships is that, way too easily, cliques can reinforce the paranoia girls feel that they're all losing the battle against each other. Behind every girl's concern when her friend starves herself is the simultaneous worry that "if she thinks she's fat, then I'm obese!" Her internal voice whispers, "Am I worried about her, or am I really envious that she has enough control that she can starve her body into submission?"

I recently received the following from a tenth-grade girl who has an anorexic friend:

> We used to be a lot closer, but she just seems to have pushed everyone who's concerned out of her life. But even if we don't end up being great friends like we used to, I just want her to stop feeling like she has to control every ounce of food that passes (or doesn't) through her body. I want her to feel happy with her life and with who she is, and I don't want her to carry this disease with her to college, where I fear she'll be lost forever.
>
> Of course I want to get her help, but I'm not really in any position to do that, and since she is still in stage number one, denial, then getting her help would be like trying to tell a brick wall to move. I hate to look at her because she should be in a National Geographic of poor, starving children. I'm much more aware of eating disorders than I ever was. I can tell when the people around me aren't eating. The effect of her disease is my paranoia. My conversations with other people seem to at one time or another revolve around eating disorders and how many people we know who have one.   —Laurie, 15

AND THE WINNER FOR MISS CONGENIALITY IS . . .

Girls know they'll pay a price for coming across as vain; as much as they crave the attention of being considered attractive, you can't proclaim yourself the reigning beauty queen without getting in trouble. Therefore, a few girls vie for acceptance by angling for Miss Congeniality. This is how you do it:

- When you're with your friends, always put yourself down, especially in comparison with them, and compliment them. (When you're not with them, you can say what you think.) Picture what happens when one girl tells another girl how great she looks. Does the recipient of the compliment thank her? Rarely. Instead, the response is usually some variation of "Oh no, I look so fat and horrible. I can't believe you would say that. You look so much better than me." Girls must degrade themselves after being complimented in order not to appear vain.
- Leap to your friends' defense when they put themselves down; they'll leap to yours when you put yourself down. So you say you're fat? "OMG, you look so good!" Girls literally compete with each other about who's the fattest ("You're so much thinner than me, compared to you I'm such a cow").
- Don't do any of the above too much because then it will look like you're begging for compliments all the time and that's annoying.

Crossing Over and Crossing Out

One of the things I always felt growing up as someone of mixed racial heritage was that I didn't fit in anywhere. On the one hand, I was presented with the white image of beauty as the blue-eyed, blond-haired, tall, skinny, big-breasted All-American girl. On the other hand was the Asian image of beauty as petite, slender, long dark hair, exotic features, and pale skin, actresses like Lucy Liu and Ming-Na Wen. The only thing I had in common with any of those images was that I was fair-skinned. Otherwise I never felt like I measured up. It's also true that Asian women try to look more white. My mother, for instance, puts tape on her eyelids to make them look rounder. One of my Korean friends once told me I was lucky that I had pale skin because when she went to Korea, people told her she looked like a "country girl" because she's

naturally tan. There are also operations that some girls get to make their eyes look more "white," and some girls get nose jobs to make their noses look more "white." This doesn't occur only in the States either; in Korea, plastic surgery is a huge industry. It's because they also get Western fashion magazines there and are presented with the Caucasian standard of beauty and will get nose jobs, fix their eyes, and get operations on their jaws to make their faces look less round, less Asian and more white. When you look at women like J. Lo and Beyoncé, who both have blond highlights and look like white women with tans, you real-ize that racism still plays itself out in what we are presented with as "beautiful."
— *Ellie, 21*

In the years since this book first came out, it looks like things have changed a lot regarding race and beauty. Black and Latina women regularly show up on the cover of magazines. We have an African American First Lady. But has it really changed?

Again it's a mixed answer. While it's more likely to see maga-zine covers with nonwhite female celebrities, we need to take a closer look. They almost all have the same caramel-colored skin and long, straight hair. Michelle Obama is such a transformative figure because she is a confident, darker-skinned black woman without fake hair and nails. But the question begs to be asked: Do Latina and African American girls see themselves reflected in the faces of Beyoncé, Rihanna, Ciara, Jessica Alba, Michelle Ro-driguez, and Eva Mendes? Or say it another way. How are you supposed to feel if you're a girl with kinky hair, curves, and a fuller nose?

To my mind, "beautiful women" with their light skin, thin bod-ies, "right" curves, and straight hair are not proof that our culture is race-blind or that girls aren't still getting toxic messages that cer-tain physical traits are more worthy than others. Yes, it's great that these women are included now in our definition of beauty, but it shows that the most acceptable and easiest way to be black / Latina and beautiful is to be closer to the "white" box ideals the culture demands.

Beyoncé has repeatedly said that she refuses to kill herself to be really skinny. Tyra Banks is also very vocal about loving her curves. Without taking away anything from these women's considerable accomplishments, they're talking about loving their curves, not their jiggle. They aren't loving their potbelly or flabby arms, because they don't have them. I'm not sure how much we've progressed if this is what we call accepting all different types of women's bodies.

Look at it from another side. When someone like Queen Latifah or Jennifer Hudson walks the red carpet, the commentator always says something like, "It's so great she's so comfortable in her own skin. She really is showing that beautiful women don't have to be stick-thin and still look great!" They never say, "Just look at Nicole Ritchie, Keira Knightley, or Mischa Barton! Isn't it amazing how sickly skinny they look and they still manage to walk down that aisle! They're just an inspiration to us all!"

And just to be clear, these issues aren't limited to African American or Latina girls:

The Indian standard of beauty is long hair, light skin, graceful, big doe eyes, and curves, but only in the right places. My culture has always thought that the paler a girl's skin is, the more beautiful she is. The prejudice still exists now, even among the girls in my group. My mother is always telling me not to be in the sun to preserve my relatively pale skin. My friends talk about other Indian girls, deriding them because they're dark. I used to hang out with a clique of all Indian girls, but we were full of contradictions. We say that we have friends in other groups, but we don't. You had to pretend that you belonged to many different cliques, but the reality was that you could only belong to the group to be accepted by the group. Wearing an Indian anklet (especially because Indian clothes and jewelry are trendy right now) is cool, but discussing the partition of India and Pakistan isn't. The Indian clique was exclusive, but the only way I can be proud of my heritage is not to be part of the Indian clique. Part of this is selfish because, like all girls, I want to be more special than everyone else, and I couldn't be in that group. Nevertheless, life in that group was a whole lot of pretending. The ones who take the most authentic pride aren't part of their cultural group. One of my closest friends is Japanese and she thinks the same thing.

—Nidhi, 16

Growing up and going to school in a town with a large minority population, I thought I was ugly because I didn't look like any of my friends. It didn't help that I was a late bloomer and was an extremely awkward adolescent. I had a sudden growth spurt and it took me a while to figure out what to do with arms and legs (clumsy is an understatement). I had straight hair, where most of my friends had dark curly hair, I was tall, pale, skinny, and flat chested, where most of my friends were shorter than I was, had curvy figures, and brown or black skin. Even if girls were my height or taller, they still had curves where I didn't. The prettiest and most popular girls in my school looked nothing like me and this made me feel ugly in comparison. It was a reversal of wanting to fit the blond, blue-eyed ideal; I wanted to look less white and like more of a minority. It was actually a double bind because by white standards I wasn't beautiful either, because I wasn't blond, blue-eyed, with a big chest. Even so, I rejected the blond image of beauty in favor of wanting to look like more of a minority because I wanted to be accepted in school and be pretty by those standards.

—Ellie, 21

Acting White

Even in the most diverse schools, black students often have a set hallway and designated lunch tables that they occupy year after year. If a black student doesn't want to hang out there and maintains friendships in other groups, does she still fit in with the black clique? Not usually. In fact, these girls tell me they often get grief for trying to be white. In schools with racial and economic diversity, the wealthier students of color are often torn: Where do they sit in the hallway or cafeteria? Where should their loyalty lie? Are they sellouts if they "talk white"?

For these young people, it can feel like they must make a choice between personifying "black culture" or what the overall culture allows it to show in movies, TV, music, etc.) and what their real lives actually reflect. And adults contribute to this dynamic as well!

> *Adults all believe that since I am black, I can't live in the suburbs and talk like I do. They all expect me to talk like I come from a bad neighborhood. It gets really frustrating because people are surprised when they see that I'm smart and have a good home life.*   —Nia, 18

Of course, the undercurrent running through this is that acting white is equal to acting educated, polite, and modest, while acting black is equal to being uneducated, rude, loud, and sexually promiscuous. Unfortunately, I have frequent experiences with parents who reinforce this message. For example, before I work in the community I always have a conference call with the organizers. If the people are from majority white suburban communities, they will often be worried about what I'm going to say and present to their children. It's under the guise of "just wanting to check in," but I inevitably get this comment in the form of a question, "We're just a close community and want to make sure our children aren't exposed to things they shouldn't be. They're not like those urban children you work with who are exposed to more sexual things and more violence. We don't have those kind of influences." Meanwhile, their kids are at home playing Grand Theft Auto on their flat screen while they're laughing at the latest pornography they've downloaded.

Bad Hair

Many white women have no idea how important the issue of "good" and "bad" hair is in nonwhite communities. If you're reading this and were born with naturally straight hair, did you know that perming "white hair" curls it, but perming "black hair" straightens it? That those long braids some women wear are made from hair extensions, cost hundreds of dollars, take ten hours to complete, and are braided so tight that women often get terrible headaches? Or that a girl is told she has "good hair" if it's like white hair and "bad hair" if it's kinky?

Listen to some of my students:

> *I have to sit for an hour every morning while my mother yanks my hair. It makes me cry because it hurts so much.*
>
> *I hate having to do my hair! I wish it were softer!*
>
> *Sometimes the perms can really burn your skin.*
>
> *You get your hair braided and they braid it so tight I get a really bad headache.*
>
> *People always say nappy hair is bad and I have nappy hair and there isn't a thing I can do about. It makes me feel bad.*

The white girls in the room were shocked. They had no idea their friends were going through this.

Racism Within

> *I hate when people say you're pretty for a dark-skinned girl.*
> —Monica, 16

> *You want to be the light-skinned girl with the good hair. You stare in the mirror and think, "She's so beautiful. I wish I had her color skin. Why isn't my nose thinner? Why am I so ugly?" In my Dominican community where I teach, the girls are either very dark or light-skinned. The darker-skin girls are just like the African American girls. They touch the light-skined girls' hair and say, "I wish I had her hair. She's so pretty."* —Sonia

Some of the worst racism can come from inside your own group, and it's exceedingly difficult and painful to talk about. When you add limited financial resources to that, it just gets more difficult, but it explains even more why markers are so critical to girls' sense of self. In many of the working-class and poor communities where I teach, there's always a clique of girls who have their hair, clothes, and nails done in the latest styles. The Queen Bees always have the best hair and nails. These girls spend tremendous amounts of money to maintain their markers because doing so solidifies their status.

> *The Dominican girls I work with say you have more benefits and more options if you have lighter skin. If you're darker skinned, you don't attract the right kind of boys.*   —Maricruz, 22

I was coteaching a high school class on race and beauty at a Washington, D.C., school where the student body is entirely African American. The students talked about how skinny white girls were and how they didn't have "white girl" issues like needing to be thin. But as we discussed what issues they did have, my African American colleague said, "I come from California, and no one in this room would be considered light-skinned." You could have heard a pin drop, then hostility radiated from the back row, where the Queen Bees sat—all girls who had straightened their hair, had the best clothes and nails, and the most "white" features. As I watched their conversation unfold, I noticed that I had pressed myself into a wall as if to make myself invisible because the emotion in the room was so tense. But girls have to discuss these issues because if we don't challenge this kind of internalized racism, girls will keep attacking each other's sense of self. It's not that the light-skinned girls inherently believe they're better than other girls. Instead, it's that if they aren't taught the history of racism and how it influences people of color's own perception of beauty and worth, they will unconsciously pick up on these cultural values and reinforce them.

By the way, understanding these issues should not be limited to girls in ethnic minorities. Regardless of your daughter's race, class, religion, or ethnicity, it's important for her to realize the connection between markers and cultural definitions of beauty and racism so she can recognize when it's devaluing other people and challenge it. On a more hopeful note, in spite of the fact that we have a lot more to do to address racism in Girl World, I believe this generation of girls can teach us a lot about race. While of course racism persists among young people, they are also more likely to have grown up with people of different races and/or are mixed race themselves and are more accustomed to people dating outside of their race. Again, this doesn't make kids color-blind or immune to racism, but it does mean they can teach us a lot about how to live in a more multiracial world.

CHECKING YOUR BAGGAGE

Parents' conflicts with their own issues of weight and appearance can be impenetrable blocks that stop them from helping their daughters. There's no way you're going to help your daughter unless you deal with your own baggage about this first.

How do you feel about your own weight and appearance?
How would your daughter answer that question about you?
How often do you talk about your weight? Every week? Every day? Does your scale decide whether it's a good day or a bad day?
When someone compliments you, do you thank them or put yourself down?
What have you said to your daughter about how she looks?
Does your daughter understand how you feel about yourself? Do you want her to know?

Think back to when you were a teen.

What part of your body or appearance were you most self-conscious about?
Did you ever look at certain people when you were growing up and think they were perfect?
What were your markers or your style when you were a teen? Why did you choose them?

Since first writing this book, a somewhat uncomfortable situation has come about between educators and moms who have had a lot of plastic surgery. I could never have predicted this as an issue when I started teaching. The first time this was brought to my attention, I was teaching in Southern California. Earlier in the afternoon I had worked with a group of eighth-grade girls who were wearing the school uniform of conservative plaid skirts and button-down shirts. Later that evening, I was scheduled to address the parents. About a half an hour before the parent presentation, the principal pulled me aside, sat me down in his office, and said, "Ms. Wiseman, it would really help me out a lot if you could tell the parents, I mean the moms, if they could stop wearing such revealing clothes to school. What kind of message are we sending to the girl students if we're telling them they have to wear a uniform but moms are coming into the school showing their cleavage and wearing really tight clothes? And it's really confusing for our male students and faculty. But as a man, I can't tell them. So could you tell them to be more appropriate?" In the last five years I have lost count of the school principals who have pulled me aside with the same request.

So moms—you should be proud of your bodies if you are taking care of yourself and you look good. More power to you. But there's a big difference between that and being caught up in the same body image craziness that you transform your body into something more resembling a female superhero—or your teen daughter. On top of that, you need to remember that school is a professional place. I'm not saying you need to wear a suit to drop off your kids. But tiny yoga outfits or tight jeans with little tops are inappropriate.

Please stop competing with us. It's really uncomfortable.
—Mia, 17

Now that we are on the topic of plastic surgery, teen girls don't need breast augmentations either. I don't care if she's obsessed with how flat chested she is. By allowing her to have this procedure you are putting her on the road of feeling that her body and her internal worth are never good enough.

WHAT YOU CAN DO TO HELP

There's a lot you can do to help your daughter deal with the incredible pressures she feels from both our cultural ideals and prejudices about beauty and the peer group she faces every day. In the next sections, I take you step-by-step through the Beauty Pageant and offer tips on handling the most common flashpoints where parents misread what their daughters tell them and intervene in counterproductive ways that undermine the very relationships they want to have. My goal is to help you strike a balance between understanding your daughter's preoccupation with style and beauty and nurturing her to appreciate her intrinsic beauty and individuality.

Beating the Evening Gown Competition: Cease-Fire in the Clothing Wars

Because it's so easy to see your daughter's behavior and appearance as a reflection of yourself, it's excruciating when she presents herself in a way that makes you want to scream or hide. Think about the clothes and hairstyles your daughter wears from day to day. What message do you think she's trying to send you? What message is she sending to her peers? What should you do if she dyes her hair purple or wants to be supersexy?

She's Super Scary

I admit that I cringe looking at the piercings I see on some girls. Let's say your daughter is dressed in the latest emo style: she's wearing all black, her makeup is dead white, and her eyes are heavily rimmed with black. No doubt about it, she's frightening. Your first impulse is to say, "Go upstairs right now and change into clothes that don't scare people." Instead, put aside your feelings about what it's going to look like to the neighbors. Find out what your daughter wants to express through her dress and makeup. You've got to seriously watch your tone here because you need to come across as respectful, not hyperanxious and embarrassed. As soon as you see her changing her style ask her why. Remember what I said on page 128 about really listening to her? Here would be a very good time to take me up on this. "Why the black lipstick? What do the combat boots stand for? Are they comfortable? How do you feel walking around in them?"

If your daughter is defensive, say, "I really want to know; why is this important to you? If it's important to you, it's important to me." If your daughter responds that she's doing it because she hates how superficial everyone is, say, "Okay, I respect that, but I'm not going to lie to you and say it's not hard for me to take you to church on Sunday. But I totally accept that this is your choice to make." It's okay to admit that you don't like your daughter's choices, but it's important to understand why they are so important to her and affirm them anyway. And honestly, if your daughter is doing these things, it tells you one very good thing—unless she's wearing all black only because all her friends are doing it, there's a very good chance she's thinking about her place in the world. That means she's an engaged critical thinker—this is a good thing.

I'm aware that many parents will pose the "slippery slope" argument; if you "let" her choose her hairstyle, makeup, and clothes, what power will you have to forbid her to do drugs or have sex? Guess what? You don't have that power anyway. What you do have is the ability to instill in her the values that enable her to make decisions well. Remember your Bill of Rights. If your rights include honesty, respect (for self and others), and accountability, and your daughter knows and has internalized them, that's your best defense. The question to ask yourself is: If I asked my daughter what my Bill of Rights is, would she know the answer? She needs to understand your rights and expectations.

If your daughter wants to dye her hair green, the reason why doesn't change if you forbid her. So let her. In a few years, she'll have only herself to blame when she winces at pictures of herself because her skin looks sallow next to that green hair, and she has a nasty, sullen expression on her face. You, on the other hand, then and now look like the reasonable and wise parent.

Now, I just said that she can choose her makeup and clothes but I have to qualify that statement. That is directed at girls fourteen and above. I don't mean she can start wearing makeup at eleven. You and your daughter need milestones. A generation ago parents would often put down rules like no makeup or dating until sixteen. There's a fine line between handing down rules that create power struggles between you and your daughter and rules that create safety, provide structure, and signify maturity milestones in her life. So if your tween daughter is begging you to wear makeup, tell her that before she's allowed to wear makeup, she has to learn how to take care of her skin. Then get her some good, not too expensive facial products. And as a compromise, let her get one lip gloss.

The problem with these power struggles about beauty and appearance is that they're annoying and unproductive. Why? If you fight her on this, you'll lose your credibility when it comes to talking about things down the line: making responsible choices about alcohol, drugs, and sex. You'll prolong the period of rebellion. Your daughter will be so busy fighting you that she won't admit to herself that she's making stupid decisions. Sometimes the cliché is true: you need to pick your battles.

Your Daughter Is Dressed So Sexy You're Embarrassed to Let Her Leave the House

What should you do if your daughter wants to wear something so sexy that it really goes against your core values?

> Dressing sexily is about wanting to be mature. Condemning your daughter's newest miniskirt will only serve to make it more attractive. You can't simply put your foot down. You have to find some kind of middle ground.   —Cherise, 16

Here is where you really have power with younger girls. Because it's up to you to buy the sexy outfit for her hip-hop dance recital. You choose the Halloween costume. You are the one who is driving her to the glamour-shot studio at the mall. I can't emphasize enough how important it is that you take a stand when she's young and that you explain your reasons.

Yes, this is one of those times when you explain, because in this situation, saying "Because I'm the parent" or "Because I said so" is an ineffective response. I'm not saying you have to reason with your child to the point where they agree with you. What I am saying is that this is an opportunity for you to share information with her about the power of Girl World culture over her and how it is your job as her parent to help her withstand it. If you do this now, it will be considerably easier to do it when she's older when she has much more freedom to do what she wants, buy what she wants, and wear what she wants.

But let's fast-forward a bit and imagine you now have an eighth-grade daughter and you're sitting in the living room on a Friday night. Your daughter walks down the stairs and quickly darts past the living room but not quite quickly enough. You can see that she's wearing a really short skirt, knee-high boots, and a shirt held up by two strings. You want to go ballistic. This is how you have the conversation.

Mental preparation: Take a deep breath and let go of any anxiety and/or anger. Remember, she isn't wearing this outfit out of disrespect for you.

Check to see if she has any friends with her. If she does, ask to speak with her privately, but don't say, "I want to speak to you privately," because then you'll have embarrassed her in front of her friends and she won't listen to you. Instead, say something like, "Hey, can you come into the kitchen for a minute? I need to ask you something." Keep your tone casual!

Check in with her about her plans. Then say something like this but in your own words:

You probably don't want to hear this, but I want to tell you how I feel about the way you're dressed. [Wait until she stops rolling her eyes.] I know that if I forbid you from wearing what you're wearing right now, you could change as soon as you leave the house.

But the way you're dressed makes me nervous because you look older and sexy, which may be the point. I'm worried that people are going to treat you as if you're older and you'll feel pressured to maintain that image. I want you to be proud and confident when you walk into a room. So, after you leave here, during the night, ask yourself if your clothes are making you act differently than you feel is the real you.

Then, the next morning, over breakfast, ask her if she thought about the question.

If you've ever seen a girl dressing in a way that you think is too sexy, have you ever asked yourself, what kind of mother lets her daughter out of the house dressed like that? Here's the deal. First of all, there's a double standard because I've never heard a parent say, "What kind of dad lets their daughter leave the house dressed like that?" We have to stop blaming moms. Second, that girl dressed so inappropriately in front of you could have left the house in sweatpants. Or she could have thrown a bag with her "cute" clothes out the window and picked it up when she left the house. Or she could have left the house and gone to find something cute to wear at a friend's house. So . . . be careful about throwing stones.

The Fashion Diva

You might be just as confused with how to deal with a daughter who is a fashion diva. If you're not, you should be. Ideally, most parents want to raise a strong, capable, interesting person. What if your daughter is obsessed with celebrity magazines and websites? What if she slavishly grooms and dresses to look exactly like her friends? Just as you shouldn't freak out if your daughter is dressing in all black, you shouldn't freak out here. I just want you to look at what she wears and her style (no matter what that is) as one of the best ways to tell you what she values in her world. And if her appearance is telling you she is blindly following others, that's a problem you need to pay attention to because she'll likely do it in any other areas too.

Do You Think I'm Sexy? Halloween Immunity

Have you noticed that girls will use any excuse to dress up in sexy costumes? Halloween is the most obvious example, but girls will do it whenever they feel they can get away with it. Note that I don't mean get away with it with you but with their peers. These situations are cease-fires in girls' battles with each other where they get to dress as sexy as possible with less fear of recrimination ("Did you see the way she was dressed? What a slut!"). It's the freedom to be a "bad" girl.

> I love Halloween! You can be a devil, angel, or a French maid. It's an excuse to be sexy without worrying about what anyone else is saying.   —Lynn, 16

> We had celebrity day and everyone used it as an excuse to wear short skirts, low-cut shirts, and no one could say anything about it because you can dress up however you want without people calling you a whore.   —Nia, 18

So, when your daughter dresses up as a belly dancer or the latest celebrity with what you consider to be totally inappropriate clothes (and it doesn't have to be something so dramatic as a whole costume, it could just be a pair of shoes), before you react to her, know her motivation. Like it or not, she's test-driving her power. You have to be able to say to your daughter, "When you wear X, you have to know that people will think of you in a sexual way. And some will see you as a target. Be clear about what your boundaries are and what you do and do not want to do with someone."

If you've communicated how you feel in a clear, respectful way and allow her to experiment (even if you think it's a mistake), your words will be in her head when she needs them most. (I'll discuss this issue in more depth in Chapter 11.)

Outlapping the Swimsuit Competition

Don't wait for your daughter to come to you. Know with absolute certainty that sometime in fifth or sixth grade she'll be comparing her physical development against that of her peers. It doesn't matter if she has big breasts or is completely flat. Talk to her about it. Sit down and say, "I want to talk to you about something that's totally normal for someone in your grade (notice I didn't say 'normal for your age' because that is a parent thing to say). I'm not sure if this has happened already, but I'm sure people are physically developing at different rates in your class. Some girls may need to wear a bra and some don't. That's totally normal. But it's also normal for girls to be teased because of it and that isn't okay. Have you ever seen anything like that happen?"

If the answer is no, then end the conversation by assuring her: "Well, I'm glad it hasn't happened, but if it ever does and you want to talk about it or anything else, I'd be happy to talk to you." If the answer is yes, listen and keep asking questions about how she feels. Brainstorm with her about what she can do and say to make herself feel better. If she's an early developer and you tell her that other girls are jealous, explain why. But advise her not to accuse her tormentors of jealousy as that will make them even angrier and more vindictive. Tell your daughter she's beautiful, that bodies come in all shapes and sizes, and that they're all beautiful. Make sure she has access to the books and websites that reassure her that what she's going through is normal. It's great to hear it from you, but if possible, find someone your daughter thinks is cool and stylish (remember, this is your daughter's choice, not yours—you just have to think the person is sane) and have that woman share with her the similar insecurities she had when she was your daughter's age.

Just one last word on the puberty thing. Sometimes parents get a little too caught up in trying to make it sound wonderful and exciting "now that your body is changing." While of course you want to teach your daughter to be proud of her body as she goes through puberty, you also need to give her the space to think puberty is embarrassing and not so wonderful. Girls need to talk about how physical development makes them feel about themselves and their peers and place it into the context of their lives—not just what happens when you get your period.

If you're reading this and your daughter is an older teen, don't worry, you can still have the talk with her. Just start the conversation by saying, "I just want to check with you about something." Start with yourself. What does your style say about you? Why do you think that? Then ask your child, "What does your style say about you?"

MORE THAN ONE STANDARD OF BEAUTY

Go through the pages of a fashion or celebrity magazine with your daughter and talk about the homogenized images of beauty you find there. Mute the volume during the ads when you are watching TV with her and ask her what it's teaching her about what is beautiful. Go to your daughter's favorite websites and analyze them. What are they telling you that women need to fix? What are they telling your daughter about girls' value and what they believe about Girl World? This probably won't be news to your daughter, but it's important to get her to articulate it. What does it take out of her to try to measure up? Now talk about how looks matter to her group of friends. What kind of pressure does she feel to uphold the standards of the clique? What happens when she breaks the rules? Your goal here is to increase her awareness of how media images and her friends influence her feelings about her attractiveness and self-esteem. As you'll do in so many other situations regarding her relationship with friends, ask her, "Who's making the decisions about how you look and feel about yourself?"

My daughter came home one day after school and told me that she wasn't pretty because she had darker skin than me.

When I asked her why she thought that, she told me that some-one at school had said that darker-skinned girls aren't as beau-tiful. I have to tell you I wanted to go over to that school and find out who had said that to my daughter, because it was so painful.
—John

So what did I tell that dad? First, you have to be clear with your-self about how these issues have impacted you. Look at pictures of when you were growing up and then share them with your daugh-ter, including your feelings about yourself at the time. Tell her she's beautiful. But don't shy away from telling her that, unfortu-nately, she's not alone in how she feels. Girls in many different cultures grow up hearing the same things about darker skin, broader noses, curlier hair, etc. So ask her to imagine a girl in India, Korea, or Africa who is being teased or looked down on just because she doesn't have as light skin or straight hair as other girls. Then ask your daughter if she could give advice to that girl, what would she say to her? Now your daughter needs to tell herself those same words. You don't want your daughter feeling ashamed or less worthy because of how insidiously racist the world is. She needs to see this issue in a larger context so that she doesn't feel alone and she realizes this problem is bigger than her. That way she begins to understand the context for the comments and hope-fully will be empowered to stand up for all women being valued as beautiful.

DEALING WITH WEIGHT: "I'M SUCH A COW!"

You're getting new jeans for your daughter. Sometime over the last year she's developed hips. You have brought no less than twenty different styles and sizes into the changing room for her to try on, yet she hates all of them. After what seems like hours, she opens the dressing room door and she's near tears. She says to you, "I hate how I look, I am so fat." If you're still wrestling with your own issues about weight, these situations can be light-ning rods between you and your daughter. For her sake, get yourself together about it so that you can be an effective role model.

If you think your daughter is overweight, the first thing to do is stop and check your baggage again. Is she truly too heavy, or are you projecting your own issues onto her?

Could you be panicking when there's no reason? Do you "need" her to be thin to satisfy your standards of beauty? Are you judging her as weak-willed or lazy if she's chubbier than you'd like?

I can't tell you how many heartbreaking discussions I've had with girls whose parents have given them the most toxic, and sometimes unintentional, messages about how "fat" they are. You see her eating a cookie and you say, "Do you really need to be eating that?" which is parent code for "Can't you see how fat you are?" Other messages are just as unhelpful: "I'm only saying this because you'd be so pretty if you just lost weight. Don't you want to look your best?" And please forget about the bribes like, "If you lose ten pounds, I'll give you that cell phone you really want."

If your daughter really is eating junk food all the time, and she's genuinely overweight, you do need to address that. What does help: healthy dinners, teaching her to slow down while she's eating so she can listen to her stomach when it's full, and enrolling her in physical activities where losing weight is a by-product of the fun she's having and skills she's learning.

She's also a prime candidate for a martial arts class. Have her check out a couple of schools and enroll her in one for three months. I used to teach martial arts, so here's a word on the kind of teacher you're looking for—and this would be the case for any "coach." They encourage their students through hard work, clear goals, and group support. They never brag about their own exploits or put their students down for their weight or physical abilities.

This is a tough battle; girls often hear "eat healthy food" as code for "you're fat." If weight issues are an ongoing struggle for you, it's best to admit that to your daughter up front (but remember there's a good chance she already knows that). Acknowledge the powerful influence of the media. Even the most emancipated women can't escape the impact of all those messages our culture sends us about what we have to be. Discuss the issue with your daughter. For younger girls, eight through twelve, look through magazines together and ask your daughter to create a collage of what she considers healthy images of women. Then ask her to do another collage of all the unhealthy images you find in the women's magazines. Help her analyze what's right and wrong with these images. Then, talk to her about the messages she gets about body weight from her friends and clique. Are these messages that make her feel good about herself? What kind of pressure is she feeling from the group to change how she looks?

The message your daughter needs to hear from you is that you love her just as she is, that you acknowledge that the world we all live in is horribly judgmental about people's weight, and that any conversation about her weight is based on developing strength and confidence in her body.

COULD YOUR DAUGHTER HAVE AN EATING DISORDER?

If you suspect your daughter has an eating disorder, either anorexia (she's starving herself or is headed that way), or binging, or bulimia (she binges and purges), it's essential to see a qualified therapist who specializes in treating these problems. For that reason, in addition to the signs to look for that are included in this chapter, you'll find other resources in the back of the book. We all have a stereotype of the little girl lost, starving herself to please her perfectionist, controlling parents. I can tell you that I've worked with many girls whose parents were truly loving and supportive and didn't conform to this stereotype at all. Don't waste time blaming yourself for your daughter's eating disorder. Get professional help right away.

Signs and Symptoms of an Eating Disorder

Emotional
Sudden change in attitude
Talks consistently about dieting, being or feeling "fat"
Denies problem
Constantly asks for reassurance about appearance

Behavioral
Seems constantly moody
Wears baggy clothes, either to hide weight loss or to conceal body
Compulsive behavior, appears "on edge," talks a lot about food, carries food around, possessive about food
Avoids social functions where food is present
Suddenly stops eating around other people; always claims to have previously eaten
Ritualistic about food (cuts food into small pieces, takes a long time to finish meals, avoids food other people have bought or cooked)

Physical
Sudden fluctuation of weight (loss or gain)
Abdominal pain
Constantly tired, forgetful
Feeling faint, dizzy, cold
Lanugo hair (a fine, downy, white hair that grows on the body to regulate temperature)

What to Do If You Suspect a Friend Has an Eating Disorder

If your friend admits to having an eating disorder, encourage her to get help and talk to a trusted adult (parent, school counselor, coach, teacher, pastor, rabbi, etc.).
Avoid making comments about your body shape or size, food, dieting, or weight loss or gain.

Try to avoid making situations awkward. Keep inviting your friend to social functions, even if she refuses to go.

Set boundaries and remember that you are not responsible for your friend's eating disorder. You cannot fix it, but you can always be there for support.

What to Do If You Have an Eating Disorder

Tell somebody—a trusted adult, friend, or professional. You cannot heal from an eating disorder alone. Ask to talk when you both have some time and are not in a hurry. Practice what you are going to say. Write it down, say it out loud, or go over it in your head.

Many adults do not understand eating disorders. Don't be discouraged if people are shocked, deny the problem, or get angry.

Be proud of yourself for coming forward and remember that you deserve to be healthy and happy.

Understand that eating disorders are not about food, size, weight, or shape.

Preoccupations and obsessions about food and weight are merely symptoms.

Ask for help from a qualified professional who has experience with eating disorders and body image concerns.

Be honest about your needs. Eating disorders are difficult to treat, and you will need a lot of support. Ask for help and be specific about your needs.

For More Information

The Something Fishy Website on Eating Disorders:
www.somethingfishy.org

National Eating Disorders Association:
www.nationaleatingdisorders.org

Eating Disorder Referral and Network Center:
www.edreferral.com

BACK TO THE MALL: DEFINING YOUR "SHOE MOMENTS"

When we last left you at the beginning of this chapter, you were rationalizing your defeat as your daughter texted her friends about the shoes she just got out of you. But now you know why they mattered to her so much: a Queen Bee probably made a snide comment about her shoes last week or maybe she's desperate to have another pair because the ones you're talking about were cool last month and now she needs *these*.

So when do you give in and help your daughter fit into the clique and please the Queen Bee, and when do you encourage her to go for it and stand on her own? I'm not saying that you should give in every time she "has" to have something. Far from it. She should never be rewarded for whining, acting entitled, or being rude. What I'm saying is that before you say no, remember how important these things were when you were her age. Remember the pressures she's under in the Beauty Pageant. If you can empathize, it'll be a lot easier for you to take her seriously, which makes you come across to her as a reasonably sympathetic person. And that more likely results in a mutually agreeable solution. You want flats, she wants four-inch heels: you compromise on two-inch heels. You want black, she wants sparkles: she gets something with some decoration. You just shelled out for last month's shoes and don't want to pay a penny more; she has to split the cost with you, do extra chores to pay for them, or it comes out of an agreed-upon clothing budget, beyond which every dime comes out of her own pocket.

Remember, it's never just about the shoes. A precedent is being established. She goes to you for help. You say no. She feels that you "just don't get it." She does it anyway but now sneaks behind your back. When she's thirteen, it's shoes; when she's fifteen, it's a nineteen-year-old boyfriend. Whether she grows up too fast is in large part determined by your recognizing the cultural pressures she's under, and establishing yourself as someone who listens and respects her problems and then works with her to come up with mutually acceptable solutions.

Most of us struggle with Beauty Pageant issues throughout our lives. If you can admit and reflect on how the pageant impacts you and your daughter, it takes some of its power away. No matter in which category your daughter falls, the Beauty Pageant is a ruthless competition. Even if she wins, she still loses, because she may have to sacrifice so much of herself to carry the scepter. You can't pull her out of the pageant, but you can teach her to walk across the stage with grace and dignity, believing in her inherent self-worth.

Mean Girls: Teasing, Gossiping, and Reputations

Samantha just found out that Megan is behind the gossip bomb that has been ruining her life for the past month. Last night, Samantha got an anonymous voice mail saying she was a fat cow, and she could hear Megan laughing in the background. Today Megan is acting like there's nothing wrong. But last period, when Samantha walks by Megan and her friends and they laugh, Samantha can't take it anymore.

SAMANTHA: You want to grow up and say whatever you're saying to my face?

MEGAN: What are you talking about? (She says this sarcastically, not subtly rolling her eyes to the other girls.)

SAMANTHA: You don't think I can hear you laughing? What's your problem?

MEGAN: No offense, but I don't think I'm the one with the problem.

SAMANTHA: What's that supposed to mean?

MEGAN: Don't take this the wrong way but it's completely pathetic to see how you're throwing yourself on Dylan. He doesn't even like you. But whatever, if you want to act like a total slut I guess that's your choice.

SAMANTHA: What's your problem, Megan?

MEGAN: I don't have a problem. I didn't say anything to you until you came up to me. If you can't take it, you shouldn't have asked. Come on, you guys. Let's get away from drama girl before she completely loses it.

Can you blame Samantha if she gave up and slugged Megan? If you were Samantha's parents, wouldn't you think Megan was horrible, and that Megan's parents were equally guilty for raising this monster? What should you do if you're Samantha's parent? What should you do if you're Megan's parent?

WHAT YOU SHOULD KNOW

- 99.99 percent of girls gossip, including your daughter.
- The longer and more adamantly you deny this fact, the worse of a gossip she'll be.
- While we're on the subject, the worse gossip you are, the worse your daughter will be (and you thought she didn't listen to you!).
- Girls will almost always blame their behavior on something or someone else. Let's say your daughter is accused of spreading a rumor. Instead of admitting her guilt, she'll demand to know who exposed her as the information source, as if the snitch were the person who's really at fault—conveniently forgetting that she was the one who gossiped.
- If she's over twelve, girls have probably called your daughter a slut and/or bitch. And it's just as likely that she has called other girls a slut and/or bitch (that you have never heard these words out of your daughter's mouth is immaterial).
- Technology increases the power and damage of gossip. Your daughter could easily and understandably feel that once gossip is "out there," it will never go away. She'll never be able to escape its clutches because everyone will know about "it" forever.
- The younger your daughter is when you give her a cell phone, the younger she'll be exposed to gossip or more likely she will participate in gossip herself.

- Starting from the age of around five years of age, "Just joking!" is used way too often as a way to tear someone down and then deny you did anything wrong.

In this chapter I will look at how teasing, gossiping, and reputations impact your daughter's sense of self, social competency, and friendships. I will break down different ways of handling gossip and teasing whether the target is inside or outside the clique. I will give you more strategies so you'll know which battles to fight for her and which ones you should let her fight on her own. But I will also challenge you to take action when your daughter is the one who starts the rumors. Most girls who are gossiped about gossip themselves. It's more than possible that your daughter has been cruel to someone else. It's up to you to teach her differently.

I know for some of you it's hard to imagine your daughter being unkind or downright nasty to other girls, especially if she's never shown this kind of ugliness around the house. On the flip side, you may know your daughter is a gossip but be so frustrated with her that you secretly side with her friends if they drop her.

> I hate to say this, but I'd understand if my daughter lost all her friends right now. She's so gossipy I think it would be good for her if someone in her group stood up to her. And I can't believe I'm saying this because two years ago if you had told me I'd feel this way or my daughter would act like this, I wouldn't have believed you.   —Meg

> I can't believe what I overhear my daughter and her friends saying about this one girl. And believe me I talk to her about it! I get so mad at her but nothing I do seems to make a difference. She really feels like it's not that big a deal to be talking so badly about people.   —Karen

When your daughter walks down the hall to her history class, what's she more likely talking to her friends about: the upcoming class or the latest gossip? Teasing and gossip swirl around your daughter's head every day, and they're the lifeblood of cliques and popularity. Although your daughter may feel that they provide the forum for bonding with her friends, teasing and gossip can also act as powerful weapons to pit girls against each other and destroy their self-confidence.

Your goal is to teach your daughter to identify when teasing and gossiping get out of hand and to do something about it. This is an ambitious goal to say the least, because it often means your daughter will have to go against her friends and risk her comfortable place in the group. But this is the Champion moment I talked about in Chapter 3. She may not think that standing up for someone else is worth the price of losing her status. Or she may know in her gut that what's happening is wrong, but can't really put her finger on it or feels powerless to stop it.

Let's go back to the classroom. I often ask girls between ten and eighteen to tell me what they like about their friendships with other girls. These are their common responses. You can:

Be yourself
Tell her anything
Trust her
Depend on her support
Be silly
Hang out
Share clothes
Tell secrets

But, as you now know, these same friendships aren't always so supportive. Just as the girls want to talk about "good" popularity for thirty seconds and focus on "evil" popularity instead, they would much rather get to my next question: "So, what are the things you don't like so much about your friendships with girls?" These are their common responses. She can:

Talk behind your back
Gossip about you
Be two-faced
Be jealous

Be competitive
Be critical
Be judgmental
Tell your secrets
Be a tagalong
Take your boyfriend
Make you choose friends
Betray you

As the girls call out their answers, they laugh and crawl over each other to complete the list of mean things they do to each other. The amazing thing is that no matter the girls' race, geographic location, class, or religion, I always get the same answers. Take a closer look at the "negative" list; a theme should become clear. They're all about competition, about looks, style, friends, popularity, and boys—things girls think they need to secure a place in the Act Like a Woman box.

Are girls competitive about grades and sports? Yes. But there's a nuance to it. About a third of the girls I teach include grades and athletics on the list. Girls tend to consider these attributes as part of the overall package you need in order to be successful. Simultaneously, they know they can't be too overt about their academic or athletic accomplishments. The general rule in Girl World is you can't make people uncomfortable with your success. This is not a lesson we want girls to learn and take with them into adulthood.

TEASING

My students love to ask me if I was teased when I was in school and I was—but no worse than most kids. In seventh and eighth grade I was part of a powerful clique, but I was at the bottom of the totem pole within that clique. From the outside, I looked like I was popular. From the inside, I didn't feel that way at all. The girls in my clique teased me all the time about precisely the things I was the most insecure about. I put up with it because I didn't want to risk being expelled from my group. I was so intimidated by them that years later, after I'd graduated from college and was living in

San Francisco, I saw the Queen Bee from my old clique in the grocery store and without hesitation ran out of the store.

Almost everyone has been on both sides of teasing. So how serious is it? Teasing is multifaceted, and just as I define popularity in two ways, I have different definitions of teasing. If you're going to be credible to your daughter, you must distinguish between them. I struggle all the time trying to figure out when girls are teasing each other or being serious, and sometimes they do too. Things you would think are serious often aren't, and sometimes your daughter sounds casual precisely because she's covering up what she really feels. Depending on your daughter's intention and the power dynamics between her and her friend, there could be a lot more going on than even she understands. How do you tell which one is which and how does your daughter? I break down teasing into three different kinds.

Good Teasing

Good teasing is one of the cornerstones of great friendships. Someone who cares about you, knows you well enough, and is comfortable with you can tease and joke around with you—"with" (not "at") being the operative word. With good teasing, there's no intention to put the other person down, and the teaser understands what your "No Joking Zone (NJZ)" is—the specific things you never want to be teased about.* Your daughter will know if she feels liked by the teaser and doesn't feel that the teaser's motivation is to put her down. If your daughter says she doesn't like it, the behavior will stop.

Unintentional Bad Teasing

It's easy to tease someone and not know you're hurting her feelings. We've all done it and we've all been on the receiving end of it. It's always hard to tell someone you like that you're not happy with something they did. It's extremely difficult for girls and

---

*Rachel Simmons, *The Curse of the Good Girl*, Penguin, 2009.

women to be in situations like this because we're taught to not make waves. But when the intent isn't malicious (which isn't to say it couldn't be insensitive), once the teaser understands the impact of her behavior, she'll get over her defensiveness and make a sincere apology because she recognizes she's hurting someone she cares about. Your daughter will know when she doesn't feel the teaser's motivation is to put her down but instead that the teaser doesn't know how she feels and that it hurt her.

Bad Teasing / Verbal Cutting

Bad teasing isn't really teasing because that would imply it's harmless. It's really more akin to being cut with words, because the person is being attacked precisely where they feel most vulnerable and exposed and where it is most likely to cause the most pain. Verbal cutting targets the NJZ I mentioned earlier. And who knows what those things would be more than the people we're closest to? It can occur both inside and out of the clique, and either way, it's ugly and done to put the recipient in her place (i.e., below the teaser on the social totem pole).

The classic strategy is for a relentless attack on a subject guaranteed to cause the most humiliation. Then, the perpetrators dismiss the target when she defends herself by saying, "Can't you take a joke?" "What are you making such a big deal of this for?" What is so frustrating about being dismissed with "I'm just joking!" is that it lets the person who hurt you off the hook. Even worse, often the girl who is being teased ends up apologizing for speaking up in the first place ("I'm sorry, I'm such an idiot") or swallowing it lest she lose her place within her group of friends.

A girl can't tease like this "up" the ladder. If she does, the girls with more power will punish her by saying something that puts her back in her place. Sometimes it's the girl who puts herself down by making a self-deprecating comment or apologizing profusely, which restores the equilibrium in the group.

Bad teasing within a clique is about maintaining order or demoting someone who has broken the group's rules. Bad teasing outside of the clique is about maintaining the power of the group in relation to the overall community it is a part of.

Why do girls do this to each other, even when they "know" it's wrong? Especially in early adolescence, girls change friendships frequently, and it's common for those changes to create a high degree of anxiety. When this happens, it's common for girls who used to be friends to turn on each other, and the verbal cutting can be brutal. When a girl leaves one group for another, the friends she's left behind feel rejected. But they often cover that feeling by convincing themselves they should be angry at her for being "stuck up" and "fake." Although there certainly may be a degree of truth in that, it is also usually the case that underneath the initial feeling are much more troubling questions, like "Why did she leave me? What's wrong with me? What does her leaving say about me? Do other girls think the same thing?"

At the least, these dynamics can make it extraordinarily difficult to concentrate in school, and many girls will do anything to avoid the people making them miserable. Here are a few strategies girls have shared with me to avoid their tormentors:

- Being so slow in the morning that she misses the bus. Meanwhile her parents are hitting the roof because she's lazy, not taking school seriously, or being immature because she doesn't realize how missing the bus makes them late for work.
- Refusing to use the bathroom at school all day.
- Taking a longer route to class, even at the expense of being late.
- An unwavering commitment to listening to music with headphones or earplugs.
- Always reading, so she can pretend (or not) to selectively hear what people are saying around her.
- Pretending to be sick.
- Pretending that she's not hungry and she has to study so she doesn't go to the cafeteria.

Sometimes I would make a pretty feeble attempt to tell my friends to stop teasing me that probably came off as whining that no one took seriously. And these girls were supposed to be my friends. . . . If the girl protests, even weakly, the teasers will say, "We're just joking. Stop making such a big deal of this."
                                                        —Jordan, 17

You don't say anything because you hope things are going to get better. But then you always end up talking to another girl about it because you're angry or you just want someone to talk to about what you're feeling. But then sometimes she tells other people and then everything gets into a huge mess. I really don't get why we do this.   —Pamela, 16

These girls are my best friends. I can tell them anything. They'll back me up. But if we're so close, then why do they tease me all the time? If they really are my friends, then why do they make me feel bad? Why am I so frightened to say anything?   —Greer, 14

Things would be a lot easier if your daughter asked herself to answer Greer's questions. But girls, like many of us, often make excuses for their friends or convince themselves that they really don't care so they won't have to take action. And in any case, it's hard for a young girl to get all of those feelings organized into thoughts, much less be able to ask you about them.

It feels like a no-win situation. She's trapped hanging out with friends who make her miserable, and if she doesn't address this, she'll be angry with herself because she can't hold her own against bullies who masquerade as her friends. Keep this in mind later when you ask yourself why your daughter dates someone you don't think is respectful to her. She is learning to be silent in the face of intimidation. It feels less painful to put up with the intimidation than take a stand against it.

ARE BAD WORDS A BIG DEAL?

"But, Mom, that's just what we say. We don't mean anything by it."

Does your daughter use "bitch" as a term of endearment? Like when she answers her cell phone with a cheerful "Hey Bitch" to her friend? If so, you may (a) think this is a problem and (b) feel blown off when she dismisses you with the above response. Well, you're right. It *is* a problem, and here's how to get her to think about it differently. The reason children and teens believe words like *bitch* and *slut* don't mean anything is because they hear them so often it seems normal.

That's exactly the problem. Just because it may be common doesn't make it right. So this is what I'd say to your daughter:

> I get that you think I'm overreacting but there's something you need to know. Originally and even now, the word *bitch* has been used to silence a woman when she expresses her opinions and rights. The word *slut* or any other word like it is used to define women as only sexual objects with no right to an opinion. I don't believe you're a person who believes women should be shut down for demanding respect. I know I can't control what comes out of your mouth, but now that you know, I'm asking you to be a strong woman by taking responsibility for the words you say. That is what powerful women of character do.

Gossiping

Gossip is like money. We exchange it, sell it, and lend it out. It's what we have of value.   —Jane, 16

I'm never mean to people without a reason.   —Celia, 12

Whoever gossips to you will gossip about you.   —Courtney, 15

Let's face it. We all gossip: on the phone and at parties, meals, and family reunions. Girls are no different. In fact, why do you think adults are so good at it? Because we've been sharpening our skills since we were young, and it's almost impossible to stop. So do I tell my friend to stop when she calls me at work with some juicy information? Of course not. But there's a difference. While gossip still has the ability to ruin your day, its impact on your adult life is usually superficial and fleeting. Hopefully, you shut your mouth when you know you'll hurt someone. But it's very different when you're a teen. Along with teasing, gossip is one of the fundamental weapons that girls use to humiliate each other and reinforce their own social status.

As I said in the beginning, the power of gossip has dramatically increased with the advance of technology. It often feels like kids have lost any internal braking system to stop the automatic response to join in the gossip mill. Someone else's embarrassment and humiliation becomes everyone else's entertainment or opportunity to make the person feel even worse. Gossip has always been humiliating because girls literally feel like the whole world notices everything they do, and with everyone texting right under their parents' noses, it's true.

Most likely you've seen your daughter's egocentricity in full bloom when she becomes embarrassed by something you've done or said in front of others. In *Reviving Ophelia*, Mary Pipher describes the "imaginary audience syndrome," where a girl was humiliated by the way her mother clapped at a play. In reality, no one but her daughter thought she was clapping strangely, and even if they did, who cares? However, this girl truly believed that everyone was totally focused on her and, by extension, her mother. If you can embarrass your daughter by doing something no one notices, imagine how she feels when rumors are spread about her. She feels as if she's wearing a neon sign advertising her shame and humiliation. And now that everyone can spread the gossip by texting, Facebooking, and instant messaging each other before, during, and after school, your daughter's paranoia is actually justified.

GOSSIPING VERSUS VENTING

Girls often pretend they are venting or getting advice from a friend when they're really gossiping. Now, there's nothing wrong with bouncing things off other people to get advice and feedback. So what's the difference? Gossiping is when a person spreads information about someone else to embarrass or isolate them. Venting is expressing your feelings about an experience you had. For example, you get really mad at another girl and then tell another friend what happened and how you're feeling about it. That's venting. Your friend takes that information and tells other people to stir up drama and make people not like the girl. That's gossiping. Your job as a parent is to teach your daughter the difference between reaching out to a friend to express her feelings and get advice versus trashing another person.

In some of my classes, we spend the entire time discussing gossip. When ten minutes are left in class, I ask the girls to sign a pledge not to gossip for any amount of time they think is realistically possible. They giggle and argue. Is it possible? Can they do it? Why would they want to? Most are doubtful they can make it past thirty minutes. During this time, they are encouraged to think about how much of their conversation with friends revolves around gossip. Here are some of their pledges:

"We the class of 8B promise not to gossip or be exclusive when we leave this class and go to our next class."

"We the class of 6C promise not to backstab, lie, gossip, or spread rumors about each other for two hours today, April 2."

Occasionally, the girls aspire to greatness.

"We the class of 9B promise not to gossip for three days."

I don't assume the girls will uphold their pledge. The purpose is for them to realize how much of their daily conversation revolves around gossip. Through this exercise, they get it. Their most frequent comment at the next class is "It was weird to realize that gossiping is all we talk about!"

What Do Girls Gossip About?

In Fourth Grade
Which girl is boy crazy
Who is "girlfriend and boyfriend"
Which girl in the glass is being stuck-up
Which boy in the class has "germs"

In Sixth Grade
Friendships
Conflicts with friends
Rivalries in/between cliques
Boys and crushes

In Ninth Grade
Who's trying to become friends with upperclassmen
Who's popular
Which girls are stealing boys away from other girls
Which boys are being used by girls
Which girls are being used by boys
Which girls in the class are getting attention from older guys
Which parties you're invited to and which ones you aren't
Who's drinking, doing drugs, or having sex

In Eleventh Grade
Which freshmen girls are throwing themselves at the upperclassmen
Who hooked up with whom at the last party
Who cheated on whom
Who got drunk and/or did drugs

Who made a fool out of themselves at the last party
Who's getting used and why or why not they deserve it

REPUTATIONS

Gossip and reputations can't exist without each other. Reputations are a by-product of constant gossiping and, good or bad, they end up trapping girls. Like cliques, your daughter will probably perceive reputations more rigidly in her early teens than in her later teens. When I first discuss reputations with girls, I ask them the following three questions: (1) If a girl gets a bad reputation, is it her fault? (2) Once you get a reputation, good or bad, will you always have it? (3) Should you back up a friend when she gets a bad reputation?

The majority of younger girls and teens believe that you're to blame for the reputation you get, you will always be stuck with it, and they're torn about backing a friend. Older teens know that people can get reputations without "doing" anything to deserve it and sometimes you can leave your reputation behind, even if that means you have to switch schools.

The impact of reputations can last throughout your daughter's teen years, because somewhere along the way, girls start believing it as truth. Who they are (their character, sense of self, and personality) gets tangled up with their reputation. This is another reason why girls are often confused about their own motivation when they know they're doing something foolish and/or dangerous. Because they want to please their friends, boys, and/or you, they will do things against their better judgment to uphold their image.

The following is a compilation of different reputations I've seen or heard girls talk about. The first four are relevant for girls up to sixth grade. These and the ones that follow are found from seventh grade up.

Drama Queen

She has to be the center of attention. She gets to decide which boys like which girls. When she's mad, she puts out her hand to stop you from talking. She is an expert liar and thinks she's better than all the other girls. She tells you what to do all the time.

Girly Girl

She loves pink and maybe purple. She freaks out when she sees any kind of insect. She hates to get dirty. She gets her nails polished or if she can't do that, expertly colors her nails with Magic Marker. She has a cloud of boys around her. She wants to be a fashion designer and talks about clothes all the time. She loves websites with princesses or dress-up games.

> She wants people to open the door for her even when the door is already open.
> —Keria, 11

> Sometimes you get a girl who is a girly girl and a drama queen. That's the worst thing that could possibly happen. It's like your house catching on fire and then exploding.
> —Annie, 10

Suck-Up

Girls don't trust her and, for the most part, teachers don't like her either. In younger grades, she often makes things much worse for herself by becoming the rules enforcer when the teacher isn't there. Her peers often find her incredibly annoying but will use her if she helps them with their homework.

Tomboy

Same as when you were growing up. The girl who won't play with dolls or makeup kits and would much rather play dodgeball or four square with the boys.

Perfect Girl

Everyone thinks her life is perfect while she feels like a fraud and thinks that at any moment someone will pull back the curtain and expose her. She tries desperately to avoid making any mistakes, and she is impossibly hard on herself. She finds fault with herself easily and never thinks she's doing enough. She runs herself into the ground trying to keep up with her image. She either never drinks or does drugs because she's too afraid to lose control or can be a binge drinker/drugger to escape the pressure she's under.

Guy's Girl

She insists that she "always gets along better with guys" because girls are "too dramatic." One of the most frustrating things the guy's girl does is back up the boys when they argue with girls about politics or gender issues, and the boys love her for it. She often neglects her own feelings and pretends she "doesn't get attached" to guys. She ends up treating herself like a sex object, and guys treat her that way too. She tells herself she feels powerful so she can sleep at night.

Preppy

She likes school, has had a boyfriend for three years, and is one of those preppy, peppy people. She's on all the committees. Like the Emo/Goth Girl, this reputation seems to stand the test of time. Many parents love having a preppy kid because it appears that their internal lives are as clean-cut as the clothes they wear. This can be true, but it's in no way a guarantee.

Emo/Goth Girl

People have called it different things over the years, but this is the girl who wears all black, dyes her hair (usually black but not always), listens to dark music, and scares people who can't see past the cynical expression and morose style. She comes across as having no patience for popularity and the people in the popular cliques. Sometimes she says things just to freak other people out. Notwithstanding her hard exterior, she can be easily hurt by others but feels like there's no point in going to adults if the popular clique is making her life (or her friends) miserable.

Lez/Dyke

In the sixth grade she played football with the boys, but by eighth grade the boys won't play with her—and neither will the girls. She's reluctant to join groups, is quiet, and often feels out of place. She can speak out defiantly if she has to, but then goes back into her shell. It's common for her peers to spread rumors about her being gay (which she may be but not always). What's important to realize is that this reputation is based more on her gender-neutral or more masculine appearance than her sexual orientation. Parents and teachers (myself included) can have a really hard time getting her to open up. But once you do, there's usually a really interesting, compassionate kid.

Social Climber

She's the chameleon. She changes herself constantly to fit in with the girls she emulates and the guys she likes. She looks to others for her opinions because she's afraid to express an original thought. She can be horrible to a target and is easily manipulated by more powerful girls. Boys and girls can laugh at her behind her back for trying too hard.

The Über-Rep: The Slut

Ho. Freak. Skank. Whatever. There are few other words that carry so much weight, have so much baggage, and control a girl's behavior and decision making more. One of the biggest difficulties in my work is encouraging girls to be proud of their developing sexuality while making sure they understand how vulnerable they are in a world that constantly wants to exploit their sexuality.

When it comes to the "slut" reputation, girls accuse each other of two things: acting like a slut, and being a slut. The fear of being accused of acting like a slut controls girls' actions in a particular situation. For example, when your daughter chooses what to wear to a party, she's trying to balance looking sexy while not coming off as slutty (i.e., being attractive to boys yet not incurring the wrath of other girls).

> *I was playing basketball with three friends. One of my friends was a girl and the other two were boys. We had been playing for a while when a girl in our school who was in seventh grade asked us if she could play. We said yes. After a while, she took off her sweatshirt and pants and she was only wearing a tiny tank top and shorts. We kept playing, but the boys couldn't pay attention. I thought she was really showing off and flirting with the boys. The whole thing got really weird. I think she was acting like a total slut.* —Brett, 11

When I asked that girl how she felt watching this scenario unfold, her reaction was far more complex. As much as she didn't approve of the seventh-grade girl's behavior, she was conflicted because she envied the boys' attention. Girls often feel they have to choose between being themselves and displaying a sexy costume, which is a huge conflict. If a girl opts for the costume and acts the part, she'll get the boys' attention, but she'll also risk the girls' resentment—and the spiteful talking behind her back. So she'll try to achieve the impossible by pleasing groups with two competing agendas. She might also feel that once she interacts with boys in a sexual way, she won't be able to hang out with them without her sexuality being the only thing they value about her. These conflicting emotions and confusion increase when girls accuse each other of acting like sluts.

For younger girls, the threat of being called a slut defines the limits of acceptable behavior and dress. They use it to describe a girl who is perceived as flirting "too much" and dressing "too" provocatively. They're easily and understandably confused about their own personal comfort level regarding how they come across to others, because they're literally transforming from little girls into women in a world that often perceives them first and foremost as sexual objects. It can be confusing, exciting, and terrifying all at the same time.

So, acting like a slut is a label a girl gets from her appearance and behavior in "public," like the school hallway, movie theaters, malls, and parties, where people might see her drunk and/or "throwing" herself onto someone. The accusation of being a slut most often doesn't come until eighth grade, when at least some girls are not only making out with guys but also giving oral sex and having intercourse. Then the slut reputation is more about pointing fingers at a girl's sexual activity, whether she "gives it up" easily, hooks up with a lot of boys, and so on. It's a reputation that's almost impossible to shake because the accused is the repository of everyone's judgment, jealousy, curiosity, and fear. When I work with girls with bad reputations, they're initially wary of me. Why should they trust me? They've learned to build big walls around themselves to block out the judgment and rejection they so often feel from others.

When I have girls like this in my class, I can usually pick them out by their defiant expressions. The worst expressions come from girls who aren't only on the outside of the Act Like a Woman box but are really suffering at the hands of the other girls in the group. At first, talking about these issues can feel dangerous for them. We're talking about things that hurt them, and they have no reason to believe I'll do right by them.

Kate was a student in one of my tenth-grade classes. The first time she came to class she was late, and her expression was both challenging—waiting for me to call her out for being late—and hostile, because she anticipated that the class would be boring. She started off sitting in the back of the room, but within five minutes she moved in front of me. The Act Like a Woman box was on the board and the girls were discussing the different roles girls play in cliques. Kate scowled and said something I couldn't quite hear. When I asked her to repeat herself, one of the popular girls said, "Oh, don't pay any attention to her. That's just Kate." Kate's face clouded over and her back stiffened as she repeated herself, "I said that I hate girls. You can't trust them. Girls are petty, stupid, and jealous. Like in this grade, the girls are just jealous because I get more attention from the boys. I know I'm known as a slut but I don't care." As she spoke, I felt the ripple of anger and resentment in the classroom in response. There are few things popular girls hate more than being accused of jealousy.

Consider this quote from a senior girl remembering what it felt like to see girls like Kate.

In seventh grade, I watched a girl who constantly flirted with boys. The problem was that she alienated herself from other girls. She pretty much accepted the slut role that people made her into. The boys she flirted with didn't take their relationships with her seriously. Even though I didn't want to be treated like she was, I wanted the attention she was getting. But whenever I was around her, I felt incredibly prudish and uptight. —Grace, 17

Girls are at best uncomfortable with girls like Kate, and at worst treat her like dirt and refuse to have anything to do with her. In turn, Kate doesn't trust girls and she has good reason not to. In her mind all girls are bad, and her mistrust of girls clouds her thinking about which boys to trust. Naturally, she seeks out people who'll make her feel better; often the easiest, fastest way for Kate to get the attention she wants is hanging out with boys. The boys who will want to hang out with Kate the most are the ones who need to prove their masculinity by interacting with girls only as sexual objects. Kate, not wanting to turn away the attention she's getting, will do what the boys want. She won't reject someone who isn't rejecting her.

But one of the saddest things about girls like Kate is that while many convince themselves that they can't depend on anyone but themselves or that they are in a position of power over the boys, they still often romanticize love and sex. They're still girls caught up with wishing someone will see them for who they really are and love them. Every time they hook up with someone, there's a little part of them hoping this person is the one who will.

Boys may call me a slut. But at least they call.   —Sasha, 15

CHECK YOUR BAGGAGE

- Did you ever feel trapped by a reputation you couldn't shake?
- Were you ever teased? What were you teased about? How did you handle it?
- When you were your daughter's age, did you ever spread gossip and get caught?
- Were you ever gossiped about? How did you handle it?
- Write down a list of your daughter's closest friends. Do you think they support her or discourage her?
- If you were mean, what would you tease your daughter about? How do you think your daughter would respond?
- Do you gossip and tease other people today?
- Does your daughter hear you gossip?

WHAT YOU CAN DO ABOUT IT

The first step to help your daughter is to acknowledge the role of teasing and gossip in your own life. As I said at the beginning of the chapter, if you gossip or dismiss hurtful words by saying "Just joking," "No offense," or "You're too sensitive," you're modeling bad behavior for your daughter. Turn off the gossip shows and stop reading the gossip magazines. I know they're a guilty pleasure for many people but this is your daughter we're talking about, and you want to be a credible role model for her.

Now you need to arm your daughter with a battle plan for when she's been ridiculed, dismissed, the object of bad teasing, or saddled with an unfair reputation. Let's use an example that one of my students shared with me to show you how to proceed:

When I was a freshman, there was this new girl that a bunch of guys liked. Two girls in the grade made a Facebook group called "Lori Shore is a mega-whore." The next day, another girl told her about the group. Lori confronted the girls. One of the girls flat-out said, "Yeah, I did it and what are you going to do about it?" The other girl was a really good friend of Lori's and kept denying it.

—Hope, 16

As despicable as this story is, it involves all the issues we've been discussing. Let's assess which girls did what:

- The Queen Bee (the girl who admitted she did it), the one who made the Facebook group, is doing it to bring Lori down and to demonstrate her power over the other kids.
- The Bystander keeps denying she was involved. She's intimidated by the Queen Bee and too ashamed to come clean with Lori.
- The Messenger is the girl who told Lori about the group.

If this happened to your daughter, how would you handle it? First things first. You're allowed to hate the Queen Bee or any other girl who is being mean to your daughter. It's easy to see how parents get so angry they feel totally justified going over to the other girl's house and screaming at her parents. Honestly, I'd totally understand if you read that story and thought if it happened to your kid there's no way you'd allow her to go to school the next day unless those girls were expelled.

If Your Daughter Is the Target, Don't Say, "Just Ignore It"

Even in this situation, there are parents who believe ignoring it is still the way to go. This may sound like a mature strategy, but it's exactly the kind of parental advice that makes girls feel that their parents don't understand the world they're living in. When girls have problems, they need help right away. Immediately. And it is absolutely realistic that every student in the school knows about the Facebook group and that even if the adults at the school knew about it, they would refuse to punish the girls because Facebook isn't associated with the school and the girls did it off school grounds. Imagine if you were Lori. You wouldn't care about anything else but how you were going to show your face at school the next day. Lori isn't thinking in the long term. Next week may as well be next year.

Lori knows that everyone else in school, especially the girls who created the Facebook group, will watch her the next day to see how she'll respond. She has to know what to say, how to hold her body, and what tone of voice to use so she can feel some control over this situation.

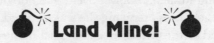

Land Mine!

Other things not to say:
They're just jealous.
They're just insecure.
You're better off without them.
Just be strong.
Just don't let it bother you.

What Do You Say

If you're Lori's parents, unless Lori comes home crying (which is possible because this is such a horrendous situation), it may be hard to know that something's wrong, or what that something is. Review the strategies in Chapter 4 for how to tell if your daughter's upset. Remember, you must be ready to talk when she's ready to talk.

If your daughter wants to talk to you but also couches it as "no big deal," don't believe her; it's a big deal. If you know she's upset, approach her gently: "I may be totally wrong here but you seem upset. Do you want to talk about it?"

If she does approach you and you absolutely can't talk to her that minute, tell her when you can. Always remember that by the time you're ready, the opportunity may be gone, because in the interim she'll have talked to her friends and/or reconsidered whether talking to you is a good idea in the first place. If you have to postpone, set up a time as soon as possible and don't forget to keep your promise!

You have two goals in addressing your daughter's problems with teasing and gossip. The first is to have a productive conversation with her. This means that through the process of your conversation, you want to affirm her and confirm that you're a good resource and a nonjudgmental listener. The second is to help her come up with realistic strategies to confront the problem effectively—meaning you aren't going to freak out and make the problem worse. You'll never accomplish the second goal without the first.

Here's how the conversation might go:

YOUR DAUGHTER: Um . . . well . . . can I talk to you for a minute?

YOU: (Paying bills, balancing bank account, in the groove of getting things done) *Huh?* (Your brain slows and the gears start to shift.) What's up?

YOUR DAUGHTER: It's nothing really. I mean it's not that big a deal, but there're these girls at school who did something on Facebook about me.

YOU: (Paying more attention but keeping a casual tone) What are they doing?

YOUR DAUGHTER: If I tell you, you have to promise not to freak out.

YOU: Can you define freaking out so I know exactly what you're talking about?

YOUR DAUGHTER: You know, call the school, call their parents. Not let me go on Facebook ever again. If I tell you, you have to promise you won't do anything like that.

YOU: OK—I can promise I won't immediately start calling people. And I also can promise whatever it is you tell me, we'll think about what to do together and take it step-by-step. But I can't promise I won't do anything else because I may have to and I don't want to go back on my word.

YOUR DAUGHTER: (Silence. Tears welling in eyes.)

YOU: Listen to me, I don't know what I'm dealing with here but I'm ready to listen. Later, if we do need to tell someone we'll decide together who and when that will be. So . . . what are the girls doing?

YOUR DAUGHTER: They just say really rude things. It's so annoying!

YOU: Can you describe specifically some of the things they do or say?

YOUR DAUGHTER: This girl at school made up a group on Facebook that she called "Lori Shore is a mega-whore."

YOU: (Take a deep breath! Sit down next to her and give her a hug.) I'm really sorry that happened to you. I can't believe anyone would say that about anyone, let alone you. But thank you for trusting me to tell me. I think the most important thing is to figure out what you can do to feel like you're getting a little bit of control over this situation.

Now it is time to come up with strategies.

There are five options and if the first option doesn't work, go to the next one. The goal is to have your daughter take the most ownership in addressing the conflict. For our purposes, I'm calling the girl who perpetrates the gossiping the RMG (Really Mean Girl).

- Your daughter can confront the RMG.
- She can ask a teacher or counselor for help.
- You can call the RMG's parents.
- You can talk to the teacher.
- You can talk to an administrator.

Option 1: Confronting the RMG

Step One: Preparing Your Daughter

As horrible as this situation is, it wasn't a death threat—it just probably feels like one. So if your daughter doesn't feel physically unsafe, then skip this part and go to Option 2. But you want to at least try to encourage her to confront the RMG—which is probably the last thing she wants to do. However, she's going to take small steps to get to that moment. To get started, take your daughter to a quiet place and suggest she write down the specific details of the event, including dates, times, what was said to her, and what she said or did in response. She should include how she felt in the situation, her feelings now, and what she wants to happen so the behavior stops. Basically, she's taking the horrible feelings in her stomach and putting them down in words.

There's another reason to document the misdeed. You never want to assume the worst, but you want to be prepared for it. Your daughter needs to show a history of what happened and the steps she took to address it. And, if you show specific dates and times, the perpetrator's pattern of behavior, and the steps your daughter took to address this problem, the school will take you more seriously because it's more difficult to dismiss it as a she said/she said conflict.

Next, have your daughter practice having the conversation in front of a mirror. Her tone of voice needs to be calm and level and her eyes steady but not challenging. Her body language needs to be confident: standing up straight, face-to-face. You can even suggest that she practice the conversation with you or another adult she trusts. Remember to utilize SEAL (see Chapter 2 discussion of this technique) while your daughter practices what she is going to say. She needs to:

- Stop and strategize.
- Explain what she doesn't like and what she wants to happen.
- Affirm her right to exist without having people humiliate her.
- Lock in / lock out the relationship (or take a vacation).

Step Two: Speaking to the RMG

If she feels physically safe, she needs to make at least one attempt to speak to the RMG. It needs to be somewhere she feels safe and secure and other people can't observe for their entertainment. For many girls, the library is a safe zone; the librarian patrols there and it has a reputation for being a calmer place, but your daughter should choose a site she thinks is best. Under no circumstances should she confront the RMG electronically.

When your daughter's ready, she should confront the RMG when she's away from other people so she's not making the RMG lose face and other girls can't buzz around her. If your daughter confronts the RMG in front of her friends, even if the RMG feels bad about what she did, her need to appear in control in front of her peers will trump any motivation to do the right thing. If the RMG is in a group, your daughter should request a private meeting. ("Can you meet me during study hall in the library at 11:00?") There's one thing to watch out for: sometimes girls will bring their friends to a meeting like this for physical support. If that happens, your daughter must request that the other girls leave because this is a "private meeting" between her and the RMG. This may create huge drama among the girls, but the situation is huge drama anyway so it doesn't really matter.

Here's how the private conversation might go:

YOUR DAUGHTER: Can I talk to you for a minute?

RMG: What about?

YOUR DAUGHTER: I know you did the Facebook group. I want it stopped and I know you have the power to stop it. I don't know why you hate me, but there's nothing I can do about that. I know you can blow me off or try to make my life worse, but I am asking you to stop.

RMG: Whatever.

YOUR DAUGHTER: Look, I don't need to be friends either, but I have a right to be at this school without you attacking me online.

You may read this and think two things: (1) there's no way my daughter would do this and (2) it would never work; why bother if the RMG is just going to blow you off? Here's my response. Any step of this that your daughter does is a success. If she writes down her feelings, even if not as articulately as the above, but then decides not to confront the RMG immediately, it is still a success because she has to take the first step of learning to confront people.

SEAL's overall goal is to give a person who feels stuck in their anxiety and anger a way to move. In this scenario your daughter was specific about what happened, how it made her feel, and what she wanted stopped, and she finished by saying something positive. She lost nothing by admitting that the other girl "won." In fact, it can be empowering for the targets to say, "I admit it. You did something to me and it's making me miserable—but I'm strong enough to stand here and call you on it."

Notice that the RMG concluded the conversation by saying "Whatever." Please tell your daughter that almost all mean people when confronted with their behavior will blow you off. It's not like the RMG is going to say, "I'm so sorry! I had no idea that calling you a mega-whore was going to hurt your feelings! I promise I'll never do it again!" And even if the RMG did that, your daughter wouldn't believe her anyway. So "Whatever" is probably as good as it'll get. Girls often feel they've failed if the RMG doesn't immediately apologize and then the two become friends or your daughter has verbally destroyed the RMG, leaving the RMG regretting she ever did it. The immediate goal is to stop the RMG's behavior. The only way she'll do that is if Lori communicates that she's not easy prey. Just like any predator, RMG goes after easy targets first, and Lori's proving to be too difficult. The unfortunate reality is that your daughter can't control the way an RMG will respond to her. She can only control her own actions.

If the RMG tries to sidestep the issue by asking "Who told you that?," don't let your daughter get distracted. Girls typically avoid taking responsibility for their actions by blaming the person who got them into trouble. If the RMG raises this red herring, your daughter can say, "It doesn't matter how I know. What matters is that it stops now."

If the RMG is a friend inside the clique, your daughter can "take a vacation" and spell out exactly what it will take for the friendship to continue. "Look, at some point maybe we can be friends again, but only if you understand how much that hurt me. Friends don't do that to each other."

Option 2: Talking to the Teacher

Lots of children and teens are extremely reluctant to tell their teachers when they are experiencing a problem like this. In my experience, the reason is because by third grade, many kids have been told by bullies not to tell or else their lives will get worse, and if and when they do tell, adults rarely know how to handle the problem effectively. They tell the kids to apologize, remind them of the community values posted on the walls, and leave it at that. But like I've said before, not all adults are useless. Your daughter needs to go through the process of learning when to go to an adult and which one to go to.

You need to go to a teacher if your daughter talks to the RMG and the behavior continues or this problem has gotten too big for her to handle on her own. But just the thought of "tattling" or "snitching" will make many girls shut down because they are certain the RMG will want revenge if they do. Now, that's true if she doesn't have a good strategy and have good people to help her implement this strategy. But the reality is that if she doesn't do anything but hope the problem goes away, it probably won't and she's letting her tormentors have all the power. I'm guessing that your daughter, just like anyone else, doesn't want to go through life letting the bullies have all the control.

So the next step is to talk to a teacher or counselor. Your daughter should choose a teacher she feels listens to her, respects her, and follows through on her promises. Remember the ally from Chapter 4; you should use the same criteria here. Here's how the conversation might go in person or by e-mail:

YOUR DAUGHTER: Ms. Wiseman, can I talk to you privately after class today?

ME: Sure, is this something we are going to need some time for or privacy?

YOUR DAUGHTER: Maybe.

ME: No problem. Why don't you come back after last period today?

Notice that this is the Stop and Strategize part of SEAL.
After last period . . .

ME: Hey, Lori, what's up?

YOUR DAUGHTER: Well, some girls did something that really bothers me.

ME: Can you tell me what they did?

YOUR DAUGHTER: (The Explain of SEAL) RMG and her friends made a Facebook group about me being a whore.

ME: I'm so sorry! Coming to school today must have taken a lot of courage. And I want to thank you for trusting me to tell me because I can imagine how hard this has been for you. So how can I help you?

YOUR DAUGHTER: I just want it to go away.

ME: I totally understand. Let's figure out together a strategy for dealing with this. Tell me what you've done so far.

YOUR DAUGHTER: I told her to stop, but she wouldn't listen.

ME: I can talk to her. Let's decide together what you would like me to say.

YOUR DAUGHTER: Okay, but I don't want her to know I told on her.

ME: No problem. I can say I found out about it on my own.

Your daughter should then give the teacher a copy of everything she's written about the incident. Your daughter's goal is to come up with a mutual agreement that she can write down between her and the teacher about what will be done and when. After the meeting, you should e-mail the teacher, thank her for the meeting and for being a resource for your child, and reiterate your daughter's understanding of what will happen as a result of their meeting. Request to hear back within forty-eight hours, because everybody works better with deadlines. If the deadline passes, your daughter should ask the teacher two days later about what's going on—which you follow up with another e-mail for confirmation.

If that deadline passes, it's time for you to get involved.

For any teachers reading this, please note: if you are a good teacher and have created a positive learning environment in your classroom, chances are good that your students will come to you for help with serious personal issues. It's one of the rewards of being a great teacher; you can literally transform or save lives. But it can also be really scary because you may have not been trained for it. Just remember you are the bridge for your students to a person with more expertise. You don't need to have a counseling degree to do that—all you need is a relationship with the child. So when a student comes to you, use the same script I describe when the child comes to the parent looking for help. "I'm so sorry that happened to you. Thank you for telling me. Together we're going to work on this." If the student requests you not to tell anyone else, follow the same strategy I outline on page 61. Don't underestimate your importance in this situation. By handling these situations effectively your student is affirmed for going to an adult for help and they have had a positive experience emerge out of a horrible situation.

Option 3: Talking to the RMG's Parents

No matter how tempting it may be to call the RMG's parents and scream at them about their evil child, this is not an effective way to handle the situation. And even if the other parents did exactly what you want—get off the phone with you, then scream at their daughter and ground her for a month—guess what happens next? The next day your daughter goes to school with an RMG bent on revenge. At some point, the RMG's and your daughter's paths will cross without adult supervision around. The harassment will escalate.

Your involvement is critical, but you have to be smart about it. Assume that the RMG's parents don't know what their kid is doing. Go to them asking for their help in solving this problem, not accusing them of bad parenting or having bad kids. Now it's *your* time to implement SEAL.

YOU: Hi, I'm Lori's mother. This is an uncomfortable call to make, but I need to talk to you about something that's going on with our daughters. Is now a good time to talk?

RMG'S PARENT: Well, I'm really busy right now but sure.

YOU: Thanks (which you try to say sincerely, not sarcastically). We need your help and I have to tell you, parent to parent, this is really hard. Your daughter created a Facebook page that said my daughter was a whore.

RMG'S PARENT: What?!! Are you sure? How do you know it was my kid?

YOU: Lori has talked to your daughter to try to get her to stop, but it hasn't. Lori is dreading going to school, so I really need your help to make this situation better.

RMG'S PARENT: But why do you think my daughter did it?

YOU: (Take a deep breath and remember the goal) Your daughter admitted it. We've really tried to work it out between the girls but that hasn't helped.

RMG'S PARENT: Well, I'm going to talk to my daughter but what do you want me to do?

YOU: Lori would like the Facebook group pulled down immediately, and I would really like to request that your daughter apologize to her. I'm also worried that when the adults aren't around, Lori will suffer even more, because your daughter will be mad she got in trouble. Do you have any ideas about what to do so that won't happen?

If Lori has a dad who is actively involved in her life (like if he has a heartbeat), he is more than capable of making this call. So, dads, don't shy away from this opportunity to show your daughter she can rely on you as a sane advocate on her behalf.

If You're the One Called

It's 6:00 and you're blissfully alone, heading up to your clean bathroom to take a bubble bath (or more likely, desperately trying to get dinner on the table and telling your kids to stop fighting) when the phone rings.

LORI'S MOM: Is this RMG's mother?

YOU: Yes . . . what can I do for you?

LORI'S MOM: I need to talk to you right now about your daughter. (Voice trembling with self-righteous anger)

YOU: OK . . . what is this about? (You glare at your daughter, who is beginning to clue in that this conversation is about her and it's not about her latest community service project.)

LORI'S MOM: I just need to tell you I have never been so disgusted in my entire life! I know girls can be mean but your daughter is absolutely the worst. And I have no idea how you're raising her but if my daughter did what your daughter did, I would ship her to reform school.

YOU: Excuse me????

LORI'S MOM: Your little angel created a Facebook group calling my daughter a whore. My daughter is crying herself to sleep every night and won't go to school because she's so humiliated. (Your head begins to throb and your eyes narrow. Where is your daughter? You walk into the living room and find her talking on her cell phone. You begin to wonder, "Is my daughter capable of doing something to terrible? Am I a horrible parent? Does everyone at the school meeting I am about to leave for already know about this?" Put all those thoughts out of your head and immediately acknowledge the other parent's feelings.)

YOU: As hard as this is to hear, thank you for calling and I'm really sorry. Can you tell me what happened and when? Can you give me more details? (Write them down.) Let me talk to my daughter, and then I would like to call you later tonight. When is a good time?

Because Lori's parent usually wants to vent, these calls can take a long time. So if you don't have the time, apologize, tell Lori's mom why you can't talk, and let her choose another time to talk. Then call exactly when you agreed.

One of the things I think also happens in a situation like this is the mom of the RMG would hold her daughter accountable, but the mom of the victim is so over the top that the RMG's mom gets

defensive and her kid's offenses pale in comparison to this psy-
chotic woman's response. So basically, this mom shoots herself
in the foot by being crazy from the get-go. —Emily, 20

I listen to them and then listen to my daughter. It's her responsi-
bility. I think it's wrong to be accused without seeing the accuser.
I also don't use pronouns. For example, I will say, "A call came
in . . . it reported X. Do you know anything about it?" Then I think
my daughter has to make a choice. She can continue her crappy
behavior or she can change. Now, this doesn't work all the time
because I'm so pissed off. —Peggy

Option 4: Parent Talking to the Teacher

If the first three strategies haven't worked, you and your daughter
need to meet with her teacher. Before your meeting, familiarize
yourself with the school's policies and state law concerning student conduct, bullying, and/or harassment. Think of yourself as an
advocate for your daughter, not a mama or papa bear out for the
kill, and approach any school professional with an attitude of col-
laboration and respect. Don't assume, unless you have direct evidence, that they're part of the problem.

This is really important, as most teachers and administrators
interact with parents only when something is wrong. As a result,
parents are often perceived as overly emotional micromanagers
who are often defensive and unwilling to take responsibility for
their child's actions. In addition, far too many parents go over the
teacher's head as soon as something goes down in the classroom
they don't like. Believe me, doing that will make the problem bigger rather than smaller.

In preparation for this meeting, I want your daughter to go
through SEAL again while you write down what she says. Then,
there should be an agreement that if at all possible, your daughter
does most of the talking during the meeting. If she is too uncomfortable, reassure her that at her request you will speak for her
using the things you have just written down.

Once you are in the meeting, thank the teacher for being there and then implement SEAL. In this conversation, one of you needs to state that your daughter must feel safe at school so she can learn her best. The Facebook group isn't allowing her to feel safe and focused. You have already made different attempts to solve the problem, but the situation hasn't improved. Get a firm deadline for action from the teacher. If you feel disrespected or dismissed by the teacher and/or the deadline isn't kept, write a short note or an e-mail telling the teacher you are contacting the principal.

REPORTING VERSUS SNITCHING

As girls get older, the pressure to not snitch and never tell an adult gets increasingly intense. For this reason, even when kids do attempt to tell someone, they can be unclear or very general in their description of what's happening. It is also true that as kids get older, the bullying gets more extreme and therefore more humiliating and difficult to talk about. If adults aren't trained to understand these dynamics, they won't be able to hear what the child is really saying and ask the right questions to get a better picture of the problem.

So it is critical to review the section on Tattling vs. Telling to help you and your daughter overcome this challenge.

Option 5: Parent Talking to an Administrator

If you're unsatisfied with the teacher, you now have to speak to the principal. I wrote extensively about this in my *Queen Bee Moms* book, but in sum you're there to establish the following: your daughter has asked for help from a member of the faculty, you've also asked for help, and help hasn't been forthcoming. There's a consistent pattern of behavior where your daughter is going to the school for help and the school isn't providing assistance, and, as a result, your daughter's ability to concentrate in school is suffering.

If Your Daughter Is the Bystander

Remember when I first described this situation? There was another girl who participated in all this as a semi-involved Bystander. Should she have stood up to the RMG and risked her wrath, or kept quiet? How responsible is she when she didn't help create the Facebook group but she joined it?

First of all, you may not hear anything from her about it. You'll hear it from other parents or you'll get called into the school yourself. Either way, once you hear something and your daughter's friends are involved, even if she wasn't as directly responsible as our Bystander is here, she'll still know about it and would have been in a position to do something—no matter how small. You're going to have to ask her about it. Why won't she tell you? She's afraid of four things happening: (1) you're going to be angry with her; (2) you're going to make her do something about it (i.e., apologize); (3) you won't let her hang out with the RMG anymore; or (4) probably most important, you're going to cut off her Internet access or take away her phone.

So, if you do find out, here's how you use SEAL to frame what you want to say.

> YOU: So I heard about the Facebook page. You want to talk about it?
>
> YOUR DAUGHTER: No, not really.
>
> YOU: Well, I want to talk about it. Was there really a group calling Lori Shore a mega-whore?
>
> YOUR DAUGHTER: Yeah, things just got totally blown out of proportion. It's so stupid! I really didn't want to do it. I wish RMG would back off a little, but she never does.
>
> YOU: What does RMG have to gain by doing it?
>
> YOUR DAUGHTER: I don't know, RMG just hates her.
>
> YOU: But there must have been a reason in her mind that this was something she needed to do.
>
> YOUR DAUGHTER: She's just really mad at all the attention Lori's getting from the boys. She thinks Lori's getting really stuck-up about it.

YOU: Now I want to ask you a question. What do you have to gain?

YOUR DAUGHTER: What are you talking about?

YOU: Well, tell me if I'm wrong, but does it sometimes seem easier to let RMG have her way when she gets mad?

YOUR DAUGHTER: Maybe.

YOU: Well, I'd understand that it'd be really hard if I were in your shoes. But, with that said, it's really important to me that you stand up and do what's right in these situations. And by not trying to stop it or telling an adult, you contributed to the problem. So what do you need to do right now to make it right? (Possible options include: using SEAL to frame a conversation with RMG, apologizing to Lori and her parents, Internet/cell phone restriction)

If Your Daughter Is the Nasty Gossiper

I do gossip all the time. And I do tell my parents most things. A lot of things. But if I've done something sort of mean, I don't usually tell them. Or at the most I'm selective about what I say.
—Eve, 13

When you confront your daughter about her nasty behavior, tell her the facts as you know them. No matter what her excuse or justification, she should be punished in a way that communicates how seriously you take this issue. It's hard to admit that your daughter has behaved like a jerk, but it isn't a reflection of poor parenting if you admit her misbehavior. Quite the opposite. Guess which parents teachers and people like me complain about? The parents who think their daughters are little angels and blame everyone else for corrupting their little darlings.

So say you just hung up with Lori's parent and you ask your daughter to meet with you privately—away from any siblings. If possible, both parents should be involved in this conversation so she can't take advantage of any information gaps between the two of you. If you're divorced, and have any kind of working relationship with your ex-spouse, please apprise him or her of this situation so he or she can be part of helping your daughter take responsibility for her actions.

YOU: OK—as you may or may not know, I just received information about your creating a Facebook group calling Lori Shore a whore. Did you in any way participate in making and/or creating this group?

RMG: (Crossing her arms and grumbling) This is so stupid! That girl just blows everything out of proportion!

YOU: I need you to answer my question.

RMG: Well, I knew about it, but it wasn't my idea. It was Monica's.

YOU: Did you have any part in writing it?

RMG: Fine! Whatever you say! (Rolling her eyes)

YOU: Well, there are a couple of things you need to know about what I think about this. Most important, I don't really care whose idea it was. I hold you responsible for participating.

RMG: Fine! Ground me forever!

YOU: Not quite. First, I'm going to need your cell phone, which I will keep until I think you've learned to handle technology more responsibly. You will also be forbidden from using Facebook for the next month and I will be checking your page to see when you last logged in. I'm going to call Lori's family and see if we can come over, and you will apologize to Lori in front of me and her parents.

RMG: No way! You are totally insane!

YOU: When you do something that is unethical, it is my responsibility to you to hold you accountable. I love you with all my heart, so I can't stand by and do nothing about this. You must have the courage to right this wrong. I know it's going to be difficult to do this but I'll be beside you the whole time. And, while I believe what you are

telling me, you need to know that if I find out that you are
more responsible for this than you are telling me right
now, then that will mean additional consequences. There
is a chance I won't find out, but there's also a chance I
will.

RMG: Fine. Believe whatever you want. I don't care!

YOU: This is a hard situation, so if after this conversation
tonight you remember anything else about what happened, you can come back to me and I won't consider it
lying. After that, however, I will. The last thing that I
really need for you to get is that if Lori's life becomes
more difficult because of this conversation or anything
the school decides to do, I will be forced to take much
more severe actions. I'll put it to you this way—I understand if you're really angry about this, but under no circumstances are you allowed to seek revenge. You aren't in
trouble because Lori told. You're in trouble for what you
did to her.

Then, call Lori's parents and ask them if you can come over to
apologize. If they say yes, set up a time the next day to go over
there. If they say no, then have your daughter write a letter of apology, which you should drive over to her house and have her physically put in the mailbox.

Just a little note on how hard apologies are to give: it's natural
to feel defensive when someone has told you that you messed up
or you were caught doing something bad. So the child may need
some time to reflect on what's happened and what she needs
to do. Ideally, give your child a night to sleep on it. That way
you have a better chance of having them process and internalize what's happened so they can take true ownership of their
actions.

Land Mine!

When parents see someone else's child being rude or mean, they usually do one of two things: look away or march up to the offending kid and yell at them—often demanding an apology (that even if the child gives is insincere). But neither of these options is effective. If you run away, the kids feel like you don't care or are too scared. If you get in the kid's face, you can be so overwhelming that the offending child shuts down or fights back by being disrespectful so she can save face in front of her friends. The goal here is for all the children involved to believe adults can handle conflict with calm, ethical authority.
So, instead, use SEAL to frame your approach and your words.

THE ART OF THE APOLOGY

Teaching your child to apologize is one of the most sacred responsibilities you have as a parent. Unfortunately, true apologies are precious and rare. Our public figures apologize when they get caught, not when they realize they have done something wrong. The media often portrays apologizing as a loss of face and respect, when in fact the opposite is true. We just don't get to see good apologies role-modeled. We have to change that.

Apologies are powerful because they're a public demonstration of remorse, an acknowledgment of the consequences of hurtful behavior, and an affirmation of the dignity of the person who has been wronged.

A true apology has to be:

- Given with a genuine understanding of what the person did. Especially when your daughter is younger, make sure she understands what she's apologizing for. Otherwise, she may very well hurt the other person again. Don't let her put the best possible spin on her actions ("I didn't mean to say X to her, I think she just took it the wrong way").
- About the apologizer's actions alone—her apology can't include what she thinks the other person did or said.

- Given without including any "last licks" in which the speaker buries another insult within the apology ("I'm sorry you're so sensitive that you need an apology. But here, 'I'm sorry.' Feel better?").
- Given without qualification. It's not an apology if it includes "But I only did it because . . ." or "I wouldn't have said that unless you . . ."
- Genuinely contrite—there's nothing worse than an apology clearly rendered only because the girl was told to apologize ("My mom says I have to apologize" or "I guess I'm supposed to say I'm sorry").
- Given without the expectation of a return apology. If the listener has the grace or goodwill to say "I'm sorry, too," that's a bonus.
- Rendered with the understanding that it may invoke further recriminations ("Yeah, well, you really hurt me! I can't believe you did that!").

Beware that apologies can be manipulated! Girls in lower positions in the social hierarchy apologize when they inadvertently challenge a more powerful girl. Then they aren't apologizing for something they did that hurt someone, they're apologizing for challenging the other girl's right to make her miserable.

What If an RMG Refuses to Apologize or Apologizes but Doesn't Mean It?

Just remember you're on a long road with her toward becoming a decent human being. You're going to have to role-model what it looks like. Both of you should go over to Lori's house and you can apologize to Lori in front of her parents on your daughter's behalf like this:

Lori, on behalf of my family, I want to apologize for what my daughter did to you. That was an incredibly hurtful thing to do and it should never have happened. If it ever happens again, I want you to contact me. Here's my e-mail and phone number. Thank you for seeing us.

Look, if your teen daughter insists on acting like she's five by not apologizing herself, then you need to treat her like she's five. It's her choice.

Accepting Apologies

If your daughter gets an apology, there's one last thing you have to teach her. Instead of saying, "That's OK, don't worry about it," she should say, "Thanks for the apology." This is critical. Because when you say it's OK, you are dismissing your feelings that you needed the apology in the first place. And one of the things I realized this year from working with a group of eighth-grade girls is that a great way to know if someone is truly your friend is if, when they apologize to you, you believe it. And, if you apologize to them, they believe you too.

RESILIENCE

You and your daughter could use every strategy I've described and girls may still be mean to her. And I wish I could give you a magic spell that would make girls stop gossiping and tearing each other down. But you know I can't do that. What we can do is have your daughter create, maintain, and communicate her personal boundaries to other girls through difficult experiences like these. We can teach her to give and accept apologies in a way that transforms her relationships. And as I tell my students, if you can handle these situations using SEAL, no matter what the outcome, the sting of cruel words will lose their venom, and you gain a degree of mastery, pride, and competence as you face some of the most difficult conflicts you'll ever experience.

Power Plays and Politics: Speaking Truth in Girl World

Lila has just come in from fifth-grade recess and can't find her backpack. She knows she left it underneath the stairwell but it's not there. As the other students collect their books to go to class, Lila looks for it in the hallway, the bathroom, and the classrooms, but she can't find it anywhere. She starts to panic. She has to turn in her project for Mr. Thompson, and he won't believe that she so suddenly and conveniently couldn't find her backpack. In desperation, she goes back outside to the playground to retrace her steps like her mom tells her when she loses something; there it is, sitting in the middle of the playground. Lila is confused. She knows there's no way she left her backpack there. She hears laughter behind her and turns around to see Jackie and Abby giggling and staring at her. When they see her looking at them, they hurry away to class.

Three weeks ago, Abby couldn't believe how lucky she was to get two tickets to her favorite concert. And, even though she hasn't been hanging out with Christina like she used to, of course Abby invited her. The night of the concert, Christina comes over early and they're getting along great. Everything is amazing until Christina gets a text from Isabella—the girl she's been hanging out with more recently—who is at the concert too. At intermission, they agree to meet, but, as soon as they do, Abby completely regrets it. Christina barely acknowledges her existence in front of the other kids. They go back to their seats, and Christina gets more texts. She tells Abby she needs to get something from Isabella and leaves—and doesn't come back. Abby texts her, but she doesn't answer until the end of the concert, when she tells her, "Don't worry about me, just text me when your dad gets here." When her dad does get there, it takes twenty more minutes to find Christina, but Abby lies to her dad about it—which makes her even more angry. The next day, Christina refuses to admit she did anything wrong.

Power plays in Girl World are awful because the person who does them can so easily dismiss what they've done. It's all smoke and mirrors. The person is mad, but she feels like she can't complain about it. What's important about power plays is that they teach your daughter to dismiss her own feelings or those of others. In this chapter, I dissect the group dynamics of several typical power plays and rites of passage and offer some advice on how to help your daughter stand up for herself and get more support from her friends. Power plays are when girls reinforce their power without leaving concrete evidence of their actions for others to specifically put their fingers on. With power plays, the victim is unsure if she has the right to her reaction, and the girl in power can deny or rationalize her motives and actions. Parents are often vulnerable to denying when their daughter is instigating a power play because they dismiss the complaint by believing that "not everybody can be friends with one another" and that "people are going to experience rejection and disappointment." Their daughter was trying to be nice; the other girl just took it the wrong way.

WHAT YOU SHOULD KNOW

- It's inevitable that your daughter will experience power plays and politics in Girl World. You can't stop them from happening, but you can teach her how to trust her reactions to power plays and believe she has the right to confront them.

- Just as these experiences are rites of passage for your daughter, they are also rites of passage for you as a parent. Don't underestimate how painful they can be for both of you.
- Most girls aren't stuck in one role, which means your daughter will likely have experiences as the one who excludes, the one who watches but doesn't say anything, and the one who's excluded.
- Strange though it may seem, in the mind of your child, there is always a rational reason for what she's doing, whether as the victim or the aggressor.
- Reconciliations are often fleeting. Two girls previously in a fight may say that they've worked it out, only to have one attack the other again. This is especially true when the girl in the weaker position believes everything's okay.
- Technology makes power plays much easier to conduct. Girls say and do things to each other electronically that they would never do face-to-face. They often literally can't believe what they did once it has blown up and they've been caught. Conflicts that would have been settled don't, small conflicts grow immense, and everyone in the school knows the drama, infighting, and intrigue.

From the time your daughter was three and she got invited to her first playdate, it has been reassuring when your daughter was invited to parties and sleepovers, had a BFF (Best Friend Forever) or BFFL (Best Friend For Life), and when you've dropped her off at school and she's been enveloped by a group of kids. There have been few more comforting moments in my life than when I've watched my children walk down the school hallway and people look genuinely happy to see them. It's like everything in the world, in that moment, is good. So, whenever you have these experiences, hold on to them and realize each and every one of them has a devastating flip side: exclusion from parties, the breakup with the best friend, excommunication from the clique without a moment's notice.

Power plays in Girl World are all-important rites of passage because they teach girls about their own personal power and their ability to change something in their world that they don't like. The goal for any girl is to learn how to navigate these sometimes-painful experiences, go through a process of self-reflection that leads to wisdom and a personal code of ethics, and develop a fundamental understanding of who they are.

Let's go back to what I wrote in the introduction: dignity is not negotiable—not your daughter's, not anyone else's. Treating yourself and others with dignity isn't hard when everyone is getting along, but treating people with dignity when you are angry is when your character is really tested. So, as you and your daughter think through how to process and get through these difficult situations, keep this principle in mind.

This isn't to say that watching your daughter go through these experiences is easy. Her friends will sometimes walk all over her, and yet she may always forgive them. Can't she just believe you when you tell her that she needs to find new friends? She goes to a dance with a boy who dumped her two months ago. Does she realize that she's being used? Does she have to hang out with people who are always getting into trouble? Does she really have to make huge mistakes while you sit back and watch?

Most parents know that their role is to offer gentle guidance and support. They don't want to be micromanaging helicopter parents. The problem occurs when social conflicts and power plays arise. They bring up such anxiety and anger for the parent that all you can think about is fixing the problem—and doing so right away. But remember this is about teaching your daughter social competence, ethical leadership, and how to speak her truth (to herself as well as those around her) so that she has the best chance of being taken seriously. This takes patience and time.

RULES OF ANGER IN GIRL WORLD

The Act Like a Woman box and Girl World teach distinctly rigid rules for how girls can communicate their anger. The funny thing about it is that if girls follow the rules of the clique, they only learn to communicate in a way that prevents their being taken seriously or really heard. Without even realizing it, most of us follow these Girl World rules of expressing our anger:

- Internalize and suffer silently.
- Laugh it off to convince yourself that you don't have to take your feelings seriously.
- Give the person the silent treatment until (hopefully) they notice and ask you what's wrong. When asked, deny your anger by saying "It's fine" or "Whatever," and then get mad at the person when they can't read your mind.
- Finally ask for the behavior to stop, but the other person dismisses you by saying:

You can't take a joke. You're so uptight.
You're so emotional and oversensitive. Are you PMSing?
Why are you being so mean? Or, *Why are you being such a bitch?*
I'm just sarcastic—you know that's the way I am.

- Internalize until something small (to everyone else) makes you explode in tears and/or screaming, only to have your feelings be dismissed again.
- Have a "You have no idea who you are dealing with" attitude and then try to destroy the other person.
- Verbally or physically fight.
- Use drugs or alcohol to deaden feelings.

None of these eight methods result in your handling yourself with dignity and being able to articulate how you really feel in situations where you are in conflict with another person. By diagramming the roles people play and using SEAL, we're going to change these rules for you and your daughter.

UNINVITED TO THE PARTY

I don't care how old you are—few things are more likely to make you insecure than not being invited to a friend's party. Meanwhile, the party girl gets to be Queen Bee for the day as she decides (in consultation with her best friends) whom to invite and whom to leave out. (And, if you allow your daughter to invite boys, as I'll explore further in Chapter 9, the drama escalates to a fever pitch.)

MARY: Did you get Amanda's text about her birthday party? It's going to be amazing!

ANA: I didn't get it yet . . . but my phone's been acting really weird this week.

MARY: Oh, I'm sure you're invited. I'll go find out and let you know.

That afternoon . . .

MARY: Amanda says that her mom is only allowing her to have a few people. You know, like her really good friends.

ANA: That's okay.

MARY: Maybe I can talk to Amanda and get you invited.

How should Ana process this? On the following page I have diagrammed each girl's feelings, motivations, likely outcomes, and a better outcome (called "make herself proud") for a few typical power plays. I suggest girls use this grid whenever they have a conflict with friends to sort out competing interests and the roles girls play. Show your daughter this format and help her through a few examples so she understands how they work.

Understanding girls' motivations can help her figure out what she wants to do. In the preceding example, Amanda is a Queen Bee (i.e., person with power, at least temporarily), Mary is a Messenger (in the middle), and Ana is a Target (person left behind). Here's how the birthday party drama would look:

	Ana	Mary	Amanda
Feelings	Rejected	Torn but feeling important because she's in the middle	Enjoying being the center of attention
Motivations	Torn—wants to be invited but doesn't want to beg	Torn—wants to help friend and affirm her own social place	Wants to have her birthday her way
Likely result	Feels she's at the bottom of the totem pole	Feels important	Gets what she wants
What she learns	Has to change herself if she wants to be accepted	Her Messenger position is powerful	Has control over others
Makes herself proud	Recognizes it isn't a reflection on her	Feels torn, but doesn't make this an opportunity to feel important	Realizes she's hurt others' feelings and opens party to others

If you're Amanda's parent, you want to do something special for your birthday girl, but you don't want to make other children feel bad in the process. If your daughter goes to a large school, you're also not obligated to invite everyone in the class, nor is it good role modeling to throw a party that flaunts your wealth. If she goes to a small school, make sure the invite list isn't including everyone but one or two girls. This is an opportunity to work together with your daughter to show your values in action.

Start by empathizing with her and saying you can understand why she would want only the people she likes best at her party and that she wants it to be nice, but that it's very important that she makes decisions that are inclusive and respectful to others. Don't force her to invite certain girls, but encourage her to explore how she'd feel if she were left out. Suggest she do something less grandiose so she can invite more kids rather than do something exclusive. Make up the guest list together and stick to it. If a delegate comes to her on someone's behalf and your daughter changes her mind and invites Ana, be aware that it usually backfires. For example, Ana might come to the party only to have your daughter be mean to her because she was "forced" to invite her. Then you have that horrible experience of hanging out with Ana in the kitchen waiting for one of her parents to pick her up and glare at you for being a bad parent.

If your daughter is a Wannabe and she's the birthday girl, the Queen Bee and Sidekick may look like they're deferring to her when making up the guest list. Don't be fooled. This is a tactic. They'll almost certainly try to get your daughter to exclude people they don't like or pressure her to invite boys. Please understand that no matter how mature and kind she is, if she's having a party or going somewhere like a concert, there's very little chance she'll be able to control herself from talking about it at school. You can't invite everyone to everything, and girls have to accept that they aren't going to be invited to everything all the time. That said, there have to be some general rules for navigating these situations. Here are mine.

When distributing invitations, encourage your daughter to mail them—the old-fashioned way. Yes, I know it's way more time-consuming than doing an e-vite, but it's better to do it old-school—it will decrease the drama because the girls can't forward them to each other.

This is what I would say to her:

1. *I expect you to keep the talking about your party to a minimum. I know I can't control every word that comes out of your mouth, but I need you to be aware that other people may feel hurt or excluded because they weren't invited. You're allowed to invite friends, but you aren't allowed to make others feel bad in the process. This is my law.*

2. *I expect you to honor both the spirit and letter of the law. This means you can't do anything obnoxious like obviously try to cover up that you're talking about the party with your invited friends by falling silent, starting to whisper, or running away*

when someone who wasn't invited comes up to you. I consider that unacceptable behavior.

3. *If I find out that you have used this party, which is my gift to you, to make someone feel bad, I will cancel it. (If you issue this threat, you must make good on it, no matter how your child whines, apologizes, or promises to never do it again.)**

During the party, it's equally important that she be gracious to all her guests, meaning she's not allowed to invite people and then ignore them at the party, nor intimate that they're only there because "Mom said I had to invite you" or "Dad made me ask all the kids." I would also consider holding all the guests' cell phones in a designated place during the party so they can't be used to take embarrassing pictures of other kids or send mean texts to each other. If they need to use them to call their parents, they can always come get them from you—and then return them.

Of all the parents in this "uninvited to the party" scenario, Mary's parents have the most difficulty discovering her role in the situation. If you find out what's going on, the primary question you should help her figure out is her motivation: Is she getting in the middle because she feels bad that Ana isn't invited or because it makes her feel important as a Messenger? If she's the star of the story, she's more likely to intervene to solidify her position in the clique. You both should ask yourselves why it's important for her to be in this role of Messenger and "star." If her description centers on her empathy for Ana, then you have a great opportunity to ask her questions about what she gains from being invited and going (she feels popular)? What she loses (is she making decisions based on popularity or on her friend's feelings)?

If you're Ana's parent, you should respond to your daughter's exclusion with your version of "I'm so sorry, thank you for telling me, what would you like to do about it?" This is also a good time to share a personal story if this ever happened to you. By the way, this is one of those times when your daughter might share something with you but doesn't need anything done about it. She just wants to vent. She doesn't want you getting on the phone with

*This is from *Queen Bee Moms and Kingpin Dads*.

the birthday girl's parent and begging for an invitation. *Nor should you.* Under no circumstances should you call the parents of the party girl to angle for an invitation. If you do this, you are teaching your daughter that social status is more important than her personal dignity and that parental love is based on her social value. As painful as it is to see your daughter excluded and as bad as she feels about it, *it's more important to affirm her ability to cope.* When the party day arrives, do something with her that she wants to do so she's reminded that there's life outside the party. Now, if your daughter wants to use SEAL to address the birthday girl (e.g., if they have been friends for a long time and she is really surprised and hurt that she's not invited) this is what she can say:

YOUR DAUGHTER: This is really uncomfortable for me to admit, but I know you're having a party and you didn't invite me.

BIRTHDAY GIRL: Well, my mom said I could only have like four people (or other excuses).

YOUR DAUGHTER: I'm not talking to you so you feel guilty and invite me. But I was pretty surprised. I just wanted to ask you if there's something I did that made you not want to include me.

Then, she needs to be prepared to listen and apologize, if appropriate (but no groveling to ingratiate herself to the birthday girl), because she may hear that she's doing something hurtful to the other girl that led to her making the decision. Remember, the goal is not to get an invitation. Instead, the goal is to think through the problem and address it.

THE THIRD WHEEL: DIVIDED LOYALTIES AND THE TAGALONG

Jennifer and Kimber are in sixth grade and very good friends. Sometimes they play with Sara, a girl who really wants to be in their group. Kimber and Sara used to be really good friends, but now Kimber thinks Sara is boring. Jennifer invites Kimber to her house for a sleepover on Saturday night. Sara overhears them talking about it and asks if she can come. Jennifer tells Sara that she's sick of her and that she should make her own friends. Kimber doesn't like what Jennifer said to Sara, but she doesn't say anything.

On Sunday morning after the sleepover, Jennifer and Kimber are playing when Jennifer's mother marches into the room, obviously angry, and asks to speak to Jennifer alone. Right outside the room, Jennifer's mother tells her that Sara's mother called her and told her what happened at school. Jennifer's mother is really angry with Jennifer and she's now forbidden from having sleepovers for a month. The first thing Jennifer does is to complain to Kimber.

JENNIFER: Can you believe what Sara did? She cries to her mom and now I get into trouble. This sucks!

KIMBER: Yeah, I can't believe it.

On Monday, Jennifer and Kimber are walking down the hall at school when they see Sara.

JENNIFER: Sara, what did you think you were doing? You ran to your mom so I would get into trouble! My mom thinks I wouldn't let you come over because that's what your mom said. Now I can't have anyone over ever again!

SARA: What are you talking about?

JENNIFER: Don't pretend like you don't know what I'm talking about.

SARA: I'm sorry. I didn't know. I mean, I'm so sorry. I was upset but I told my mom not to tell anyone. What can I do to make it up to you?

JENNIFER: You already did enough damage. Come on, Kimber, let's go.

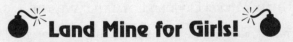

Land Mine for Girls!

Don't use the word *annoying*—as in "You're so annoying!"—when you're telling someone you're mad. Why? Because there are a million different things a person can do to be annoying. So in order to stop the behavior they have to know what they're doing.

Using the grid again, let's break down each girl's role.

	Sara	Kimber	Jennifer
Feelings	Excluded, rejected, upset, maybe angry	Depends on what kind of bystander she is: torn would feel guilty, powerful would feel justified and angry	Angry and defensive; wants to put Sara "in her place"
Motivations	Wants to be liked and is hurt by the other girls' rejection	Torn between friendships and doing the "right" thing	Got in trouble; doesn't want to be forced to be Sara's friend
Likely result	She'll apologize to the group, change her personality to fit with the group, or find other friends	Weakens friendship with Sara	Bullies Sara to stop hanging out with them and bullies Kimber to follow her lead
What she learns	She'll get in trouble if she admits that her feelings are hurt or confronts powerful girls; won't talk to her mom again	Jennifer is a strong Queen Bee; don't cross her	Bullying people works
Makes herself proud	Stands up for herself by telling both girls how their actions make her feel; walks away proud of herself; knows that she should make new friends because the old ones come at too high a price	Tells Jennifer she doesn't like how she treated Sara and gives suggestions for handling the situation better	Takes responsibility for her behavior and apologizes to both Sara and Kimber

If you're Sara's parent: In this situation, Sara has learned that people in positions of power can bully weaker people and that if the victim of the bully "tells," it'll come back on her. Remember, as I said in Chapter 2, kids often believe that if an adult gets involved, the situation will get worse. When a parent finds out their child has been slighted, they sometimes forget what kids know well: if you get the bully in trouble, at some point she'll find you and no one will be around to help. In this situation, involvement should be limited to strategizing with her about what she wants to do and then affirming that she has the strength to carry it out by herself. It's a fine line because your daughter needs to know that you're watching her back, but she also needs to know that you have confidence in her ability to take care of herself. That means not calling the other girl's parents to complain about your daughter's exclusion and keeping her complaints to yourself when she confides in you. If you keep trying to fix life for her, she'll think that she can't do it herself, or that she can't trust you with her feelings. This becomes proof that going to you makes the problem worse.

Your first step, as always, is to empathize with your daughter. It hurts to be excluded, especially if you're put down as a tagalong. It's hard to admit that other girls see your daughter as a nuisance. But, if she is, you need to talk to her about it. Otherwise, sixth through eighth grade will be even more painful for her. Review your daughter's Bill of Rights with Friends (see later) with her. Ask her if she knew that Kimber and Jennifer felt this way about her. If she did, why does she still want to hang out with them?

The hardest question that both you and your daughter need to think about is why is this happening? Whatever the answer to that is, the next question is equally difficult. For example, if your daughter is annoying her friends because she's not as into boys as they are, is this something she wants to change about herself? I would say no. She should be interested in boys at her own pace and in her own time. On the other hand, if your daughter is annoying because she interrupts people and is constantly getting in people's business, that may be something she needs to look at and change.

It's critical to get your daughter to understand the difference between her actions and her personality. She might want to change how she acts, but she shouldn't try to change who she is. Talk out why she thinks she and Kimber grew apart. Are they into different things? If so, is Sara feeling any pressure to "catch up" to Kimber's interests? Remind her that every girl has her own schedule, and that Sara shouldn't give in to pressure to fake being into boys, clothes, or whatever else Kimber thinks is a more "mature" interest. At the same time, Sara needs to recognize that it's fair for Kimber to have her own interests and to want to hang out with girls who share them. She shouldn't ask Jennifer to invite her, but she can tell Kimber how she feels when she's left out. And she needs to do it in person, not by texting, e-mailing, or IMing. For example:

SARA: Kimber, can I talk to you for a minute?

KIMBER: Sure . . . what's up? (She probably knows something's up.)

SARA: This is hard to say, but I'm pretty sure that you don't want to hang out with me as much as you used to and I want to know if we can talk about it?

KIMBER: That's so not true! I don't know what you're talking about!

SARA: I'm not saying this to make you feel bad, I just want to talk about it because you're a good friend. Can you tell me why you don't want to hang out? I promise I'll do my best to listen to what you're saying.

Please remember that Sara doesn't have to say everything perfectly in this conversation, and she may not get the response from Kimber she wants. Encourage her to tell Kimber politely and directly how she feels and that real friendships are built on people honestly and respectfully communicating face-to-face, even when what's being said is hard to hear. That said, she also needs to prepare herself for hearing something that may make her feel bad, but she's learning and implementing social skills that enable her to take care of herself.

It's painful to realize that a friendship may be ending, but remind your daughter that a lot of friendships have natural ups and downs, and that she and Kimber might be more in sync later. On the other hand, if Kimber is more interested in being part of a clique than being a good friend, Sara needs to assess whether this is a friendship worth trying to keep.

If you're Kimber's parent: What would you want Kimber to do in this situation? Girls do have the right to choose their friends. They just don't have the right to make the girl they don't like feel like dirt in the process. On the other hand, a girl can be too "nice." Of course, you want your daughter to be kind to others, but you don't want her to feel that she must always put other people's needs before her own. Being too much of a "people pleaser" can lead to people taking advantage of her.

Even if you don't agree with what she did, empathize with her first and let her raise her initial defense on her own. See it from her perspective and don't show anger that she hasn't done the "right thing." These situations are complex and demand your thoughtfulness. During adolescence, girls' loyalties are frequently divided. If Kimber sides with Sara, she'll earn Sara's undying loyalty, but she'll "betray" Jennifer. Betraying Jennifer makes her extremely vulnerable, because Jennifer will seek revenge by getting other girls to gang up on and exclude her. If she betrays Sara, there's no social liability, and most likely Sara will forgive her later. If you were twelve, in Kimber's situation, dealing with Jennifer and her friends all day, every day, what would you do? Going with Jennifer is often the only answer that makes sense. Jennifer is intimidating. Acknowledge how hard it is to stand up to someone who seems to hold all the cards.

Your next step is to get Kimber to take responsibility for her actions. Girls are masters at convincing themselves that their bad behavior is a result of someone else's actions. Jennifer believes she never would have been in that situation if Sara hadn't complained to her mother. Almost anyone in Kimber's position will back down and do anything to stay in the good graces of the powerful girl in the group. The girls' social hierarchy supports Jennifer's denial of responsibility because the other girls won't challenge it and the parents aren't there to know what really happened.

Girls always get angry with the person in Sara's position, but it's just a diversionary tactic. Don't let your daughter get away with it. This is a great time to teach your daughter about the need to treat others with respect. She needs to admit that she should have stood up for Sara. Then, ask her about Jennifer. Does she want to be a person other people push around? Does she want to be a person who says nothing when another person is bullied? Ask her how she would like to handle the situation in the future. Encourage her to talk through with you what she would like to say to Jennifer and Sara.

If she's really brave, the best thing she can do is apologize to Sara in front of Jennifer (see Chapter 6 for more on apologies). She should say to Jennifer that she didn't feel right about what happened to Sara (don't say "what Jennifer did to Sara" because, first, Jennifer will get defensive, and, second, Kimber needs to take responsibility for her actions that backed up Jennifer).

If you're Jennifer's parent: You may be angry and embarrassed, but focus your energy on what lessons Jennifer can learn from this experience. Because another parent is blaming your child for bad behavior, it's easy to feel that your parenting skills are being questioned. Take Jennifer's behavior seriously, but also look at this as part of the unfortunate yet realistic parenting process. Thank Sara's mom for telling you and apologize for Jennifer's behavior. Then, get Jennifer's side of the story (which will likely initially focus on how she was pushed to be mean because Sara wasn't listening to her). Empathize: "There's nothing wrong with wanting to spend time with Kimber alone, but that doesn't excuse or justify treating Sara the way you did." Just as if you were Kimber's parent, emphasize that it doesn't matter how she feels about Sara, because it was wrong to be cruel. Tell her how you want her to act instead: "You don't have to be friends with everyone, but that doesn't justify being mean to people. The next time you are in this situation, I want you to first ask yourself why hanging out with this person is such a problem. What is making you not want to be with her? What is making you want to show her that you don't like her?" Ask her to call Sara to apologize for her rudeness (see the "Art of the Apology" in Chapter 6) and follow up to make sure she did. Have her call Kimber, too, and apologize for putting her in the middle. Last, say something like, "I know you might be mad at Sara for telling on you, but I don't want to find out you're making her life worse because of this."

BFF: BEST FRIENDS FOREVER OR A DAY?

I'm convinced that the best-friend relationships girls have can be the most intense relationships girls will ever have and that nothing can threaten these friendships more than power plays.

Other girls and boys perceive BFFs as living in their own world. They have their own language and codes. They wear each other's clothes. They may even have crushes at the same time on the same person (that may seem strange, but what better way to start exploring the scary boy-girl world than with your best friend?). It's common that they'll break up around seventh grade (if not before) when one wants to expand her social horizons.

From then on, they may make up, then break up, then make up again. Sometimes it becomes a friendship where they only hang out one-on-one when they're at each other's house, but the minute they're around their peers, one of them will barely recognize the existence of the other. Or worse, she'll be mean.

> *I have a friend who is so nice to me when I'm alone with her but in public she's so mean. The problem is our parents are friends. I like to be with her alone but I'm sick of her other side.* —Kelly, 13

Sometimes your daughter will be the dumper, sometimes the dumpee. When your daughter is on the outs with her friend, discourage her from demonizing her friend or the friendship by focusing only on the negatives, and don't you do it either, because where will you be when they're back together next week? Again, remind your daughter that friendships have a natural ebb and flow, and that she doesn't need to burn her bridges behind her. Help her appreciate that people can grow apart and still be genuinely nice. Don't minimize her broken heart over a lost friendship. Emphasize the importance of talking one-on-one and not relying on e-mail and texts. It's always better to face these situations in person; this way, not as much is "lost in translation." There's little you can do to "fix" the situation, but this is your chance to hone your listening skills and help your daughter realize she can survive the pain and difficulties of the situations that naturally arise from these kinds of relationships.

EXILED FROM THE PROMISED LAND

It all started in October. I began to feel left out of my group. One of the girls in the group, Brittany, was moving, and I wanted to be closer to her before she left. Every time I went near her, she ran away. I was very upset. So I expressed my feelings to her. She told me that I was following her. I agreed, I was. After we talked, I was happy because I thought I wouldn't be left out again. I was wrong. Then a soccer teammate of Brittany's told me she saw Brittany and my friend Brianna imitate me before their soccer game.

I decided I would hang out with Kim. The next day, I went to lunch with my head high, but when I walked into the cafeteria, Brittany and the other girls in my group were taking up all the seats. I was very hurt by what the girls did. I cried uncontrollably. I just couldn't stop crying. When I talked to the guidance counselor, she suggested that we talk to one of Brittany's best friends, Krista. Krista was one of my close friends, too. Krista offered to have a party inviting Brittany and the others that were in my group. At the party, Brittany and I apologized to each other and we're now friends again. The party turned out so well that I looked forward to Monday.

The next day at school, nothing had changed. Brittany, Krista, and the others in the group were still sitting at the opposite side of the table. So I said to Kim, "Fine! Let them sit there, I don't need them." And to this day, I have not talked to any girl in the group. Kim has stuck by me during the hardest time of my life. I'll always have eternal gratitude for Kim. She's a true friend.

—Amy, 14

You're in. No, you're out. One day your daughter will go to school and her group of friends will have decided that she's no longer one of them. Or it may happen to one of her best friends in the clique.

The reasons may look superficial to you—maybe she has the same shoes as the Queen Bee and everyone knows the Queen Bee told everyone else not to copy her because purple Pumas are *her* signature item; maybe your daughter's hanging out with the "wrong" person, she took the "wrong side" against a Queen Bee or Side-kick, and/or she committed some other act of high treason. Some-times there's no easily identifiable reason except that the leaders of the group decide she no longer belongs. Whenever and whyever it happens, it's devastating. Girls come away from these experiences learning that girls—even the ones you think are your true-blue friends—can turn on you on a whim. As is the case here, this is also a time when girls can learn the meaning of true friendship.

Amy's mom told me her daughter's seventh-grade year was completely horrible. She watched her daughter go from being rel-atively happy to miserable. Here's how I would help Amy and her mom break down what happened so Amy (with her mom's guid-ance) could figure out the best next steps. I spoke to Amy's mom on the subject. She is honest in her assessment of her daughter ("She can be bossy and sometimes self-righteous"), but compas-sionate as well. She talked openly with her daughter and sup-ported her. She even called Brittany's mom because she thought Amy might have contributed to the problem. Unfortunately, Brit-tany's mom chose to act more like Brittany. For more information on how to talk to other parents, see Chapter 6, but suffice it to say that these are difficult yet critical conversations to have. You'll be more effective if you approach the other parent as an ally and re-source than you would as an attacker.

If you're Krista's parent: When a counselor has a good idea of the power dynamics and the pattern of the relationship between the girls, sometimes it can be effective to bring the girls together for a facilitated discussion. But, in this situation, it wasn't a good idea to bring Amy and Krista (instead of Brittany) together. Doing so sends the message that Brittany is either operating below adult radar or is above the law. As a result, Krista's party became an op-portunity for Brittany to steamroll over the other girls and call all the shots. If your daughter is in Krista's position and asks you if she can have this party, she may feel so excited about being the social nexus that she'll tell you what's up. If it's clear that she's doing this mainly to cement her social status, nix the party. If Krista explains that she was only trying to patch things up between Amy and Brittany, ask her why she joined Brittany in snubbing Amy at school. You need to get her to admit to herself what she is getting out of this situation. (Girls are never nicer to each other than when they're fighting with someone else.)

If you're Brittany's parent: Brittany may be feeling anxious because she's moving—but, even though that may be a reason for her behavior, it doesn't justify it. Maybe she snubbed Amy because she wanted to confirm that her status as Queen Bee is secure; that is, she's doing it just to prove that she can. In your discussions with her, talk about what's making her feel anxious and out of control. Your job is to make her see the connection between what she's anxious about and the things she's doing to feel more in control. Empathize with her about what's motivating her to act out in this way. Then, insist she apologize to Amy. Follow up to make sure she not only made the apology, but also is continuing to act consistently afterward. (Freezing Amy out at school clearly violates the spirit of the apology.) Watch out for this: many girls agree to a truce or reconciliation and then start a war all over again as soon as they get the opportunity.

THE BETTER OFFER: BLOWING EACH OTHER OFF

Amber and Michelle are in high school. They used to hang out all the time, but recently they haven't been spending as much time together because their interests are changing and they're hanging out with different groups—Amber is hanging out with the more popular group, while Michelle still hangs out with their old group. Amber likes Michelle, but when she's with her, she feels as if she's missing out on the fun things her new group likes to do.

Amber and Michelle make plans to hang out on a Saturday night. Michelle is supposed to come over at 7:00. At 5:00, one of

Amber's new friends, Nicole, calls her and asks her to go to the movies. She also tells Amber that Will, a really hot guy in the group, is interested in her; he's going to the movies, too.

At this point, Amber has three options.

1. She can tell Nicole she wishes she could go, but she already has plans with Michelle. She tells Nicole to have a good time without her.
2. She can blow off Michelle with a lie and go with Nicole.
3. She can try to have her cake and eat it by getting Nicole to invite Michelle to the movies, too.

I've role-played this scenario hundreds of times with girls in my classes and I've had only a few stick to the plans with Michelle. About 20 percent invite Michelle along, and the rest lie. There usually isn't a moment of hesitation before they decide to lie, and the lie usually blames the mother: "My mom is so mean! She won't let me go out because I have to do chores for her/ babysit/finish my homework." ("My grandmother died" is another popular option, which never ceases to amaze me—don't these girls think the truth will come out?)

Whichever choice they make, girls learn critical lessons from this situation.

- If Amber sticks with her original plan to hang out with Michelle, Nicole may not respect that Amber is doing the right thing. Consequently, if Amber stays, she may resent Michelle for "keeping her down" and worry that Nicole will think she's not cool enough to hang out with again. Amber learns that "doing the right thing" isn't all it's cracked up to be, no matter what her parents may say.
- If Amber lies, Michelle will usually find out about it. (In our role-playing, we make the girls run into each other at the movies so that they learn that if you lie, you usually get caught.) Michelle will think that Amber is two-faced, but she'll also be confused about what she should do about it; would she have done the same thing in that situation?

Michelle may not have the same social aspirations, but it's a clear indication that Amber has been anointed by the powers that be (Nicole), so it will be harder for Michelle to confront Amber now that her value on the social index has increased.

- Nicole brings a person like Amber into her group for a reason. Amber is most likely a Pleaser/Wannabe or Torn Bystander. Michelle is hurt and rightfully angry at being blown off, but the social pecking order is reinforced. Michelle learns that she should try to change herself to be more like Amber and Nicole so she won't get left behind. If she tells Amber how she feels about being blown off, Amber will probably accuse her of jealousy, so Michelle learns to keep her mouth shut.

- Nicole, despite her high social status, often feels that the only way to maintain friendships is to make people prove themselves to her. She's just as trapped as everyone else, maybe more so. Girls in Nicole's position can get so caught up in maintaining their high status that they may not even develop a solid sense of self to lose in the first place.

Let's diagram the situation:

	Michelle	Amber	Nicole
Feelings	Betrayed, rejected, and angry	Confused, defensive, and flattered by Nicole's attention	Say what? Amber should feel grateful she's being accepted into the group
Motivations	Wants things to go back to the way they used to be with Amber	Wants the status of hanging out with Nicole and the attention of the guy	Wants to demonstrate her power
Likely result	Gets into a fight with Amber where she has to justify her feelings and then gives up on Amber	Couches any apology by accusing Michelle of being jealous and holding her back	Dismisses Amber's friendship with Michelle and flatters Amber with more attention
What she learns	Popularity is more important to Amber than their friendship	She can't have friendships with Michelle and Nicole; she has to choose one	She's in control of Amber
Makes herself proud	Talks to Amber and responds effectively to the accusation of jealousy. She feels good about how she handled herself.	Apologizes to Michelle and decides which friendship she wants and why. Is able to stand up to Nicole.	Realizes that she's making people choose her over others. Apologizes and stops.

If you're Michelle's parent: Don't make her feel better by talking about how badly Amber or Nicole behaved. You need to help your daughter feel better about herself because she is who she is, not by putting someone else down. (Besides, chances are you'll come home in a week and see Amber hanging out with Michelle and then she'll worry that you don't like Amber.) Acknowledge how difficult this is right now, but point out that in the long run, her situation is probably less difficult than Amber's. Michelle doesn't have to change herself to be accepted by her real friends; Amber does.

Encourage Michelle to tell Amber how she feels and brainstorm how to respond if Amber tells her she's just being jealous. ("I know you think I'm jealous, but that's not the issue here. The issue is that we agreed we were going to hang out. Good friends don't blow each other off the second a better offer comes along.")

If you're Amber's parent: The biggest problem you have is a daughter who's willing to do things against her better judgment to increase her social status. Acknowledge that Nicole may be more fun to hang out with, but she needs to keep any commitment she makes, regardless of whether a better offer comes along. Ask her what she's giving up in the process. If she says, "Nothing," review her Bill of Rights for Friends (page 260). What does she want and expect from her friendship with Nicole? Can she be herself with Nicole or does she edit herself to please Nicole? If she assures you that Nicole is a really good friend, don't press the issue, because you don't want her to feel she has to defend Nicole to you. Let her think about it on her own.

If Amber were your daughter, there's a chance you'd know about her plans with Michelle. If she changes her plans to go with Nicole, she has to figure out how to get past you (because you'd make her keep her plans with Michelle). You become the biggest obstacle in her way, and she might lie to get around you. Once she lies, you won't know where she is and/or who she's with. It's at this point, when Amber may feel more secure in the life raft than ever, that she's actually swimming in shark-infested waters because she's with friends who aren't going to respect her boundaries—even if she articulates them, which is doubtful because she doesn't want to be uptight.

In any case, Amber owes Michelle an apology, and if at all possible, she should tell Nicole how she feels. If she went with Nicole and blew off Michelle, then she needs to tell Nicole: "Look, I need to tell you that I made a big mistake. When you invited me out, I actually had already made plans with Michelle and I blew her off. I feel bad about it and I don't want to do that again. So next time, I'd like to invite Michelle."

If she invited Michelle along and Nicole was mean to her, then she needs to tell Nicole that she won't hang out with her if she's going to treat other people like that. Rest assured, there's a selfish reason to do this, because if Amber stands up to Nicole now, Nicole will be a lot less likely to turn on her later. You need to impress upon her that there's real danger in trying to please everyone around you all the time, because it usually results in pleasing no one and losing yourself in the process.

If you're Nicole's parent: Your daughter will appear in control. Do some soul-searching before talking to her. What motivates her to build and sustain friendships like this? She didn't technically do anything wrong, she just tried to persuade a friend to hang out with her. But when I do this role-play in class, the Nicoles can be very convincing because they make Amber feel like she's losing out on the opportunity of a lifetime. It's often presented as a choice that's not a choice: either you can come with me and you'll have the keys to the kingdom, or you can stay home and spend forty years in the social desert. You need to hold her accountable for her behavior (and perhaps hold yourself accountable for encouraging it, too. Are you perhaps a little too invested in your daughter's popularity?). If you're convinced that your daughter is inviting Michelle along to be inclusive, that's something to be proud of.

THE AMBUSH

In the world we live in, your daughter's power plays are frequently played out on a virtual platform. The conversation below is just one example—keep in mind that all of the preceding scenarios could have occurred online as well. I hope you can see exactly why online conflicts can be so much worse than conflicts in person. Online, conflicts are all consuming. All of a sudden, your heart races as you wait to see what happens next.

Your daughter, Zoe, is sitting at the family computer doing her homework when she receives an instant message.

SXXYDIVA (Olivia): heyy, there r some things i thnk u should kno.
GLITTERGIRL (Zoe): what r u talking about?

SXXYDIVA: no offense, but every1 thinks ur totally throwing urself on Derek.

GLITTERGIRL: why can't u just leave me alone?

SXXYDIVA: im just doing this for ur own good. id wanna know if ppl were talking behind my back.

GLITTERGIRL: whatever, I could tell u things too.

SXXYDIVA: really? what could a fat, ugly loser like u possibly tell me that id care about?

GLITTERGIRL: im not going to say.

SXXYDIVA: exactly. y do u even value yr life? its not like anyone wd care if u killed urself.

This is how Zoe would SEAL it—offline and in person. With your guidance, she'd strategize where to confront Olivia. Zoe remembers that Olivia is usually in the art room fifth period without her friends.

ZOE: Can I talk to you?

OLIVIA: (Pretending she has no idea.) Sure, what's up?

ZOE: You said a lot of mean things to me last night, like I was fat, ugly, and I should kill myself. I want you to stop.

OLIVIA: What? I have no idea what you're talking about.

ZOE: You're telling me that you didn't send me any instant messages last night?

OLIVIA: Seriously.

ZOE: Well, whether you did or someone else did with your account, I'm asking you to stop. If you're mad at me, then don't attack me online. Tell me to my face and we'll work it out. But no matter what, I have the right to not have people telling me I should kill myself.

OLIVIA: Sure. I have no idea what you're talking about, but whatever you say. (Rolls her eyes.)

By calling someone out in the daylight with your voice and real words, you take the conflict out of that imaginary space. That person who said things online they'd never say in real life is faced with the reality of their language, making much more powerful that person's speaking out against it. Even if the girl doesn't acknowledge the truth, she'll hear the message.

> *She'd be pretty ballsy to keep going. If she did, I guarantee it's*
> *from a completely different username.*   —*Emily, 17*

THE VOICE MAIL BOMB

Emily has a really good point that most parents rarely consider. Girls will use fake names, set up other accounts, or use someone else's account to hide their identities.

Naomi is good friends with Caitlyn, but there are some things Caitlyn does that she really doesn't like—but Naomi's never told her. The most recent thing Caitlyn did was get really mad at another girl in their class named Eliza. In front of Naomi, Caitlyn disguised her voice and left a really bad message on Eliza's voice mail. Caitlyn ended the message by laughing and saying, "Just kidding!" Here's the SEAL:

NAOMI: I've been thinking a lot about the voice mail you left on Eliza's phone.

CAITLYN: And . . .

NAOMI: You shouldn't have done it.

CAITLYN: Well, you were standing right there, and I didn't see you try to stop me. In fact, you seemed to think it was funny.

NAOMI: I was wrong, too. If it looked like I was laughing, it was because I was too uncomfortable to tell you to stop. But I thought about it later, and that was a mistake. I should have told you right away. But that doesn't take away from the fact that you shouldn't have done it.

CAITLYN: Whatever. I had no idea how ridiculously uptight you are. It was just a joke.

NAOMI: Caitlyn, it would have been way easier not to say anything and just keep this to myself, but I think we are better friends than that. I'm going to apologize to Eliza.

CAITLYN: If you do that, I'm never talking to you again.

NAOMI: I can't control what you do, but I'm not going to let
    Eliza feel miserable.

As a Bystander's parent, your responsibility to your daughter is
to help her recognize the challenges in this situation yet point out
the ethical responsibility she has to acknowledge her own behavior and speak out. Remember that most Bystanders believe if they
don't protest in the moment, they have lost their credibility to
come forward—especially if they have done something that either
appears to or actually does back up the bullying—like laughing
does here. But the truth is, when Bystanders speak out, including
against their own actions, their words have even more power.

FISHING FOR COMPLIMENTS

Clara is your daughter's good friend. Recently, though, Clara has
been getting on your daughter's nerves because she is always complaining about how fat and ugly she is. For months, your daughter
has tried to reassure Clara about her appearance, but nothing she
says makes Clara feel better. Your daughter comes to you complaining about Clara and says she's really tempted the next time
she puts herself down to agree with her. Worse, your daughter tells
you hanging out with Clara is making her question her own
weight and appearance.

Ask your daughter, "What do you think is motivating Clara?
Why does she say she's fat when she's not?" (If your daughter says,
"She's insecure," dig deeper to find out what lies behind this inse-
curity.) Ask her to describe the physical feeling she has when
Clara starts putting herself down and your daughter gets annoyed.
Have her think about the place and time she could talk to Clara
with the best chance of her listening.

Here's a sample SEAL dialogue you and your daughter can use
as a starting place to create her own.

Stop and think about her feelings and strategy.

YOUR DAUGHTER: Clara, I need to talk to you about some-
    thing important.

CLARA: Okay, sure. Are you mad at me or something?

YOUR DAUGHTER: No, I'm not mad at you, but I need to talk to you about the things you say about yourself.

CLARA: Okay . . .

YOUR DAUGHTER (Explain): When you say you're fat or put yourself down about how you look, I tell you you're not, but it doesn't make a difference. I want you to feel good about yourself, but I don't want to feel like I have to do this all the time.

CLARA: I'm sorry. I'm sorry. I know it's so stupid.

YOUR DAUGHTER (Affirm/Lock): Don't apologize for feeling bad. As your friend, I want to be able to help you and I think the best way to do that is to figure out what's going to work here beyond the two of us. Who do you think could help?

CHECKING YOUR BAGGAGE

- When you were your daughter's age, did you blow friends off if a better option came along?
- What and how have you communicated your values about friendships and commitment to your daughter?
- What do you think your daughter would say if I asked her the same question about you?
- Do you have close friendships where you can tell people when you're upset with them and they'll respect what you're saying?
- How do you handle power plays when you see them occurring in your own life?

WHAT YOU CAN DO TO ALLEVIATE THE FRUSTRATION OF POWER PLAYS

You may feel that it's not worth making a federal case of not getting invited to a birthday party or letting your daughter blow off one friend for another. You may have heard someone say, "We need to let the girls work it out." Remember, involvement isn't all or nothing. You don't want to micromanage them. You don't want to fight their fights for them. But you have to be behind the scenes using these opportunities to show what you stand for as a parent. These may seem like trivial issues, but they aren't. They lay the groundwork for girls faking their feelings, pretending to be someone they're not, pleasing others at their own expense, or otherwise sacrificing self-esteem and authenticity. The skirmishes that in earlier years are limited to hurt feelings can transition into parents' worst fears: vulnerability to drinking, drugs, and bad relationships. You can use these early power plays to help your daughter figure out why it's worthwhile to be true to herself and to think through what real friendship is all about.

You should also appreciate that sometimes the values you teach your daughter will be in conflict with the way she feels she needs to act to feel comfortable in her clique. Let's suppose that you've always taught her that championing the underdog is the right thing to do and that she should stick up for people who are being bullied or picked on. If your daughter stands up for an unpopular girl and the result is that her friends in the clique are angry at her, she's bound to feel burned by your teaching her to do the right thing. To her, she only ends up feeling punished. She needs to know that you understand how she feels. Acknowledge that sometimes, doing the right thing will bring her grief in the short term, but in the long term, it's more important to be true to her character and values. Tell her you're proud that she took the rougher road and that sooner or later, she'll feel just as proud of her actions as you do.

This is how I explain it to my students:

I'm not going to lie to you and say people are going to thank you for doing the right thing. If you complain about this stuff, people very well may turn on you. They may make your life more difficult. This is absolutely true. You have to decide what price you would rather pay. If you decide to speak out, the price will possibly be some kind of social rejection, but you will know that the people who stand by you are your true and loyal friends and that you treated yourself and others with dignity when it was hard. If you decide to say nothing, people won't get in your face. Things will be calm on the outside. But there is a cost and it is your dignity. Another cost is people being able to take advantage of you or believing that even if you don't like something going down, you won't say anything about it. It's up to you to decide which price is higher.

Talk to your daughter about what she should expect to give and get from her friendships with others. Every friendship will have its ups and downs, so there are benefits to encouraging your daughter to take a longer view so she doesn't burn all her bridges. That said, you should help her identify patterns of inconsiderate behavior that suggest she rethink the relationship. Help her clarify her expectations with the Bill of Rights for Friends.

Bill of Rights for Friends

- What does she want and need in a friendship? (Trust, reliability, loyalty, telling you when they're angry with you in a respectful way)
- What are her rights in a friendship? (To be treated respectfully, with kindness and honesty)
- What are her responsibilities in a friendship? (To treat her friends ethically)
- What would a friend have to do or be like for her to end the friendship? (Not listen to her, not honor her values and ethics)
- Under what circumstances would she go to an adult for help with a problem with a friend? (When the problem feels too big to handle alone)
- What are her friends' rights and responsibilities in the friendship? (To listen even when it's not easy to hear)

Then, ask the hardest question: How do her experiences with her friends compare to her Bill of Rights? If they aren't similar, why does she have those friendships?

If and when your daughter makes the decision that her friend(s) aren't right for her, it'll be a very lonely time for her. She may know that she has made the right decision in ending a friendship, but that'll be only a small comfort. It takes incredible strength of character to decide to break up with a friend who doesn't respect her Bill of Rights and even more strength to remain resolute. Praise her courage. I present some examples from my teaching on how to do this in the next section.

What If and How Do You . . .

Following are common "What if" and "How do you . . ."questions girls ask me when I am teaching them about the role of power plays.

What if one of your really good friends is someone everyone talks bad about but if you stand up for her everyone will hate you too?

This is a particularly difficult situation because it feels like there's no way to win. First I would begin with baby steps. The next time someone trashes your friend, pretend there is something really interesting about ten feet away from the group and go over to it. This is another way of my saying, "Walk away." If you get a text, e-mail, voice mail, or instant message trashing your friend, train your brain and your fingers to immediately press delete—no matter how much you "really just want to find out what they're saying." Just try it once and see if you can actually do it. Once you have accomplished those two goals, you can start preparing for the second goal, which is to talk privately to the person who is the most focused on hating your friend. Then you would use SEAL.

What is the best way to approach a friend who you feel doesn't like you anymore?

You can't make people like you. So I think you initially back off a little and give your friend some space, for about a week. Then the beginning of the second week you are casually friendly with the person. Like "Hey, what's up?" when you see her in the hall, in class, or at lunch. After a couple of days of that, if you still want to, I'd ask her to hang out and see how she responds. If you do hang out and you have a good time, then that's good and you can think about putting energy into maintaining the friendship. If it doesn't go well, then you've given yourself some space from the last couple of weeks' break so it'll be easier to walk away.

What if I feel like I can't trust people because they'll make fun of me. But I have so much on my chest. What do I do?
Just like it's not good to distrust all people, it's not good to trust all people. So overall, it's never good to make judgments that begin with "all . . . and always," because both are rarely true. What you need to do is write a list of any people you think are trustworthy and slowly build relationships with them—both people your own age and adults. From that list you need to find someone you feel comfortable sharing your problems with.

What do I do if I have a friend who constantly embarrasses me in front of other people?
You have to give the friend one chance to seriously tell her how you feel. So the next time it happens, wait until you are alone with that person and say:

> YOU: Remember two hours ago when you teased me in front of those guys about how awkward I was in front of my ex? It seriously has to stop. I know I laughed but I did that because I didn't know what to say at the time because I was so frustrated.
> FRIEND: I didn't mean anything by it. It was nothing!
> YOU: It wasn't nothing to me so please listen to me about it because otherwise it's really hard to hang out with you and not worry about what you're going to say.
> FRIEND: Fine . . .
> YOU: Thanks, so did you like the movie . . .

And if they still do it, I seriously think it's time to "lock out" the friendship. Or at least take a vacation.

How do you tell a good friend that her new "best friend" is a terrible influence and is using her for her connections?

The biggest risk you're taking by saying something is that your friend will tell her BFF what you said and then you have a big problem on your hands. If you think that's what is the most likely outcome, I wouldn't say anything. Why? Because even in the best of circumstances, there is a low chance that your friend will hear what you're saying anyway. I'll put it to you this way: if or when your parents tell you they don't like a friend of yours, what's your most likely response? I doubt it's, "Mom, Dad, thanks so much for bringing this to my attention. I had no idea she was such an un-trustworthy person. I'll stop being friends with her right now."

But, if you really think it's the right thing to do, this is what I'd suggest you say to her: "I admit it's hard to see you being such close friends with someone else. But beyond that, when I see her do X, it seems like she's using you for Y. I totally could be wrong but as your friend at least I thought I should talk to you about it."

What do you do if one of your BFFs was best friends with your enemy and then she turned against you? You want to be friends again but the whole time she was just getting info out of you.

You ask yourself what this girl has that makes it so important to you to be friends with her. Then ask yourself, Do I trust her? Why would I trust her? Why do I want a friend who uses me? What am I getting by being friends with her and what am I sacrificing?

What do you do if one of your best friends that you've been friends with forever has totally changed and you don't like it?

Usually in situations like this one, the friend is acting in ways where she comes across as less intelligent, and more into style, fashion, guys, and flirting and you don't like it. First, you have to come to terms with the fact that there's probably nothing you can do to make her change back to the way she was before. But you *can* say something like this:

> YOU: Jaden, you and I have been friends for a really long time. Part of me really still wants to be friends with you but when you act like (explain exactly what she's doing that you don't like) I don't like it because it seems like people only know you as that kind of person. I want them to see the things I like in you, like you're funny and smart.
>
> JADEN: Why are you so mad at me? I haven't done anything to you! It's not my fault that I like to do different things now.
>
> YOU: I'm not mad. I'm telling you what I think. As your friend, I want us to be able to talk honestly with each other. It would have been much easier if I had said nothing and kept these things to myself. But I don't think real friends hide what they're thinking.

What if the girl denies that she's mad, or if she tells you she's angry but refuses to tell you why?

This is a classic power play. The reason a girl does that is because Girl World is controlling the way she expresses her anger. If the girl denies she's mad, this is how I'd respond:

> OK, you're saying you're not mad but if you change your mind later and decide you are angry, the only thing I'm asking is that you come to me directly instead of talking to other people about it—because I want to work it out with you.

Then, don't wait around for her to change her mind. Let her think about it and make her own decision.

If she's established that she's mad but won't discuss it further, you might talk to her like this:

> I'd really like for you to tell me what I've done to upset you. I don't want to guess because I don't want to assume it's one

thing and have it not be. So, when you're ready to tell me, I'm ready to hear it.

What if you try to talk to your friend about why you're mad or why she's mad at you and she accuses you of flipping out?

First of all, using SEAL to communicate substantially decreases the likelihood that you will flip out (i.e., cry, yell, get all red and splotchy, etc.). But if that accusation is still put on you, this is how I suggest you respond.

Take a deep breath.

YOU: Lauren, why do you think I'm flipping out?
LAUREN: I didn't do anything, and you're acting like I killed your dog!
YOU: I'm telling you that I don't like it when you embarrass me around Mike and Jack.
LAUREN: OMG! I am totally not doing that! You are being so overly sensitive!
YOU: (Remain calm.) I'm asking you to stop. That's all I want. You can do what you want but that's what I'm asking. If we're going to be friends, I need you to take this seriously.

What if you think a friend's apology is insincere?

She says something like, "Fine, if it's that important to you . . . I'm sorry."

You say, "Thanks for the apology but I have to tell you that the way you said it came across as if I don't deserve to get an apology. I don't know if that was what you meant to do but that's the way I heard it."

What do you do if someone apologizes to you and you think she means it and then she does the same thing again?

You need to do the Bill of Rights and compare your friendship standards with what is actually going on in your relationship because it sounds like your friend is acting inconsistently with what you say is important in a friendship.

What if my friend refuses to accept my apology?

Sometimes people have a hard time accepting your apology because they think you're apologizing insincerely. If you have apologized before, acknowledge that in your apology now and really try to be more mindful of your future actions. But sometimes people would rather hold on to the hurt and anger they feel than accept the apology. People like this say things like "I forgive but I never forget," which really means they don't trust the apology so they really haven't accepted it. All you can do is take ownership of your actions, apologize sincerely, and walk away. Nothing you are going to do beyond acting respectfully will change their feelings—and sometimes that's not enough. Just keep in mind that while it is frustrating to have someone refuse your apology, it's way worse to not apologize at all.

What if I'm just not a confrontational person? I will never be able to talk to someone like this.

People getting angry at you is not the end of the relationship. You actually will only know who your true friends are once you have gone through a conflict and your friendship has come out the other side—not with words unspoken, assumptions intact, not with your true feelings still buried, but where you have had a conflict in which you have actually shared what you really think and listened to your friend's own emotional truth. No one has said, "No offense, I was just joking, you're being too sensitive." You know you have a true friend. One who you can believe in. One whom you can depend on.

DO ASK, DON'T TELL

It's very hard as a parent to hold your tongue when you can see your daughter being used or mistreated in power play situations. You'll be sorely tempted to tell her what to do and summarily banish the mean girls who steamrolled her heart. But remember, these situations give her a chance to test her own strength, hew to her own standards, and affirm her self-sufficiency. And when your daughter is the steamroller, you'll be tempted to control her behavior by grounding her or taking away her privileges. That may be appropriate, but it's not enough. Your most important goal is not to punish her for her actions but instead to get her to take responsibility for them.

CRITICAL THINKING

Your daughter will almost certainly pass through the rites of passage that I've just described, and in addition to the advice above, here's a general strategy for communicating with her about girls' power plays:

- Even if you think she's behaving abominably, appreciate the awful pressure of the clique and her fear of losing her social status.
- Ask her questions to articulate her motivations and those of her friends. (Drawing a diagram similar to the ones in this chapter can help.)
- Have her review the Bill of Rights for Friends (page 260) to clarify whether she thinks her behavior or that of her friends has stepped outside bounds.
- Articulate your values and ethics and how you would like to see them reflected in her behavior. Ask her what she thinks your values look like in the situation she is facing.
- Brainstorm and role-play with her about how she can respond so that she stands up for herself while communicating her feelings respectfully, and emphasize the importance of one-on-one communication so she can clearly

ask for what she wants. Remind her that success in these
situations is not being best friends with everyone or the girl
she wants to get back together with, and it isn't about getting
even. It is simply about handling herself well so she can be
taken seriously and she can be proud of herself at the end of
the day.
• Hold her accountable when she makes mistakes.

What I have diagrammed in this chapter is a methodology for
your daughter to develop the critical thinking skills she needs to
think her way through these difficult rites of passage. If she is able
to accomplish that goal, she will develop social competency—the
necessary coping skills to navigate her personal relationships and
the social hierarchy. From social competency comes high self-
esteem. I see high self-esteem as a by-product, the end goal of all
the work you and I are doing to raise healthy girls with a strong
ethical foundation who can make sound decisions. This is hard
and you have to manage your own reactions as you watch your
daughter muddle her way through. Just don't forget that it's only in
going through the process that your daughter will reach her full
potential.

Boy World

Getting involved in a girl fight is like putting your head up when you're surrounded by sniper fire. —Will, 15

A guy has to be funny and act cool. He can look like a nerd, but he has to play basketball and have social skills. —Theo, 15

If you're a pretty boy, that's bad because you can't put too much attention to your appearance. There's no way to win. Too much attention . . . you're like a girl. Too little and you won't get girls. —Jake, 16

Girls want us to treat them with respect and take them seriously. They get really mad at us when we call them names. Sorry, but it's hard to take girls seriously about this stuff when they do the same thing all the time. They just need to get over themselves. —Dylan, 15

We don't gossip unless it's a real emergency. —Rob, 11

Your daughter lives in a world with boys. I know that's obvious, but it's important to remember because boys and Boy World are inextricably tied to all the drama in Girl World. Their presence in her life and the quality of her interaction with them is critical, and therefore you need to take it seriously. So no matter how young your daughter, how innocent her interactions with them, or if you feel like she's still too young to have a serious boyfriend, you need to acknowledge this part of her life so that you can help her navigate through it. You are laying the groundwork for her to form strong, healthy relationships with boys, either as friends or as young men with whom she is or will be intimate.

But . . . before we talk about what happens when your daughter comes home devastated because her best friend just got together with her ex-boyfriend, we have to spend some time understanding what's going on with boys. And if you have a son, you need to know this too. Why? To start, let's look at two common things parents say:

You're so lucky you have two boys! Boys are so much harder than girls when they're little but just you wait. Boys are so easy compared to girls when they're older!

You know, boys will be boys . . . (shaking their heads and shrugging their shoulders as if this statement explains everything).

These are unquestioned statements many parents love to tell one another. As a mother of sons who also works with girls, people particularly like to say both to me. But besides being a mother of sons, I've always worked with boys and I'm convinced that what looks like "easiness" is actually silence. Parents mistake the fact that their son isn't coming to them with problems as proof that he doesn't have any. Like when he just got dumped by a girl but to admit he's hurt would invite ridicule; when he's failing his classes because he has a learning difference but assumes he's stupid; when he feels inadequate because he isn't living up to your expectations of him; when he's being relentlessly bullied but thinks he should be able to take it or is too ashamed to admit he's the target. So yes, boys may be easier—but often it's because they are suffering in silence. We have to get them to speak out.

And we all really need to stop ourselves and other adults in boys' lives from saying, "boys will be boys," as an explanation for their behavior, in particular, "bad" behavior. I'm not talking about boys' love of fireworks or fart jokes. I am talking about when boys are cruel or degrading to other people. This phrase normalizes these actions because if it's something that boys just do, then there's an assumption underneath it that there's nothing wrong.

I'm going to ask you to be mindful of how we contribute to this problem. Let me give you one example: what we say to boys when they get dumped. The common response adults say is, "There are lots more fish in the sea. Why would you want to be tied down to one person anyway?" "Get over it, it's not that big of a deal." It would be unlikely for someone to say, "Wow, I bet that feels awful. It's OK if you want to cry about it. Breakups are tough. I know you really liked her." His real feelings aren't acknowledged because people want to replace them with, "Look at all the other girls you can have now."

A girl, on the other hand, may be told, "You're so much better than him," and the "more fish in the sea" part is usually framed as "You'll find the right guy for you," or "You just have not met 'THE ONE' yet." Very few moms and dads would say to a girl, "There are so many guys out there, why would you want to pick just one?"

Last, it's important to recognize that girls can be horribly mean to boys and vice versa. Our collective attention on Queen Bees and Mean Girls has meant that boys' verbal and psychological aggression is overlooked and the pain they experience is dismissed. And if there was any doubt before, technology encourages boys to wage psychological warfare on their peers—and I'm not just talking about violent video games. You give a boy a cell phone with a camera at a high school party and he has a weapon of mass destruction.

WHAT YOU SHOULD KNOW

- Boys need strong meaningful relationships with people.
- Boys easily and often can have their heart broken.
- Especially if you're a woman, it can be really hard to know the difference between boys playing and fighting. Boys often

don't know the difference until it's too late—meaning people are going for blood.

- In general, boys and girls have a completely different sense of humor. What's funny to a boy is usually absolutely idiotic to a girl.
- Boys are controlled by this culture just as much as girls are.
- Technology encourages boys to be mean in much the same way as girls.
- Boys have a very hard time taking girls seriously if the girls who surround them act less competent than they are and/or are obsessed with their weight or clothes.
- Ironically, boys can be intimidated by girls who are really competent; that is very frustrating and confusing to girls.
- When girls complain about boys calling girls sluts, bitches, whores, and worse, boys won't respect those complaints when they hear and see girls do it too.
- Boys, just like girls, aren't allowed to complain when they see someone being ridiculed or humiliated. The only difference is that instead of being called uptight, they're called gay, fags, or bitches.
- Most boys think the worst thing that can happen to them is to be publicly humiliated.
- Most boys aren't violent and abusive. A few are and the rest have no idea how to stop them.

WELCOME TO BOY WORLD

To help you get a handle on this, I'm going to give you a primer on Boy World in much the same way I did with Girl World.

Here's the comparison between the dictionary definition of *femininity* and my Girl World definition:

Dictionary Definition: The quality of nature of the female sex.
Girl World Definition: You have a great body, guys like you, you're not a prude but you're not a slut, you're in control, you're not uptight, and you're smart enough to get people to do what you want—preferably without them noticing.

Here's my parallel definition for *masculinity*:

Dictionary Definition: The qualities or appearance traditionally associated with a man; for example, strength and aggressiveness.

Boy World Definition: Nothing is ever serious. You don't make an obvious effort for anything, especially not for the right style or a great body (if it's not effortless or your goal is to look good, you'll be accused of being gay,) you laugh off emotional and physical pain, the right girls like you and you like all attention girls give you, you're competitive about everything, and, by five years of age, you can discuss professional sports with authority (although it's permissible to trade knowledge of sports for expertise in martial arts or cars).

In my boys' classes, I also conduct the same "in the box" exercise as I do for girls. I begin by asking them to describe a guy with high social status. This is a person everyone knows. If he has an opinion, everyone listens and agrees. Then I ask them to answer these questions: What does he look like, and how does he act? What is a boy or man who doesn't have high social status like? Is this someone who is likely to be teased, ridiculed, or dismissed? What does he look like, and how does he act?

These are their answers, incorporated into the Act like a Man box.

Backs down	Strong	Funny	Doesn't like
Weak	Verbal	(nothing is	to play video
Short	Tall	serious)	games/bad at
Poor	Tough	Good style/	video games
Acts like a girl/	Athletic	right gear	Gay
flamboyant/	Likes girls	Good at	Snitch/
effeminate	Girls	video games,	tattletale
Bad style/	like him	but not	Learning or
wrong gear	Money	obsessed	physical
Whipped			disabilities
Awkward			

Just like in Girl World, not everyone buys into the idea that you have to stay in the Act Like a Man box, but everyone has to deal with people who do. A boy may not care about conforming to what's inside the box, but he still interacts with people who judge themselves and him according to its rules. He's still getting a constant stream of messages from the culture about what a real man is like. The Act Like a Man box controls boys' behavior in countless destructive ways. For example, boys want to have strong friendships, but many boys don't feel they can talk to even their closest friends when they're upset because they'll be teased. Asking for help is often the same as admitting you're weak and sensitive. And I'm not just talking about social problems boys experience. When boys have learning disorders, they don't ask for help because it seems weak and shameful. But overall, one of the most profound things the box teaches is that the easiest way to prove your "in the boxness" is to demean and dismiss girls and out-of-the-box boys.

Land Mine!

If you look closely, you'll see that "acting like a girl" is the basis for many of the characteristics outside the box. One of the ways you can most easily see this dynamic played out in our daily lives is how often people still try to motivate boys by not being girls. Without even realizing what we're doing, we say to our sons, "Don't throw like a girl!" "You're screaming like a little girl!" or "Don't cry like a girl!" Some people dismiss the problem of these comments by saying, "But it's true. Most boys throw better than most girls. Little girls scream at a higher pitch. Girls cry more easily than boys." That's not the issue. When people say those things to boys, they set up a parallel in boys' brains between acting incompetently or in a way that people can ridicule and being like a girl. If you want boys to respect girls, you have to stop saying things like that.

Just because I like violent video games doesn't mean I'm going to go out and start killing people. I know the difference between real life and a video game.

Many boys have said this to their teachers and parents, and it often stops adults in their tracks. After all, the boys are proving their point just by standing there and not shooting someone. And by the way, I get why boys like to play these games. It's a huge adrenaline rush and it makes you feel a sense of mastery and dominance in a world where you may not feel like you have any. Don't let their response stop you from understanding what is really at stake here. For the record, I don't think video games "cause" violence. The problem is that violent video games normalize violence, humiliation, and degradation, especially of out-of-the-box men and women. They also normalize all of these dynamics as entertainment. And the really tricky thing about calling these things "entertainment" is that as soon as you call them that, their influence sneaks under your radar. It's no different than having your child understand the power of how most popular music is now packaged to value power and domination over others and devalue those who are perceived as weaker.

Do Boys Have Cliques?

In our school there is a group of junior guys who act just like they're a group of middle-school girls. There's a Queen Bee that all the guys are afraid of. I'm not joking. They don't do anything without checking with him first. One day, I saw one of the guys sitting outside on a bench waiting for class. I wanted to talk to him because we used to be a lot closer but since he's been hanging out with this guy he doesn't want to. So I came up to him and tried to talk to him and he wouldn't and he was all nervous. So I looked around and there was the guy coming over to our direction. It was so messed up. He used to be such a great guy and now he's so arrogant. It's really hard to believe he's the same person and he'd let this guy have so much control over him.

—Ellie, 17

So boys can have cliques. Just call them groups. But it is true that, in general, boys do have more flexibility than girls do to have different friends. However, in moments when boys have to prove where they fit in the Act Like a Man box, especially when there is conflict between boys, these roles come to life and control boys just as profoundly as girls.

The Mastermind

He is charismatic, persuasive, and socially intelligent (he can read people's strengths and weaknesses) and feels strongly that his influence in the group should never be challenged. As he gets older he doesn't like to admit his position in the group because he's smart enough to realize that it appears as if his group is acting like a clique of middle-school girls. If his decisions or actions are challenged, he sees the challenge as disloyalty. He often makes members of the group prove their loyalty. He is a vocal proponent of individual rights over his responsibilities to others. As in, "I have the right to say whatever I want. The other people are just too weak to be able to take it." If he gets a picture of someone in a compromising or embarrassing picture, he loves to forward it and then blame them for being so stupid for allowing the picture to be taken—therefore, whatever happens after that is their fault (even if he was the one who forwarded it).

> *What Does He Gain?* Has power and control over his environment. Is the center of attention.
>
> *What Does He Lose?* Because he's in a position of high pressure and responsibility, he can lose real sense of self. Can use people so much that he loses true friendships. Feels that he can't admit to anyone when he's in over his head because he must maintain the appearance that everything's under control.

The Muscle

He is less socially intelligent than the Mastermind. He doesn't question people who have more power than he does. He often thinks it's funny when people are treated disrespectfully. He loves ridiculing boys for being "gay" or "fags." When he's challenged about this behavior, he feels attacked and justified to ridicule, dismiss, or humiliate even more. He is also a big proponent of forwarding humiliating photographs of other kids. He loves to binge drink or makes sure alcohol is available at social gatherings.

What Does He Gain? Has power over other boys that he wouldn't without the Mastermind. Has a close friend who makes him feel like he has status because he is connected to someone who does.

What Does He Lose? His right to express personal opinions. Is controlled by the Mastermind.

The Banker

With the increase in technology, there are *a lot* more boy Bankers now. Information, especially about other people's personal insecurities, is currency in Boy World. The Banker creates conflicts with both boys and girls by banking information about others in his social sphere and dispensing it at strategic opportunities. The Bankers love to know people's passwords.

What Does He Gain? Has power and security of his position in the group. Other boys are afraid of him.

What Does He Lose? Other boys don't trust him but are not really sure why, and he may not trust other boys.

The Messenger

The Messenger also trades personal information; however, he differs from the Banker in that his motivation is to feel important in the moment. By doing this, he hopes to gain recognition from others, especially those with higher social power.

What Does He Gain? Feels valued because friendships will be made or broken based on his involvement.

What Does He Lose? Others can easily turn on this person, especially if he gets the information wrong or others deny what he's claimed. Easily used, manipulated, then discarded when no longer useful.

The Torn Bystander

He doesn't want to go against the more powerful people in the group and usually convinces himself to not challenge them. He wants to help the Target but is not sure how or thinks it won't make a difference. He may rationalize his own silence or apologize for others' behavior.

What Does He Gain? His silence enables him to be accepted by the group. If he doesn't speak out, people aren't going to get mad at him or think he is disloyal. Also, by associating himself with more powerful boys, he has access to popularity, high social status.

What Does He Lose? Sacrifices his sense of self—may not try new things or may hide things he's interested in because others in the group would make fun of him. May dumb himself down. Feels powerless to stop Mastermind behavior.

The Pleaser/Wannabe

He wants recognition from the Mastermind or the Muscle and looks for opportunities to prove his loyalty to them. He often observes and imitates their behavior, clothes, and interests.

What Does He Gain? Is in the middle of the action.

What Does He Lose? Never feels completely in the group. Loses personal authenticity—hasn't figured out who he is or what he values. Constantly anticipates what people want from him but doesn't ask himself what he wants in return. Feels insecure about his friendships. Has trouble developing personal boundaries and communicating them to others.

The Target

He is the object of the group's anger or ridicule. He may apologize after he complains about how people are treating him. He can be inside or outside of the group.

> *What Does He Gain?* Learns empathy and understanding for people who are bullied or discriminated against. Can see the cost of fitting in and so may decide he's better off outside the group, where he can be true to himself or find good friends who like him for who he is, not his social standing.
>
> *What Does He Lose?* Can feel totally helpless in the face of other boys' cruelty. Can feel ashamed of being rejected by other boys because of who he is. Feels tempted to change himself in order to fit in. Feels vulnerable and unable to affect the outcome of his situation.

The Champion

The Champion is not controlled by the Act Like a Man box. He can take criticism, doesn't make people choose friends, and doesn't blow off someone for a better offer. He has friends in different groups and doesn't treat people differently when groups are together. People can challenge his masculinity without his having to prove it. He can and will stand up to the Mastermind in a way that treats them both with dignity.

> *What Does He Gain?* Has an authentic sense of self. His peers like him for who he is as a person. He is less likely to sacrifice himself to gain and keep social status.
>
> *What Does He Lose?* Can be lonely when people turn on him for doing the right thing.

THE RULES OF ANGER IN BOY WORLD

Just as there are cultural rules guiding girls when they're angry, the same is true for boys—it's just that the rules are a little different. Your daughter needs to know this because it will help her understand boys better when they are in conflict with her or vice versa. Here's the general breakdown:

- Internalize and suffer silently.
- Blow it off and say, "It's not a big deal. Don't worry about it. I'm fine."
- Laugh it off. Convince himself that whatever he experiences or observes is funny or nothing he can or should do anything about.
- Refuse to admit he's angry.
- Rely on other boys to help him manage his anger and justify physical outbursts by saying, "You can't push me like that. I just lose it." Or even better, his friends will say it for him.
- Verbally dominate the other person.
- Physically dominate the other person, but only if he has numbers or he knows he is tougher or not afraid to fight if the other person doesn't back down.
- Drink alcohol or do drugs to deaden feelings.

The rules of anger go right to the heart of why boys are conditioned not to complain when they are being bullied or when they see someone being bullied. I have asked many boys, "What would it take for you to intervene if someone was getting bullied?" And their response is inevitably, "They'd have to be really hurt," "Like someone was going to die," or "Something would have to happen like what you see on TV."

So we have to counteract boys' belief that the threshold for coming forward is only when someone is at risk for or is actually being assaulted because by then it's too late.

TOOL VERSUS DOUCHE BAG

I don't know if boys use these words in your community but in the last two years wherever I've taught, they're commonplace. I actually wasn't sure what the difference was until I asked boys. Here's their answer. A tool is someone who can't help himself. He's like a tool in the hands of another guy. He doesn't really intend to be annoying and obnoxious but he is. A douche bag (also a douche, or d-bag) has the intention of being a douche bag. He wants to degrade people. Other people's embarrassment is his entertainment. Tools are often used by douche bags. But isn't it strange that *douche bag* is the word teens use to describe this boy? If they knew it was something women used to "clean" themselves after their periods, I doubt they would use the word.

WHAT HAPPENS WHEN GIRLS GET MAD AT GUYS?

Girls are so vindictive—especially those with a bigger social life. They get mad at you but then they wait to unleash their anger. This one girl was angry at me and she waited for a couple of weeks and then she exploded. She embarrassed me in front of all my friends. She completely caught me off guard. She could have taken me off to the side.   —Matt, 17

When a girl says something negative, she's expressing her feelings. When a guy says something negative, he's an asshole.
                                                        —Brandon, 16

When girls are mad, it's all about the numbers. What numbers? The number of other girls they bring with them to destroy you.
                                                        —Alan, 14

Girls in a group get mad at one guy and then they corner him and attack him. If a group of guys did that to a girl, everyone would hate them.   —Jacob, 13

When teachers get mad at you, it's really boring. When girls get
mad at you, they surround you and then give you a no-nonsense
lecture.   —*Malesh, 11*

The dynamic described above and its impact on girls and boys
expressing their anger to one another is one of the most important
things I realized in the course of my research for this book. Before
girls become teens, one of the most common ways they confront
someone is to do it with several other girls for support; that is, they
gang up on the person. Although some of them are conscious of
the fact that they are ganging up on the person, most girls do it because they are insecure about expressing their anger or being
taken seriously; the other girls are there for reinforcement. Of
course, this strategy exacerbates the conflict because the other person feels attacked and defensive—which means it will be impossible for her to hear anything the angry girl is saying.

This is exactly the same strategy girls and young women use
with boys, especially in high school and college. There are understandable reasons for this. Girls anticipate being blown off for
being uptight. So, just like they did when they were twelve, a
girl can bring other girls with her to publicly humiliate the person she's angry at, without realizing what she's doing because she's
so focused on what was done to her. She is also prone to saying things like, "Do you realize that everyone in the grade hates
you?"

One of my female students said that to a boy her whole grade
hated, mainly because of his constant need to make sexist, racist
comments. That girl had every reason to be angry and I would
never take that away from her. But there's no way the boy isn't
going to respond exactly the way he did—which was to verbally attack her again.

This problem becomes so pervasive in some schools that it in-
fects the entire atmosphere of the community. Then a pattern
emerges where the other boys rationalize not calling the guy out
because "it's not worth it" and the burden of expressing the anger
falls on a few girls, who really become labeled as the "uptight
complainers"—and I am being really polite in how I am writing

that. Although the girls don't like admitting it, this experience is frustrating and exhausting. They lie low for a while until there's a buildup of smaller insults that makes these girls blow up. But the blowup is usually about something that can be easily dismissed—and does not reflect the other indignities that preceded it. Therefore, a cycle emerges where the complainers explode in anger, usually with other girls surrounding them. The targets of their anger feel attacked, so they dismiss or ridicule the complaint. This in turn reinforces to everyone else that it is futile to speak out, and the complainers shut up until something else makes them blow up and the whole thing begins again.

All of this results in boys who believe that they have the right to put people in their place, who think making fun of someone is amusing and more important than treating people with dignity, and who silence boys by questioning their heterosexuality (the ubiquitous calling of boys "fags" etc.) and girls by calling them bitches, whores, or worse. Their behavior continues unchecked— until occasionally when their behavior becomes so untenable that an adult like a coach or principal must intervene.

Once girls get into high school and college, these issues become even more complex because the boys who dismiss the "angry complaining girls" are reinforced by other girls. A girl who calls a guy out, and in particular uses the label of "sexist," "racist," "homophobic," or any other adult word to describe the behavior becomes the "political" girl who is always making a "statement." The result is that being a truly outspoken woman becomes something you don't want to be.

That is, unless you back up the boys who are going after the girls. Then you can be as outspoken as you want to be (for adults, think of popular female political commentators). Other girls, who want to prove they belong in the Act Like a Woman box, won't back up the "uptight angry girl" (even if, deep down, they agree with her), and they will use her intensity to make them seem more relaxed, friendly, and inoffensive. Unfortunately, this strategy usually works for a while because the boys who want to fit into the Act Like a Man box like girls who aren't calling them out and making their lives difficult. Then girls learn to believe that in order to keep any guy happy she will need to stay quiet, not think critically, and believe in gender stereotypes because the position that she chose appears to work for her.

> *She will feel stuck many, many times in her life. She won't know why she feels like she can never say anything but she will know it's an unwritten truth. She knows the most desirable girl goes with the flow, doesn't make too much noise, and when she does make noise it's laughter.*   —Emily

I realize that some girls and young women may read this and say, "That's not the way it was at my school." If this is true, you should be very grateful for your experience. But you have a responsibility to role-model for women who weren't that lucky. Don't look down on them when they lose their voice. Show them by your words and deeds what it means to be a courageous, competent, substantive woman of dignity who isn't afraid to say what she thinks and doesn't put down other girls.

Apologizing in Boy World

Boys are better apologizers than girls—when they are apologizing to other boys. If you can get boys in a room to sort out their differences, in general, unless there is a really powerful Mastermind in the room, boys can apologize, mean it, and actually let go of their anger.

But just as girls struggle to give and accept meaningful apologies, boys do, too, when they are apologizing to girls. As I said in Chapter 6, girls can have a really hard time trusting apologies—from both boys and girls. They don't trust apologies from girls because many have seen girls apologize and not mean it or continue to hold a grudge. But by the time girls get to high school, girls don't trust a lot of boys' apologies because they've had the experience of a boy apologizing, who then goes right back to what he was doing before that got her so upset in the first place. Why would boys apologize and not mean it? I think it's for one of two reasons. One, boys are conditioned to not take girls' feelings seriously. Two, boys often find girls' display of emotions overwhelming. And an emotional or, way worse, crying girl is top of the list for what must be stopped. So they say anything (i.e., apologize) to placate her or "calm her down," sometimes without listening, to get the girl to stop.

HOMOPHOBIA, BULLYING, AND BEING A MAN

As I write this, two boys, both under twelve, have recently committed suicide because their peers relentlessly teased them for being gay. Throughout this chapter, I've been talking a lot about boys calling each other fags and gay without fully explaining its power. Homophobia is the invisible hand in Boy World that guides boys to assigned roles of Perpetrator, Bystander, or Target. Some boys threaten and/or perpetrate violence to prove their power and control—their masculinity—daring other boys to stop them.

Boys who witness these acts have a choice. They can be a passive bystander by looking the other way; an active bystander who backs up the bully by words and deeds; they can run away; or they can stand up to the bully. Standing up to the bully by physically fighting him isn't too tough—that's condoned behavior in Boy World. Standing up to a bully by saying his actions are wrong, however, challenges the foundation on which Boy World is built.

The irony of this cultural definition of masculinity is that it represses courage—not the kind where a boy will fight someone if challenged, but the moral courage to raise his voice and stand up for what's right. Kids calling each other "gay" and "fag" and parents not understanding its wide-ranging implications create an environment where we all suffer. Starting around fourth or fifth grade, boys are called gay or fags not just when they are acting like girls but when they speak out against bullying. You see a kid in school being teased and you want to say something about it? If you do, any boy by sixth grade knows he's going to be labeled gay for doing it. In high school, this dynamic is so powerful and pervasive that most boys don't realize its viselike grip on their behavior. So whether you see a boy being teased for being a fag or watch your junior friend try to get a freshman girl drunk so you can hook up with her, if you speak out, you will be labeled a fag.

And then there are the tragic stories of kids killing themselves because they are living with this every day. When you read these stories, your heart breaks. If you have kids, you may be worried this could happen to your kids or already gone through it. If it hasn't, you worry they will be targeted. Then we wonder what is wrong with children who torment others. They're heartless. They have no sense of decency. We shake our heads and then don't know what to do, so we go back to our lives hoping this problem won't touch the kids we know and love. Of course there are countless more who aren't killing themselves but daily must deal with this ridicule and cruelness.

But we really could stop this. By "we" I mean parents, teachers, administrators, and anyone who works with kids. Because when we don't, we become the bystanders who could have helped but chose to look the other way. How can we help? My challenge to you is to start a conversation.

With any child you are close to or work with you say:

> I don't know if bullying is a problem for you (at school, in your youth group, athletic team), but I need to get really clear with you about where I stand. When people use the word "gay" or "fag" to put something or someone down, that is intolerable to me. It is against everything that I stand for. If there is someone in your class, someone you don't even know well, who is being teased or humiliated in any way, I want you to come talk to me about it. When you tell me, I'm not going to freak out and randomly start calling people. But we will bring it to the attention of the right people so the target can get help.
>
> If I find out that you have been involved in humiliating someone in this manner either in real life or by using your cell phone or computer, I will work with the school to discipline you in a manner where you learn that a person's dignity is more important than your right to demean them.
>
> If you are targeted, I will support you every step of the way to

get the help you need. You have the right to exist in this life without people making you feel miserable and unworthy.

We also must get ourselves straight (pun intended) about homophobia. It should go without saying that everyone—gay or not—has the right to be treated with dignity. This dignity is not negotiable. You do not have to change your religion or your politics in order to have the basic human decency to respect another person's right to exist in this world.

What's so frustrating and ironic about this is that calling boys fags for speaking out makes no sense. Guys who speak out about social injustice don't want to have sex with other guys—but that's what the bullies are saying when they try to silence others with, "Don't be a fag." More important, being gay is now being connected with speaking out against degradation and violence. So are we saying that a real man is a heterosexual man who says nothing when he sees someone being degraded?

We've got to do better. We must individually and collectively change the definition of masculinity to standing up for social justice so that real men speak out when they see someone being targeted. Go to your children and talk to them. If you're a parent, talk to them tonight before they go to bed or do it on the way to school tomorrow. If you're a teacher, start the class tomorrow making sure that your students know your classroom is a sanctuary. And if you're straight, you have an even larger responsibility to speak out—because you won't be so easily dismissed for trying to advance "an agenda."

Seen in this light, homophobia becomes much more than whether you "tolerate" or "accept" homosexuality. Homophobia is one of the cornerstones of the culture of masculinity. If you want your daughter or son to be treated well by boys and men, you have to actively take a stand against homophobia.

What do you do if you hear your son or daughter teasing someone for being gay? Or worse, what if you're hanging out with a bunch of boys and one of them says, "Don't be so gay! You're such a fag!" to another kid in the group. You say something! You don't have to give them a lecture for an hour or show them a documentary. You say something like this:

> You: Guys, when you said to Mike, "Don't be gay," what did you mean by that?

Then they're going to get all defensive and try to worm their way out of answering you.

> You: Seriously, what did you mean?
> Son/Daughter: I don't know! We didn't mean anything by it! It's just what we say!

Ignore your son/daughter rolling his/her eyes and hyperventilating because he/she is so embarrassed.

> You: But what do you mean?
> Son/Daughter: I don't know. Stupid, dumb. Mike doesn't mind, do you?
> Mike: No, they're just messing with me. I know they don't mean it.*
> You: Here's the deal. This has nothing to do with Mike. If you're calling someone gay or a fag to put someone down, that is unacceptable. I expect better from all of you.
> Son/Daughter: OK, fine. (In his/her head, "Whatever, crazy woman.")

*Please note that in this situation Mike had no choice but to agree with his friends that he doesn't mind what they're saying. If he did, he would risk further ridicule.

I know there are some schools where openly gay students are accepted by the student body. But I think this is conditional acceptance. If a kid really is gay, then it sometimes can be unacceptable to tease him/her, but if you're a boy acting effeminate or a girl acting masculine, then you are open to ridicule. Calling someone gay/dyke/fag is still the way kids shut others up for complaining, so we still have farther to go.

DO THE RIGHT THING

Most boys really want to do the right thing, they just have no idea how. They want to be courageous, valiant, loving, emotional, strong men. But how can they be when their public role models are men who are idolized for being tough and always in control and when they themselves are vilified and emasculated when they demonstrate characteristics associated with women and girls? Where are the role models who look like the strong men they want to be but who are also emotionally articulate, engaged, and morally courageous? Actors and music artists may protect the beautiful woman from gunfire and shower women with money and gifts, but what are boys learning about empathy and "real men" when their heroes limit communication to a clenched jaw?

If we believe that most boys are out of control, uncaring, and thoughtless members of our communities, and if we believe that the best response to this problem is to toughen them up and punish them, we'll create a self-fulfilling prophecy. Instead, if we demand the best from boys, hold ourselves accountable for what we do that contributes to Boy World, and reach out to them with respect, we will raise strong men who believe that "being a man" is about standing up and speaking up when someone is being degraded.

Talk about this chapter with your daughter—and with your son. Show her the Act Like a Man box and ask her how it corresponds to her experience. Does she know boys who fall into the categories in this chapter? Ask her to imagine what it would be like to be a boy. Talk to her about homophobia, and how it affects not only attitudes toward the gay community but how people behave. Talk to her about how issues of race and religion intersect with boy culture. Most of all, help her appreciate that boys are in their own life raft. Just like girls, they're looking to break out and be appreciated for who they are. If your daughter can empathize with how difficult it is in Boy World, she can work toward seeing boys as equal partners on the path toward healthy adulthood.

Girl World Meets Boy World

My dad told me that if a boy hits me then he likes me. But I can't tell the boy that so I still don't know what to do. —Madeline, 11

One time a boy punched me in the nose so his parents made him come over to my house to apologize to me and bring flowers. But then everyone in school started teasing us. So then we had to hate each other and now I punch him. —Abby, 10

Boys are asking us out but we aren't going anywhere.
—Molly, 13

The Drama Begins

Emily and Kristi are seventh graders, and both are in love with Jason. Each spends considerable quality time with Jason, including sending him notes, writing his name on their notebooks, calling and texting him, hanging out after school to see if she can bump into him, and "accidentally" walking by when his team practice is over. When the competition for his affections becomes unbearable, they make a pact that both will stop liking him. Of course, neither girl has any intention of keeping her word, but each also believes that the other will. Each is also convinced that she reserves the right to be angry with the other if she goes back on her word, but both girls quietly do everything they can behind each other's back to win Jason's affection.

Things become much more complicated when they discover that four other girls in their grade like Jason as well. Making matters worse, one of the four girls, Liza, threatens Emily and Kristi's position as the front contenders for Jason's affections. Emily and Kristi's response is to go after Liza, assured that they're in the right because (a) Liza knows they like him, (b) Liza is throwing herself at Jason, and (c) they staked their claim first. Within a day, the grade is abuzz watching the drama unfold. Messengers are dispatched. Queen Bees are consulted. Delegations confer.

In the situation described above, the parents of Emily, Kristi, and Liza are largely clueless that anything's going on. Jason's parents figure something's up because their son's cell phone is going off all evening. There have even been calls on the landline that give Jason's parents flashbacks to their own adolescence as they hear giggles on the other end, then a quick *click* when the mysterious caller hangs up.

I've talked to many parents like Jason's. They perceive their son as a deer in the headlights with these girls barreling toward him like a Mack truck. Is this true? Are the Jasons of the world clueless and terrified as girls vie for their attention? If one of these girls were your daughter, would you know about this drama? Should you? Why do girls turn against each other over a boy they may barely know? How does girls' competition for boys influence your daughter's future friendships with girls and her intimate relationships?

In this chapter, we're going to examine how Girl World and Boy World work together. Here is where you'll see girls begin to turn themselves inside out trying to be attractive to boys. You may have to witness your daughter being blown off by a close friend for a boy, or suddenly insecure when all the other girls are obsessed with boys and she's more interested in soccer. You'll see your daughter question her self-worth if she doesn't think she fits the model (pun intended) she thinks the boys want. She'll fall madly in love and not know why. Or she'll know why, but she'll think she has no chance because everyone else is so much prettier than she is.

What You Should Know

- Around twelve years of age, girls' bonding often extends beyond navigating their friendships with other girls to include drama with boys.
- If one girl is getting attention from boys or is more "boy crazy" than her friend, it will strain the relationship and put pressure on the other girl to play catch-up.
- At some point, almost all girls will pretend to be not as smart, strong, or capable around a boy they like. A girl may be embarrassed by her behavior but not know how to stop.
- Her girlfriends will see this, be secondhand embarrassed, and talk behind her back. They may also wonder if this is the right way to get boys' attention.
- As in their friendships with girls, girls often communicate unclearly with boys because they don't want to say something that will ruin the relationship.
- A girl will have a crush on someone who doesn't treat her or other people well. She'll know this, but won't stop liking the person.
- Not all girls are boy crazy. Some girls aren't that interested until they're older, or they may be sexually attracted to girls.
- Regardless of her sexual orientation, your daughter will likely have strong friendships with boys. Some of those friendships can become sexual, but that doesn't take away from the depth of the friendship.

"Friend Boys" and Boyfriends

I'm sure you remember this concept from your teens. There were boys or girls who were friends and then there were boyfriends and girlfriends. Girls still make those distinctions. Most girls have strong friendships with boys that they value highly, and ironically, girls don't seem to be so constrained by gendered behavior within these friendships. These friendships are defined by the fact that the girl has no problem clearly communicating what she really thinks. As Mike, age sixteen, puts it, "My girl friends will tell me when I'm acting like a dumb ass." But far too many girls don't communicate like this with boys. As I'll discuss in this and upcoming chapters, girls often hide their true selves as soon as the boy goes from being a boy who's a friend to a potential or real boy-friend.

Girls will tease each other about the boys they are friends with. If your daughter has close male friends (this seems to be especially true with boys she grows up with and/or who live in the neighborhood), tell her that she doesn't have to lose those friendships if they aren't romantic. I have talked to many confused girls who don't want to lose these close friendships but can feel them slipping away under all the scrutiny and pressure to pair up.

> *One of my best friends is a boy I grew up with. My friends tease the two of us all the time and I don't know what to do about it. He's like my brother and all these people want us to be boy-friend/girlfriend.* —Rachel, 12

At the risk of repeating myself, it's really important to remember that girls have individual responses to boys. Some are totally boy crazy and have been since kindergarten when they chased the boys around the playground trying to capture them and put them in the "jail." But that doesn't mean that all girls are like this. They can be anywhere from very interested to sometimes interested to never-going-to-be-interested. What's important here is to understand that your daughter can often value herself and other girls based on the belief that the more into boys she is, the better. So starting around third or fourth grade, you need to say to her, "Honey, girls can think all different things about boys. Some are boy crazy, some only want them as friends, and some girls are in between. But whatever you think and feel about boys is totally fine. No matter how old you are, that will never change." And then keep reminding her that wherever she is on the spectrum of boys, it is totally and completely acceptable.

CRUSHES

Sooner or later, your daughter will have her first crush, and it'll feel like she's been hit between the eyes, with butterflies in her stomach and cheeks burning. Girls fall in love with someone "who is so hot, you don't understand," and then overnight change their affections to someone else. These are typical descriptions of crushes from the girls in my classes.

> *I feel like I'm going to throw up. And I'm sure right in front of him.*
> *I get butterflies in my stomach.*
> *I get excited, can't breathe, and then I start to giggle uncontrollably. It's humiliating and also fun at the same time.*
> *I'm so nervous. I'm sure I'll do or say something stupid.*

But sometimes the problem with crushes goes back to the Act Like a Man box, because girls tend to be drawn to boys who fit in the box. And, when you add in the difference in biological maturity between most junior high boys and girls, it's easy to sympathize. Compare and contrast. Do you remember what boys were like in sixth and seventh grade? Maybe two grew proportionately. The rest were awkward and gangly. Now I want you to picture a typical eighth-grade girl and an eighth-grade boy. If you were a girl, who would you fall for? Exactly—the 2 percent of hot guys in your class who look like they belong in the box, or . . . older guys. Even though the awkward ones now will be the hottest at the high school reunion, girls don't know that, and even if they did, why should they care? Girls want someone who's cute and cool now.

We also have to hold up a mirror here. Parents love boys who fit in the box. They like to have them as sons, and when their daughters date, they like boyfriends who fit this mold. I'm not saying all those boys are jerks. Far from it. But for many of them, the power and privilege they get lends itself to the belief that they don't need to treat girls with respect.

> *Those guys develop an ego. One of my best friends did this. The girls were all over him and he treated them like trash. They accepted it and came flocking back.* —Jake, 16

One of the things girls have to learn is why they're attracted to boys who aren't going to treat them with dignity or why they go back to these boys when they know from previous experience that it isn't good for them.

OBSESSIONS

Why Are Girls Obsessed with Celebrities?

> *The girls in our class are completely in love with famous people. They have shrines in their lockers and they doodle their names all day. When they talk about this guy that they don't even know in real life, they start to scream. It's really really weird.* —Keith, 10

Do you remember your first crush? Maybe it was someone you actually knew. But depending on your generation, chances are it was Sean Cassidy, Scott Baio, Luke Perry, or Scott Wolf. Remember them?

Why do girls do it? It's an easy and timeless answer. Because liking boys can be so stressful and weird, it's way easier to fall in love with someone who you have no chance of actually meeting. That way, you are free to fall in love as intensely as you want, without actually having to deal with all the unnerving feelings of developing sexuality. That's why girls make shrines, are possessive of the person they love, and forbid other girls from liking the person, as if he was someone they actually knew. Plus an imaginary boyfriend can be and feel anything you want. If you were a girl in fifth, sixth, and even seventh grade, wouldn't you look at the clueless boys around you farting and jumping on each other, and choose the guy in your head instead?

Obsessions with People Whom the Girls Actually Know

I was obsessed with this guy named Scott. I have no idea why. I look back and laugh at this now, but at the time I was totally serious. I would write [in my journal] the different things he had done that brought me closer to the conclusion that he liked me. I would show off, try to be near him. Every day during recess, my friend and I would play tag near where he played soccer with his friends and count the number of times he smiled at me. It was pathetic. —Julia, 12

Obsession in middle school is worse because you have nothing to compare it to. Someone who humiliates you, you like even more. I was obsessed with a guy in seventh grade. I dated him and then he broke up with me. Then he fell in love with someone else and I hated it. But then she did a little Mexican hat dance on his heart by hooking up with five guys and I felt a lot better. —Angie, 17

In fifth grade I was obsessed with this guy. I naturally told my friends I was crazy about him and they spread it around that I liked him. He stayed as far away from me as possible and wouldn't say a word to me after that. —Nina, 13

Land Mine!

What not to say to your daughter about boys:
You're not at that stage yet.
You're too young.
He only wants one thing.
All teenage boys are pigs.

POWER BROKERS IN PUBERTY: MATCHMAKING

For all the difficult things I write about, early adolescence is an exciting time to be a girl. Some girls eagerly anticipate when they'll be old enough to have boyfriends and all the accompanying drama. But they're also cowards (which is totally understandable). They want to check out the whole boy thing and be involved in the drama, but without putting themselves on the front line. So in many different ways, girls push one another to be the first one to jump off the cliff.

For example, Julia, twelve, is on her way to math class when one of her best friends rushes up to her . . .

ANI: I was just talking to Jeremy and he says that Matt likes you! That's so cool! You guys would make such a cute couple! I knew he liked you!

JULIA: Are you sure? What did Jeremy say exactly?

ANI: He said Matt thought you were really pretty and nice.

Julia is so happy because she's had a huge crush on Matt since the beginning of the year but hasn't known how to tell him. After class, she discusses with her two closest friends what her next step should be. Later that afternoon, they send Matt the following text:

Do you like Julia? Yes No

Between classes Julia's friend checks her phone every thirty seconds until she gets an answer.

If Matt's answer is "Yes" and maybe even a request to meet after school, this means high drama. Julia gets to figure out every nuance of what she should do in full consultation with her friends, who offer their opinion and analysis. She will be the center of attention the entire afternoon, and it will seem to her that all is right in the world.

But more often than not, Julia and every girl in her situation is quickly disappointed, because the meeting with Matt isn't nearly as good as she anticipated. Where is the romantic boy from the magazines and TV shows? Why is this boy answering in monosyllables? Why, if his friends are around, is he acting like he doesn't know her? To make matters worse, without being aware of it, Julia's expectations of Matt are also based on her closest friendships. Remember, girls' friendships are often characterized by endless conversations. It's hard for the awkward first crush to measure up to the intimacy of girl-girl friendships, or even the camaraderie of friendships with boys. That's one of the primary reasons why the first thing a girl does after hanging out with her crush is to call, text, or IM with a girlfriend to analyze every word of the conversation. In these early romances, she may spend more time talking to her girlfriend about the boyfriend than to the boyfriend himself.

A lot of girls' first crushes never even get to the stage where girl meets boy. Some follow dramatic trajectories from first inklings of attraction through flaming breakup without the boy even knowing he was the object of affection ("It is so over with Jason"). Some girls run through a series of "boyfriends" without any of the relationships advancing, as one girl put it, "all the way up to holding hands." What's often true of a lot of these early experiences is that the reality is a little disappointing compared with the anticipation.

But let's go back to why Julia and Matt are getting together in the first place. It may have been a crush at first sight, but Julia and her friends could have collectively decided that Matt is a worthy object on which to experiment. Is he boyfriend material? Usually beginning around sixth grade, matchmaking becomes a prime directive. Girls love to be in each other's business as they dissect the boy mystery. What better way to deal with boy anxiety than setting up a friend? No matter who made the initial push, the whole group can analyze every stage of the relationship, from the first mutual flirtations through the intense phone calls, text messages, and IMs to the inevitable conflicts that send the whole thing crashing down in flames. As girls go through this phase in their lives, their friendships solidify around these dramatic moments. And not surprisingly, the social hierarchy is operating at full force.

In the social hierarchy, although I am not the super Queen Bee, I'm fairly close. I'm not hated by anyone (hopefully) and have many good friends. The people I've set up are not outcasts or dorks, but they aren't the Queen Bees. The people close to the Queen Bees are the matchmakers. —Kim, 15

The Queen Bee set me up and I didn't feel like there was anything I could do about it. —Molly, 18

It was really hard to like a guy my friends didn't think was cool enough. I liked him because he was nice. But he wasn't that cute. They made fun of him all the time. It made me feel bad but I didn't know what to do. —Raquel, 14

Queen Bees are careful to regulate the popularity of other girls. When they set up another girl, one of the ulterior motives is to bind the girl more closely to the Queen Bee. The girl set up for her first boyfriend, and hence her moment in the sun as the focus of attention, is now beholden and bonded to the Queen Bee. In Julia's situation, she is likely a Wannabe, Pleaser, or Messenger, and Ani is a Banker or Queen Bee. Note that both girls' stock goes up when Julia gets her first boyfriend. One way to solidify your place on the social totem pole is to be a Banker or Messenger whose information on who likes whom is vital to the unfolding drama. If you're wondering what your daughter texted in those three thousand messages she sent to her friends last month, a situation like this easily provides the answer.

The Queen Bee can also influence when the girl stops liking the boy. Real conflicts between girls occur when the girl who is set up begins to act independently.

And what if Julia didn't like Matt or really didn't want a boyfriend? It'll be hard for her to resist the encouragement of her girlfriends, the gratification of being the center of attention, and the excitement of this new kind of intimacy. So she's forced into relationships with boys that she might really rather not have. When a girl is twelve or younger it's generally about a crush, and the scope of what she'll most likely do with this boy is limited. But the consequences are there: she's learning to stifle her personal boundaries with boys so she can maintain her friendships with girls and fit into the Act Like a Woman box.

THE BIRTH OF FRUIT CUP GIRL

Of all the topics I have ever taught girls, Fruit Cup Girl is definitely one of their favorites. I came up with this term after teaching a group of seventh graders who had had a big blowup after a field trip. Why? Because one of the girls (let's call her Mia) had a huge crush on a boy but was too shy to talk to him. Her two best friends decided to take on the cause, and they set their sights on putting them together at an upcoming field trip. The big moment came during lunch when they orchestrated having the boy sit next to Mia—while they sat at the next table so they could overhear everything. When Mia was finally alone with her crush, she had no idea what to say. So without even thinking about it, Mia pretended she couldn't open her fruit cup and asked the boy to do it for her.

That was the conversation opener, and, from Mia's point of view, it was a good one because everything went well from that moment. So well that they sat next to each other on the bus ride back. At the same time, however, Mia's friends noticed how "weird" she was acting with this boy. She was laughing really strangely, acting like she was incredibly stupid, and pretending she was clueless. For the next two days, every time Mia was around this boy, she acted like this, causing the girls to get more irritated with every passing minute.

That's when rumors started circulating that Mia had done "things" with the boy on the bus ride home. (This was before text messages. Now everyone would be texting one another on all the buses that went on the trip.) Mia was very upset about the rumors and then she found out one of her friends was behind the gossip bomb. The morning I had my class with them, Mia was understandably furious at her friends for betraying her, but the friends were also angry at Mia for acting stupid around the boy.

And that's how I came up with the Fruit Cup Girl (FCG). This girl personifies girls' internal conflict between expressing personal authenticity and codified gendered behavior that they believe gets them attention from boys. But girls aren't clueless—it's just usually one of those things you know but don't have the words to explain it. Girls know they're not supposed to act incompetent, but this is really where you and your daughter can see the power of the culture (remember: everything you know but have never been sat down and taught) controlling girls' behavior, even the girl she sees in the mirror. To help girls think through FCG, I go through the following cost-benefit analysis with them.

Benefits of Being Fruit Cup Girl
- She gets the boy's attention.
- It's easy. She can do it without thinking about it. Somehow she knows how to play the part (even while criticizing herself for doing it).
- It works.

Costs of Being Fruit Cup Girl
- She feels ridiculous.
- Girls can and will make fun of her.
- She feels like a fraud.
- She fears the only way guys will like her is if she acts in stereotypically feminine ways (i.e., weak, laughing at their jokes, etc.). She's afraid to show her real self.
- She's afraid people won't take her seriously. She's right.
- She conditions herself to be Fruit Cup Girl whenever she's around a boy she likes.

So FCG gets the guy, but feels like a fool. And by the way, the vast majority of boys don't really get or like FCG either. While they don't want girls beating them at everything or making them feel stupid, they also don't want a girl who seems incredibly superficial and brainless.

I constantly see girls act superficially around guys! It's amazing how girls instantly become charming and flirty when a guy steps

into the room, as if they can't let down their guard for a split sec-
ond and just be themselves. Although I hate to admit it, I'm sure
I've done this before.   —*Jenny, 17*

Girls feel they're not perfect enough and try to make up for that
by acting. Same with me.   —*Jessica, 13*

But the larger issue is that FCG makes girls feel ashamed to be girls. You look at girls acting like FCG and you understandably don't want to be associated with that because you know boys don't respect it (which of course doesn't stop some of them from hooking up with her). And the big problem with that, beyond the fact that we want girls to be proud of being a girl, is that as girls get older, this dynamic is the reason why girls won't help a FCG girl who's in trouble with a boy and/or if she's intoxicated.

When girls are younger, being a FCG is the easy way to get a boy's attention. By eighth grade, girls know that acting like that is only going to get you so far without inviting even more ridicule. Older girls still bring out FCG to get boys' attention, but now they need an excuse to openly fall back on her. That's where drinking comes in. As long as a girl has a beer in her hand, she has an excuse to be FCG. The metamorphosis from Fruit Cup Girl to Beer Cup Girl sets the stage for girls to use alcohol and drugs as excuses for doing what they want to do but are too afraid to do sober because they'll get a bad reputation.

When I was twelve, I remember wondering why girls had to act
so fake around guys. They would stand around in clusters and
scream and giggle and shoot looks over at some guy. Maybe one
of their friends would come over and give you a message. If they
act like that now, I would think they were trying to hook up. It's
obvious. No one acts like that much of a moron unless they want
to hook up.   —*Patrick, 16*

By the way, it's not like boys don't have their own version of FCG. His characteristics aren't like FCG but he too has in-the-Box attributes (just for guys this time) to get attention from girls.

When he's younger, he likes to show off and everything's a joke to him. When he's older, you're sure to find him in social situations as the loud one, making fun of people and trying to be the center of attention by forcing other people to notice him.

FIGHTING OVER BOYS

Girls competing over boys can get very ugly, and they often drag their friends into the mess with them. I teach a semester course for sixth graders as part of their health class. Last year before the class started, a teacher gave me the lowdown. The girls were off-the-charts cliquey and mean. They had already been talked to several times with no improvement. The teacher described one girl by saying, "I'm sure Morgan's the Queen Bee; I've been trying to catch her all year and haven't been able to." When I met this girl, she was tiny, pretty, and didn't say a word in class. Meanwhile, there was another girl in the class named Brianna, also tiny and pretty, who talked constantly in class and asked for my advice afterward. Of course, being a sucker for anyone who asks my advice, I thought Brianna was sweet and Morgan was mean. I was wrong. They were both mean. They had been waging a protracted dirty war against each other all year, and the pivotal battle peaked at a boy/girl school event in the spring. At this event, where adults were everywhere but no one was officially chaperoning, Morgan and two of her friends met up with three popular boys who Brianna thought were "hers." When Brianna found out, she began a systematic campaign to get the boys to switch their allegiance back—and she was successful. Practically the entire grade was polarized between these two girls, with savage consequences threatened for any displays of disloyalty. Morgan vowed revenge, although she justified her actions because it was "only equal to what she did to me." The only thing that stopped them was the end of the school year. The next year, many new students joined their grade, and they had about a day to decide which girl they aligned with.

When girls are younger, the fighting over boys is usually limited to things they say to the boy to trash the other girl or telling the girl something to make her feel terrible under the guise of "I think there's something you should really know." For example, an eighth-grade girl recently asked my advice for the following situation:

"I like this guy and he likes me too but he's still talking to this other girl. She doesn't know that he likes me. Shouldn't I tell her?"

Here was my answer:

Yes, you should, but you have to be honest with yourself about your motivation. If you're telling her because you feel bad that this boy is manipulating her, then by all means say something. But let's be clear that she isn't the only one being manipulated here—so are you. If you're telling her because you want her to know that he likes you more or she should back off your property, then, no, I wouldn't. I would tell the boy you're not going to allow him to use both of you and that until he stops doing that, whatever you've got going with him is over.

REJECTION: DUMPING AND GETTING DUMPED

No matter how old you are, being rejected is awful. When a girl is younger, it hurts because she's having these feelings and experiences for the first time and her inexperience can blind her to the warning signs of an impending rejection. It ends up being a cruel surprise. When she's older, her relationship is more physically intimate and/or emotionally complex. Her life could be more connected with his because they have the same friends. She could feel that her image in her school community is tied to the relationship. Since a girl's sense of self is often tied to her perception of her sexuality, she could feel used, manipulated, and foolish when rejected. Last, rejections now are rarely kept private between the people directly involved. Technology now makes getting dumped a public event that everyone can have an opinion about. Are you mad because you just found out your boyfriend has been getting together with someone else behind your back? Dump him by making a YouTube video that everyone in the world can see.

When a girl is dumped, she usually tries to figure out what she did wrong and then change that part of her personality. Even if she knows that the person who dumped her is a jerk, she can convince herself easily to get back with him—even if she knows he'll treat her poorly.

In sixth grade he wrote a script to break up with me and read it to me in the lunchroom. He said, "Erin, it's over, I can't be with you anymore," and I said, "Okay," and he goes, "No, you're not following the script! Your line is, 'I need you, don't leave me.'" In seventh grade I gave him another try. That time he tape-recorded him breaking up with me. —Erin, 18

Why do girls take back boys who dump them? Because most humans have a weakness for wanting what they can't have. Girls want easy, quick fixes that reassure them that they fit in. The Act Like a Woman box is an obvious place for answers, and it tells them that a boyfriend is important to their status. So they turn themselves inside out trying to be the girl they think the boy wants them to be.

A breakup's silver lining is that it creates great girl-bonding moments. The intimacy that comes out of these experiences can be unexpectedly rewarding. Especially if the dumped girl has been blowing off her girlfriends for her now ex-boyfriend, those friendships can experience a honeymoon period. The dumped girl can pour out her sorrows, anger, and confusion to her friends while they analyze the ex-boyfriend's baggage and problems that made him reject her.

Girlfriends can be similarly helpful when a girl is considering breaking up with someone because they help in sorting through the pros and cons of the relationship and strategize what to do when the girl wants out. This can be a hard task for girls. They may date someone longer than they want or may then find it impossible to communicate clearly when they want to end the relationship. They'll look for excuses so they won't have to face the situation directly. Friends in the clique can help them find the backbone to confront the boy. Or the clique can allow a girl to abdicate responsibility for the unpleasant job by bringing the bad news themselves or supporting her while she simply ignores the boy, hoping he'll go away.

BREAKING UP ONLINE

Getting dumped online is the worst! This is what this guy e-mailed me. "It's not you. It's me. I don't like you. You're bossy and I don't like the sound of your voice. I used to like you and now I don't. Sorry. PS I want my PlayStation back." Then he forwarded it to all his friends before he sent it to me. So by the time I got to school everyone in the school knew. —Zoe, 18

I broke up with a girl once by text message and it was a huge mistake. You can't tell the person's reaction. I really shouldn't have done that. —Dylan, 14

Technology has created a whole new system for breaking up—and that's not a good thing. Think about it. What better way to go through the discomfort of getting out of a relationship than doing it online where you don't have to face the person, and if they do anything you don't like, you can forward their response to all your friends to justify your actions?

Going from worst to least objectionable, here are the most common ways my students are breaking up online:

1. Changing their relationship status on Facebook from "In a relationship" to "Single"
2. Texting
3. Sending an IM
4. Leaving a voice mail on a cell phone
5. Sending an e-mail

I got rejected, and I'm shy when it comes to girls. I mean, I had a huge crush on her, and she kind of liked me back. She dumped me by leaving it on my voice mail. I hated it because it feels like you're leaving something unfinished. —Chris, 15

As a parent, you need to know how your daughter could get rejected or how she could reject someone else. From there, you need to present her with some guidelines. Here are mine:

1. No one should find out they got dumped by having their ex (which they don't even know is an "ex" yet) change their relationship status on Facebook from "In a relationship" to "Single." It's just cowardly and mean. And adding to the humiliation is the likelihood that five minutes later all the "friends" are going to see it and then post things on the rejected person's wall like, "I'm soooooo sorry!" "When did it happen???????" "WHATTTTTTT!!!!! U MADE THE CUTEST COUPLE!!!!!"

2. Text messaging is unacceptable. It's impersonal and disrespectful.

3. Instant messaging isn't much better and has a higher risk for sketchy behavior. You don't even know if you're really talking to the person you think you are, and even if he or she is there, the person can leave you hanging. So there you are at your computer typing "Hello? Are you still there?" right after reading, "I hope we can still be friends." Also a big negative is that instant messages are easy to copy, paste, and forward. Last, there's little personal investment on the part of the person doing the rejection because he or she could be doing ten other things at once.

4. Voice mail—you've taken the risk that the person may pick up, unless you deliberately call when you know he or she will miss the call. If that's the case, voice mail is like text messaging. You're rejecting a person without giving him or her the respect to have the conversation.

5. E-mail's benefit is that it can give the person being dumped the opportunity to read it on his or her own time and decide when to contact you back. However, e-mail still isn't that great of an option because people are more than capable of dumping someone meanly and forwarding any part of the exchange to other people. Also remember that e-mail can be misinterpreted, even at its best.

This leads me to the conclusion that the best way to end a relationship is to do it face-to-face, without other people around. A good time to break up is before a school break. A bad time to break up is on the person's birthday. I know this is hard because I am asking your daughter to tell someone he is being rejected in a clear and direct manner. But nothing about this situation is easy. By the very nature of what she's doing, she'll hurt the person's feelings. Accept that as fact, but remember that she can control how she conducts herself so she treats him with dignity. She can do so by preparing what she's going to say, and being clear so there are no false hopes that she'll get back together with him.

> They [the person who gets dumped] are going to trash you no matter what, so timing is important here. Don't do this when you're about to see them in the next few hours, so don't do it in the middle of school. After school like when they can go to practice and run out their frustration is good. —Alex, 18

> You can't take steps backwards in a romantic relationship and say, "OK, we're just like we were before we started dating." Before dating you were on the path to dating. You need to give the other person space and let the friendship re-form between the people you are now. —Faith, 17

CHECKING YOUR BAGGAGE

- Close your eyes and remember your first crush: Where were you when you first saw this person? How did you feel?
- What makes you most nervous about boys and your daughter?
- What do you want to teach your daughter about boys?
- Were you ever dumped by a girlfriend or boyfriend? Where and how did it happen?
- Who, if anyone, did you go to for support?

Just as you've brought your baggage from your own experiences with friendships, you'll do the same thing when your daughter begins to be sexually interested in people. Somewhere in your daughter's adolescence you'll go from telling her what to do, with a good chance she'll do what she's told, to guiding her and recognizing that she needs space to make her own decisions. Nowhere is this more true than with boys.

HER BILL OF RIGHTS WITH BOYFRIENDS

Lots of girls get all red in the face as soon as you bring up the whole boy thing. Here are some suggestions for how to have those conversations. Remember, this may be a great time to see if she's interested in talking to that ally. You don't have to wait until your daughter has a boyfriend to have this conversation. As soon as you see your daughter or her friends being interested in boys (age nine or ten is what I'm thinking here), you can start to have these talks.

When you sense that your daughter is ready to start talking about an interest in boys—either because she comes to you or because you see the unmistakable signs, such as the new monthly phone bill—it's time for a discussion to clarify what she wants and has the right to expect out of any relationship. Your goal is to help her understand how her feelings when she likes someone may impact her Bill of Rights. Ask her how she feels when she likes someone (don't use the word *crush* because then she'll think you're patronizing her). Then, ask her what her Bill of Rights should be with someone she likes. If the discussion is too uncomfortable for her, suggest she write it down in her journal. It should look like this:

When I like someone I feel . . .
  Nervous
  Excited
  Butterflies in my stomach
  Distracted

When someone I like treats me with dignity they:
  Respect me and other people.
  Don't make fun of me with bad teasing.

Listen to what I say.
Don't treat me differently in front of other people than when
we're alone.

The question you need to get your daughter to think about is this: If she likes someone and they don't act according to her Bill of Rights, what should she do? She should reread her Bill of Rights for her friendships with girls (see Chapter 7) and then ask herself why she would hold a person she likes to a lesser standard than she would a friend. How can SEAL help her strategize and frame her words? Reassure her that you're there to listen or to help.

> *A girl sometimes discounts her Bill of Rights with boys because she thinks if she lets him get away with more, he'll like her back. What she doesn't realize is that that will only make him respect her less.*   —*Nidhi, 16*

Remember, dismissing her Bill of Rights is the first step (or more accurately, misstep) your daughter can take toward believing that what boys want is more important than what she wants or feels is right.

DADS, PAY ATTENTION!

When your daughter starts to like boys, you have a crucial opportunity to reach out to her. If you establish a rapport with her, she'll see you as a critical resource for the boy perspective. If your inclination is to sum up what your daughter should know about boys in the sentence "All boys want is sex," think again. Even if you believe this is the case, your saying that will totally shut her down. She needs to hear about boys from your vantage point. For example: "I know this may be uncomfortable, but if you ever want to talk about guy stuff I'm here anytime to talk."

When she opens up, this is a great time to talk about the first person you liked and/or your first relationship. Your daughter needs to be reminded that you were her age once and you may have gone through similar experiences. Feel free to tell her what confused you about girls and how you figured things out. Invite her to ask questions about what a boy might be thinking in certain situations.

Most of the time there is so much focus on the special relationship that mothers and daughters share that dads kind of get pushed to the sidelines when it comes to their daughters.

Girls want their father's approval. There's something really powerful about being "Daddy's little girl" and most girls don't want to tarnish that image. At the same time, it's also difficult to talk to fathers because it seems like they don't know what to say and they can seem kind of clueless. Dads seem to have a really hard time letting go of the image of their "sweet little baby girl" and fear what will happen when guys start to find their "little girl" attractive, because dads know how guys think and "no one better be having those thoughts about my daughter." It's good to warn daughters that not all guys may have the best intentions, but it's also important to let her know that there are some good guys out there, because your dad can't be the only exception to the rule. I've noticed that my friends who grew up with their mothers and have really bad relationships with their fathers end up having bad relationships with their boyfriends. It often seems like they date guys who share some character traits that their fathers have. —Ellie, 21

Remember Frank, the dad from Chapter 2? He's a great example of someone who almost lost an opportunity to be present in his daughter's life but didn't because other adults in his family reached out to him and he was open-minded and -hearted to his daughter's changing needs. He went from a relationship of conflict and misunderstanding with his daughter to understanding and deeper connection.

THE GAMES BEGIN: THE BOY-GIRL PARTY

It's happened. Your daughter has just received her first invitation to a boy-girl party. Should you let her go? I would let her go if she wants to. If, however, there's a hint that she doesn't want to go but is feeling pressured, always give her the out of you saying no, so she can "blame" you for not letting her. If she does go and she's open about it the next day, try to have a conversation with her about it. Don't start by asking if she had fun (that's like asking how her day was), but ask her what she thought about the party. Ask if people acted the way she thought they would or if they acted differently. (If she answers that some of the girls acted like FCGs, you have a great opportunity to ask her why she thinks girls act like that.)

Now, suppose your daughter is in sixth grade and relentlessly begs you to allow her to invite boys to her birthday party. Remember why this could be so important to her: having a boy-girl party is a huge asset in ascending the social pecking order. In sixth and seventh grade, these parties can cause an amazing amount of drama. Girls will get upset over a boy, someone will make out in your basement, and your daughter will be at the center of it all. I guarantee tears and fights culminating in a Messenger going back and forth between two cliques brokering a peace accord. What could be better?

Then why, you ask, would you volunteer to be the sacrificial host here? You don't have to but if you want to try, you have to use this as an opportunity to demonstrate parental responsibility. If you agree to have the party, make sure your daughter understands your parameters for invitations and the importance of diplomacy in issuing them, especially if she can't invite everyone. This is a tough call for girls, as they know their stock goes up if they have a boy-girl party.

Before the party, clarify with your daughter where you'll be during the proceedings. Will you stay upstairs with occasional policing reconnaissance missions? Circulating is one way you can minimize drama. It's also an informal but clear statement about who is in charge. Go over your house rules for appropriate behavior and what will happen if kids behave inappropriately. Adopt a zero-tolerance policy for cigarettes, drugs, alcohol, and nasty exclusive behavior. Most important, make a plan with your daughter for how she can ask for your help if things get out of hand and she doesn't want to lose face and risk losing a sense of acceptance among the other girls.

YOUR ROLE AS PARENT: THE ETERNAL "OUT"

One of the cardinal rules you want to establish with your daughter for a boy-girl party is that she can always use you as the "out" and blame you for any rules she may secretly want enforced but doesn't want to take the rap for in front of her friends. Two examples: "My mom and dad will kill me if you bring that in here," and "My parents absolutely freak if anybody goes upstairs to any of the bedrooms."

This rule isn't just for parties, however. Make sure your daughter knows she can always pin it on you if her peers are pressuring her to do something she doesn't want to do: "Sorry, but my mom doesn't let me go out on weekdays." "Sorry, but Dad would go ballistic if I went to the mall without his permission." It's a fair deal: you're the fall guy, and she stays safe.

I did it a lot freshman year, and it worked! —Vivian, 15

For any "Hip Parent" types, if your daughter uses you like this, it won't make you lose face with her friends: valid excuses (which these almost automatically are) don't get a second thought from them. —Katelyn, 18

OFF TO THE MALL: RUNNING IN PACKS

It's normal for teens to run in packs. A lot of major boy-girl interactions will take place at the mall, the movies, or school functions. It's also normal that once in packs, kids do things they never would if alone. You can't stop your daughter from running in packs, but you can guide her about how to behave in these packs.

Having a check-in time is very important. Make an agreement (and, you know, I think it should be written down and put in the alarm of her cell phone—here's a time when cell phones are good!) about when she'll check in with you. If you say she needs to be home at 10:00, then you have every right to expect her home by then. If not, apply appropriate consequences.

MAKE NEW FRIENDS BUT KEEP THE OLD

In the excitement of girl-meets-boy, it can be easy for your daughter to forget to maintain her friendships with both girls and boys. Just as you've reinforced the lesson that it's not okay to blow off one girlfriend when an offer from another girlfriend comes along, make it clear to your daughter that it's not okay to blow off a girl when a boy comes into the picture. As you'll see in the next chapter, this is a crucial lesson. As intimate relationships become more important to girls, they are more likely to devalue their girlfriends—the very people who can support and protect her if she gets into an unhealthy relationship.

LATE-NIGHT PHONE CALLS

Here's yet another reason for your daughter to hand over her phone at night . . .

When you were a teen, did you ever wait by the phone at night for a boy to call? When the phone rang, somehow your mom or dad would answer before you could get to it? Then you would have to suffer the humiliation of your dad saying things to the caller like, "Do you know what time it is? No, she doesn't talk to people at this time of night!"

Today, if your daughter goes to bed with her cell phone, she misses this experience because she'll get all the calls she wants without parental interruption. Don't deny her this experience! Take her cell phone with you when you go to bed, and if someone calls answer the phone and do the same thing your parents did.

Think of it this way: You owe it to your daughter and the caller to teach them about boundaries.

THE STOMACH CHURNER . . .
SHOULD YOU ALLOW BOYS IN THE BEDROOM?

Maybe the rest of the group took off, and it's just your daughter and the guy she currently is obsessed with. Or maybe he came over to study. Are you uptight if you forbid your daughter from having boys in her bedroom? Who cares? This is exactly the kind of rule you have to make. My opinion is that you shouldn't allow your daughter to have boys in her room. Of course, having this rule may not stop her, but it's important to make the rule anyway. There are several reasons to have this rule. First, if you aren't home and she's with a boy she's attracted to, she may feel nervous about "going upstairs" with him. She can blame you, the "eternal out," again. Second, when she tells the boy he isn't allowed upstairs or she's obviously nervous about it, it transfers critical information to him about you: this is a house with rules and your daughter respects your rules; therefore, he should too. You are reinforcing your values about personal space (yours and hers) and it gives her the feeling that you're watching her.

SO HOW DOES SHE BREAK IT OFF?

I broke up with my boyfriend over the phone and my mom got so mad at me. And I said, "What do you want me to do, ask you for a ride so you can drive me there? I can't break up with him while you're waiting for me outside. There's no way I am doing it at school because everyone will see. How else am I supposed to do it?"
—Katelyn, 18

You really have to be careful how much explaining you do when you break up with someone. I know it's necessary but at the same time the breaker-upper may come across as willing to take the person back if they changed. So if she really wants to break up, she has to be clear about it. It's not fair to leave them with false hope.
—Alex, 18

As I mentioned earlier, your daughter might run through several boyfriends, with varying degrees of seriousness. Even if she's with someone who turns your stomach, encourage her to break up with him respectfully, clearly, and on her own (meaning no Messengers doing her dirty work for her or breaking up online). She can use the same SEAL strategy I've outlined in earlier chapters. She should Strategize where to do it privately and Explain: "When you tease me in front of your friends and won't listen when I ask you to stop, I feel like you don't respect me." When there's no reason other than that she just wants to move on, she can say, "I just don't like you like that anymore." Recall that this is very tough for girls; she may be tempted to be unclear. "I'm not sure we should see each other anymore" or "Maybe it isn't a good idea for us to keep dating" are fuzzy statements that invite misinterpretation. Finally, she should Affirm and Lock. She doesn't have to say anything cheesy and patronizing (saying "I still want us to be friends"), but she still needs to affirm him by saying, "I'd never talk behind your back." She's communicating that her own needs matter and she can set her boundaries with respect while treating him in a way she can be proud of.

When someone breaks your daughter's heart, what can you do to make her feel better? Honestly, there's really nothing you can do to make her pain and feelings of rejection go away, but you can give her a hug, if she lets you, or tell her you're available to talk anytime. Let her sulk and lick her wounds in her room and let her cry; when she does want to talk, just listen and don't rush in with your judgments. Empathize with her feelings, even if you don't believe they could be that intense. Give her some time. Offer to do something fun with her and if she says no, wait for a while and ask again.

I'd be incredibly depressed and I would take it out on my family. They would probably think I was back in some phase or something. Which of course would be really annoying. Chances would be that my mom would know that I was dating him, but she'd probably be happy that I broke up with him. If I thought I was in

*love with him, she would think I wasn't. So then I wouldn't want
to go to her. Girls are going to talk to someone else or keep it
inside.*   —Nidhi, 16

Support your daughter without tearing the boy down. That way
she learns that she doesn't have to put someone else down to take
care of herself. Also, if she gets back together with him (which is
quite possible), she'll still feel she can go to you without looking
weak.

WHAT DO BOYS AND GIRLS MOST WANT TO KNOW ABOUT EACH OTHER?

At strategically placed times in my courses (meaning when our
students are capable of having a meaningful conversation without
putting each other down or yelling over each other), we bring the
boys and girls together and have them write down anonymous
questions to ask each other. Of course, some of our students can't
resist asking questions that are meant to shock, and we weed those
out first or ask the question in a more appropriate way. Then we let
the boys have the opportunity to answer the girls' questions (without the girls' commenting) and vice versa.

So, what do boys want to know about girls? These are their
common questions and the girls' most common answers:

1. *Why do girls like jerks?* Girls' reason: Because he's hot and
   can be really cool when he's alone. My reason: He fits in the
   Act Like a Man box. He's the Misunderstood Guy who looks
   like he has things under control. Girls find it especially attractive if he shows them his sensitive side and feel that only
   they can understand him.
2. *What are girls looking for in a boyfriend?* Or *Why do girls say
   they're looking for someone who listens and respects them and
   then date the guys that don't?* Girls' reason: We don't know.
   My reason: The Act Like a Man box gives them bad boyfriend criteria.

3. *Why do girls always go to the bathroom together?* The girls and I agree: It's a big-time bonding opportunity. Girls check in with each other and gossip. If they're on a date, they discuss if they're into the date (or, if not, strategize how to get out of it).

4. *Do girls think about sex like boys do?* The girls and I agree: Yes, and they talk about it with each other in detail. When girls say this, the boys giggle nervously.

5. *Why don't girls tell you what they're really thinking?* Girls' reason: We do, but you don't listen. My reason: For one of three reasons: (1) girls think they are, but they're communicating in a way that makes their opinions unclear; (2) they're so conditioned not to that they develop severe anxiety just at the thought of telling boys something they may not want to hear and they shut down; or (3) they're putting up a front.

6. *How do you tell a girl you like her?* The girls and I agree: Directly.

7. *Why do girls ask so many questions when you're dating them?* Girls' response: We don't, but every time we want to ask anything, you all freak. My reason: Because talking and sharing personal information makes girls feel they're getting to know you.

8. *Why do girls wear tight clothing if they don't want the attention?* Girls' response: Don't even go there! We have the right to wear what we want, when we want. My response: Girls do want attention, but not the kind that makes them feel like a piece of dirt and/or a slab of meat. When girls wear revealing clothes, don't make the assumption that they want to have sex. Wanting to feel sexy is not the same as wanting to have sex.

What do girls ask boys? Here are their common questions and boys' responses:

1. *Why are boys such jerks in front of their friends and totally nice with you when you're alone?* Boys' reason: I don't know what you're talking about. Girls want too much when my

friends and I are together and it gets on my nerves. My reason: To get their friends' respect, boys put up a front that they're tough, in control, and funny. They may feel more comfortable showing their vulnerable side to a girl because a girl won't tease them.

2. *How should I tell a boy I like him?* The boys and I agree: Directly.

3. *Why do boys get mad when you don't want to date them?* Boys' reasons: Because girls give mixed signals, play games, and never know what they want. My reason: Some boys believe that girls don't have the right to say no. Much more likely is that the boys' feelings are hurt, but they don't want to show it because it makes them look weak. Instead, a more masculine response is to adopt an angry "Who does the bitch think she is" attitude.

4. *Why do boys think about sex all the time?* Boys' reason: Because we're obsessed and we have no control. My reason: Like girls, boys have hormones, and sexuality is new and exciting. Unlike girls, society more readily condones sexually aggressive behavior in boys, so they have more freedom to express it. For example, boys talk about masturbating more easily than girls do.

5. *When a boy talks to you, why does he look at your chest?* Boys' reason: Because we can't help it, especially when girls wear things that make it impossible to look anywhere else. My reason: (1) He could be objectifying you because that's how he generally sees women. (2) He could be distracted by your breasts because he's attracted to you but really does like you. (3) You are wearing clothes that really do show off your cleavage, so don't pretend you're not.

6. *Why don't boys talk about their feelings?* Boys' reason: Because we don't make a huge deal out of things like girls. We have nothing to talk about. My reason: It's a sign of weakness. They feel that girls have power over them if they give personal information.

7. *Why can't boys ever be serious?* Boys' reason: Girls take things too seriously. My reason: "Serious" to boys often means

emotional, which equals weak and vulnerable or up for public humiliation.

COMMON QUESTIONS YOUR DAUGHTERS ASK ME ABOUT BOYS

What if a boy says, "I'll tell you who I like if you tell me who you like?" Should I tell him?

The only reason to answer this question is (1) if you all are talking about each other; (2) if you want the person you like to know and you want them to find out through a Messenger. But, if you send it through a Messenger, you can't control the information the person gets. So even though this is unbelievably uncomfortable to think about, wouldn't you rather have the person find out directly from you?

How do you get someone you like to notice you?

You can stare until he notices and then smile. And you can still flirt and not be Fruit Cup Girl. If you share something in common, like you both write for the school paper, you can use that as an opportunity to talk.

What do you do when you have a friend who has done things with boys that you don't agree with? I want to be her friend but I don't want to live in the shadow of someone like her. She wasn't always this way.

First off, when you prepare to talk to her using SEAL, you have to get your judgments out of your head. For whatever reason, what she's doing with boys probably makes sense to her right now. So, if you tell her something like, "You're being really trashy right now" or "Do you realize that everyone thinks you're acting like a slut?" it's going to backfire because she'll only get defensive. Think about it: if you were her, wouldn't you get defensive too? I would focus instead on what you liked about your friendship and the way she used to be and say something like:

YOU: (Explain) This is sort of hard to talk about but you're my really good friend and I'm worried about what you're doing with guys.

FRIEND: I know you don't approve but you're not my mom and I don't think there's anything wrong with what I'm doing. I'm having fun.

YOU: (Affirm) This isn't about whether I approve or not [and by the way it isn't]. But as your friend, I have to tell you when you're doing things that I don't think are a good idea. And I need to tell you that I don't want to hang out with you when you are hanging out with X guy.

FRIEND: Then don't! And I really don't need you worrying about me.

YOU: (Lock) Friends are supposed to worry about each other. I'm just telling you what I think. If we can hang out, just the two of us, that would be great. I miss our friendship.

If my best friend has a new boyfriend and I like him, what should I do, just grin and bear it and pretend not to care?

Yes. You are absolutely not allowed to flirt with him to try to get him to dump her and go out with you. That is against the rules of how women should treat each other—best friend or not. Now keep in mind, this rule applies with a current relationship. Girls don't have the right to stop their friends from dating "ex's."

THESE EXPERIENCES ARE IMPORTANT!

I hope you now have a better idea of what's going on when Girl World meets Boy World. These early boy-drama experiences set the stage for your daughter's expectations for and understanding of her personal rights in intimate relationships. As she gets older, these relationships become more mature, and her friendships will become even more important as a safe place to reflect on and analyze these new and often confusing experiences. Unfortunately, battles over boys will continue. As her parent, your ability to guide her in these earlier times will be crucial as she takes her first steps into the complexity of intimacy. And that's what we're going to talk about next. Remember, an essential part of your guidance involves todays' technology, since using technology ethically in intimate relationships is going to become increasingly critical as she gets older.

Pleasing Boys, Betraying Yourself

Dear Rosalind,
Please help me. There's a boy that I really like and he likes me
also and we went out and were boyfriend and girlfriend but then
he broke up with me and he told me that he wanted to listen to
his mom and not have a girlfriend because he can't sleep at night
and it's a distraction to him. So I said OK that's fine. Then I
found out about three days later he was dating a girl named
Katya and he kept it from me and they didn't tell me and Katya is
my BEST FRIEND and I knew her since fifth grade and we are
now in eighth. We made a promise to each other that we would
never date a guy that we went out with.

Thanks! Jasmine

Dear Rosalind,
There is this guy that I really like and he says he likes me a lot too
and then the other day I found out he was making out with one of
my closest friends and it was like a dagger in my heart and he
calls me and tells me that he's sorry and that I wasn't supposed to
find out. I spent 1 hour crying in the bathroom and I don't know
what to do cause we are very close friends and now he pulls this
on me and it made me sad and mad. What should I do?

Yours truly,
Alisa please help me !!!

In the last year, I have created a web video program called Rosalind's Inbox where teens, parents, and teachers ask me questions. Then I post my answers on a variety of social networking sites such as Facebook, YouTube, and my own website. I get hundreds of questions like the ones above, which begs the question: why are girls so willing to betray each other for a guy? Why are girls so good at talking about how unforgivable boy stealing is and then do it anyway?

If your daughter was Jasmine or Alisa, how could you help her think through this situation without condoning an attitude of "girls can never be trusted"? How can you give her the skills to use SEAL to have a conversation with the girl and the boy who have betrayed her? And this is only the beginning. How can you channel your own concerns, fears, and frustrations as she develops these relationships so she'll listen to you instead of tuning you out? Because let's be honest: if you knew your daughter was being knowingly used by boys or betrayed by her best friends, wouldn't you be slightly annoyed that she was putting up with that? Wouldn't you wonder what in the world was wrong with her? After all, you didn't raise her to be a doormat, did you?

All of these issues reflect major challenges girls face as they get older. This chapter looks at how Girl World traps girls in a vicious cycle of craving boys' validation, pleasing boys to obtain that validation, and betraying the friends who truly support them. It will show how you can help your daughter stop the cycle. This chapter, and the one that follows it, will be intense for some people. So I'd like you to keep two things in mind as you read. One, I've made a conscious effort to write the earlier chapters in a way that girls fourteen or younger can read. These two chapters are more appropriate for eighth grade and high school girls. If you're reading this and are under age fourteen, ask your parent, ally, or an older sibling to read it first and see if it's relevant for what you're going through. Two, up to this point, the format of this book is to describe the issues, ask you to think about them from your own experience, and then I provide strategies. I'm doing the same here. So if you start getting really anxious about what you're reading, remember, solutions are coming.

What You Should Know

- Getting validation from boys boosts a girl's self-confidence and confirms that she's in the Act Like a Woman box.
- Girls understand that their social status and identity are tied to relationships with boys.
- Even when she knows better, a girl may sacrifice her personal boundaries and do things that defy common sense, in order to please a boy.
- In trying to please a boy, she may betray and sacrifice her friendships with girls.
- At some point, most girls will lie, connive, or backstab to get the boy they want.
- Your daughter may lie and sneak behind your back to be with her boyfriend, especially if you don't like him and/or forbid her to see him.
- Girls, just like everyone else, have trouble defining the difference between acceptable flirting and sexual harassment.
- Technology is encouraging girls to present themselves in ever increasingly sexual ways to prove they're not uptight or as a way to get boys' attention.
- Denial is a reasonable response to your daughter's developing sexuality. For her welfare, get over it.
- Your daughter can become trapped in an abusive relationship even if she's confident and self-assured and there's no history of violence in your family.

For most teenage girls, guys are everything. Boys validate their existence; they define who they are and where they stand in the world. You can talk to boys differently than your girlfriends. Until they screw you over, they can be really fun and comforting.

—Ling, 17

DATING, HOOKING UP, AND GOING OUT

As girls get older, their relationships with boys become more serious. Do boys and girls still date? Does it count as a date when people go out in a big group of friends? First, let's define some terms. As you'll see from the comment below, definitions have probably changed a lot since you were a teen. With my students "dating" means going out—one-on-one. Dating is rare and it's a big deal. Much more common is the umbrella term, "hooking up," which usually refers to a spectrum of behavior, from literally hanging out to making out to having sex—but the common denominator is it's always no strings attached, whereas dating refers to a more long-term, exclusive relationship.

> *Group dating is the best. It makes dating a whole gray area. Group dates are safer because you don't have to be alone with the person and if you decide you don't like him, you can ignore him.*   —Isa, 16

> *This whole hooking up thing is a gray area. It allows people to not communicate straightforwardly or bank on the fact that the other person is too uncomfortable.*   —Aliesha, 16

The quality of your daughter's experiences with boyfriends and her perception of her choices within those relationships are based on four things: (1) what examples you and other adults she's close to have modeled, (2) what she absorbs from the media, (3) her past and current friendships with girls, and (4) her role in the clique.

> *Being in a clique is an easy way to meet boys. Whichever clique she belongs to, there's a boy group that goes with them. If she strays outside of the accepted group of guys, then that's a problem.*   —Portia, 18

There's often a boys' group that's linked to the girls' clique, and the girls may date those boys. Relationships usually don't develop by going on one-on-one dates, but rather when both cliques hang out together. By the end of high school, it's common for boys and girls within a large group to have hooked up with almost everyone in the group. This doesn't mean they're having sex with each other, but sexual interaction is often a part of the group dynamic.

> When I was in high school, the clique I was in had two "Queen Bees," which divided us up a lot but we were still all friends. One of the Queen Bees made a hookup map with the other Queen Bee as the center (the "sluttiest" girl) to show how we all connected through our hookups. —Charlotte, 19

The girls' social hierarchy can dictate how much flexibility a girl has in her choice of dates. To a certain extent, a powerful Queen Bee has dating immunity, as she can date whomever she wants because the guy she anoints as her current love interest automatically becomes cool. At the same time, she'll be careful to be interested in someone who has some of the Act Like a Man box qualities because she has her image to protect.

> It's gossip central [if a Queen Bee dates outside the box]. People will joke and say, "Is he paying her?" Or they'll ask her "What are you doing?" They won't be supportive of it until she breaks up with him. —Dawn, 15

Girls learn that one of the fundamental criteria for group acceptance is dating someone who has the group's approval. There's powerful pressure for a girl to discount her feelings and her own personal standards to date someone who superficially looks the part even if he doesn't treat her well.

MATCHMAKING AND THE OLDER CLIQUE

By fifteen, most girls have one or two very close friendships—the kind people develop when they go through boot camp together. But most also continue to have the kind of friendships with other girls that are an extended, although more sophisticated, version of their friendships in late adolescence and junior high. It's hard to convince older girls that their individual behavior is still affected by what they learned in the clique from earlier years. It's still there, it's just more sophisticated and subtle so it flies under the radar.

Older Queen Bees now focus their attention on boys as the final arbiter for measuring their power among girls.

> *The summer before my sophomore year, my best friend set me up with her boyfriend's best friend. I felt obligated to go out with him but I didn't like him. He was extremely sexually aggressive, and he really scared me. Alyson said it was "cute" to have two guys who were best friends go out with two girls who were best friends. I would consider Alyson a Queen Bee and I would be the Pleaser. When I told her what the other guy was doing, she said that I was being a prude, so I just shut my mouth and kept going out with him. I was miserable. Finally, I talked to her boyfriend about it. He understood and apologized for setting us up. He helped me break up with my gross boyfriend. It's really hard to be the girl being set up. I said no numerous times, but she kept pushing!*
> *—Ella, 18*

Here you can see the direct connection between girls' friendships and girls' unhealthy experiences with boys. Ella, in spite of being miserable, dated and couldn't break up with a boy she was frightened of because she wouldn't risk going against her friend. She was more afraid of displeasing the Queen Bee than of being with a sexually aggressive boy. People often link girls' vulnerability to making poor sexual decisions and even sexual violence to their difficulty standing up for themselves with a boy. Yet one of the reasons Ella found herself with this sexually aggressive boy is that she was unable to hold her own with a girlfriend.

WHEN BOYS ARE THE BETTER OFFER

In previous chapters I discussed how girls often jockey for position within their cliques by blowing off friends for a better offer—a better party, a more popular friend, or a chance to see a new movie with the more popular friend. As girls get older, more and more the "better offer" involves boys. A girl makes plans to hang with her friends at someone's house, then "he" calls or texts, and all bets are off. This is where older girls follow the invisible rules of the Act Like a Woman box, which values boyfriends over almost everything else. According to its rules, girls are allowed to blow off girlfriends for a guy. Girls don't like it. They'll complain and talk behind the back of the friend who blew them off, but girls will almost always take her back.

> We all do it to each other. It's understandable. It's part of the code. If she ditches us, then we talk behind her back and say she has no self-esteem and how pathetic she is, but we'll take her back. Sometimes it gets out of control [with the boy] and we never see her anymore.   —Melanie, 14

> We have to forgive each other if we hope to be taken back.
> —Ellie, 21

Ironically, girls often blow each other off for the same reason girls blow off their parents—it's safe. A girl knows her parents won't reject her if she decides to go out with her friends instead of staying home and playing Scrabble with them. Likewise, her friends won't reject her because she's choosing a boy over them. It's the rare girl who will stand up and tell a girlfriend how hurt and angry she is that she was dumped for a boy. And if she does, she often gets accused of "holding the girl back" or "not letting her have her own life." There's a point in most friendships where the girl being blown off won't take it anymore, and it can cause huge fights between close friends. This dynamic sends girls the message that their friendships don't count as much as romantic relationships. It teaches them to discount themselves and to value themselves as less than males.

> This happens A LOT, and when the relationship with the boy ends, the girl is left friendless.   —Lily, 15

BOYFRIEND STEALING

By high school, girls' friendships are often made or broken over boys, and this can have a chilling effect on the support girls can expect from one another. Some girls become so mistrustful of other girls that they shrink down their circle of friends, confiding in only one close friend, or deciding that only their diary is trustworthy. When a girl betrays another girl by hooking up with her boyfriend, she has violated a sacred bond between girls. No matter who in the new couple took the initiative, rarely do girls blame the boy as much as the girl, if they blame him at all.

> *Girls will excuse his behavior by saying that the girl was all over him, she was being a slut and what was he supposed to do.*
> —*Amanda, 17*

Many girls are conditioned to believe that boys are less capable of fidelity, so they don't hold them to the same standard they would a friend. Since girls' friendships are still often more intimate than the sexual relationships they are having with a boy, the feeling of betrayal often runs correspondingly deeper. Girls excuse boys' behavior. They don't excuse girls' behavior. This double standard of not holding the boy accountable has repercussions in other aspects of intimate relationships, as we'll see shortly.

Two things happen when girls can't trust each other. First, they miss out on having strong relationships now and in the future. Second, when girls don't watch out for each other, they often walk away from or ridicule a girl who is caught making bad decisions with guys. Girls often turn away from each other in situations ranging from being drunk and having sex with someone a girl met a few hours ago to being "stupid and weak" if she's in an abusive relationship. The sad and frustrating truth is that so many girls forget or never learn how invaluable they are to one another. But look what happens when they do:

> *I have about five close girlfriends who have stood by me during this long process of trying to break free from my ex- and now-*

again "boyfriend" (this word would entail responsibilities, none of which he possesses, so I have trouble referring to him as such). Rather than tell me I'm stupid and weak and shouldn't care so much, they have tried their best to understand that the relationship is hard to break free of because he was my first everything. No matter how much pain he causes me, my friends understand that he has played an important role in my life and understand why it's a long and winding road. This, to me, is major support and tolerance. —Brooke, 18

I had a friend stay up all night with me as I finally talked about how mean my boyfriend was. She told me I didn't have to put up with it and there was nothing to be embarrassed about. I really think she gave me the strength to break it off with him.
—India, 17

RELATIONSHIPS ON ANY TERMS: PLEASE PLEASE LIKE ME

I hooked up with someone who told me from the beginning that he was not interested in monogamy. I said it was fine because I thought I could be happy with what I could get, but I wasn't. When he hooked up with friends of mine, I'd get so jealous and so angry, but I couldn't tell him why. —Zoe, 17

Think about the many dynamics that intersect when girls become more interested in boys. They want true love the way they see it in the media. They want boyfriends to show off to their friends and to increase their social status. They want to explore the excitement and drama of romance. In the course of achieving these goals, they learn that they can get away with blowing off their friends for a boy, that it's hard to trust a friend around their man, and that maybe the more valuable relationship is with the guy.

Combine that with what they learned in early adolescence about maintaining relationships no matter how they are treated, how they learn from the culture to express their anger and depend on online platforms as the way to communicate, and you can see how girls face major challenges to have healthy relationships with boys. Pleasing boys governs what girls say and their perception of their power within a relationship. The desire to please affects the way they date, how they communicate what they want or don't want with boys, and even the way they dump a guy. Girls are looking for an insurance policy against their own insecurity. When Girl World is set up to increase your daughter's insecurity, she'll seek validation from a boy and can become desperate to please him.

COMMUNICATING WITH BOYS

Of course, it's harder to please a boy if a girl can't figure out how to talk to him. And now it's that much harder when the default method of communication to create and maintain intimacy is online. In addition, communication moves to a whole new level when girls have to figure out whether boys are being nice because they genuinely like them, or flattering them because they're physically attracted to them. By the time they're ready to date, girls have had years to hone the fake compliment. Girl World compels girls to compliment each other, so girls realize how hollow words can be. Picture yourself in the fitting room at a clothing store; the saleswoman tells you with a fake smile how great you look in a skirt that obviously makes you resemble a large bran muffin. You know she's lying, but there's some small part of you that wants to believe her. When a boy compliments a girl, it's the same thing. She wants to believe him, even if her gut tells her that there's an ulterior motive. She'll feel grateful and then obligated to him.

> *Your insecurity kicks in. At some point the fact that the guy wants something sexual doesn't matter because getting the validation is more important.*   *—Zoe, 17*

Many girls initially give in to boys and agree to things they may not want. Later it may make them angry with themselves and resentful toward the person and situation. They start to smolder and simmer, waiting for the boys to understand and reach out to them.

Of course, boys rarely do this, because they've been trained to dismiss what is stereotyped as overemotional behavior.

> *Many of us feel that our negative emotions aren't as worthy as guys'. This is certainly true for me and it's aggravating. When I finally tell my boyfriend how I feel, I immediately apologize. So girls end up saying yes when we really mean no. I think a lot of girls also feel like they need to keep up this mystique—it's in everything we do. We cover ourselves in makeup, we wear clothing just short of being completely revealing. Most of us (including myself) never let down that barrier when it comes to our emotions. We don't say "It hurts me when . . ." Or "I feel like . . ." We just aren't speaking up and very few boys listen when we do.*
> —Anna, 16

> *You're either supposed to know everything about everything or be an innocent little angel. There's no in between. I'm confused a lot.*
> —Katia, 16

Communication is another place where the expectations girls bring from their intimate relationships with girls inform their relationships with boys. Girls define a great relationship as one in which the other person knows what you're thinking and you can finish each other's sentences; you're totally in sync with each other. This is essential to girls' closest friendships. They think they're going to get it with the boys they like, and when they don't, they feel betrayed. They want to be understood without having to explain everything.

> *Isn't it easier to hope someone will guess how you're feeling than gathering your thoughts in your mind and bringing it up? Even now I watch my mom do the same things with my dad.*
> —Jordan, 18

Let Me Make Myself Perfectly Unclear

I wanted to break up with this guy and I just couldn't. It was so hard! I sat down with him and gave him a million excuses why I couldn't go out with him anymore. "I'm having a lot of personal problems right now, I just can't handle it right now." The more he questioned me, the more excuses I made up. —Ella, 18

All this miscommunication, further complicated by cell phones and computers, is the stuff of romantic comedies and the subject of bestsellers. Part of the joy of a girl's first more serious relationship is figuring out how to get on the same page as the boy. And it does happen. But the process is hampered by a girl's ingrained need to please and not say what she really feels. This dynamic creates a coded, unclear language when a girl wants to break off a relationship. "I didn't want to hurt his feelings," "I didn't want to be rude," "I didn't want to assume what he was thinking," and "I didn't want to tell him what I wanted because I didn't want him to not like me" are all examples. The result is often a seriously mixed message, and it's more of a problem in relationships among older teens because the stakes are so much higher.

Recently I went on a date with a guy that I have had an on-and-off thing with for about six months. Today was our first official date. Right when he gets to the movie he hugs me and gives me a kiss on my cheek. When we sat down he tried to kiss me on the lips. What I haven't mentioned is the fact that this is my first kiss. I didn't tell him that though. All he wanted to do was make out and that bothered me a little. If we are on a date I understand if he wanted to kiss me but he kept whispering to me, "you are soooo sexy," and "you are way too hot." And when I finally gave in and made out with him, I got really into it and sort of lost control. Before I knew it he was trying to stick his hand in my shirt and he grabbed my butt. This bothered me A LOT and I pulled away. At the end of the movie I gave him a kiss good-bye, but I'm not going out with him again. —Caroline, 15

Caroline's experience encapsulates most of the dynamics I am describing. I didn't talk to her date, but I would bet any amount of money that he thought the date went well. She was sexually attracted to him, she was excited to be on the date, she did want to make out with him. But she didn't know what her personal boundaries were or how to communicate them until she felt like it got out of control. From his point of view the only thing she communicated is that she was into him but didn't want him going down her shirt or pants at that moment—because she kissed him at the end of the date. To her date that probably means she wants to keep going—just at another time and maybe not in public.

A sixteen-year-old girl recently asked my advice about how to tell a boy she wasn't interested in dating him. Part of her liked him and part of her didn't, but she was fairly sure she didn't want to be his girlfriend. On the phone, she had told him that she couldn't date him because she wanted to get to know him better and her parents wouldn't approve. Because she felt obliged to explain this to him in more depth, she made plans to have dinner with him alone—something her traditional parents wouldn't have approved of, so she lied to them about what she was doing that night. She told me she believed that she had clearly communicated to this boy that she wasn't interested in being his girlfriend. I really don't think so. First, instead of explaining her own feelings, she blamed the barrier to a relationship on her parents. When the boy heard this, he could reasonably assume, "If we get rid of this obstacle, then we're back on." When she said, "I can't date you until I get to know you better," what did the boy think when she made plans to go out to dinner with him? That she wanted to get to know him better. What she said and what he heard were totally different. Just imagine your daughter having this conversation secretly with a boy in her bedroom.

Flirting Versus Sexual Harassment

Flirting is a time-honored ritual. It's how teens test their fledgling romantic social skills, and it can be a lot of fun. It can also be another haven for miscommunication. Hardly anything about teens is subtle, and flirting is no exception. Walk down any school hallway and you'll probably be disconcerted by the way teens overtly display their bodies, talk to each other in sexually explicit ways, and constantly touch each other. It's a huge part of teen culture, but that doesn't mean that all teens like it.

This is the environment where sexual harassment occurs. When does flirting cross the line? Flirting makes both people feel good, and sexual harassment makes the recipient feel small, uncomfortable, powerless, and/or intimidated. What is relevant to your daughter is that sexual harassment can create a hostile educational environment.

When I give presentations on sexual harassment at high schools, I ask the students to give me examples of sexual harassment separated into categories of verbal and written, visual, and physical examples. These are their responses:

Verbal/Written	Visual	Physical
Sexually explicit notes	Hand gestures	Pinching
Cat calls	Licking lips	Grabbing
Showing lewd pictures	Staring at body parts	Hugging/kissing
Calling someone bitch or ho	Flashing	Blocking a path
"Can I get some of that?"	Grabbing crotch	Rubbing
		Grinding (when boys grind their bodies against girls at dances)

Then I ask the students if everything on the list is always sexual harassment. The answer is always no, but it never fails to spark a heated argument. The key to understanding why sexual harassment is so confusing is appreciating that it's defined differently by different people, and that calling it harassment places a huge burden on those who speak up about it (Targets) and who subsequently may be labeled an "uptight complainer."

Several criteria determine whether the action in question is considered sexual harassment: what relation the person doing the action has to the Target; how comfortable or uncomfortable the

Target feels; the boundaries and personal space of those involved; and the threshold for harassment. If the Target is attracted to the other person, she might have a higher threshold for what she considers sexual harassment.

Girls and boys each have distinct and different reasons why it's often hard to tell a harasser to stop. The following are two stories that may shed some light on these difficulties.

Girls Are Silent Because . . .

Jim, Craig, and Jess are friends who have history class together. One day during class Jim convinces Craig to write a note to Jess that details the various ways they want to have sex with her. Jim encourages Craig to give Jess the note after class. When Craig hands it to her, he realizes, by the look on her face as she reads it, that she's upset, but she doesn't say anything. Craig immediately realizes how stupid it was to give the note to her and just hopes she'll blow it off. However, when she leaves the classroom she tells her friends. She didn't realize that boys she considered friends would think about her like that. With the encouragement of her friends, she tells the principal, who then suspends both boys. The boys are infuriated. If Jess is as upset as she claims, why didn't she say anything to them when she first got the note? Why did she go to the principal first instead of telling them?

Why didn't Jess tell the two boys off? First, she was so flustered—guy friends of hers think that way about her?—that she couldn't think of anything to say, much less the perfect comeback. Second, these boys didn't pick her by chance. They picked someone they weren't intimidated by. They didn't pick a girl who would have gotten right back in their face. Jess is a quiet pleaser. It would be hard for her to stand up to them. Jess is programmed to not want to make a big deal out of it. What if people think she's uptight, frigid, or a bitch? She's confused about the boys' motivations—maybe they meant it as a joke, or even a weird kind of compliment?—and her own reactions—maybe it's good that someone thinks you're sexy, even if the note makes you feel bad? With the Act Like a Woman box controlling her actions, Jess says nothing to them to their faces. Only when she has the support of her clique does she feel she can take any kind of action.

Boys Are Silent Because . . .

I was teaching a coed class on sexual harassment with juniors and seniors. The girls had just explained how violated they felt when they walked down the hallway and boys tried to put their hands up their shirts. When I asked if there were any boys who had been sexually harassed, a handsome guy raised his hand. He was on the track team and when he was practicing, girls would call out suggestive things to him as he ran by or slap his butt. He didn't like it.

The same girls who'd complained of harassment moments earlier now screamed with laughter. This is the double standard boys are up against. Some girls and boys don't believe that boys can be sexually harassed because they "always want to have sex with anyone at anytime." If a boy complains, he's called gay.

It comes down to this: boys can never say they don't want sexual attention for fear of being called gay, and girls worry that if they say they don't want sexual attention, they'll be called frigid or a bitch. Both boys and girls are conditioned to never say no.

> *Aggressive girls corner boys when they're drunk and have their way with them when the boy doesn't want to hook up.*
>
> *—Ben, 18*

> *A girl in my school sent a really dirty e-mail to my friend about all the ways she wanted to have sex with him, but she never would have gotten in trouble for sexually harassing him. Never.*
>
> *—David, 17*

Let's go back to my school auditorium presentation. Examples of sexual harassment are written on the flip charts, and I think the students are getting it when a boy stands up and challenges me. "What about people's First Amendment rights? Don't people have the right to say what they want? If they want to talk about a girl in the boys' locker room, that's their right and how does that hurt the girl?" I pressed him, "Why would you want to have the right to say something that would make someone else feel bad? Why is it so important that you have that right? Do you think people will like you for exercising this right?" He answered with, "You're trying to control the things we say. You can't do that." I said, "You're right. I have no control over what you say, but don't you want people in your community, including yourself, to be able to walk down the school hall and not be preoccupied with what someone is going to say to you?"

A teen girl gave a very eloquent summary of how that locker room chat does indeed violate a girl's rights:

> *The First Amendment gives you your personal rights as long as, in practicing them, you don't take away someone else's. A guy should have the sense of responsibility enough to know that talking to a bunch of random guys about a girl will have repercussions on that girl, and those repercussions will violate her rights of expecting safety and comfortable surroundings in a school environment. He will indirectly take away her sense of safety and security in an environment where she should be concentrating on studying. However, it's not that indirect because he knows that she will get a disrespectful or some type of sexually harassing response from the guys in the locker room based on what he tells them.* —Nidhi, 16

Most sexual harassers don't realize the impact of their behavior. There are also people who do realize and don't care, or are intentionally using sexual harassment as a way to intimidate. How can your daughter tell the difference? It's actually a lot like the different definitions of teasing I discussed in Chapter 6.

- An unaware perpetrator doesn't realize the consequences of his or her actions, but will stop if told in an effective manner.
- An insensitive perpetrator harasses to impress his peer group and can dismiss girls' feelings by laughing or making stereotypical comments; for example, "You are so emotional. You are so uptight."

- An intimidating perpetrator most likely intimidates boys as
  well through verbal and/or physical bullying, but he can have
  excellent social skills.

Some people think sexual harassment is totally blown out of
proportion by the media and a few overzealous school administrators and teachers. We've all read about the five-year-old boy sus-
pended for kissing a girl in his class. Forget about the extreme
cases. The goal, as I say to students, is to have a school environment where people feel safe and comfortable so they can focus on
their education. If there are students who feel uncomfortable because other people are doing something in a sexual manner that
they don't like, shouldn't we address the problem? We all have to
be honest. Girls and boys both act inappropriately with each other
all the time—usually because they're trying to figure out what is
appropriate. Girls rub up against boys as they're pushing them
away and saying "Get off of me!," and they mean both. Boys are
often deaf, blind, and dumb when girls send clear but nonverbal
messages like tensing and pulling away when they're hugged or
running away when someone asks if they can be their boyfriend.
While it would be better if all girls could tell a boy directly when
they don't like his behavior, it doesn't help the problem when we
blame the girl for not speaking up or accusing the boy of being insensitive.

Instead, our goal should be to create a way for girls and boys to
live together in a civilized, respectful way. The challenge is to educate girls and boys about the obstacles they face that make listening to each other so difficult. They have to know how the Act Like
a Woman and Act Like a Man boxes guide their behavior and take
responsibility when they behave in confusing, threatening ways.

OLDER GIRLS VERSUS YOUNGER GIRLS

*The senior girls don't like freshmen hooking up with "their" [se-
nior] guys. The girls of higher social status feel like this girl who
isn't as cool or pretty as they are takes "their" guys. They feel
threatened. If they're close to the guy, the girls make comments*

to the guy when the girl isn't around or they'll try to hook up with
the guy not because they like him, but because they want to get
the "lowly" girl away from him.   —Ella, 18

By far one of the most frustrating and recurring problems I deal with is senior girls bullying a freshman girl because they have decided that she doesn't know her place. In some senior girls' minds, that girl's place is underneath their feet apologizing for her existence.

This isn't something that happens *all* the time, but it is a problem. What's going on is the seniors are jealous and threatened because their male peers think that freshman girl is really hot or "frosh meat" (the "o" in the word indicates that sophomores are included). But the senior girls rarely admit that to themselves, let alone anyone else. It's much easier for them to humiliate the freshman girl. Here are things senior girls have done to freshmen in some of the schools I work at:

- Laughed at a freshman girl at a party because she's drunk and vomiting.
- Laughed and yelled "Slut" and "Skank" as they see the freshman girl go into a bedroom with a senior boy.
- Created a rules list for all the freshmen (which included not hooking up with any senior guys or any ex-boyfriend of a senior girl), stating that if they didn't comply their lives would be made into a "living hell."
- Getting a can of sardines, opening it, and rubbing the contents into a freshman girl's bed (that was at a boarding school, which is why they had access to her bed).

What's absolutely amazing to me about this is the consistent belief among these groups of senior girls that "This year's freshmen girls don't have any respect for the seniors. It's not like when we were their age. We didn't dress like whores. We didn't throw ourselves on guys. We treated the seniors with respect. These girls deserve what they're getting." There's no empathy. They have no sense that treating these girls so horribly isn't the right thing to do.

It's all about the older girls' right to teach the younger girls their place.

On the other hand, if your freshman daughter is hooking up with a junior or senior boy, especially an Act Like a Man box boy, there is a good chance she's attracted to him precisely because she won't be able to hold her own with him. You can imagine how angry girls can get with me when I say that but this quote sums up what boys tell me perfectly.

> I guess there's a possibility that an older guy in high school would hang out with a freshman because he actually liked her but not very often. What freshmen girls need to realize is that when you go out with a guy like that, his friends tease him relentlessly about it. And we talk behind his back because it's so obvious why he would do that—and it's not because he likes you or respects you. It's because you'll do what he wants.
> —James, 18

FRIENDS WITH BENEFITS

Teens don't use this term anymore to describe when two people are friends and have sex—with the expressed acknowledgment that there is nothing more to the relationship than friendship. More likely, they're going to call it a "booty call" or a "fuck buddy."

Most teens I work with see it as a way for girls to be sexually active without getting the tag of being a slut. It lets her escape the slut/player double standard because it looks like she's in control of the situation and isn't emotionally invested in its outcome. But for many girls and boys alike, that's easier said than done.

You constantly have to convince yourself that it doesn't mean anything. And if you do feel something, then you feel guilty about it because it's not part of the agreement.

THE BAD BOYFRIEND

Unfortunately, it's almost inevitable that your daughter will date a guy you don't like or even hate. Your daughter doesn't have to date someone who physically abuses her to sustain a serious blow to her self-esteem.

This is my criteria for a bad boyfriend:

- When they argue, he questions her perspective and feelings.
- He tells her she needs to lose weight or makes other denigrating remarks.
- He questions her intellect and makes her doubt herself.
- He blows her off by saying she's uptight.
- He calls her a slut or a bitch.
- He insults her.
- He humiliates her.
- He does all of the above and then says "I'm just joking. You know I don't mean those things."

Please notice that this list is basically the same criteria as those for a bad friend. All relationships have drama, but anytime your daughter is in a relationship where she is made to feel "less than" or smaller, where her perspective is questioned, she shouldn't be in that relationship. Later in the chapter, I'll offer some advice on how to help her handle that kind of situation.

HEALTHY RELATIONSHIPS

I realize I've focused in this chapter on the more negative aspects of relationships, since these are the issues girls most often ask about. Not all boyfriends are bad, however, and your daughter may have a wonderful boyfriend. (And, although you might not want to admit it, she can even have a healthy and responsible sexual relationship with that boyfriend.) Remember, girls develop their personal standards for relationships from watching you, their friends, and the world at large.

A healthy relationship is one where the people respect each other and can be themselves without being criticized or corrected. When the person is mad at you, he or she still treats you with dignity. If the person has a moment where he or she doesn't treat you with dignity, the individual apologizes and stops. And of course all of this goes both ways.

SECURITY BLANKETS

There are always a few couples who date exclusively throughout high school. Parents and teachers think they're cute, and other students refer to them as married. But often, one of the two eventually wants to hook up with other people but is unwilling to let go of the security blanket that the old relationship has become. If the boy wants to play the field ("I really think we should see other people, but I still want to see you, too") and the girl doesn't want to let go, she may feel that she has to go along with what he wants. She'll put up with his being nonexclusive in the hopes that he'll come back, because it's better to have something than nothing. She'll say she doesn't need or want monogamy when she really does. She doesn't communicate what she really wants and hopes for the best.

The result is that they're still a couple but they aren't technically going out. They can use this technicality to treat each other like dirt. They can still have casual sex with each other, but it will be casual to one and not to the other. The girl in this situation is in a terrible bind. She's upset about the status of the relationship, but knows that she has no "right" to complain. If she does, her "agreement" will be thrown back in her face ("You said it was okay if we saw other people"), her feelings will be dismissed, and she'll have no one to blame but herself. The only thing she can do is create dramatic situations where she either drinks too much, does a lot of drugs, or does something reckless so he can come to her rescue. And he will, because he does still care for her and her request fits in the "Act Like a Man" box. He feels special because he's the only one she wants to rescue or soothe her. The end result of these dramatic moments are long (I'm talking hours) tear-filled conversations, often at a party where the happy couple locks themselves in a room to discuss their relationship problems.

Checking Your Baggage

- Close your eyes and remember your first serious love: Do you remember the first time you saw this person? How did you feel? What did it feel like to be alone with that person?
- Did you ever date someone your parents didn't like? How did you react to their disapproval?
- Have you ever been sexually harassed? How did you handle it? How do you think your daughter would? How would you want her to?
- Did you ever have a girlfriend hook up with a person you were dating? Whom did you hold responsible? How did it impact your future friendships and relationships?
- Did you ever go along with something a romantic partner wanted because you didn't know how to say no?
- What has your daughter learned from you about relationships? What have you modeled, for better or worse?
- What would you look for to know that your daughter was in a healthy relationship?

What You Can Do to Help

OK—I just described some very difficult situations girls get into. Now I'm going to give you my best suggestions for how to address Girl World meets Boy World issues.

1. Teach your daughter to not blow off girlfriends for a boy. This is an ironclad rule that begins when she's little. It doesn't matter if it's the love of her life; keeping her commitment to what she's promised is more important. Ask her about the unwritten code that says it's okay to blow off a friend for a guy. Where does it come from? What would happen if she told a guy she liked that she already made a commitment to someone else? Why would she like a guy if he wouldn't accept that she already had other plans? What's important to focus on with your daughter is that breaking or

keeping plans has nothing to do with how much you like the person or vice versa. Keeping commitments is about honoring an agreement you made—regardless of the relationship you have with the person.

2. Help your daughter create criteria for dating on her own terms and on her own timetable. Remind her that every girl has her own pace and interest in guys and wherever she is with that is fine.

3. Help your daughter frame her difficult conversations with boys using SEAL. For example, here's what she can say to a boy she wants to break up with:

Stop and Strategize: She thinks about what exactly she doesn't like and where she can tell him.

Explain: She articulates what she doesn't like. For example, "I don't feel respected when you're around your friends and you make fun of me or you laugh along with your friends when they're making fun of me. I don't want to hang out with you if that is going to happen."

Affirm: "I realize talking to your friends about it before going to you looks like I was going behind your back and I'm sorry for that."

Lock: "Right now I feel more comfortable not hanging out or calling/texting/IMing each other [meaning he should feel respected as a person but still know that the relationship is over]."

Unfortunately, breakups are rarely clean and dignified. Most people aren't going to feel comfortable having an extended conversation about why your daughter doesn't want to date them any longer. Most will run away and lick their wounds privately. Sometimes they'll get angry and retaliate, doing things like this:

My friend dated a guy for only like two months when he went crazy. After she broke up with him, he was devastated. Apparently he felt the need to get back at her so he went on her Facebook and commented on every single picture she had taken on a trip with him with some version of "ruined," "fucking whore."

This wasn't like one or two pictures, it was a full 60-photo album.
Needless to say the album had to be deleted. —*Margaret, 18*

Or he could do it the old-fashioned way by spreading rumors about her. If your daughter has this experience, here's an example of what she can say:

YOUR DAUGHTER: You've been saying that I'm a slut/frigid bitch who wouldn't give it up. I have the right to break up with you without you saying mean things about me to other people (or going after me online). I can't stop you from doing it, but I'm requesting that you stop immediately. If you feel I disrespected you or you didn't have the chance to talk last time, I'm open to it, but only if you treat me respectfully.

THE GOLDEN RULES OF HOOKING UP WITH A FRIEND'S EX'S AND PREVIOUS/CURRENT LOVE INTERESTS

In an ideal world, parents would talk to their kids about this subject but it may be a little too close to the sun for everyone involved. However, there really need to be some ethical guidelines about when a person is in her or his rights to hook up with other people. So this is the part where you hand the book over to your daughter and let her read the following.

First, if you are going to do this, you have to know that 99 percent of the time, you won't get out of this free and clear. And you can't say, "She's not allowed to get mad at me because . . ." "It's not my fault, he likes me better." Your friend can get mad—even if she doesn't necessarily still like the guy, it can still bother her. Know that you're in for drama. But, if you still want to go for it, here are my suggestions:

- If there is any possibility of hooking up with the ex on the horizon, you prepare your friend by telling her that you're interested.
- If you have an unplanned hookup with a friend's ex, you tell your friend within twelve hours. Don't assume you can get away with

it, because you won't. Someone will text something or send a photograph, and you will be discovered. There are no private hookups anymore.

- If you think there is a possibility your friend still likes the person, think about that in your SEAL preparation

You don't owe her anything except to treat your friendship with respect. Which means under no circumstances are you within your rights to make out, and so on, in front of her. Also, there should be no gratuitous flirting, like sitting on laps, pushing, being picked up and thrown around, and shrieking. Especially don't ditch her to go out with him. You're not doing this to kiss up to get permission to be with him. Rather, your actions should reflect a conscious effort to be sensitive to how she may be feeling.

If you are the ex: Your position is really uncomfortable and it can easily feel like you have no power. The reality is that you always have the right to your feelings, but you can't control what people do or how they feel. If you find out that a friend has hooked up with someone that you are currently interested in or involved with, then you would have two conversations. One with the friend and one with the hookup, using SEAL to frame both conversations. But under no circumstances are you within your right to get revenge on this girl, talk smack about her, or try to get everyone to hate her.

And last, both of you can't let the object of all this attention get away free and clear. Seriously, he knew what was going on. He is just as guilty, if not more so. Don't let this person sit back and watch girls fighting over him.

4. Help your daughter respond to sexual harassment—this includes applying the same standard of behavior to boys. Just as she wants boys to respect her body, so she must as well with boys. Overall, what's most important here is to "denormalize" the behavior. If she's seeing it every day, then it will be logical for her to think that there's nothing really wrong with the behavior—except for the fact that she doesn't like it. One of the best things adults can do is challenge this reality. And

remember, just because it's something you may see every day doesn't make it right.

Because sexual harassment is so common, there is a good chance that the person who harasses your daughter doesn't realize his behavior is a problem. And if at all possible (meaning your daughter feels physically safe with this person) she should make the first attempt one-on-one, using SEAL.

YOUR DAUGHTER (Explain): Todd, can I talk to you for a minute? This is difficult for me to say, but I really need to talk to you and for you to take me seriously. When you hug me in the hall, I often feel like I'm being felt up. I want you to stop.
(Affirm) As friends, we have to be honest with each other and not let that ruin the friendships.

If he gets defensive or accuses her of sending mixed messages:

YOUR DAUGHTER: You're my friend, and as your friend it's important for me to tell you when something is bothering me, that it's respected, and that you feel I'm doing the same for you. I'm sorry if you think I've sent mixed messages, so the next time you feel I'm doing that, you need to tell me directly.

If he knows that what he's doing is a problem:

YOUR DAUGHTER: Todd, I need to talk to you. I want you to stop making comments to your friends when I walk by your locker. Maybe you believe girls like that kind of attention, but I want to be clear to you that I don't. Now that I have said this to you, I assume you'll respect my request.

If he laughs at her:

YOUR DAUGHTER: Let me be absolutely clear. I want you to stop. I have now asked you several times to stop. If you won't, you will force me to go to (best person in the school) for help.

If he does it again, she should go to her adult advocate in the school for assistance.

What if she does any or all these things to him? It is more than possible that your daughter could be on the giving side of things. She could be the one who gets dumped and goes after her ex. She could be the one who isn't respecting his boundaries. So just as you would with a son, I'd sit down with your daughter and be clear about respecting people's boundaries. She can't trash her boy online. She can't make fun of him if he breaks up with her. So just as you need to talk to your daughter about her strategy when she is on the receiving end of these conflicts, you must also be clear with her that being hurt and feeling rejected doesn't justify revenge.

5. Help your daughter recognize the difference between a good boyfriend, a bad boyfriend, and an abusive boyfriend; and have the best strategies possible to help her get out of an unhealthy relationship.

YOU DON'T LIKE HER BOYFRIEND

Many parents have shared with me how unbearable it is to watch their daughter date someone they believe is unworthy.

Or is he? Before you pass judgment, invite the boy over to dinner and attempt to get to know him a little better. He may have more piercings than you would like, he might have horrible posture, or he may be shy. Forget all that. Does he treat your daughter respectfully? Is he polite? Does he seem to value her opinions? Many kids with green hair and tongue studs turn out to be terrific guys. Frankly, I'd worry more about the Masterminds and the Muscles.

I'd make a huge effort to get to know him better by inviting him over to dinner. If I still didn't like him, I'd give her a factual list of why, like if he smokes or he's lazy about grades, not that he burps at dinner.   *—Nina, 17*

I have a policy that my best friend and I devised which originated sophomore year when I dated this guy named Rick who I was really into, but he could never get it together to call or see me. I knew he liked me, but he was just dumb. But my parents would always be on my case about it, and thus I would end up defending him! We then created the "Defending Rick" philosophy, which has come to describe just about every relationship I've encountered since then. The worst has been with Dylan (the one I'm struggling to break free of) because I've had to defend him in order for people to understand why I've let him back in my life after he broke my heart nine months ago.   *—Carmen, 18*

Okay, you've tried your best and you still can't stand him. The thought of him makes your skin crawl. What can you do? You know that if you voice your disapproval, she'll stay with him forever. Try to keep your mouth shut and wait for her to come to you. Girls want their parents and people they respect to approve of their boyfriends. When asked, you can be honest, but first check your baggage. If you don't like what he wears, forget about it. If you don't like the way he talks to your daughter, that's something else entirely.

If you don't like him for a superficial reason, you can say: "I may not like his choice of clothes, piercings, hair color, etc., but I respect your right to make your own decisions and I have faith that you want to be in a relationship with someone who treats you with respect. But please come and talk to me about it anytime and don't feel uncomfortable bringing him around."

If you don't like him for a really good reason, you can say: "I would like to talk to you about Seth. Yesterday, when you came home from school together, I was really worried about how he was talking to you. Maybe I'm wrong or making too much of something, but I felt like he was belittling you. You have the right to have a boyfriend, but you also have the right to have a boyfriend that doesn't tell you things that make you feel bad about yourself or doubt yourself. What do you think about what I just said? Can you see why I'd think these things?"

To which your daughter will say, "Thanks, Mom/Dad, for telling me what you were feeling. I didn't see it before, but now that you've said it, you're right and I'll break up with him right now." Yeah, right. And then the Lotto van will back up to your driveway with your jackpot winnings, you'll fit into your high school jeans, and your gray hairs will disappear.

Or perhaps your daughter will flip out and tell you that you don't understand her relationship. Then you need to respond with: "I'm not asking for answers or telling you I want you to stop seeing him. All I'm asking is for you to think about what I've said and talk to me later."

What Do You Do If You Find Out She's Sneaking Behind Your Back?

The times when I get into trouble are when I'm sneaking around and can't talk to my parents. —Grace, 16

I'm 14 years old and a freshman in high school. Now, my parents have always been overprotective, but lately things have gotten out of hand. I love my parents, don't get me wrong, but sometimes they are just too much. My mom is more understanding, but my dad just will not listen to anything I have to say. I've gotten into multiple arguments with him before, and every time I try to get my point across he is always interrupting me telling me that I'm wrong and that I don't make sense. He says that I shouldn't date because he doesn't want me getting distracted from my schoolwork. But the thing is that I'm doing perfectly well in school. I've also had a boyfriend for about two months now. I really want my parents to meet him, because he's such a nice guy and I know for a fact that they will love him once they get to know him. But they (especially my dad) are really quick to judge.

But I really want to tell them that I'm actually dating him, so I wouldn't have to sneak around and lie about where I'm going all the time. How can I tell them the truth without having them freak out on me? —Hayden, 16

I'm a 15-year-old girl with Hispanic parents, so they're really like protective when it comes to guys. I'm okay with them being concerned, just not going overboard. They believe I should just concentrate on school; there is no room for boys. I have a boyfriend that I do really like (no I'm not going to say love, I don't think I know what that is yet). We have been "dating" for a month but I have known him for a year. It's getting real hard to see him since I always have to be sneaking around. I really don't want to keep lying to my parents, but I feel that if I tell them I will lose a lot of privileges. My mom always tells me that guys are a distraction from school, but I have actually continued getting straight A's. I wish my parents and I could communicate better; they still want to believe I don't know what sex is. Manuel, my boyfriend, doesn't really seem to pressure me into telling my parents, but I can tell he wants me to. He is a genuinely good guy and I want my parents to know about us without them flipping out like they normally do with me. How do I ease them into the idea about me dating? —Pilar, 16

Like so many girls, Pilar and Hayden want their parents' approval, and they understand their parents' concerns. However, they want an increased degree of freedom and for their parents to recognize they can make good choices. This is what I say to girls who come to me for advice:

Although I totally understand why you are sneaking, you have to stop, because eventually you'll get lazy, make a mistake, and get caught. Then your parents will be so mad about the sneaking that it will be harder for them to see the merits of your argument. Plus, they may also think that the boy is influencing you to sneak, so that doesn't put him in a very good light with them. And it is true that guys can be a major distraction. But if you are handling the distraction by keeping up your grades and your other responsibilities, then I think you go to them like this: "Mom, Dad, I really respect you and I want you to be proud of me and the decisions I make. I know you don't want me to have a serious boyfriend but I really like a guy and I would like to go out with him. I'd like to go out to the movies with him. How can we work this out so I get a little more freedom and you feel good about how I'm conducting myself?" Now, if you get them to agree, it is REALLY IMPORTANT that you abide by the terms. So if you say you will be back by 11:00 P.M., do yourself a favor and plan to get back home at 10:50—because you will lose all credibility if you don't do what you say.

HELP YOUR DAUGHTER RECOGNIZE AN ABUSIVE RELATIONSHIP

Of course, you want your daughter to have positive experiences with the people she dates, and no parent expects that their daughter will be involved in an abusive relationship. But if you know four girls (your daughter and three of her friends), you know a girl who has been or will be in an abusive relationship. How will you know, and how can you get her the help that she needs?

Girls don't get involved in abusive relationships out of the blue. They're vulnerable when certain ingredients combine. Those ingredients include wanting to be that someone special in another person's life, loving someone and wanting the best for them, being part of a community or family that doesn't admit that family violence could occur within it, seeing verbal and/or physical abuse in the family, and a peer social system that measures social status based on a boyfriend.

What Is Abuse?

At its core, an abusive relationship is one in which one person verbally, emotionally, financially, and physically (but not always) dominates, intimidates, and controls another. Abuse is at once terrifyingly simple and complex. "Why doesn't she leave?" people ask. Because she loves him and it's impossible to fall out of love overnight, even when the person who loves you treats you like dirt. Because she has been brought down so much that she has lost any confidence that she can make any decision. Because her clique thinks they look good together. And even the most abusive relationships have good moments, especially because abusers can make you feel like the most special person in the world. And if you love someone, you want to believe him. You see no other option, so you hope for the best.

Have you ever gone to a party and stayed later than you wanted to because a friend, spouse, boyfriend, or girlfriend wanted to stay? Ever gotten into a car with someone who drank enough wine at dinner that you knew they shouldn't be behind the wheel and you had no business being a passenger? I've done both. If you've stayed at that party or gotten into that car, you did so because you didn't want to offend someone, go against someone else's needs, or openly acknowledge that someone was doing something dangerous and irresponsible. Now imagine that if you did stand your ground, people would ridicule you or talk about you behind your back. If it's so hard to stand up to someone in these situations, imagine how hard it is for someone dealing with abuse.

Girls are particularly vulnerable to abusive relationships simply because they are who they are—teens. They think in extremes and in the short term (next year may as well be the next century), are prone to narcissism and drama, and have little experience with which to compare the relationship.

Why Wouldn't She Tell You?

Notwithstanding some of the jokes I've made about girls not wanting to talk to their parents, it's not hard to imagine why your daughter wouldn't want to tell you if she's in an abusive relationship. Look at it from her point of view:

- She wants her privacy: Abusive relationships are maintained by creating a sacrosanct sphere around the couple.
- She thrives on intensity: She could be in love for the first time. An abusive relationship feels like a drug. She needs the

fix. The lows are very low, but the highs are amazing. She can feel like the most loved person in the world. The drama reinforces the feeling that she's in a mature, adult relationship and it's them against the world.

- She feels special: She feels as if she's the only one who understands her boyfriend and can take care of and save him.
- She's afraid of your response: She worries you won't let her see him anymore or date anyone else again for the rest of her life.
- She cherishes her independence: Because of this, she'll resist going to people she sees as an authority. She could easily feel, rightly or wrongly, that if she seeks help, her newly gained independence will be taken away or her future relationships will be controlled.
- She's afraid of disappointing you: She's ashamed and feels as if she let you down. You may like him, and if she tells you, you won't like him. Or you tried to warn her, and she didn't listen.
- She's afraid she'll lose her status: Most likely she attends the same school and shares the same friends as her abuser. She could easily perceive her social status as dependent on her relationship with him.
- She's stubborn and feels invincible: She won't admit to anyone (sometimes including herself) that she's in over her head.
- She's inexperienced: She could believe that his jealousy and controlling behavior are expected and normal aspects of relationships and has little to compare them to. She could see both as proof of his love (that's why what she sees modeled in her home is so important!). So, by the way, texting and leaving voice mails every hour is not healthy.
- She feels helpless: She feels the abuser has complete power over her, so nothing will make it better.
- She's afraid he'll hurt others: He could threaten to hurt people, animals, or things she cares for.

- She feels it's normal: She sees it in her own family and thinks she doesn't deserve better.

What Does Abuse Look Like?

- She apologizes for his behavior (either to herself and/or others).
- She's stressed out. She's hypervigilant and overreacts to minor incidents because she's living under extreme tension. Reacting to this kind of constant stress may cause her to explode or become hysterical over things she can give herself "permission" to get upset about—like lashing out at you.
- She gives up things or people that are important to her, such as after-school activities or friends.
- She has difficulty making decisions on her own, from the clothes she wears to what classes she wants to take. An abuser is very effective at making her feel that any decision she makes is stupid and a mistake, so she becomes paralyzed. She has to check with him for every decision, such as if she can go somewhere.
- She changes her appearance or behavior because he asked her to.
- She comes home with injuries that she cannot explain, or whose explanation is inconsistent with the nature of the injury.
- She believes jealous, controlling behavior is an expression of love.
- She tries to be the "perfect" girlfriend and seems frightened of her abuser's reaction if she isn't. Or she believes if she can just be better in the ways he wants, he won't treat her badly. That way it becomes all her fault.

How Should You Talk to Your Daughter If You Think She's Being Abused?

Do

- Ask about the relationship.
- Maintain open and respectful communication.
- Help her recognize controlling behaviors in the relationship.
- Use all resources at your disposal, including counseling, school, and the legal system.
- Check how often and how long she is spending online and texting with the person. (This would be an example of the importance of needing her passwords. If something goes wrong, you need to able to see what she's been saying online.)
- Plan for her safety.
- Call your local domestic violence agency for help.
- Assure her confidentiality. If you need to tell someone else, ask her permission first. If you need to tell the police or other authorities, tell her first and then jointly agree about who she wants to talk to. Make a plan with her so she feels safe and in control.
- Appreciate that she believes that sometimes the relationship is good for her and that the two may feel that they're in love with each other. She may feel that she can't survive without her abuser.
- Ask, "What can I do to help you?"
- Tell her that you're sorry she feels bad, but you know that you can't understand how she's feeling (teens hate it when adults pretend they know what teens are feeling, unless they have their own story to prove they do).
- Ask questions to help her recognize that her relationship is abusive.
- Support her courage for asking for help and respect her limits. You're helping her establish boundaries with others, including yourself. For example, if she wants to remain in an abusive relationship, don't tell her that her decision is wrong, but do tell her that you're worried for her safety and help her

see the danger she's placing herself in if she returns to the relationship. Explain to her how you would intervene if you felt she was in immediate physical danger.

- Help her recognize that the explanations and excuses for his violence don't justify his behavior.
- Help her see that her feelings are valid. The abuser does not have the right to dismiss her feelings or recollection of events.

Don't

- Present her with ultimatums. Don't make her feel that she has to choose between you and her abuser.
- Assume she wants to leave or that you know what's best for her. If you make decisions for her, you reinforce that she can't make decisions for herself.
- Ask what she did to "provoke him." This type of question reinforces her feelings of self-blame.
- Talk to her and the abuser together.
- Take secondhand information. If you want to use information, say what it is and then ask, "Is any part of that accurate from your perspective?"
- Pressure her into making decisions.
- Threaten or physically attack the abuser. Not only is this dangerous, but it will likely make her side with the abuser.

How to Spot a Potential Abuser

- He exploits a victim's sympathy and guilt.
- He lashes out, calls her names, or demeans her.
- He causes fear through intimidating statements and actions.
- He calls her persistently or texts her incessantly.
- He shows up without warning at home, at her classes, or at her after-school job.
- He follows her.
- He tries to enlist family and friends in attempts to maintain the relationship.
- He's possessive to the point of controlling her behavior.

- He fights with others "over" the intimate partner.
- He has public displays of anger or ridicule toward women.
- He feels entitled—the community's rules do not apply to him.
- He has a two-faced personality. He's charming in public and mean and degrading in private.
- He's abusive toward others, especially small children or animals.

You'll never have a more important opportunity to practice your listening skills. Remind your daughter that she has more courage and resilience than she knows, and that no matter what, you're there for her.

You'll All Get Through This

In preparing yourself for the worst, it's easy to forget that watching your daughter learn to navigate more adult relationships can be fulfilling for you both. Remember, this can be your time to shine. You can role-model positive, honest, caring, loving relationships with men. Dads, if she comes up against a guy who is treating her poorly, she'll know by your example that it's not right and she doesn't have to take it. Moms, you are important role models, too. Show her by your own actions how to have loving relationships based on mutual respect and equality. All of this can be over-whelming, but you can be an involved parent who guides her toward respectful, responsible relationships that will give all of you joy.

Sex, Drugs, Alcohol, and Partying in Girl World

People say your friends will change in high school and you never believe them and then they do. One of my friends does drugs now; I don't even know who she is. I haven't talked to her in two months.
—Makayla, 14

I was 18, my sister was 15, the party started out as this well-organized little event, and I was the cool big sister that got us booze from another friend, and all our friends were hanging out and then she totally lost it. She drank almost a full 12-oz water bottle full of vodka by herself. She couldn't sit up or open her eyes. She was 5'8" and 110 pounds. Then her best friend pulled me into my room and told me that the reason Morgan was so drunk was because she wasn't eating. She was never, ever eating. How at school she would always say she'd already eaten and her friends thought she was throwing up. Before that moment, I had suspicions that she had an eating disorder but after that, all of how she had been acting fell into place. But I remember thinking, "How do I tell my mom what I've seen and heard without getting us both in trouble?" Because part of the proof was in how badly she handled her booze.
—Emma, 20

WE WILL GET THROUGH THIS CHAPTER!

Full disclosure—this was a hard chapter to write and it's probably going to be a hard chapter to read. It's not like I enjoy talking to parents about how ugly things can get at parties or the mess of teen drinking, drugging, and sex. And, in all honesty, I'm not including the most extreme stories my students have shared with me because my goal isn't to shock you. Rather it is to give you information that applies to most teens and to present strategies to help them. So here we go . . .

Word has spread . . .

Gabby is in tenth grade. On a Thursday night, Gabby's mom tells her that her grandmother slipped on black ice in the driveway and broke her ankle. She'll be in the hospital overnight and needs help getting home and through the weekend. Her grandmother lives six hours away, so Gabby's mom plans to leave right after work tomorrow. Then Gabby's dad decides to go because he doesn't want her to make the trip alone. They don't want to leave Gabby behind, but she has a big paper due Monday that she needs to finish over the weekend.

On Friday morning, Gabby tells her friends Anna and Kara what happened to her grandmother and says she wants to have people over Saturday night—but with some ground rules. They have to decide who can come, the parking strategy (because everyone can't park in front of the house or they'll arouse suspicion from the neighbors), no hanging out in the front yard, and all smoking has to be outside. An hour later Gabby texts fifteen of her friends: "Small PARTY Sat. 10 PM My house! Be there!" At Anna's request, Gabby invites Tye, Anna's forever on-again, off-again boyfriend, and Colin, his best friend.

The night begins:

8:30: Pregaming begins. The girls get dressed, put on music, and drink whatever they can find in the liquor cabinet.

9:30: People arrive. Gabby is momentarily anxious about the number of people in her house but then she looks around and tells herself to calm down. It's only fifteen people. They're all following her rules. There's nothing to worry about. No one is trashing anything. It's all good.

WHAT YOU SHOULD KNOW

- Facebook and cell phones are the primary ways kids get the word out about parties. Word of mouth still works but it's a secondary outreach strategy.
- When parents go out of town, even the "best" kids have a hard time resisting the temptation to have a party. Teens can be like caged animals. They are acutely aware of opportunities for freedom and usually jump on these opportunities in case they don't happen again. The risk is worth the reward or consequence.
- There are girls who don't drink, do drugs, send naked pictures of themselves to boys, or have random sex. But almost all of those girls have friends who do and could drag them into difficult and potentially dangerous situations.
- Now that I have said there are girls who abstain from any or all of the above, don't assume I'm talking about your daughter.
- Teens trust one another. At parties, it's common for a girl to meet someone she doesn't know well but feels she does simply because he goes to the same or nearby school and/or has friends in common. When that happens, a girl can trust someone she shouldn't.
- Girls love having a reputation for having a high tolerance to alcohol, and they'll drink themselves under the table proving it.
- Pregaming (hanging out before a party) is a sacred ritual where girls drink, get dressed, and dance. You don't eat during the pregame because then it's harder to get drunk.
- The postgame analysis is also a sacred ritual where girls usually eat, discuss who got together with whom, who humiliated themselves, and who got totally wasted.
- Teens in any community know which parents will let them

party in their house The worst offenders are the Hip Parents I referred to in Chapter 4. These are the parents who buy the alcohol, give it to their kids, lie to other adults, and justify their actions by saying, "I'd rather they drink at my house than somewhere else where they can get into more trouble." These parents are ruthlessly manipulated and ridiculed by their own children and everyone else's children.

When you party at a friend's house and their parents let you do it, you know you're going behind your parents' back but there's something really wrong with other parents doing it. I had one friend whose mom let us drink at her house and then she'd sit next to my mom at swim meets and chat. She was the one who would call my mom and say, "The girls are sleeping over at my house and everything's cool," and then let us drink. I feel really bad about it now and I never had any respect for those parents.
—Emily, 20

Back to the party . . .

Saturday, 7:00: Tye has invited Ally, a ninth grader, to Gabby's party. Ally doesn't know Gabby, and this will be her first high school party. When she asked Tye if she could bring a friend, he said sure, but jokingly (she thinks) said her friend had to be hot. Ally's parents wouldn't approve of her going to the party, so she lied and told them she'd be going to the movies with Bianca and sleeping over at her house. Ally and Bianca are really excited about going to the party. No one else in their grade is invited, and they want to look good, not like pathetic freshmen trying too hard to be cool.

9:00: Ally's dad drives them to "the movie" while Ally sits in the back and texts Tye that they'll be at the mall in ten minutes. As they walk away, Ally's dad wonders if he should have checked in with Bianca's parents but doesn't know their cell numbers. He brushes off his concern while watching the girls walk away and thinks how lucky he is that Ally is steering away from everything he did in high school.

9:30: Tye and Colin pick them up. They drive to Gabby's house while Tye talks to Colin about a lot of people Bianca and Ally don't know but have heard about and who seem very cool.

10:00: They arrive at Gabby's house. Tye and Colin are greeted by a group of guys with affectionate yells and grunts. Ally thinks she hears one of the guys say "Easy" under his breath as she walks by.

10:05: Tye and Colin start drinking. Tye asks Ally if she wants a Watermelon/Raspberry Smirnoff Ice. She's conflicted. She wants the drink, but she also doesn't want to be one of those freshman girls who gets really drunk and makes a total fool of herself. As she's deciding what to do, she realizes that a group of girls are standing by the sink and one in particular is looking at her with full-on hatred. Ally grabs the drink. Tye introduces Ally and Bianca to Anna and Kara. Anna responds by refusing to acknowledge Ally's existence. Tye shrugs and pulls Ally out of the room behind him, which prompts the following conversation.

KARA: Please tell me you aren't going to let him ruin your night. He's just doing it to rub it in your face! It's so obvious! She's a freshman. How much more obvious can you get?

GABBY: Who is she? Can you believe what she was wearing?

KARA: She can't help herself. She's a pathetic freshman. Seriously, Anna, he so clearly invited her just so he can use her. Please tell me you're over him. He's such a loser.

ANNA: Yeah, I can't believe he would bring such a little skank . . .

10:10: Anna pulls out a bottle of Ron Rico and fumes, "How dare he embarrass me like this and bring that little slut here? I'll show him he can't do this to me and get away with it."

10:12: Anna grabs Kara and drags her to the living room, where they start dancing together . . .

I was at a party and watched a girl who weighs a hundred pounds and had never drunk before drink five shots of vodka in

fifteen minutes. Her eyes rolled back into her head, she fell on the ground, and she was twitching. It was scary and we had no idea what to do. Someone eventually took her to the hospital.
—Emma, 15

If I see a hot guy and he's drinking beer, I try to avoid going up to him because I know it'll be really hard to say no. Half the time I'm successful.
—Lynn, 16

When you're at a party, the real girl comes out. A lot of girls say, "I don't need drugs. I don't drink beer." Then you see someone you like and they're really cute and this is one of the few times when you can really talk, so you'll do it [drink or do drugs].
—Nia, 18

When a girl gets drunk at a party, guys look at her like it's a golden opportunity. She's vulnerable.
—Matt, 17

11:00: Gabby is now in full police mode. She stopped drinking hours ago because she's so busy making sure people don't trash the house. She looks over at Anna and Kara, who are being encouraged to make out with each other by some guys—and they do. All the boys start clapping and laughing. Anna smiles, takes a swig out of the bottle of vodka, and walks out. Kara follows Anna out to make sure Anna doesn't do anything stupid and then gives up because she's sick of cleaning up after Anna's messes.

When it's your own party, you can't really drink that much because you have to make sure nothing gets out of hand so people trash things or the cops show up. But even if they [the cops] do shut down the party, you still had the party so it's still worth it.
—Maddy, 17

Parents need to realize that Gabby in this situation thinks she's being responsible, even though she knows she's not allowed to have this party.
—Jaden, 16

Meanwhile, Ally is at a table in the kitchen having a great time sitting on Tye's lap playing drinking games. Tye keeps telling her how good she is. She's not sure where Bianca is, but the last time she saw her, she was dancing with Colin in the living room. Meanwhile, Bianca is getting a little worried about Ally, but doesn't know how to bring it up and get her away from Tye.

11:30: Gabby is miserable. She just went into her parents' room and found two random people in their bed. It dawns on her that she's going to have to clean the sheets before her parents get home.

11:30: Ally becomes aware that the girl who had been giving her death stares is now above her, arms crossed.

ANNA: Tye, we need to talk right now.
TYE: Can it wait? I'm sort of busy right now.
ANNA: No, it's really important.

Tye follows Anna out, leaving Ally behind to continue playing drinking games with his friends. As soon as they're outside, Anna falls apart crying, and Tye tells her that he still cares a lot for her but wants to be able to do his own thing. He suggests doing something next weekend, after his game. When they come back inside, Anna goes back to Kara to dissect the conversation with Tye and Tye goes back to Ally.

TYE: Let's go somewhere else, away from my crazy ex-girlfriend.
ALLY: Sure, but is she OK?
TYE: Oh yeah, she's fine. Come on, let's get away from all these people.

They go to a bedroom; he closes the door, locks it ("So no one will bother us"), and sits on the bed with her. He confides in Ally that he used to go out with Anna and he's tried to let her down nicely, but she just won't drop it. But he's really glad Ally is here. Tye kisses her, and Ally can't believe she's hooking up with a guy like Tye. A few minutes later, he pushes her back so she's lying on the bed. Ally laughs nervously and says, "Maybe I should check on Bianca. She seemed pretty drunk." Tye keeps kissing her and now he's putting his hand up her shirt while he says, "Bianca's fine. I'm the one you need to worry about. I've been wanting to get you alone all night." Tye keeps going and Ally laughs nervously again and kisses him back.

Downstairs, Bianca is having such a good time dancing with Colin that she's completely lost track of Ally.

Why Is It So Hard for Ally to Hold Her Own in This Situation?

There is a small chance that Tye and Ally make out and that's it. But it's far more likely that Ally will do whatever Tye wants her to do, which could run the spectrum of making out, to giving him a blow job (very likely), to sexual intercourse (less likely). But overall, she's not the one in control, he is. Why? The most obvious is that she's been drinking. But that's only the beginning. Here's my complete list:

- She's flattered that he's paying attention to her in the first place, because he's older and has higher social status.
- She feels special because Tye is confiding in her (and in her mind, someone only does that when you trust the person and are close to them). He knows that telling Ally that another, older girl covets him makes Ally feel special. Now Ally is part of the drama—with a senior, no less—and it feels good because it feels like she won.
- She doesn't want Tye to get mad at her and stop liking her.
- If she pushes him away, he'll think she's immature or a prude.
- She may want to do something sexual with him but she hasn't thought about her own sexual boundaries before getting into this situation, and then it's an almost impossible time to start making them.
- She believes that if she gives him what he wants, he'll want to have a relationship with her. And because he

already confided in her, they're already on their way to couplehood.

- For his part, Tye, has grown up conditioned by the Act Like a Man box to be unintentionally or intentionally blind and deaf to the subtle, or sometimes very obvious, signs that he has created a situation where it's virtually impossible for Ally to tell him what she wants or doesn't (from trying to distract him with the Bianca question, to having tears in her eyes, to saying, "No").

In general, I'm not a big proponent of statistics, because they can be easily manipulated to prove what you want. But sexual assault statistics have consistently shown that the vast majority of sexual assaults, including rape, occur when girls are between the ages of eleven and eighteen; and the perpetrator is someone they know and of the same racial and socioeconomic background. In other words, sexual assault is rarely perpetrated by a crazed stranger who jumps out of the bushes. It is much more likely to happen at parties like the one I just described.

I hear versions of this story constantly. A girl walks up to me before class, eyes down, and whispers that she wants to talk to me after class. Later, she'll tell me, often with tears welling in her eyes, "Last Saturday night, I went to this party . . . and I sort of hooked up with this guy. He seemed so nice and I don't really know what happened . . ."

Don't forget, like I said in the last chapter, many older girls' feelings of competition only make the younger ones more vulnerable at the hands of the boys who are proving they belong in the Act Like a Man box. Even though they probably had the same experiences when they were her age, many junior and senior girls believe that a younger girl deserves to make her own mistakes. Like Anna and Kara at the party, older girls justify their behavior by saying, "What was she doing all over him like that? What did she expect? She should know better. Freshmen know they're just being used." They don't. As much as a ninth-grade girl may tell you she knows this, when she's in the situation, most girls will think they're the exception. In the moment, she believes the guy really likes her. Meanwhile, the older girls spread around their version of events, so this fourteen-year-old girl has not only just been coerced into sex but also has been labeled a slut in the process.

If you are a guy and you can figure this stuff out, you can play girls off each other. All a guy needs to do is tell her she's pretty.
—Katy, 15

Are All These Girls Really Lesbians?

At the party, Kara and Anna made out with each other in front of the boys. Many parents hear stories about girls making out with each other and want to know what this means. Are the girls lesbians? Are there more lesbians than there used to be? Why? Is it a phase? What's going on here?

OK, here's the way I see it. Yes, it has become "cool" to make out with a girl—particularly in front of other boys. But this doesn't necessarily mean that these girls are gay. In fact, girls making out in front of boys is usually more about turning the boys on than their sexual attraction to each other. Those girls are "crazy," "fun," and "open-minded." But that's not about being lesbian, that's about pleasing boys. There's nothing more heterosexist than that. Of course, it can also be a cover for girls who really are sexually attracted to other girls but don't want to admit to themselves that they really are. That's why so many of them, if they do it, will talk about it being a "phase."

Now, I know more people have become more accepting of gay people in our lives—which I couldn't be more happy about. No matter who your daughter is attracted to, your job is to accept that and love her unconditionally. And of course everyone must be treated with dignity—period. What you don't want your daughter doing is expressing her sexuality and being sexually active only to please someone else and be objectified.

Land Mine!

If you see that your daughter is "married" to a girlfriend on their Facebook page, this doesn't mean she's coming out. It's just a new public way to say you're BFFs with someone, just like those "Best Friend" necklaces were used in the 1980s and 1990s.

Putting your actual relationship on Facebook can be really awkward. It's official, intense, and binding. So you put that you're married to a friend mostly because it's a symbol that you're really good friends. When a boy does it to a girl, it's like he's being a gal pal. —Katie, 16

GETTING ATTENTION: WHATEVER THE COST

I don't care if we're talking about girls making out with each other in front of other guys, wearing T-shirts that say #1 PORN STAR, sending pictures of themselves to guys they want to impress, doing a striptease, or having sex with multiple boys in one night—it all has a common theme of trying to get attention, no matter the cost to your dignity. The girls I know who do this have a couple of things in common. They are slaves to the consumer, celebrity culture—and their parents are usually right along with them. They don't have things in their lives that they feel good about—beyond what they wear and what they have. They don't have adults in their lives who unconditionally love them but also hold them accountable.

At my school if a girl doesn't hook up it's because she's either not attractive, a prude, or a lesbian until proven otherwise (the same thing is for a boy). It's sad but it's true. Thus the girls here crave the attention of the boys. They must be the hottest to win. There are girls that will have sex with boys on the first hookup. When I started at this school, I learned of something called the rule of 3 . . . meaning you should be getting pretty far (if not the furthest) by the third hookup. But at the same time we have girls that when they come as freshmen will have sex with boys even before the foreplay. I guess what I'm trying to get at is that yes there is an expectation for girls here but it seems to me that most of the girls that participate go above and beyond the expectations. —Nathan, 17

I want you to understand that there is a possibility that your daughter could do any or all of the things I listed above. If you don't give her a strong sense of self and make her feel valued for her character, she can fall prey to needing this kind of attention. And she sees role models all around her in this culture to show her how to do it.

Drugs and Alcohol

You don't want to be the drama drunk. You want to be the fun drunk. The girl who plays drinking games and drinks just enough that she's fun, social, flirty, but not throwing yourself on anyone, and not so wasted that someone has to take care of you. You are in such a good mood that you'll do anything. —Annie, 17

Alcohol and drugs are a part of everyone's life—whether you drink or use any kind of drugs is not the point. And if you have cough syrup and an old prescription of Valium or Xanax in your medicine cabinet, you have exactly what a lot of teens are looking for to get high. But, seriously, cough syrup will do. You just add it to a can of Red Bull and you're good to go.

Where are your children getting alcohol and drugs? This is what my students answered:

Your liquor cabinet—and filling bottles back up with water or similar-color liquid
Fake IDs
Shoulder-tapping (when a teen gives an adult money to get the alcohol for her)
Older friends

Older siblings

Younger siblings (especially if they have a prescription for ADHD, depression, anxiety, etc.)

Visiting grandparents

Housesitting/babysitting

Buying from dealer at school or neighborhood

Garage hopping (usually takes place in the suburbs where kids can take alcohol out of garages of friends)

PRESCRIPTION DRUGS

I can't emphasize enough the difference in "pharming," the abuse of prescription drugs, in the last eight years since I first wrote this book. Maybe you know the smell of pot from five hundred feet away or the telltale red eyes and slurred words when someone is drunk. But in my experience, far fewer people know the signs of prescription drug abuse. In general, they are as follows:

Uppers/Stimulants

Dilated pupils

Nervous or "on edge"

Loss of appetite → weight loss

Euphoria/enhanced movements

Preoccupation with constructing and deconstructing objects

Compulsive grooming

Profuse perspiration

Dehydration

Jaw clenching/teeth grinding

Muscle twitching/jitteriness

Depressants/Antianxiety Medications/Sedatives

Extreme sleepiness/fatigue

Impaired coordinated/slurred speech

Paranoia/mood swings

Short attention span

Slow, shallow breathing

Desensitization/numbness to pain
Constricted pupils
Itching
Flushing

Sources for More Information

- www.merck.com/mmhe/index.html
- www.eap.partners.org/default.asp
- www.homedrugtestingkit.com
- www.pdrhealth.com/home/home.aspx
- www.adolescent-substance-abuse.com

Land Mine!

Yet another reason cell phones make your parenting more difficult is that your child can buy and sell drugs and you'll never have a clue.

CHECKING YOUR BAGGAGE

- When you were a teen, did you drink, do drugs? Was it fun? Did you use it as an escape? What were you running away from?
- Are you conflicted about how to talk to your child about alcohol and drugs?
- Have you ever been drunk and/or high and done something (either as a teen or adult) you wouldn't have if you'd been sober?
- What are the ways you run away and escape from problems? Why?
- What would your child say is your position about their use of alcohol and drugs? Would they think your words are consistent with your actions?
- Do you still use alcohol and/or recreational drugs? Does it impact your relationships?

WHAT YOU CAN DO

When most parents think about what can happen to their daughters at parties, their first instinct is to put their Rapunzels up in the tower and throw away the key. But parties are a part of life. If the tower isn't a viable option, your best bet is to help your daughter enjoy herself responsibly at the parties she throws and those she attends. That means she has to take certain steps to make sure she's safe, thinks clearly about her boundaries ahead of time, and understands what situations will compromise those promises to herself.

If She's Giving the Party

And you thought the boy-girl invitation issue was a tough one. If your daughter wants to host a party when she's in high school, don't veto the idea out of hand. Certainly there are downsides: it's your house that could get trashed; it's your house the police will visit if the volume on the stereo is up too high; and in some parts of the country, it's you who will be held accountable if guests break the law on your premises or after leaving your premises. On the plus side, letting your daughter host the party gives you a chance to supervise her and model how a party should go and provides an opportunity to meet her friends and observe them in action.

The rules of engagement begin the same way as in Chapter 7, although the stakes are higher for older girls. Sit down with your daughter before and write down guidelines for both of you. For example, you can insist that there's no drinking or drugs, that admission is by invitation only (i.e., she can't let in anyone she doesn't know, even if it's a "friend of a friend"—she can blame you if her friends complain), and that the number of people invited not exceed a predetermined limit. You can insist that you must be on the premises during the party. She can ask that you stay upstairs unless she needs your help and/or you're concerned the party is getting out of hand. You may want to discuss what that means, because your definitions could be different. You think having a hundred people in your home is too much, while she thinks that's a definition of a successful party. Clarify under what circumstances you will interrupt the party (too loud, evidence of alcohol or drugs, too late) and the actions you will take (escorting guests out personally, calling parents). Go over her personal degree of accountability, including rules for reimbursement of costs and cleanup. Remind her once again that you'll act as the "eternal out"—her guests have to stick to the rules "because Mom and Dad said so, and they'd kill me if we broke them."

If you're harboring any notion of becoming a Hip Parent (see Chapter 4) and buying beer or other alcohol for the party, remember that not only is it illegal (and you could be held accountable for repercussions), and teens are ridiculing you behind their back, you are exposing yourself to long-term risk that really just doesn't justify the short-term reward of sucking up to a bunch of adolescents. You're a parent, not an older friend with an ID.

Parents who buy the alcohol and have the parties at their house think they have the control but they don't. They never do in high school parties. They assume that if they have the party at their house instead of going to someone else's, they don't get into trouble. Why don't parents get how wrong they are? —Malia, 15

My friend's mom has no control over her kids because she drank and did drugs when she was young so she feels hypocritical about it. So she just lets them drink. —Faith, 16

Teens and parents drink together. During the summer, my parents and their friends wake up, have coffee, go to the beach, and then start drinking and they don't stop until late—like 2 A.M. They're so drunk that they aren't paying attention when their kids walk by the cooler and pick out whatever they want. —Morgan, 14

BUSTED: THE UNPLANNED PARTY

It's not fun to contemplate, but your daughter might take advantage of your plans to go out of town to throw a party at your house. The best way to prevent this is not only to have a clear conversation about why you won't allow this (which should focus largely on safety issues), but to have a trusted friend or relative stay at the house with your daughter. Yes, she'll complain that you don't trust her and are treating her like a baby, but your house and child will be safe.

Signs She's Planning a Party
- You have the feeling that your daughter is rushing you out of the house.
- You find a large amount of Doritos or other junk food in her closet.
- She's nervous and superficially nice around you.
- She's a little too helpful around the house or with anything you need to do to get ready for the trip.
- She's superfocused on the details of your trip, like when you're leaving, getting back, etc.
- You look at her texts and see that she's planning a party.

Signs There's Been a Party at Your House
- Fresh carpet stains and scuff marks on the walls.
- Empty food cabinets and/or refrigerator.
- Mysterious items of clothing found about the house.
- The outside of your house is littered with cigarette butts.
- The house is cleaner than when you left it; the carpets are so recently vacuumed that you can see the vacuum marks and the trash cans in the rooms are all empty.
- Your daughter tells you she had a couple of friends over, then jokes about having a party (to distract you from the fact that she really did have one).
- You ask another parent who is Facebook friends with a friend of your daughter's to scan the wall for recently posted pictures, and she sees kids partying in your house.

- There is not one roll of toilet paper anywhere in the house.
- She's really nice to you.
- When you ask her what she did over the weekend, her answers are very specific.

Usually when our parents ask us how we are or about what we did, we say "Fine" and "Nothing." But if we had a party, we talk to our friends so we all agree about what we did. So if we talk to the parent about the movie we went to and how much we liked it, we had a party.　　　—Lynn, 16

What do you do if you make plans to be out of town and learn your daughter is about to have a party? It depends on when you find out. If you find out twenty-four hours or more before, cancel your plans if possible and stay home. (If you leave, she may have the party anyway because she'll feel she has nothing to lose.) If you can't stay in town, leave her with a relative or family friend, or have an ally who has a strong backbone stay at the house (otherwise, she may have the party anyway).

If you find out the day of the party, take her cell phone and tell anyone who calls that the party is canceled. Monitor the door so you can assure guests that the party is off. If you can't cancel your plans, have a friend or relative go over to your house and monitor the phone and door. Around 8:00 P.M. turn off all lights in the house. If it's warm enough, the adult can sit on the front steps and tell the people the party is off. Then ground her and cut off her lines of communication for at least two weeks.

If you find out when you're away, you'll appreciate why I said earlier that there's nothing wrong with your children having a healthy dose of fear—the kind of fear that stops your daughter in her tracks from doing something really stupid, irresponsible, and/or dangerous because she thinks "If my mom finds out I had this party instead of babysitting like I told her, I'm dead."

This is also why you need to have at least one neighbor who will watch over the house and have no problem breaking up the party if he or she sees kids over there. Punish your child when you return. If you've caught her sneaking out to go or come back from a party, waiting in the dark and watching her quietly sneak back into her room is always fun, and you definitely have the surprise factor on your side when you flip on the lights. Listen patiently as she attempts to correctly get out the logistics of the excuse she tried to memorize on her way home. After you do that, use the same strategies I outlined in Chapter 4 in the sneaking section.

My mom always had her sister drive by and check around 11:30. She didn't trust my older sister at all. —Becky, 16

IF YOU KNOW SHE'S GOING TO A PARTY

- You should speak to the parent who is hosting the party and introduce yourself and tell them who your daughter is if they don't already know.
- By all means ask if the party is going to be supervised but realize that the Hip Parents are going to lie to you or think they're telling you the truth when their plan is to show the kids the liquor cabinet and go upstairs to their room.
- Set a curfew and tell that to the hosting parent.

In general I think the best strategy for letting your child go to a party is to pick them up at the end of the night—meaning at the time you have set their curfew. That means your child has in the back of her mind that she has to be sober enough to see you at the end of the night. As a peace offering (because your daughter likely will hate this plan) I would extend the curfew by thirty minutes and offer to pick her up around the block so you don't embarrass her. Or you can try to get the ally to be her pickup. I would also extend a ride home to any other kid who wants to leave. If that happens and you think the kid is slightly drunk, I would give them amnesty from calling their parents—but I would tell your child your suspicions. If the child is clearly drugged or incapacitated, I would let the parent know when you drop the child off.

I know there are parents who think that it's safer to let the kids sleep over wherever they end up. I don't think so. If your daughter knows she can sleep out under these circumstances, you are giving her a free pass to get as messed up as possible. And even known and trusted hosts have to go to sleep. Once that happens, all bets are off. Someone could be sober and get really upset, "have to go home now," get their keys, and get into an accident on the way home. Someone could bring out drugs they've been stashing until they were safe to come out. Just do everyone a favor, and bring your daughter home.

IF SHE'S GONE TO A PARTY AND YOU DIDN'T KNOW

If you discover she's at a party, you need to drive over and pick her up. Even if she hasn't had a sip of alcohol, just being tired from the night or stressed out because you know what's up can severely impair her ability to drive safely. Once you know where she is, tell her to remain there until you come to get her. You should then leave immediately, and try to be alone—taking siblings is unnecessarily embarrassing, and taking a spouse along might make it seem like it's two on one and immediately put her on the defensive.

> If you want her home, go get her yourself. That'll embarrass her enough so that she won't ever do it again.   —Alex, 18

> Under no circumstances should you yell or call her and say, "You need to get home now." I know a lot of parents who freak out when their child is past curfew or out doing something they shouldn't be. When the parents call up and start yelling, it puts a lot of added stress on the kid and then they drive badly. Have her take a taxi. You shouldn't add stress to driving.   —Katelyn, 18

You might not know that she's been to a party, however, until she stumbles in the back door or her friends pull into the driveway at 3:00 A.M. Don't let her put herself to bed to simply "sleep it off" and plan on confronting her the next morning—we've all heard those tragic stories where she never wakes up for that confrontation. If her friends are drunk or high, get them inside. Take their keys and call their parents. It isn't your job to punish them, but you can communicate your anger with their putting themselves and your daughter in danger. If they, too, are physically impaired, you should take care of them as best you can until their parents arrive to take over.

Once you have your daughter home or in the car, you should take the following steps:

- Keep in mind that your primary concern is her health. Rid your mind of all punishment ideas until after she's physically stable. Your letting her know this is key to the next step. Say, "I don't want you worrying about what your punishment will be. Right now, I just want to know what's in your body and how much of it there is so that I can take care of you."
- Establish her physical condition—ideally, she'll respond honestly. If she is either incapacitated or unwilling to share, you might have to do some guesswork.
- Give her lots of food and water.
- If she is vomiting or feels like she might, encourage it—her body needs to get rid of the alcohol.
- When you finally put her to bed, make sure that she's on her side so that if she vomits in her sleep, she doesn't choke. Even if she seems okay when going to bed, her body may still be processing alcohol and not have recognized the true level in her system.
- Check on her throughout the night.
- If she is unconscious, has slow/shallow/irregular breathing, does not withdraw from painful stimuli, is choking on vomit, has blue-tinged or unusually pale skin, or is seizing, seek immediate professional medical help—she may have alcohol poisoning or be under the influence of drugs, and it's beyond your abilities to help her.

The next morning, don't give her a vacation—she made the decision to party, and that doesn't mean she gets to sleep in until 3:00 that afternoon. In fact, getting her up early for breakfast with the family and chores might be enough, in combination with a hangover, to deter her from repeating the night before. It also shows her the direct consequences of her actions, and she can better connect what she's done to her punishment. Take her aside to talk one-on-one. Emphasize that last night is exactly why you set rules in place against alcohol and drug use, and then use SEAL to communicate.

> *The worst is when they wake up really early and you have to do all the chores and they're in a good mood but they won't tell you if there's any other punishment. So you do your best all day and think, "OK, if I do a really good job, then maybe I'll get out of this" and then you sit down at the dinner table and bam, your life is over.*   —Sam, 18

GOLDEN RULES FOR BEING A GUEST

Parties are fun, and there's nothing horrible about your daughter wanting to go to one. You just need to teach your daughter how to act responsibly while she's there.

If you live in a community where there are reliable taxis, always make sure she has enough money for a taxi home. Also, teach your daughter that you don't leave a friend behind. You at least hold her hair while she's throwing up, and get her a glass or two of water.

SAFETY IN NUMBERS

Overall, the best strategy for your daughter's safety at a party is to have good friends who will look out for her and vice versa. She needs the buddy system now more than ever. She needs to strategize with one or two close friends before the party about how they will look out for each other. Do they need a signal that says, "Bail me out"? If your daughter pairs off with a date to a secluded part of the house, does she have an agreement in place that a friend will come looking for her in five minutes to make sure everything's okay? It needs to be absolutely clear that no matter what, their sacrosanct bond is to watch out for each other.

Let's go back to the moment at the party where Bianca thought she should find Ally. She has a friend who has been drinking and is going off somewhere isolated with a guy. If your daughter were in Bianca's place, what could she do? Here is an effective intervention strategy:

> Your daughter should go up to her friend (or even knock on the door if the girl is already in a room) and say, "I really need to talk to you privately. It's really important." If she gets any resistance from her friend or the guy says, "Hey, everything's cool," she can say, "I'm having my period and I need a tampon. So I need to get one from her bag."

EVERY GIRL'S GOLDEN RULES FOR GOING TO A PARTY

Go with a friend you trust.

Have a code word between you that means, "You need to help me get away from this situation right now."

Have one more code word that means, "You, my friend, have drunk way too much and you are making really bad decisions, so you need to do what I am telling you without arguing with me."

Don't leave drinks unattended.

Don't accept open containers at parties.

Watch the person pour your drink.

NEVER leave your friend because she's gotten really wasted and is now making a fool of herself and embarrassing you. Take her with you.

*Ninth-grade girls should not go to parties with older kids—period. Nothing good can come of it. If your daughter hates you for imposing this rule, have her read this chapter and blame me.

**High school girls, including seniors, should not go to college parties with their older siblings, cousins, or friends for the same reason.

Talk to Your Daughter About Alcohol, Drugs, and Sex

By now, I hope I've convinced you to see how the issues facing girls are interrelated. The decision-making skills your daughter needs are the same no matter what she's making the decision about, whether it's deciding to smoke cigarettes or pot, drink, or have sex. Your role as a parent is to communicate your values and ethics on the subject, help your daughter clarify her own, and teach her how to communicate her boundaries to others and act on her principles.

Your strategy for talking about alcohol, drugs, and sex should follow the same principles:

1. Recognize that they surround your daughter.
2. Talk with (not to) her regularly.
3. Be clear about your rules and expectations.
4. Be consistent (your actions must match what you're telling her).
5. Leave an open door for later conversations.
6. Don't be shocked and take it personally when she doesn't follow your rules.
7. Be clear about consequences and follow through.
8. Don't be in denial!

Talk About Peer Pressure

Peer pressure—where there're groups of people pressuring you to do something—doesn't happen anymore. It's not like they say, "Everyone's doing it, so come on." People are normally cool with your decision to not drink or do drugs. The only time when you will do it is when you want to fit in with an elite group or you want to impress a guy. —Sydney, 15

What else is peer pressure but people you perceive to be cool or above you convincing you to do something you don't want to do? Peer pressure today is more subtle and internalized. Kids doing drugs or drinking are not going to say to someone "If you want to be our friend or be cool, you have to drink." Or "Come on and do it. All the cool people are." It's much more sophisticated. Drugs and alcohol are so much a part of teen culture that the motivation to drink and do drugs comes from an internal pressure to belong, not from someone standing over you with a joint forcing you to smoke.

"Just Walk Away"

One of the more ineffective things to tell your daughter about sex, drugs, or alcohol is "Just walk away" or "If you respect yourself, don't do it." I guarantee that your daughter knows plenty of teens who respect themselves and regularly have sex and use alcohol and/or drugs.

Zero-tolerance strategies also won't work because they smack of the hypocrisy that teens disdain. Your daughter lives in a world where sexual imagery, drugs, and alcohol are around every corner. Parents tend to focus on drugs, drinking, and sex separately, but your daughter uses the same skills to make decisions about all of them. While refusing may be the decision you want her to make, it's a process that she must go through, not an all-or-nothing proposition, and you don't have ultimate control about the outcome. How you help her make decisions must reflect the world she lives in, where advertising and peer pressure surround her.

Here's an example of what you can say to kids; the first part really surprises them and gets them listening more seriously:

I'm not going to tell you not to drink or do drugs. I know that alcohol and drugs are easy to get, and I'm pretty sure that many people you know and like are drinking and getting high. There may be parents who allow their kids to abuse alcohol or are alcoholics or drug abusers themselves. And I know that, ultimately, this is your choice. I *will* tell you that I don't want you to drink or do drugs for the following reason: When you're drunk or high, it's harder for you to be in control of yourself, and other people can and will easily take advantage of that. The facts are that bad things happen to really smart people when they drink and use drugs. I'm also really worried about your getting into a car with someone who's drunk or high but seems sober. But I can't control what you do. When you're away from me, I've got to hope that you'll make choices that will keep you safe and out of trouble.

If you have drug addicts or alcoholics in your family, you might say this:

Your grandfather has struggled with alcoholism. It has hurt the relationships that matter most to him, his career, etc. Although you are not destined to share the same problem, you are more prone to it, so you need to take these issues even more seriously.

What if you did drugs or drank alcohol when you were her age?

Do you find yourself wondering how you can tell your daughter not to do something you did yourself, and then lived to tell the tale? Maybe you think you have no credibility, or that you'll be a hypocrite. Here's how you can do it:

1. Don't lie, but that doesn't mean share every detail either. There is, however, a time to talk about it—and that time is when she's thirteen or older.
2. Give your child some credit. Just because you're standing in front of her in one piece relatively sane doesn't mean she won't understand that you made mistakes and learned from them. Share the struggles you have experienced or observed people have while under the influence.

Your obligation to your daughter is to teach her not to abuse alcohol or drugs, and to let her in on some of the "hindsight 20/20" vision you've gained. Perhaps you *didn't* do those things as a teenager—you might find, however, that your siblings or friends have good advice for your daughter. I'm not talking about sharing advice on obtaining or consuming the drugs or alcohol, but about having those people share experiences that offer real problem-solving templates for her life. If sharing those stories sounds too awful and you can't be motivated by any other reason to divulge, remember that rehab is heartbreaking and very expensive.

Parents can be subtly involved in helping kids navigate difficult situations with alcohol or drugs. My parents, aunts, and uncles have definitely given me and my friends good advice and tips from their own experiences. My mom was pretty straight-edged growing up, but her sister and brothers weren't. They were the ones who told me their experiences, and I learned from that. I wouldn't have taken their advice as seriously if they had sat me down and lectured me, but that they talked to me from their own lives really made me listen. —Krissy, 16

One of my mom's best friends is the person who told me never to put your drink down because someone did it to him, and my uncle told me about not mixing alcohol and drugs. I know parents don't want to have their kids hear things like this, but it's really helpful. No one is going to listen to their parents about this stuff, but they will listen to their friends and relatives. —Mercedes, 18

SEX TALK 101

OK. Let's just dive in and talk about sex and your daughter. Scared? Grossed out? Flipping out? Resigned? Whatever your feelings, you need a lot of information so you can handle what your daughter is up against. And like anything else, the less you know, the more frightened you'll be. Get educated; you'll be more likely to make sound decisions.

Have Another Talk About Sex

She'll respect the values you've taught her only if she's internalized them so they've become her code of ethics—for herself and others. Again, you'll have to clarify your own values about sex so you can share them with your daughter. I'm assuming they'll be based on the assumption that when the time is right, your daughter should know how to act responsibly, respectfully, and consensually—and expect the same from her partner. Please see the books listed in the resources section for more in-depth discussion of these issues.

There's no excuse for not talking about sex with your daughter several times throughout her childhood and adolescence. If you don't provide her with accurate information, she'll learn everything about sex from her peers and the media. And don't assume that her school will take care of "the talk." The teacher may not be good or the class curriculum may be restricted. There are parents who believe that talking to children about sex and reading books with sexual content will encourage them to have sex. In my years of teaching, I've never understood this perspective. I believe that denying girls information greatly increases their vulnerability to having irresponsible sex or making bad decisions that can lead to coerced sex.

Talking to your daughter about sex can be uncomfortable. But your discomfort doesn't outweigh her safety. You're also not off the hook by having one conversation with her that superficially covers the facts. You should first talk to her at the latest when she's eight about the nuts and bolts (if she hasn't asked you before then). Talk to her again in sixth or seventh grade. Review the nuts and bolts, and now incorporate what you think is important about how to make dating decisions. If your daughter has two people raising her, both people should talk to her. If it's really too hard for you to have this conversation with her, ask your ally to do it for you. Review with your ally the facts and values you want your daughter to learn. However, if at all possible, try to undertake this task yourself. You are the rule maker and caregiver in your daughter's life, and she needs to discuss important things like this with you.

So, how do you start the conversation about boys in such a way that you both won't freak?

Knowing Her Boundaries

Go back to the party at the moment when Ally goes upstairs with Tye. She needs to know her personal boundaries way before she's walking into that room with Tye. So your daughter needs to ask herself:

How well do I have to know someone before I do something sexual with them?

How do I define knowing someone well? (Meeting a friend of a friend at a party doesn't qualify.)

What do I feel comfortable doing with someone sexually?

What do I not want to do?

How can I communicate that to the person I am with?

What would make it more difficult for me to say what I want and don't want?

Obviously, it'll be really uncomfortable for your daughter to share her answers to these questions with you, let alone have a discussion, but you need to give her the starting point to establish her boundaries and then be the person, or find a person, she can discuss it with. Again, her ally is really important here.

A common problem girls have is that many worry that if they say something about their limits too early, it assumes that their date wants to have sex when in fact he may not have thought about sex at all. Please tell your daughters that they can be safe in making the assumption that their date does want to do something sexual (not necessarily have intercourse but they're on the road). If she thinks through all the possibilities, she can be clearer about where she wants to draw the boundaries, and she doesn't have to assume that every boy is a predator to take precautions to protect herself. She needs to remind herself that drinking or doing drugs will make it harder to do that.

As I've mentioned, girls don't like admitting it, but most are really bad at saying no clearly because it feels like they aren't in control. They can sit in my class and tell me confidently that they have the right to say no whenever they want. But when they're actually in the situation, things are different. As a result, a girl often will say no while she's still kissing a boy, and he may understandably be confused by the mixed message and keep going. She may say, "Can't we wait" or "Maybe we should check on Rachel, I think she's throwing up in the bathroom" or "I'm not sure this is a good idea." None of these statements clearly communicate "I don't want to have sex" or "I don't want to give you oral sex." She must learn to say what she means: "No, I don't want to have sex." "No, you have to stop trying to persuade me to have sex."

If you haven't had any conversations, start now. It's up to you to clarify and communicate your beliefs about sexuality. When your daughter is a young teen, it's especially important to discuss puberty, hormones, changing and conflicting feelings, and the essential need to look for mutual respect in every relationship. As your daughter matures, you'll need to address the nuts and bolts of sexual responsibility. Get over your queasiness. Your girl is growing up with or without you.

Being Left Behind

Just as I talked about girls feeling left behind when some of them first become interested in boys, here comes the reality of trying to keep up, again—but this time the stakes are higher. You daughter is now trying to keep up with her sexually active friends, trying to keep up with her boyfriend who wants to have sex, and trying to keep up with a society that pushes girls to be mature and sophisticated even as it wags a finger at them for being slutty.

It's weird when you have a friend who has had sex and you haven't. They have entered a whole new realm of being. They're like light-years away from any sort of sexual experience I might have had. —Ilana, 16

Girls I know have sex to feel popular. Guys know exactly what to say to the girls to get exactly what they want. At school, they may even deny any kind of association with the girls depending on who they are, their social status, looks, et cetera, and of course, what the boys' friends' opinions/reactions are when they hear the "rumors." Sometimes [she has sex] with a boyfriend because the girl fears that the guy will "move to greener pastures" if he doesn't get what "he deserves" or what "he needs." The girl doesn't realize that especially if she has sex with him, this type of guy will still leave her eventually. She will just be prolonging the detrimental relationship and causing herself more suffering, shock, and pain. —Jane, 16

If there's a clique and one of the girls isn't having sex and the rest are, it's not like the girls are going to tell her she's a loser for not having sex. Older girls are too sophisticated for that, and they know having sex has a lot of risks. But the girl who isn't having sex may still feel the pressure. Where does that pressure come from?

There's a lot of kinship between girls who have had sex. It's another thing to bond with each other [about], because you can tell each other what you like and don't like. If there's a girl in the group who isn't sexually experienced, then you wouldn't feel comfortable sharing that kind of stuff with her. —Monica, 17

Most girls are more supportive of each other [than to pressure someone to have sex]. Having sex is a really personal thing. It's an internal battle for what she's ready for. You will always want to know what you're getting yourself into. If one person in the group has had sex, then the rest of the group doesn't think it's so scary. —Mariel, 16

It always comes down to sitting in that life raft I referred to in Chapter 3. Getting through adolescence is scary. A girl finds a group to sit with and wants to stay put. Friendships are built on going through these rites of passage with each other. Sex is a pivotal right of passage; it can feel lonely being left out.

Oral Sex: Do Teens Really Not Consider It Sex?

Girls are doing it so they don't have to have sex. It isn't seen as part of sex but a part of foreplay. A lot of ninth graders do it because the older boys will like them and think they're cool.   —Kim, 16

One of my friends was battling over a guy with another girl—and my friend was losing. So she went out with this guy and some other people and they were all in a car. She was in the backseat with him. They stopped and everyone got out but them. She gave him head! And people could look into the car! I think she did it because she felt like she had to do what he wanted or else he would like the other girl more.   —Robin, 17

Guys say things like, "You're so pretty and this would really make me feel good."   —Alisha, 15

Here's a representative sample of opinions from the girls I work with:

It's gross.
It's demeaning.
Oral sex isn't "sex."
Girls are sometimes willing to give boys oral sex to please them.
Oral sex is a bargain—girls don't think they risk getting an STD [they're wrong about that] and they know it won't get them pregnant.

First, let's get something straight. When people talk about teens engaging in oral sex, they're only talking about girls performing oral sex on boys, not the other way around. Second, when today's parents were growing up, oral sex was perceived by most people to be equal to or more intimate than vaginal intercourse; now it is the other way around. So as hard as it may be for you to believe, many girls see oral sex as safe and emotionally distant, vaginal intercourse as something you "save" for someone special.

But while it's true that many girls don't think oral sex is the same as sexual intercourse, it doesn't mean all girls are doing it or that it means nothing to them. What is clear to me is that girls believe that the dynamics of oral sex reflect the power difference between boys and girls, but it has become so normalized that they don't question it.

> *There isn't much a girl won't do to make a boy like her.*
> —*Maria, 15*

But what oral sex is also about is getting out of the room without having sex and admitting your powerlessness. It's what you can offer so you please the boy. Think about Ally at the party with Tye. She wants him to like her but she doesn't want to have sex and she doesn't want to admit to herself that she has no power in the situation. So . . . she may "choose" the best option in front of her. Give the guy a blow job and it seems like all her problems are solved.

Oh, God, They're Having Sex

The worst, most ineffective things you can say to her are:

> *You can never see him again.*
> *He's such a bad influence.*
> *You're a slut/whore/tramp.*
> *If I catch you doing this again . . .*
> *You need to think about your reputation.*

What Should You Do If You Find Condoms?

If you find condoms, you have to admit to yourself that there's a 99 percent probability that your daughter is having sex. But, as uncomfortable as that may make you, it should at least reassure you that she's practicing safer sex. And, if she's not having sex now, finding condoms is a clear sign that she's definitely thinking about it.

Some parents confront their daughters when they find condoms. If you do, here are some common things you'll hear:

I was buying/holding them for friends.
An HIV/AIDS/sex-ed teacher was giving them out as part of the presentation.
Someone gave them to me as a joke.

Please notice that none of these explanations is a denial that your daughter is having sex. They could all be true. She could be buying them for friends and using some for herself. She could have had a presentation in school but she could also plan to use them. Whatever the reason, I suggest saying something like the following:

Whatever the reason you have them, if you are thinking about being sexually active or if you already are, then it's time to see a gynecologist and get a checkup. If you're responsible enough to be sexually active, then there should be no problem going to the doctor. And I want to be clear that I don't believe someone your age should be having sex, but if you are, then we need to sit down and go over what I feel you need to know about sexual responsibility.

If You Catch Her Having Sex

This has to rank up there with the most horribly uncomfortable experiences you can have as a parent. After you get over your shock and/or embarrassment, leave the room and let them dress in private. Meanwhile, calm down and breathe deeply. And while they're getting dressed, get yourself together, and tell them to meet you in the living room.

Go sit down in the most comfortable chair in the living room. When they come in, direct them to the most uncomfortable chairs (I think you have to find a little humor where you can get it in this situation).

An ideally effective response is based on the rules you've already established and communicated to your daughter—if not both of them. If you have forbidden boys to be in her bedroom, they broke a rule and disrespected you as a parent. This is what you say:

> Diana, Ryan, I'm sure that was completely embarrassing for all of us, but that doesn't obscure the fact that you have broken a rule that is important to me and one that I believed I had your agreement on. Your violation of this rule means that I can't trust you in my house. In addition, [looking at your daughter] now that I know you're having sex, you must get a pelvic exam and get tested for STDs. Ryan, while I am not your parent, I would advise you to do the same. Ryan, I also want you to go home and tell your parents in general what happened. I would advise you to tell them sooner rather than later because I will be calling them later tonight.

Ideally your daughter has already been to a gynecologist for a pelvic exam when she began her period. If not, she needs to go ASAP. This is a great thing the ally can do with her. I went with my sister to her first exam. She was nervous, but I told her what would happen. When she came out of the exam, she walked into the waiting room and announced to me—and the ten women waiting for their appointments—"Well, I guess that makes me a woman!" We both laughed, and then we went out to lunch. Bonding moments are what and when you make them.

And I really do want you to call the other parents. I know this isn't exactly something every parent dreams of doing, but you do need to tell them in general what happened and how you handled it.

IN SUM

I worry a lot about girls. I also have my moments of serious frustration and sadness when they do things that degrade themselves or others. I worry that they will drink too much, use drugs, and not be around people who will or can help them if they need it. I worry that your daughter will meet someone she's really attracted to, who pays attention to her, and tells her she's pretty, and she'll have sex with him when she wasn't sure she wanted to but didn't know what to do. I worry about the things she'll see and experience that will make her feel less than and not good enough. I worry about the car she'll get into going home and the person driving that car. I worry that she doesn't have an adult in her life who makes it clear to her that she is valued for the things that matter, her ability to live a life of purpose and integrity. So in sum, my goals for your daughter are the following:

1. She can recognize when she is in over her head and has friends who will take care of her.
2. She understands why other girls may turn on her and doesn't let their interactions with her make her feel insecure.
3. She knows her own boundaries about drinking, doing drugs, and having sex and is able to communicate them clearly to others.
4. She trusts her gut.
5. She knows that if she makes a mistake, she can go to you or another adult you both trust for guidance.
6. If she breaks a family rule, she knows you'll be there to hold her accountable but not make her feel forever ashamed of herself for any mistakes she's made.

As uncomfortable as this chapter may have made you, I wrote it in hopes of showing you the connection between girls' relationships with one another, Girl World, their need to please, and their interactions with boys. I know it's painful to contemplate that your daughter could experience the type of pain we've talked about here. It's difficult to stomach that there are people in this world who will not cherish or respect her. As I say to my students: I want you to recognize danger on the horizon, not when it's hitting you in the face. With your help, she will.

Getting Help

So far in this book, I've concentrated on how you or your ally can help your daughter. However, there may come a time when your daughter will need to get professional help from a therapist or other mental health professional, so you should be prepared to see the signs if she does and to get her the help she needs.

One of the most significant advances we've made in the last several decades is to take away much of the stigma of seeking help from mental health professionals. We also have a language for many mental health issues that we didn't have a generation ago. One of the reasons why it was so hard for me to talk about my abusive relationship in high school was that I, along with the rest of my community, wasn't educated about abusive relationships. I had no words to define what was happening. Now many girls in my situation, and many other situations, do.

If your daughter is a victim of any kind of abuse, you both will go through a process of recovery. But you need to remember that as her parent you face unique challenges. Your love for her can make it very difficult for you to allow her to make her own decisions as she muddles through her recovery. Honestly, one of the most important things I have learned as a parent is what I mentioned in the beginning of the book. Sometimes the very fact that we are parents stops us from being the best resource for our children. Our love and anxiety blinds us from seeing the most effective course of action.

Recovery is a messy process for everyone involved. If you find out from someone else, much later and after the fact, that your daughter needed professional help, you may feel hurt that she didn't feel comfortable telling you. Remember, a girl doesn't tell her parents for one of two reasons: it's not safe to tell them because their reaction will make her feel worse, or she doesn't want to disappoint them.

People frequently ask if my parents knew about my abusive relationship in high school. No, they didn't. I didn't tell them until I was twenty-four and was about to publish my first book. But my parents were still helpful when I was going through it as a teen, even though they and I didn't know it. What did they say that helped?

My mother always told me that I, like anyone, could and would make many mistakes throughout the course of my life and that I would survive. If I made bad decisions, I could always fix them. Even though she says she didn't, I think she intuited something was wrong. One day, at the airport, while we waited to pick up my father, she said, "I don't know what's going on with you, but I know something is. Everyone makes mistakes. You're very private, but if you ever want to talk, I'm here." She opened a door, albeit just a crack, and I soon walked through it to get help. I was deeply ashamed that I had "let" the relationship get so out of my control. Her words let me see that there was a possibility of leaving the relationship behind me and I didn't have to be so ashamed.

My reasons for not getting help are very common. It doesn't matter if the problem is bullying, eating disorders, molestation, drugs, drinking, abuse, rape, depression, anxiety, or any combination. Girls feel ashamed, damaged, and unfixable, and they may not think anyone around them has gone through similar experiences. I often say that abusers' insurance policy is the silence of their victims. People don't speak out and yet there's hardly a person around any of us who hasn't been touched by painful experiences at our hands or the hands of others.

Like anyone, your daughter could easily have problems that are too big to bear by herself, let alone solve. Likewise, even if you're the world's perfect parent, your daughter could go through experiences where one, if not both of you, needs to look outside for help.

So one of the most important things to teach your daughter is that there is no shame and it's not weak to ask for help. It's courageous to admit when you're in over your head. People kill themselves trying to look like they have it together when they're falling apart inside. Unfortunately, many parents themselves are reluctant to ask for help. Why? There's no easy answer. Sometimes it's because parents see their daughter's successes and failures as a reflection on themselves. Sometimes parents don't want others to know their family business. Sometimes looking at such problems is too painful because our children's pain is a consequence of our own choices or circumstance.

For better or worse, being a parent gives you endless opportunities to admit and get over your own baggage. It's your responsibility, duty, and obligation to face your own demons and put them to rest as best as you can so that you can provide the love, guidance, and nurturing your daughter needs.

There are some other reasons why girls don't go to their parents for help. It could be any one or a combination of these:

- By the time she admits to herself that she needs help, she's in way over her head.
- She's afraid you'll deny that she's in trouble.
- She doesn't want to change the image you have of her.
- You've been known to freak out when she's come to you with other problems, meaning you do things without her consent or knowledge.
- In your home, family problems (including your daughter's) are private. The family doesn't need the help of outsiders to take care of its own.

"Allison" is one of my favorite girls. She's funny, intelligent, beautiful, and charismatic. She also suffers from anxiety and depression. Until recently, I had no idea. I knew middle school was painful for her—it was one of the reasons I got to know her in the first place, but she was so good at keeping up her image that I didn't see her struggling.

Allison is a constant achiever. She was accepted early into an Ivy League school, has been on varsity sports teams since ninth grade, and her academic and extracurricular awards are endless. After three years of volunteering with me, she told me she couldn't volunteer anymore. I was dumbfounded and angry. I immediately jumped to the conclusion that she was suffering from "senioritis" and was blowing everything off now that she'd been accepted into college. Where was her commitment? She just couldn't walk away from her responsibilities. Then she told me she had been depressed for years. She had even attempted suicide in eighth grade.

What has been her worst obstacle in getting help? That her parents didn't want her telling anyone. They wanted her to "keep it in the family." A few days later, we went out to lunch, and she shared with me that for years she had been working as hard as she could to be what everyone else wanted her to be. Her identity was so caught up in her accomplishments that she feels as if she's nothing without them. She kept a notebook under her bed with every award she'd received since eighth grade, and when she was depressed, she took it out and looked at all her awards. Allison asked me:

Why are we so special that we have to pretend that we don't have problems? When my older sister had an eating disorder, the doctors wanted to hospitalize her. My parents refused. They thought they could take care of her at home. I overheard my parents discussing that if they did put her in the hospital they could always tell people that she had mono. My sister was down to eighty-five pounds and they didn't want to get her help because they were too ashamed. When I was first depressed, they took me to a psychiatrist that I actually liked. He told my parents that they were going to have to do some "reparenting." We never went back. Next I went to a therapist my mom knew. When my mom picked me up, they would talk about things, including their kids. There was no way I trusted her. Now I go to a psychiatrist who just sits there and I don't tell him what's really going on with me. Why should I?

Maybe you're reading this and thinking, *What's wrong with Allison's parents? Can't they see what they are doing to their daughter?* Watch out. Hubris will make you blind. Allison comes from a "traditional" family—a mom and dad who live together in the suburbs, go to church, and are active members of the community. I know Allison's parents. They're caring, loving people. There's no question in my mind that they love their daughter and want what's best for her. Allison's father commuted hours out of his way to drop her off and pick her up at my office. He is warm, caring, and clearly proud of her. So why in the world are they so scared to let Allison talk about her problems? Is it really more important what their neighbors think than getting help for their daughter?

Parents sometimes make miserably foolish decisions in the "best interest" of their daughter and the family. Because it's so hard for parents to reflect on their own parenting, it's easier to close ranks around the family. So I'm asking you to keep the door open. Ask your daughter, "You seem upset. Is there anything I can help you with? If you don't want to talk to me, I'd be happy to have you talk to someone else." Keep asking gently if your gut tells you she's troubled but not ready to open up to you about it.

No matter how much you love your daughter, you won't parent her well if you let your issues interfere with getting her the help she needs. She needs to learn from you that when she makes a mistake, she'll learn from it and move on. She isn't damaged and unfixable if she made bad decisions or got in trouble. This doesn't mean you have to share your most intimate family problems with everyone you see. But don't tell your daughter to lie about her problem, pretend it's not there, and it'll go away. If she has to leave school early once a week to see a therapist, help her come up with what she feels comfortable telling people, but don't tell her to keep it a secret. If you do any of these things, you're sending the message that she should be ashamed. As long as she feels shame, she can't heal her wounds. Respect that she's her own person and you are her guide.

WHO NEEDS HELP

Every one of following signs could describe a normal teen, but if you're seeing a big difference over a relatively short time period, the actions indicate that they're coping mechanisms for dealing with whatever is bothering her.

Signs She Needs Professional Help
- Isolation and withdrawing
- Eating too little and/or too much
- Intense mood swings

Additional Signs She May Have Experienced Sexual Violence
- She takes showers all the time.
- She keeps constantly busy.
- She covers her body with huge clothes.
- She's fearful in a way she wasn't before.
- She doesn't want to be left alone.

Additional Signs She May Suffer from Depression and/or Anxiety*
- Sleeping too much or too little
- Persistent physical symptoms that don't respond to medical treatment (headaches, digestive problems, chronic pain)
- Difficulty concentrating, remembering, or making decisions
- Thoughts of death and/or suicide
- Feelings of guilt, worthlessness, hopelessness, pessimism

CHOOSING A COUNSELOR

At first, my parents had to drag me to the therapist because I thought it was going to be a total waste of time. But around the third time, I began to see why I was there. It's sort of cool to be able to tell someone what's going on in your head and think

---

*National Institute of Mental Health. See www.nimh.gov.

*through stuff. Seeing her makes me feel a lot less anxious about
the problems I'm dealing with.* —Corrine, 15

*My doctor told my parents I should go to a psychiatrist. He just
stared at me and asked why I hated my dad. There was no way I
was telling that man anything about me.* —Karen, 16

If you can find a good therapist, she or he can be a great resource for your daughter. But sometimes they're not so easy to
find. You probably don't want to have to shop around, but you
must. Think of it this way: it's probably going to cost you a lot of
money and you're going to spend a lot of time taking your daughter to the appointments, so it better be worth your while.

Prepare three to five questions to ask the therapist over the
phone. Ask your daughter to prepare her own questions. Here are
a few I ask:

- How would she describe her style? Does she like to listen and
  sit back? Will she give her opinion?
- How does she see her role as mediator between parent and
  child? For example, at what point would she notify you of
  something about your child? Don't ask this question to hear
  that the therapist will tell you when and if your daughter's in
  imminent danger. You're looking for a therapist who won't
  tell you things about your daughter. The best adolescent
  therapists have a clear understanding of their boundaries
  between themselves, the parent, and child.
- What are her areas of specialization? Find someone who
  specializes in teens and the particular issue(s) your daughter
  has (e.g., bullying, eating disorders, rape, abusive
  relationships).
- Why does she work with teens? What does she find most
  rewarding? What does she find most challenging?

Here's an example of a mother and therapist doing an effective
job. As a result, the girl, a recent rape survivor, is getting the help
she needs.

My mom called three [therapists] and said choose one. She told me I didn't have to talk, but she needed to know she tried to do something to help me. When I went to the psychiatrist, she didn't force me to speak about it. I talked about friends and other things in my life. All the other adults forced me to talk about it [the rape], but she waited until I wanted to bring it up.

—Alexa, 16

If your child needs a therapist, it doesn't mean you've failed as a parent. If you can get her the help she needs, you're doing the best you can for her—and that's all anyone can ask of you.

Grace Notes: Before You Go

Now you know Girl World. I know it can be hard to read about what goes on there. But I hope you've also been able to see how you not only can make your daughter's teen years more bearable for both of you but also can nurture her confidence and independence.

As a parting note, I've asked some girls to share the messages they'd most like to leave with parents:

Don't try to understand your daughter's every thought; just show her that her feelings are valid and are not wrong. When you need to listen, listen. When you need to talk, talk. And most importantly, treat her with the respect you'd like to be treated with, even if she doesn't do the same. After all, this is probably the hardest time in her life and no matter what she says, she does need you. —Julie, 17

Communication is the biggest part to making your relationship with your daughter the best it can be. Teenagers love to know that their parents are really interested in what is going on in their lives. The most important thing to remember is not to pressure your child into talking and being open if they don't feel comfortable doing so. Keep the lines open and always be on the lookout so you know when something is bothering her. Showing your love and concern can do wonders for a teen's self-esteem. —Nia, 18

Just be there for me. Don't judge. Don't tell me how to make it better. Just tell me you love me. —Dia, 15

Know that I love you and want to make you proud of me. —Michelle, 15

Even when I'm fighting with you, sometimes I know you're right, but I don't want to admit it. —Kia, 16

You really do make a difference and I really do listen. —Sara, 16

Resources

Cultural Commentary

Female Chauvinist Pigs: Women and the Rise of Raunch Culture, by Ariel Levy. Free Press, 2005.

Freaks, Geeks, and Cool Kids: American Teenagers, Schools, and the Culture of Consumption, by Murray Milner, Jr. Routledge, 2004.

Gender and Education: An Encyclopedia (Vols. 1 & 2), by Barbara J. Bank, ed. Praeger Publishers, 2007.

Gender Play: Girls and Boys in School, by Barrie Thorne. Rutgers University Press, 1993.

Getting Through to Difficult Kids and Parents: Uncommon Sense for Child Professionals, by Ron Taffel. Guilford Press, 2004.

The Good Enough Teen: Raising Adolescents with Love and Acceptance, Despite How Impossible They Can Be, by Brad E. Sachs. Harper Paperbacks, 2005.

Goth: Undead Subculture, by Lauren M. E. Goodlad and Michael Bibby, eds. Duke University Press, 2007.

Grassroots: A Field Guide for Feminist Activism, by Jennifer Baumgardner and Amy Richards. Farrar, Straus, and Giroux, 2005.

The Motivation Breakthrough: 6 Secrets to Turning On the Tuned-Out Child, by Richard Lavoie. Touchstone, 2008.

The Nature of Prejudice: 25th Anniversary, by Gordon W. Allport. Perseus Book Group, 1979.

Nerds: Who They Are and Why We Need More of Them, by David Anderegg. Tarcher, 2007.

Nurturing Good Children Now: 10 Basic Skills to Protect and Strengthen Your

Child's Core Self, by Ron Taffel and Melinda Blau. Golden Guides from St. Martin's Press, 2000.

Parenting by Heart: How to Stay Connected to Your Child in a Disconnected World, by Ron Taffel and Melinda Blau. Da Capo Press, 2002.

The Pecking Order: Which Siblings Succeed and Why, by Dalton Conley. Pantheon, 2004.

The Pressured Child: Helping Your Child Find Success in School and Life, by Michael G. Thompson and Teresa Barker. Ballantine Books, 2005.

Privilege: A Reader, by Michael Kimmel and Abby Ferber. Westview Press, 2003.

Queen Bee Moms and Kingpin Dads: Dealing with the Difficult Parents in Your Child's Life, by Rosalind Wiseman and Elizabeth Rapoport. Three Rivers Press, 2007.

School Girls: Young Women, Self-Esteem, and the Confidence Gap, by Peggy Orenstein. Doubleday, 1994.

The Second Family: Dealing with Peer Power, Pop Culture, the Wall of Silence, and Other Challenges of Raising Today's Teen, by Ron Taffel. St. Martin's Griffin, 2002.

Somebodies and Nobodies: Overcoming the Abuse of Rank, by Robert W. Fuller. New Society Publishers, 2003.

A Tribe Apart: A Journey into the Heart of American Adolescence, by Patricia Hersch. Ballantine Books, 1999.

When Parents Disagree and What You Can Do About It, by Ron Taffel. Guilford Press, 2002.

Worried All the Time: Overparenting in an Age of Anxiety and How to Stop It, by David Anderegg. Free Press, 2003.

Bullying, Social Justice, and Intervention Strategies

All Rise: Somebodies, Nobodies, and the Politics of Dignity, by Robert Fuller. Berrett-Koehler, 2006.

Best Friends, Worst Enemies: Understanding the Social Lives of Children, by Michael Thompson, Catherine O'Neill Grace, and Lawrence J. Cohen. Ballantine Books, 2002.

Bullying from Both Sides: Strategic Interventions for Working with Bullies and Victims, by Walter B. Roberts Jr. Corwin Press, 2005.

Bullying, Victimization, and Peer Harassment: A Handbook of Prevention and Intervention, by Joseph E. Zins, Maurice J. Elias, Charles A. Maher, eds. Haworth Press, 2007.

Creating Safe Schools: What Principals Can Do, by Marie S. Hill and Frank W. Hill. Corwin Press, 1994.

Disarming the Playground, by Rena Kornblum. Woods and Barnes Publishing, 2002.

Family Matters: How Schools Can Cope with the Crisis in Childrearing, by Robert Evans. Jossey-Bass, 2004.

Letters to a Bullied Girl: Messages of Healing and Hope, by Olivia Gardner, Emily Buder, and Sarah Buder. Harper Paperbacks, 2008.

Mom, They're Teasing Me: Helping Your Child Solve Social Problems, by Michael G. Thompson, Lawrence J. Cohen, and Catherine O'Neill. Ballantine Books, 2004.

Not Much Just Chillin': The Hidden Lives of Middle Schoolers, by Linda Perlstein. Farrar, Straus, and Giroux, 2003.

Please Stop Laughing at Me: One Woman's Inspirational Story, by Jodee Blanco. Adams Media, 2003.

Safe School Ambassadors: Harnessing Student Power to Stop Bullying and Violence, by Rick Phillips, John Linney, Chris Pack. Jossey-Bass, 2008. (Curriculum)

Salvaging Sisterhood, by Julia V. Taylor. Youthlight, 2005. (Curriculum)

Teens at Risk: Opposing Viewpoints, by Auriana Ojeda, ed. Greenhaven Press, 2003.

Your Child: Bully or Victim? Understanding and Ending Schoolyard Tyranny, by Peter Sheras and Sherill Tippins. Fireside, 2002.

Youth at Risk: A Prevention Resource for Counselors, Teachers, and Parents, by David Capuzzi and Douglas R. Gross, eds. American Counseling Association, 2000.

Audiovisual

How to Eat Fried Worms. Bob Dolman (Director). Walden Media, 2006. (www.walden.com)

Websites

Facing History and Ourselves: www.facinghistory.org

Teaching Tolerance—A Project of the Southern Poverty Law Center: www.tolerance.org

Adolescent Development and Diverse Learning

Breaking Through to Teens: A New Psychotherapy for New Adolescence, by Ron Taffel. Guilford Press, 2005.

Childhood Unbound: Saving Our Kids' Best Selves—Confident Parenting in a World of Change, by Ron Taffel. Free Press, 2009.

Delivered from Distraction: Getting the Most Out of Life with Attention Deficit Disorder, by Edward M. Hallowell and John J. Ratey. Ballantine Books, 2005.

Driven to Distraction: Recognizing and Coping with Attention Deficit Disorder from Childhood Through Adulthood, by Edward M. Hallowell and John J. Ratey. Touchstone, 1995.

It's So Much Work to Be Your Friend: Helping the Child with Learning Disabilities Find Social Success, by Richard Lavoie. Touchstone, 2006.

Key Indicators of Child Well-Being: Completing the Picture, by Brett Brown, ed. Lawrence Erlbaum, 2007.

Killing Monsters: Why Children Need Fantasy Superheroes and Make-Believe Violence, by Gerald Jones. Basic Books, 2002.

The Primal Teen: What the New Discoveries About the Teenage Brain Tell Us About Our Kids, by Barbara Strauch. Doubleday, 2003.

Thinking in Pictures and Other Reports from My Life with Autism, by Temple Grandin. Vintage Books, 1996.

Understanding Learning: The How, the Why, the What, by Ruby K. Payne. aha! Process, Inc., 2001.

Understanding Youth: Adolescent Development for Educators, by Michael J. Nakkula and Eric Toshalis. Harvard Education Press, 2006.

What Do Children Need to Flourish? Conceptualizing and Measuring Indicators of Positive Development, by Kristin Anderson Moore and Laura Lippman, eds. Springer, 2005.

Working with Parents: Building Relationships for Student Success, by Ruby K. Payne. aha! Process, Inc., 2005.

Working with Students: Discipline Strategies for the Classroom, by Ruby K. Payne. aha! Process, Inc., 2006.

Audiovisual

The Motivation Breakthrough, by Richard Lavoie. Gerardine Wurzburg (Director). PBS Video, 2007.

Masculinity, Male Aggression, and Issues for Boys

Bad Boys: Public Schools in the Making of Black Masculinity, by Ann Arnett Ferguson. University of Michigan Press, 2001.

BAM: Boys Advocacy and Mentoring: A Guidebook for Leading Preventative Boys Groups, Helping Boys Connect through Physical Challenge and Strategic Storytelling, by Stephen Grant, Howard Hilton, and Peter Motola. BAM! Press, 2006. (Curriculum)

The Bond: Three Young Men Learn to Forgive and Reconnect with Their Fathers, by Sampson Davis, Rameck Hunt, and George Jenkins. Riverhead Hardcover, 2007.

Boys into Men: Raising Our African American Teenage Sons, by Nancy Boyd-Franklin, A. J. Franklin, and Pamela Touissaint. Dutton, 2000.

Boys of Few Words: Raising Our Sons to Communicate and Connect, by Adam J. Cox. Guilford Press, 2006.

Counseling Troubled Boys: A Guidebook for Professionals, by Mark S. Kiselica, Matt Englar-Carlson, and Arthur M. Horne, eds. Routledge, 2008.

Fathers, Brothers, Sons and Lovers: Why Some Men Hurt and Others Watch, by Jackson Katz. Sourcebooks, 2006.

A Fine Young Man, by Michael Gurian. Putnam, 1999.

Guyland: The Perilous World Where Boys Become Men, by Michael Kimmel. Harper, 2008.

I Don't Want to Talk About It: Overcoming the Secret Legacy of Male Depression, by Terrence Real. Fireside, 1997.

It's a Boy! Understanding Your Son's Development from Birth to Age 18, by Michael G. Thompson and Teresa Barker. Ballantine Books, 2008.

Lost Boys: Why Our Sons Turn Violent and How We Can Save Them, by James Garbarino. Free Press, 1999.

Makes Me Wanna Holler: A Young Black Man in America, by Nathan McCall. Vintage Books, 1994.

Manhood in America: A Cultural History, by Michael Kimmel. Free Press, 1996.

Men's Lives, by Michael Kimmel. Allyn and Bacon, 1998.

More Than a Few Good Men: Strategies for Inspiring Boys and Young Men to Be Allies in Anti-Sexist Education (Working Paper Series), by Jackson Katz. Wellesley Center for Research on Women, 1999.

Our Boys Speak: Adolescent Boys Write About Their Inner Lives, by John Nikkah with Leah Furman. St. Martin's Griffin, 2000.

The Pact: Three Young Men Make a Promise to Fulfill a Dream, by Davis Sampson, George Jenkins, and Rameck Hunt with Lisa Frazier Page. Riverhead Books, 2002.

Raising Cain: Protecting the Emotional Life of Boys, by Daniel Kindlon and Michael Thompson. Ballantine Books, 1999.

Real Boys: Rescuing Our Sons from the Myths of Boyhood, by William Pollack. Random House, 1998.

Real Boys' Voices, by William Pollack and Todd Shuster. Random House, 2000.

Speaking of Boys: Answers to the Most-Asked Questions About Raising Sons, by Michael G. Thompson and Teresa Barker. Ballantine Books, 2000.

When Good Men Behave Badly, by David Wexler. New Harbinger Publications, 2004.

The Wonder of Boys, by Michael Gurian. Putnam, 1996.

Audiovisual

Raising Cain: Exploring the Inner Lives of America's Boys, by Michael Thompson and Powderhouse Productions. PBS Video, 2005.

Tough Guise: Violence, Media, and the Crisis in Masculinity (abridged). Sut Jhally (Director), featuring Jackson Katz. Media Education Foundation, 1999. (www.mediaed.org)

Wrestling with Manhood: Boys, Bullying, and Battering (abridged). Sut Jhally (Director), featuring Sut Jhally and Jackson Katz. Media Education Foundation, 2002. (www.mediaed.org)

Websites
National Organization for Men Against Sexism: www.nomas.org
XY—Men, Masculinities, and Gender Politics: www.xyonline.net

Reflections on Girl World, Female Aggression, and Issues for Girls

The Blueprint for My Girls: How to Build a Life Full of Courage, Determination and Self-Love, by Yasmin Shiraz. Fireside, 2004.

The Curse of the Good Girl: Raising Authentic Girls with Courage and Confidence, by Rachel Simmons. Penguin Press, 2009.

Deal with It! A Whole New Approach to Your Body, Brain, and Life as a gURL, by Esther Drill and Heather McDonald. Pocket Books, 1999.

Don't Give It Away, by Ilyana Vanzant. Fireside Publications, 1999.

Full of Ourselves: A Wellness Program to Advance Girl Power, Health, and Learning, by Catherine Seiner-Adair and Lisa Sjostrom. Teachers College Press, 2006. (Curriculum)

Girl in the Mirror: Mothers and Daughters in the Years of Adolescence, by Nancy L. Snyderman and Peg Steep. Hyperion, 2003.

Girl Wise: How to Be Confident, Capable, Cool and in Control, by Julia DeVillers. Three Rivers Press, 2002.

Girlfighting: Betrayal and Rejection Among Girls, by Lyn Mikel Brown. New York University Press, 2003.

The Girl's Guide to Absolutely Everything, by Melissa Kirsch. Workman Publishing, 2006.

Girls in Real-Life Situations: Group Counseling for Enhancing Social and Emotional Development (Grades K–5), by Shannon Trice-Black and Julia V. Taylor. Research Press, 2007. (Curriculum)

Girls in Real-Life Situations: Group Counseling for Enhancing Social and Emotional Development (Grades 6–12), by Julia V. Taylor and Shannon Trice-Black, Research Press, 2007. (Curriculum)

Girls on Track: A Parent's Guide to Inspiring Our Daughters to Achieve a Lifetime of Self-Esteem and Respect, by Molly Barker. Random House, 2004.

Girls Will Be Girls: Raising Confident and Courageous Daughters, by JoAnn Deale and Teresa Barker. Hyperion, 2002.

Handbook of Prevention and Intervention Programs for Adolescent Girls, by Craig Winston LeCroy and Joyce Elizabeth Mann, eds. John Wiley and Sons, 2008.

The J Girls Guide: The Young Jewish Women's Handbook for Coming of Age, by Penina Adelman, Ali Feldman, and Shulamit Reinharz. Jewish Lights Publishing, 2005.

Listen Up: Voices from the Next Feminist Generation, by Barbara Findlen. Seal Press, 2001.

Manifesta: Young Women, Feminism, and the Future, by Jennifer Baumgartner and Amy Richards. Farrar, Straus, and Giroux, 2000.

Meeting at the Crossroads: Women's Psychology and Girls' Development, by Lyn Mikel Brown and Carol Gilligan. Harvard University Press, 1998.

My Girl: Adventures with a Teen in Training, by Karen Stabiner. Little, Brown and Company, 2005.

New Moon: Friendship, by New Moon Publishing, Seth Godin Productions, and LLC Lark Productions. Knopf Books for Young Readers, 1999.

Odd Girl Out: The Hidden Culture of Girls' Aggression, by Rachel Simmons. Harcourt, 2002.

Odd Girl Speaks Out: Girls Write About Bullies, Cliques, Popularity, and Jealousy, by Rachel Simmons. Harcourt, 2004.

Ophelia Speaks: Adolescent Girls Write About Their Search for Self, by Sara Shandler. Harper Perennial, 2000.

Ophelia's Mom: Women Speak Out About Loving and Letting Go of Their Adolescent Daughters, by Nina Shandler. Crown, 2001.

Packaging Girlhood: Rescuing Our Daughters from Marketing Schemes, Sharon Lamb and Lyn Mikel Brown. St. Martin's Press, 2006.

The Period Book: Everything You Don't Want to Ask (But Need to Know), by Karen Gravelle and Jennifer Gravelle. Walker Publishing, 1996.

Promiscuities: The Secret Struggle for Womanhood, by Naomi Wolf. Fawcett Books, 1998.

Queen Bees & Wannabes: Helping Your Daughter Survive Cliques, Gossip, Boyfriends, and Other Realities of Adolescence, by Rosalind Wiseman. Three Rivers Press, 2003.

Raising Their Voices: The Politics of Girls' Anger, by Lyn Mikel Brown. Harvard University Press, 1998.

Reviving Ophelia: Saving the Selves of Adolescent Girls, by Mary Pipher. Ballantine Books, 1994.

The Secret Lives of Girls: What Good Girls Really Do, by Sharon Lamb. Free Press, 2002.

See Jane Hit: Why Girls Are Growing More Violent and What Can Be Done About It, by James Garbarino. Penguin Press, 2006.

See Jane Win: The Rimm Report on How 1000 Girls Became Successful Women, by Silvia Rimm. Three Rivers Press, 1999.

Stressed-Out Girls: Helping Them Thrive in an Age of Pressure, by Roni Cohen-Sandler. Penguin Press, 2005.

Tripping the Prom Queen: The Truth About Women and Rivalry, by Susan Shapiro Barash. St. Martin's Press, 2006.

Voices of a Generation: Teenage Girls on Sex, School, and Self, by Pamela Haag and American Association of University Women Educational Foundation. Da Capo Press, 1999.

Women's Inhumanity to Women, by Phyllis Chester. Thunder's Mouth Press, 2002.

And Words Can Hurt Forever, by James Garbarino and Ellen deLara. Free Press, 2002.

Audiovisual

5 Girls. Maria Finitzo (Director). Kartemquin Educational Films, 2001. (www.kartemquin.com/films/5-girls)

Mean Girls (Special Feature with Rosalind Wiseman, "The Politics of Girl World"). Mark Waters (Director). Paramount Pictures, 2004.

Odd Girl Out. Tom McLoughlin (Director). Lifetime Television, 2005.

Cyberbullying, Media, and Technology

Adolescents, Media, and the Law: What Developmental Science Reveals and Free Speech Requires, by Roger J. R. Levesque. Oxford University Press, 2007.

Can't Stop Won't Stop: A History of the Hip-Hop Generation, by Jeff Chang. St. Martin's Press, 2005.

Cyber Bullying: Bullying in the Digital Age, by Robin M. Kowalski, Susan P. Limber, and Patricia W. Agatston. Wiley-Blackwell, 2007.

"Cyber Bullying: The Legal Challenge for Educators," by Jill Joline Myers and Gayle Tronvig Carper. *West's Education Law Reporter,* 2008, Vol. 238.

Cyber-Bullying: Issues and Solutions for the School, the Classroom and the Home, by Shaheen Shariff. Routledge, 2008.

Cyberbullying and Cyberthreats: Responding to the Challenge of Online Social Aggression, Threats, and Distress, by Nancy E. Willard. Research Press, 2007.

"Cyber-Libel and Cyber-Bullying: Can Schools Protect Student Reputations and Free-Expression in Virtual Environments?" by Shaheen Shariff and Leanne Johnny. *Education and Law Journal,* 2007, Vol. 16.

Cyber-Safe Kids, Cyber-Savvy Teens: Helping Young People Learn to Use the Internet Safely and Responsibly, by Nancy E. Willard. Jossey-Bass, 2007.

Encyclopedia of Children, Adolescents, and the Media (Vols. 1 & 2), by Jeffrey Jensen Arnett, ed. Sage Publications, 2007.

Generation MySpace: Helping Your Teen Survive Online Adolescence, by Candice M. Kelsey. Marlowe and Company, 2007.

"Grounding Cyberspeech: Public Schools' Authority to Discipline Students for Internet Activity," by Sarah O. Cronan. *Kentucky Law Journal,* 2008, Vol. 97.

Kids and Media in America, by Donald F. Roberts and Ulla G. Foehr. Cambridge University Press, 2004.

"MySpace and Its Relatives: The Cyberbullying Dilemma," by Kathleen Conn and Kevin P. Brady. *West's Education Law Reporter,* 2008, Vol. 226.

So Sexy So Soon, by Diane E. Levin and Jean Kilbourne. Ballantine Books, 2008.

Young People and New Media: Childhood and the Changing Media Environment, by Sonia Livingstone. Sage Publications, 2002.

Youth Media, by Bill Osgerby. Routledge, 2004.

Audiovisual

Consuming Kids: The Commercialization of Childhood, by Adriana Barbaro and Jeremy Ear (Directors). Media Education Foundation, 2008. (www.media ed.org)

Hip-Hop: Beyond Beats and Rhymes (abridged). Byron Hurt (Director). Media Education Foundation, 2006. (www.mediaed.org)

Killing Us Softly: Advertising's Image of Women, by Jean Kilbourne. Sut Jhally (Director). Media Education Foundation, 2006. (www.mediaed.org)

Websites

Bully Police USA: www.bullypolice.org

Center for Media Literacy: www.medialit.org

Center for Safe and Responsible Internet Use: www.cyberbully.org

Cyberbullying.us: www.cyberbullying.us

Cyberlaw Enforcement Organization (CLEO): www.cyberlawenforcement.org

Delete Cyberbullying (National Crime Prevention Council): www.ncpc.org/cyberbullying

Free Technology for Teachers: www.freetech4teachers.com

i-SAFE: www.isafe.org

Just Think: www.justthink.org

Media Awareness Network: www.media-awareness.ca/english/index.cfm

NetSmartz Workshop (National Center for Missing and Exploited Children/Boys and Girls Clubs of America): www.netsmartz.org

Stop Cyberbullying: www.stopcyberbullying.org

WiredSafety: www.wiredsafety.org

Race, Ethnicity, and Diversity

Adolescent Boys: Exploring Diverse Cultures of Boyhood, by Niobe Way and Judy Y. Chu, eds. New York University Press, 2004.

Affirming Diversity: The Sociopolitical Context of Multicultural Education, by Sonia Nieto and Patricia Bode. Allyn and Bacon, 2007.

All About Love: New Visions, by Bell Hooks. William Morrow, 2000.

Bridges Out of Poverty, by Philip DeVol, Terie Dreussi Smith, and Ruby K. Payne. aha! Process, Inc., 2006.

The Color of Success: Race and High-Achieving Urban Youth, by Gilberto Q. Conchas. Teachers College Press, 2006.

A Framework for Understanding Poverty, by Ruby K. Payne. aha! Process, Inc., 2005.

The Gendered Society Reader, by Michael Kimmel and Amy Aronson. Oxford University Press, 2000.

Good Kids from Bad Neighborhoods: Successful Development in Social Context, by

Delbert S. Elliott, Scott Menard, Bruce Rankin, and Amanda Elliott. Cambridge University Press, 2007.

Hidden Rules of Class at Work, by Ruby K. Payne and Don L. Krabill. aha! Process, Inc., 2002.

Hopeful Girls, Troubled Boys: Race and Gender Disparity in Urban Education, by Nancy Lopez. Routledge, 2002.

Race in the Schoolyard: Negotiating the Color Line in Classrooms and Communities, by Amanda E. Lewis. Rutgers University Press, 2003.

School Kids/Street Kids: Identity Development in Latino Students, by Nilda Flores-Gonzalez. Teachers College Press, 2002.

Under-resourced Learners: 8 Strategies to Boost Student Achievement, by Ruby K. Payne and Dan Shenk. aha! Process, Inc., 2008.

Up Against Whiteness: Race, School and Immigrant Youth, by Stacey J. Lee. Teachers College Press, 2005.

Urban Girls Revisited: Building Strengths, by Bonnie Leadbeater and Niobe Way. New York University Press, 2007.

We Can't Teach What We Don't Know: White Teachers, Multiracial Schools, by Gary R. Howard. Teachers College Press, 2006.

"Why Are All the Black Kids Sitting Together in the Cafeteria?": A Psychologist Explains the Development of Racial Identity, by Beverly Daniel Tatum. Basic Books, 2003.

Why White Kids Love Hip-Hop: Wangstas, Wiggers, Wannabes, and the New Reality of Race in America, by Bakari Kitwana. Basic Civitas Books, 2005.

Women Without Class: Girls, Race, and Identity, by Julie Bettie. University of California Press, 2002.

Body Image and Eating Disorders

The Adonis Complex: How to Identify, Treat and Prevent Body Obsession in Men and Boys, by Harrison G. Pope, Katharine A. Phillips, and Roberto Olivardia. Free Press, 2002.

Body Image: A Handbook of Theory, Research, and Clinical Practice, by Thomas F. Cash and Thomas Pruzinsky, eds. Guilford Press, 2004.

Body Image: New Research, by Marlene V. Kindes, ed. Nova Biomedical Books, 2006.

Boys Get Anorexia Too: Coping with Male Eating Disorders in the Family, by Jenny Langley. Paul Chapman Educational Publishing, 2006.

Can't Buy My Love: How Advertising Changes the Way We Think and Feel, by Jean Kilbourne. Free Press, 2000.

The Cult of Thinness, by Sharlene Nagy Hesse-Biber. Oxford University Press, 2007.

Deadly Persuasion: Why Women and Girls Must Fight the Addictive Power of Advertising, by Jean Kilbourne. Free Press, 1999.

The Geography of Girlhood, by Kirsten Smith. Little, Brown Young Readers, 2007.

Go Figure, by Jo Edwards. Simon Pulse, 2007.

The Good Body, by Eve Ensler. Villard, 2005.

The Invisible Man: A Self-Help Guide for Men with Eating Disorders, Compulsive Exercise, and Bigorexia, by John F. Morgan. Routledge, 2008.

Locker Room Diaries: The Naked Truth About Women, Body Image, and Re-imagining the "Perfect" Body, by Leslie Goldman. Da Capo Press, 2007.

Looks, by Madeleine George. Viking Juvenile, 2008.

Making Weight: Healing Men's Conflicts with Food, Weight, and Shape, by Arnold Andersen, Leigh Cohen, and Tom Holbrook. Gurze Books, 2000.

The Muscular Ideal: Psychological, Social, and Medical Perspectives, by J. Kevin Thompson and Guy Cafri, eds. American Psychological Association, 2007.

Packaging Girlhood: Rescuing Our Daughters from Marketers' Schemes, by Sharon Lamb and Lyn Mikel Brown. St. Martin's Griffin, 2007.

Understanding Body Dissatisfaction in Men, Women and Children, by Sarah Grogan. Routledge, 2007.

Audiovisual

Reflections "Friends Don't Let Friends Fat Talk" Video: (https://secure.pursuant group.net/pursuant4/deltadeltadelta/fall08/dddselect/flashstory.asp)

Slim Hopes: Advertising and the Obsession with Thinness, by Jean Kilbourne. Sut Jhally (Director). Media Education Foundation, 2006. (www.mediaed.org)

Websites

About Face: www.about-face.org

Body Positive: www.bodypositive.com

Campaign For Real Beauty: www.campaignforrealbeauty.com

Eating Disorder Referral and Network Center: www.edreferral.com

Finding Balance: www.findingbalance.com

Gurze Books: Resources for Eating Disorders: www.gurze.com

The National Association for Males with Eating Disorders (NAMED): www .namedinc.org

National Eating Disorders Association: www.nationaleatingdisorders.org

Reflections: The Body Image Program: www.bodyimageprogram.org

The Something Fishy Website on Eating Disorders: www.something-fishy.org

Sex, Sexuality, Homophobia, and Harassment

Adolescent Sexuality: A Historical Handbook and Guide, by Carolyn Cocca, ed. Praeger, 2006

The Commonwealth Fund Survey of Adolescent Girls, by Cathy Schoen, Karen Davis, and Karen Scott Collins. Commonwealth Fund Commission on Women's Health, 1997.

Dude, You're a Fag: Masculinity and Sexuality in High School, by C. J. Pascoe. University of California Press, 2007.

Everything You Never Wanted Your Kids to Know About Sex (But Were Afraid They'd Ask): The Secret to Surviving Your Child's Sexual Development from Birth to the Teens, by Justin Richardson and Mark A. Schuster. Crown, 2003.

From Teasing to Torment: School Climate in America—A Survey of Students and Teachers, by Dana Markow and Jordan Fein (Harris Interactive). Gay, Lesbian and Straight Education Network, 2005. (www.new.glsen.org/binary-data/ GLSEN_ATTACHMENTS/file/499-1.pdf)

Hostile Hallways: The AAUW Survey on Sexual Harassment in America's Schools (Harris Interactive), by the American Association of University Women Educational Foundation, 2001. (www.aauw.org/research/upload/hostilehallways .pdf)

Mom, Dad—I'm Gay: How Families Negotiate Coming Out, by Ritch C. Savin-Williams. American Psychological Association, 2001.

"Oral Sex Among Adolescents: Is It Sex or Is It Abstinence?" by Lisa Remez. *Family Planning Perspectives*, 2002, Vol. 32, No. 6, pp. 298–304.

Sex and Tech: Results from a Survey of Teens and Young Adults, by TRU. National Campaign to Prevent Teen and Unplanned Pregnancy and Cosmogirl.com, 2008. (www.thenationalcampaign.org/sextech)

The Sex Lives of Teenagers: Revealing the Secret World of Adolescent Boys and Girls, by Lynn Ponton. Dutton Press, 2000.

Sexualities: Identities, Behaviors, and Society, by Michael S. Kimmel and Rebecca F. Plante. Oxford University Press, 2004.

Start Talking: A Girl's Guide for You and Your Mom About Health, Sex, or Whatever, by Mary Jo Rapini and Janine Sherman. Bayou Publishing, 2008.

Teenage Sexuality: Opposing Viewpoints, by Ken R. Wells, ed. Greenhaven Press/ Thomson Gale, 2006.

The 2005 National School Climate Survey: The Experiences of Lesbian, Gay, Bisexual and Transgender Youth in Our Nation's Schools, by Joseph G. Kosciw and Elizabeth M. Diaz. Gay, Lesbian and Straight Education Network, 2006. (www.glsen.org/binary-data/GLSEN_ATTACHMENTS/file/585-1.pdf)

Websites

American Civil Liberties Union LGBT Project: www.aclu.org/lgbt
Gay and Lesbian Alliance Against Defamation: www.glaad.org
Gay Lesbian Straight Education Network: www.glsen.org
Sex, etc.: www.sexetc.org
The Safe Schools Coalition: www.safeschoolscoalition.org

Sexual Assault and Abusive Relationships

The Batterer: A Psychological Profile, by Donald G. Dutton and Susan K. Golant. Basic Books, 1995.

Dating Violence: Young Women in Danger, by Barrie Levy. Seal Press, 1997.

Domestic Violence: Opposing Viewpoints, by Mike Wilson, ed. Greenhaven Press, 2009.

Family Violence Across the Lifespan: An Introduction, by Ola Barnett, Cindy L. Miller-Perrin, and Robin D. Perrin. Sage Publications, 2005.

The Gift of Fear: Survival Signals That Protect Us from Violence, by Gavin deBecker. Little, Brown, 1997.

I Will Survive: The African-American Guide to Healing from Sexual Assault and Abuse, by Lori Robinson. Seal Press, 2003.

In Love and in Danger, by Barrie Levy. Seal Press, 1998.

Male Victims of Sexual Assault, by Gillian C. Mezey and Michael B. King, eds. Oxford University Press, 2000.

Protecting the Gift: Keeping Children and Teenagers Safe, by Gavin deBecker. Dial Press, 1999.

Rethinking Domestic Violence, by Donald G. Dutton. UBC Press, 2006.

Surviving the Silence: Black Women's Stories of Rape, by Charlotte Pierce-Baker. Norton and Co., 2000.

Violence in the Lives of Black Women: Battered Black and Blue, by Carolyn West. Haworth Press, 2003.

Women Who Kill: Battered Women That Killed in Self-defense, by Ann Jones. Ballantine Books, 1980.

Audiovisual

Dealing with Teen Dating Abuse: Matters of Choice. Human Relations Media, 2003. (www.hrmvideo.com)

Websites

Men Can Stop Rape: www.mencanstoprape.org
National Coalition Against Domestic Violence: www.ncadv.org
National Sexual Violence Resource Center: www.nsvrc.org

Books for Younger Children

A Bad Case of Tattle Tongue, by Julia Cook. National Center for Youth Issues, 2006.

Bootsie Barker Bites, by Barbara Bottner. Putnam Juvenile, 1997.

Chrysanthemum, by Kevin Henkes. Greenwillow, 1991.

How to Lose All Your Friends, by Nancy Carlson. Puffin, 1997.

Just Kidding, by Trudy Ludwig. Tricycle Press, 2006.

Loud Emily, by Alexis O'Neill. Aladdin, 2001.

My Mouth Is a Volcano!, by Julia Cook. National Center for Youth Issues, 2008.

My Secret Bully, by Trudy Ludwig. Tricycle Press, 1995.

Odd Velvet, by Mary E. Whitcomb. Chronicle Books, 1998.

Pig Is Moving In, by Claudia Fries. Scholastic, 2000.

The Recess Queen, by Alexis O'Neill. Scholastic, 2005.

Sorry!, by Trudy Ludwig. Tricycle Press, 2006.

Stand Tall, Molly Lou Mellon, by Patty Lovell. Putnam Juvenile, 2006.

The Sneetches and Other Stories, by Dr. Seuss. Random House, 1961.

Too Perfect, by Trudy Ludwig and Lisa Fields. Tricycle Press, 2009.

Trouble Talk, by Trudy Ludwig and Mikela Prevost. Tricycle Press, 2008.

Worst Best Friend, by Alexis O'Neill. Scholastic Press, 2008.

You Can't Say You Can't Play, by Vivian Gussin Paley. Harvard University Press, 1993.

Audiovisual

Consuming Kids: The Commercialization of Childhood. Adriana Barbaro and Jeremy Ear (Directors), 2008. Produced by Media Education Foundation (www.mediaed.org).

Dealing with Teen Dating Abuse: Matters of Choice, 2003. Produced by Human Relations Media (www.hrmvideo.com).

5 Girls. Maria Finitzo (Director), 2001. Produced by Kartemquin Educational Films (www.kartemquin.com/films/5-girls).

Hip-Hop: Beyond Beats and Rhymes, Byron Hurt (Producer/Director), 2006. Produced by God Bless the Child Production (www.bhurt.com). Distributed by Media Education Foundation (www.mediaed.org).

How to Eat Fried Worms. Bob Dolman (Director), 2006. Produced and distributed by Walden Media (www.walden.com).

Killing Us Softly 3: Advertising's Image of Women, created by Jean Kilbourne, 2001. Sut Jhally (Producer/Director). Distributed by Media Education Foundation (www.mediaed.org).

Mean Girls (Special Feature with Rosalind Wiseman, "The Politics of Girl World"). Mark Waters (Director), 2004. Paramount Pictures.

The Motivation Breakthrough, by Richard Lavoie, 2005. Gerardine Wurzburg (Director). PBS Video.

Odd Girl Out. Tom McLoughlin (Director), 2005. Lifetime Television.

Raising Cain: Exploring the Inner Lives of America's Boys, by Michael Thompson and Powderhouse Productions, 2005. PBS Video.

Reflections "Friends Don't Let Friends Fat Talk" Video: (https://secure.pursuant group.net/pursuant4/deltadeltadelta/fall08/dddselect/flashstory.asp)

Slim Hopes: Advertising and the Obsession with Thinness, featuring Jean Kilbourne, 1995. Sut Jhally (Producer/Director). Distributed by Media Education Foundation (www.mediaed.org).

Tough Guise: Violence, Media, and the Crisis in Masculinity (abridged), featuring Jackson Katz, 1999. Sut Jhally (Director). Distributed by Media Education Foundation (www.mediaed.org).

Wrestling with Manhood: Boys, Bullying, and Battering (abridged), featuring Sut Jhally and Jackson Katz, 2002. Sut Jhally (Writer/Director). Distributed by Media Education Foundation (www.mediaed.org).

UK Organisations

The organisations here have been independently sourced in the UK, and as such are not necessarily endorsed by the author.

Careline
Website: www.carelineuk.com. Tel: 0845 034 7070.

Family and Parenting Institute
Website: www.familyandparenting.org. Tel: 020 7424 3460.

Parentline Plus
Website: www.parentlineplus.org.uk. Tel: 0808 800 2222.

Rape Crisis Federation
Website: www.rapecrisis.co.uk.

Relate
Website: www.relate.org.uk. Tel: 0300 100 1234.

The Samaritans
Website: www.samaritans.org. Tel: 08457 90 90 90.

Victim Support
Website: www.victimsupport.org.uk. Tel: 0845 30 30 900.

Women's Aid
Website: www.womensaid.org.uk. Tel: 0117 944 44 11.

Acknowledgments

Having people put faith in you to help them with their children is a deep responsibility and a high honor. It is my hope that this version of the book will be even more helpful than the last—and I really tried to include all the most common questions girls and their parents ask me.

Queen Bees is always a combined effort; from my students sharing their experiences with me and telling me when I am completely wrong to parents and educators reaching out, I can't do any of this without the feedback I get. And if you bought the first version and recommended it to other people, thank you so much. You can't ask for more as an author. In particular I want to thank the American School Counselor Association and all the educators who refer the families they work with to *Queen Bees*. You all rarely get the credit you deserve.

In the actual writing of this version of *Queen Bees*, first I want to thank my in-house editing team of Candace Nuzzo and Emily Bartek—I couldn't do a tenth of what I do without you both. To Zoe Wiseman (whom this book will always be dedicated to no matter how old you are and the woman you have become). To Stacey Barney for always going above and beyond even when it's not your job. To my interns, Sarah Sheya, Wes Graf, and Trina Brady, and specific thanks to Kaitlyn Haldorson and Alex Schuyler.

Your honest feedback was invaluable in making this relevant for a new generation. To Philip Patrick, thank you for making sure the book was done, and to Cindy Berman, thank you for saving me at the last minute.

I was also assisted greatly by Julia Taylor, Missy Harlin, and Melinda Kapalin. Thank you for being such incredible ambassadors for this work and for helping conduct the focus groups. Lastly, to the schools where we conducted the focus groups, while we agreed not to use their names, we extend our sincerest thanks to all of them, the faculty and students, for opening their doors to us. And the biggest thank-you to my husband, James, for keeping our family together while I finished three books in eighteen months. I promise I will never do it again.

Index

Ready to enter Boy World?

RINGLEADERS AND SIDEKICKS

How to Help Your Son Cope with Classroom Politics,
Bullying, Girls and Growing Up

Rosalind Wiseman

When Rosalind Wiseman published her bestseller *Queen Bees and Wannabes* in 2001, it fundamentally changed the way that parents, educators and the media looked at the impact of girls' social dynamics and created a road map for girls to develop better relationships and higher self-esteem.

Now Rosalind turns her attention to the tricky terrain of Boy World. Drawing on 20 years of work with boys and her own experience as a mother of two sons, Rosalind will help parents understand their tween and teenage sons better. The book will cover such timely issues as video games, online identities and social networking sites. This is an essential manual that will help any parent build a stronger, more meaningful relationship with their son.

Out now from Piatkus!

Also by Rosalind Wiseman:

QUEEN BEE MUMS AND KINGPIN DADS

Dealing with the Difficult Parents in Your Child's Life

Rosalind Wiseman with Elizabeth Rapoport

Adulthood doesn't mean an end to cliques and peer pressure; often we just graduate to a new level. In *Queen Bee Mums and Kingpin Dads* Rosalind Wiseman reveals the unspoken rules of Perfect Parent World, a place in which a few parents set the standards for all parental involvement and most parents feel frustrated or disempowered.

With candour and insight, Wiseman explores how to deal effectively with the other adults (parents, teachers) who help create the reality of your son or daughter's world, including the norms about money, fashion, alcohol and sex. *Queen Bee Mums and Kingpin Dads* is essential reading for all parents.

'*Queen Bee Mums and Kingpin Dads* is honest and wise. As a father, I found the insights, stories and practical information in this book very powerful' Michael Gurian, author of *The Minds of Boys and The Wonder of Girls*

'*Queen Bee Mums and Kingpin Dads* will be your bible for handling the adults in your child's life with dignity and grace' Rachel Simmons, author of *Odd Girl Out*

9780-7499-2749-3

Also from Piatkus:

THE SPOILT GENERATION

Why restoring authority will make our children and society happier

Dr Aric Sigman

In the space of a few decades the way we parent has changed dramatically. Something we once did intuitively has become the subject of political fashion, guided by experts.

The result? Our children – right across society – are now spoilt in ways that go far beyond materialism. They have been given so much in terms of legislation, rights and experience, yet they are suffering unimaginably, with rates of child depression, underage pregnancy, obesity and pre-teen alcoholism the highest since records began.

In *The Spoilt Generation*, Dr Aric Sigman – himself a hands-on father of four – takes issues by the scruff of the neck, among them children's sense of entitlement, the effects of television and computers, single-parent homes and blended families, parental guilt and the compensation culture. Tackling each one in a refreshingly honest and direct way, he offers a clear and practical message to us all as to how we can redress the status quo, redefine our roles and, together, cultivate better-behaved and happier children.

'An intriguing read for all parents' *Maternity and Infant* magazine

978-0-7499-4148-2

WHATEVER!

A down-to-earth guide to parenting teenagers

Gill Hines and Alison Baverstock
Foreword by Jacqueline Wilson

Raising teenagers can test parental love to breaking point, particularly if you have previously enjoyed a close relationship. But help is at hand with *Whatever!* the really practical guide for teenagers, their parents and the whole family. With tried and tested strategies for every situation, which you can put into practice immediately, you'll wonder how you ever managed without this book!

'This just could be the book that restores you sanity'
Daily Mail

'Masses of practical ideas about how to help teenagers feel good about themselves, how to keep family communications open and how to deal with problems, from parties to swearing'
Independent

'All power to these two authors. There's a real understanding of young people and practical advice . . . A good book for parents and, perhaps, for form tutors, especially those with no children of their own' *Times Educational Supplement*

978-0-7499-2723-3